INTERNATIONAL MONETARY COOPERATION

Lessons from the Plaza Accord After Thirty Years

C. Fred Bergsten and
Russell A. Green
Editors

C. Fred Bergsten was founding director of the Peterson Institute for International Economics from 1981 through 2012 and is now senior fellow and director emeritus there. He has been a member of the President's Advisory Committee on Trade Policy and Negotiations since 2010. He was formerly assistant secretary for international affairs of the US Treasury (1977–81), functioned as undersecretary for monetary affairs (1980–81), and was assistant for international economic affairs to the National Security Council (1969–71). He was chairman of the Competitiveness Policy Council created by the Congress (1991–95) and chairman of the APEC Eminent Persons Group (1993–95). This is the 44th book he has written, coauthored, or edited, including most recently *India's Rise: A Strategy for Trade-Led Growth* (2015), *Addressing Currency Manipulation through Trade Agreements* (2014), *Bridging the Pacific: Toward Free Trade and Investment Between China and the United States* (2014), and *The Coming Resolution of the European Crisis* (2012). Bergsten has received the Meritorious Honor Award of the Department of State (1965), Exceptional Service Award of the Treasury Department (1981), Legion d'Honneur from the Government of France (1985), an honorary fellowship in the Chinese Academy of Social Sciences (1997), the Distinguished Alumni Leadership Award from the Fletcher School (2010), the Order of the Polar Star from the Government of Sweden (2013), the Officer's Cross of the Order of Merit of the Federal Republic of Germany (2014), the Swedish American of the Year for 2014, and the 1st Class of the Order of Diplomatic Service Merit "Gwanghwa Medal" from the Republic of Korea (2016).

Russell A. Green is the Will Clayton Fellow in International Economics at Rice University's Baker Institute and an adjunct assistant professor in the economics department there. His current research focuses on exchange rate policies, financial market development in emerging-market economies, and India's development challenges. Prior to joining the Baker Institute, Green spent four years in India as the US Treasury Department's first financial attaché to that country. He was previously the deputy director of the US Treasury's Office of International Monetary Policy, where he led efforts to strengthen International Monetary Fund exchange rate policies and international reserve management. Green holds a BA from Pomona College and PhD from the University of California, Berkeley.

PETERSON INSTITUTE FOR INTERNATIONAL ECONOMICS
1750 Massachusetts Avenue, NW, Washington, DC 20036-1903
(202) 328-9000   Fax: (202) 328-5432   www.piie.com

Adam S. Posen, *President*
Steven R. Weisman, *Vice President for Publications and Communications*

Cover Design: Fletcher Design, Inc./Washington, DC
Cover Image: © Chrupka/iStock
Photo on back cover: © Robert Maass/Corbis
Photo on page 26: © Bettmann/Corbis. Photographer: Harbus; Rich

RICE UNIVERSITY'S BAKER INSTITUTE FOR PUBLIC POLICY
6100 Main Street, Baker Hall MS-40, Suite 120, Houston, TX 77005
(713) 348-4683   Fax: (713) 348-5993   http://bakerinstitute.org

Library of Congress Cataloging-in-Publication Data
Bergsten, C. Fred, 1941- editor. | Green, Russell Aaron, editor. Title: International monetary cooperation: lessons from the Plaza Accord after thirty years / C. Fred Bergsten and Russell A. Green, editors. Other titles: International monetary cooperation (Peterson Institute for   International Economics) Description: Washington, DC: Peterson Institute for International Economics and Rice University's Baker Institute for Public Policy, [2016] | Includes   bibliographical references. Identifiers: LCCN 2015047771 | ISBN 9780881327113 Subjects: LCSH: Foreign exchange rates—Government policy—History—20th century. | Devaluation of currency—United States—History—20th century. | Monetary policy—International cooperation. | Economic policy—International cooperation. | International finance. | International trade. Classification: LCC HG3851 .I526 2016 | DDC 332.4/5—dc23

INTERNATIONAL MONETARY COOPERATION

Lessons from the Plaza Accord After Thirty Years

C. Fred Bergsten and
Russell A. Green
Editors

PETERSON INSTITUTE FOR INTERNATIONAL ECONOMICS
RICE UNIVERSITY'S BAKER INSTITUTE FOR PUBLIC POLICY

Washington, DC
April 2016

This publication has been subjected to a prepublication peer review intended to ensure analytical quality. The views expressed are those of the authors. This publication is part of the overall program of the Peterson Institute for International Economics, as endorsed by its Board of Directors, but it does not necessarily reflect the views of individual members of the Board or of the Institute's staff or management.

The Peterson Institute for International Economics is a private nonpartisan, nonprofit institution for rigorous, intellectually open, and indepth study and discussion of international economic policy. Its purpose is to identify and analyze important issues to make globalization beneficial and sustainable for the people of the United States and the world, and then to develop and communicate practical new approaches for dealing with them. Its work is funded by a highly diverse group of philanthropic foundations, private corporations, and interested individuals, as well as by income on its capital fund. About 35 percent of the Institute's resources in its latest fiscal year were provided by contributors from outside the United States. A list of all financial supporters for the preceding four years is posted at http://www.piie.com/institute/supporters.pdf.

Contents

Preface

The Plaza Accord of 1985 was a major milestone in the history of economic cooperation among the industrial nations. It was a rare occasion when the financial and growth spillover effects of surplus economies' lower demand were addressed. Protectionist pressures in the US Congress were the main driver of the Plaza's monetary initiatives so it relates directly to the interaction between trade policy and currency issues that is playing out again in today's very different global circumstances. The current weaknesses of the international financial architecture with respect to persistent surplus economies and their currencies underline the relevance of reconsidering this successful episode from the past.

This volume brings together some of the leading international economists in the United States, Japan, and Europe to offer their respective perspectives on the array of questions posed by the Plaza Accord and its successor, the Louvre Accord of 1987. Notably, it includes analytical perspectives of economists who were involved in the Accord's design, negotiation, and implementation. The volume derives from a project launched in early 2015 by the Baker Institute for Public Policy at Rice University to commemorate the 30th anniversary of the Plaza. That institute is named for James A. Baker, III, the former Secretary of the Treasury and Secretary of State, who was the chief architect and negotiator of the Plaza Accord and its implementation.

The Baker Institute hosted a conference in Houston in October 2015, at which the papers included in this book were initially presented, and we are delighted that our Peterson Institute for International Economics was asked to coedit and publish the resulting volume—especially given our own fellows' contributions. We are honored that Secretary Baker delivered the keynote address to the conference, which is included as chapter 1 of the book, and that former Federal Reserve Chairman Paul Volcker and other key participants in the Plaza process contributed their own views both to the conference and on these pages.

The Peterson Institute for International Economics is a private nonpartisan, nonprofit institution for rigorous, intellectually open, and indepth study and discussion of international economic policy. Its purpose is to identify and analyze important issues to making globalization beneficial and sustainable for the people of the United States and the world, and then to develop and communicate practical new approaches for dealing with them.

The Institute's work is funded by a highly diverse group of philanthropic foundations, private corporations, and interested individuals, as well as by income on its capital fund. About 35 percent of the Institute's resources in our latest fiscal year were provided by contributors from outside the United States. A list of all our financial supporters for the preceding year is posted at http://piie.com/institute/supporters.pdf.

The Executive Committee of the Institute's Board of Directors bears overall responsibility for the Institute's direction, gives general guidance and approval to its research program, and evaluates its performance in pursuit of its mission. The Institute's President is responsible for the identification of topics that are likely to become important over the medium term (one to three years) that should be addressed by Institute scholars. This rolling agenda is set in close consultation with the Institute's research staff, Board of Directors, and other stakeholders.

The President makes the final decision to publish any individual Institute study, following independent internal and external review of the work. Interested readers may access the data and computations underlying Institute publications for research and replication by searching titles at www.piie.com.

The Institute hopes that its research and other activities will contribute to building a stronger foundation for international economic policy around the world. We invite readers of these publications to let us know how they think we can best accomplish this objective.

ADAM S. POSEN
President
February 2016

Acknowledgments

The editors gratefully acknowledge support for research related to the 30th anniversary of the Plaza Accord provided by The Honorable Robert L. Clarke and Mrs. Clarke and The Clayton Fund, Inc. We also appreciate the contributions of the authors of this volume, who each contributed collaboratively to the production and content of the overall volume. Russell Green would like to acknowledge the capable research assistance of Taryn Cheng and Yuan "Doria" Du.

Overview

C. FRED BERGSTEN AND RUSSELL A. GREEN

The Setting

The Plaza Accord of September 1985 represents the most successful example of international economic cooperation since the Bretton Woods agreement. It was worked out in complete secrecy at the Plaza Hotel in New York City and unveiled to an unsuspecting world on a Sunday afternoon with dramatic effects. Led by the United States, it brought together the world's five leading economies at the time (France, Germany, Japan, the United States, and the United Kingdom) in an unprecedented effort to correct the largest set of global imbalances that had ever threatened the world economy.

The exchange rate of the dollar, which had plummeted to its weakest level ever only seven years earlier and required a massive rescue operation, doubled in value in the five years before the Plaza. As a result, the international competitiveness of the United States was decimated and protectionist pressures exploded in Congress, jeopardizing the global trading system. The US current account deficit soared beyond $100 billion, an unheard of level at the time, and the United States shifted from being the world's largest creditor country to being the world's largest debtor country in less than a decade.

It is difficult, but useful, to recall from our vantage point of 30 years later how profoundly these developments affected thinking around the world. Such global statesmen as Raymond Barre, the former prime minister of France and author of his country's leading economic textbook, and Fritz Leutwiler,

C. Fred Bergsten was founding director of the Peterson Institute for International Economics from 1981 through 2012 and is now senior fellow and director emeritus there. Russell A. Green is the Will Clayton Fellow in International Economics at Rice University's Baker Institute and adjunct assistant professor in the economics department there.

the universally esteemed president of the Swiss National Bank, stated flatly in early 1985 that "a new world [of international finance] was at hand" and that "the dollar would never again drop below 3 deutschemarks" (it subsequently dropped as low as 1.35).[1] Congressman Bill Frenzel of Minnesota, the thoughtful top Republican on both the full Ways and Means Committee of the House of Representatives and its Subcommittee on Trade, posited that "the Smoot-Hawley tariff itself would have passed overwhelmingly had it come to the floor at that time."[2] The financial, trade, and economic risks were enormous.

The first Reagan administration essentially ignored the problem. Despite growing pleas for remedial action from the rest of the world, and many quarters within the United States, it basked in the boom that led to the president's landslide reelection in 1984 and portrayed the strong dollar as a vote of global confidence in America. Its "benign neglect" and doctrine of nonintervention permitted the problems to rise to unprecedented heights.

Change began in the United States with a change of guard at the Treasury at the beginning of the second Reagan administration. Incoming Secretary of the Treasury James Baker, III and his team saw the tide of protectionism rising in Congress and decided that "item one on our agenda was the dollar" as the only effective policy response (chapter 1 of this volume). Charles Dallara, the senior deputy assistant secretary for international affairs at the time, notes that he and David Mulford, the assistant secretary for international affairs, obtained Baker's approval to undertake intervention to weaken the dollar during Baker's first week in office, in February 1985 (see chapter 4). Mulford describes the total reversal of policy the new Baker team engineered (see chapter 3).[3]

With the threat of US protectionism providing them with enormous leverage, the Treasury worked closely with the rest of the G-5, bringing them to the table to agree to coordinated intervention in September. The immediate sharp depreciation of the dollar after the Plaza Accord generated enthusiasm among the major economies about cooperation that launched more than two years of intensive effort to manage exchange rates and coordinate economic policies more broadly. This ambitious agenda helped revive the institutions for major-economy coordination (primarily the G-5/G-7) that had been fading before the Plaza, largely because of US resistance to the entire process. To some extent, it also institutionalized the role of the International Monetary Fund (IMF) as a neutral participant and adviser in the process. These institutions have survived into the present, though their adequacy for addressing problems in the global economy has been—and remains—an ongoing area of concern.

---

1. Private conversations with C. Fred Bergsten.

2. Ibid.

3. See also the sharp distinction between "Reagan I" and "Reagan II" in Bergsten (1994).

The idea of the Plaza Accord remains alive today as a major milestone in the history of exchange rate policy. As Takatoshi Ito notes in chapter 7, for the Japanese "the Plaza Accord is as important as fixing the yen to 360 /dollar in 1949, the breakdown of the Bretton Woods regime in 1971, and the breakdown of the Smithsonian Agreement in 1973."[4] Its interpretation remains an important point of debate among international economists because, remarkably, they still refer to the Plaza period when thinking about important policy questions today.

This volume is an attempt to interpret the Plaza Accord with the advantage of 30 years of hindsight. It arose from work commissioned by Rice University's Baker Institute for Public Policy for a conference on the 30th anniversary of the Plaza Accord that was held in Houston October 1, 2015.[5] Fortuitously, the anniversary occurred at a particularly suitable time to examine the current state of affairs in exchange rate policy and global macroeconomic stability in light of the Plaza Accord experience, as indicated in several chapters in this book.

The volume consists of three parts. The first comprises the recollections of several key actors in the Plaza Agreement itself: Secretary Baker, who presented the keynote address at the conference and whose chapter leads off the book; Federal Reserve Chairman Paul Volcker; Baker's chief lieutenants, David Mulford and Charles Dallara, who worked out the details of the Plaza Accord over three months of intense negotiations with the rest of the G-5; and Makoto Utsumi, who played a central role in the Japanese government, the most important of the foreign participants. Several authors of papers in other sections of the book, including Volcker's chief aide Edwin Truman, also offer personal reflections of the period.

The second part of the book offers five analytical appraisals of the Plaza experience by leading experts on international monetary affairs. The third part summarizes lessons from the Plaza by four other experts, each of whom emphasizes in a different way the need for renewed international cooperation to improve the functioning of the international monetary system. Taken together, the 14 chapters provide a comprehensive assessment of the Plaza itself and its implications for global monetary cooperation today and tomorrow.

What Was "the Plaza"?

Interpreting the Plaza Accord and applying its lessons turn out to be complicated. The term *Plaza Accord* encompasses many meanings, as the range of topics addressed in this volume attests.[6] There are at least three: the movement

---

4. In Japan one can find college-age people who have not studied economics but are familiar with the Plaza Accord.

5. The video proceedings of the conference are available at http://bakerinstitute.org/events/1736/.

6. Even the name *Plaza Accord* remains controversial: The authors of the chapters debated whether it is properly called the *Plaza Accord* or the *Plaza Agreement*. In the end Google played the neutral arbiter: *Accord* beat *Agreement* 102,000 hits to 15,300.

of exchange rates per se, the broader coordination of macroeconomic policies that was attempted, and the institutionalization of international monetary cooperation symbolized by the revival of the G-5 process.

In the narrowest sense, the Plaza Accord refers to the exchange rate activity of 1985, beginning with the shift of the US approach early in the year and ending with the last portion of Plaza-linked intervention and monetary policy reaction. It is also shorthand for the large decline of the dollar from 1985 through 1987 that helped correct the large international imbalances of the mid-1980s. Because it stands as the exemplar of coordinated intervention efforts, this definition of the Plaza engenders debate about whether and how such intervention succeeds. Historical questions, such as when markets perceived the change in US policy and why Japan participated so enthusiastically, remain puzzles with no agreed upon answers.

This narrow definition of the Plaza Accord also provides a useful benchmark against which to judge exchange rate dynamics at any future point in time. Determining whether conditions are ripe for a repeat performance entails evaluating the conditions that led to the Plaza in the first place. The dollar was exceptionally strong, and the exchange rate misalignment was driving large current account imbalances. The real threat of protectionism in the United States, which provided the motivation for all parties to come together and seek a solution, was a direct result. How many of these factors have been matched in other periods, including today? Additionally, for those who are not enamored of freely floating exchange rates, this period provides inspiration that alternative exchange rate policies may be possible.

In a second and broader sense, the Plaza Accord refers to the entire period from the Plaza until at least the end of 1987, including the Tokyo Summit and the Louvre Accord, when the major economies experimented with intensive efforts to coordinate their overall economic policies. This definition of the Plaza refers to a much higher degree of ambition and indeed an effort to build a much more widespread structure. Ultimately, the arrangements attempted under this meaning of the Plaza proved unworkable and unsustainable. They nonetheless provide valuable lessons about the difficulty and limitations of coordination.

In the third and broadest sense, the Plaza stands for an effort to exercise leadership of the global economy by a group of like-minded major countries. The Plaza reinvigorated international coordination in the form of regular, concerted conversations among the G-5 about the global economy and evaluation of joint action on many fronts beyond exchange rate management, which, Mulford argues, paid important dividends in dealing with separate issues, such as Third World debt and the economic dimensions of the end of the Cold War. The Plaza gave the G-5, and soon thereafter the G-7, a prominence that sustained it for at least two decades.

The system of sorts revived by the Plaza did not succeed on all counts. It eroded in the 1990s, and its ultimate denouement came with the global financial crisis in 2007–08, after which the larger and more representative

G-20 succeeded to the title of preeminent global economic policy coordination council. The current lack of functional high-level coordination raises important questions about what should come next. Should another form of the small-group Plaza system return, or should something totally different be created? How should the system accommodate China's prominence or the reality that the international monetary system is shifting from a dollar-dominated system to a multipolar system, as outlined by Agnès Bénassy-Quéré in chapter 13?

For all its shortcomings, the Plaza Accord remains the totem of international economic coordination, providing a metric by which to judge all of these questions. This volume aims to facilitate learning from the past to inform the present, with chapters that relate to all three meanings of the Plaza Accord.

The Narrow Plaza

In the lead-up to the Plaza, there was no doubt about the misalignment of the dollar. Russell Green, David Papell, and Ruxandra Prodan (chapter 8) document its climb beyond the improvement in US fundamentals, with broad support from other authors.

There is less agreement about the historical question of when the Plaza began. The dollar peaked in February 1985, well before the Plaza Accord. Jeffrey Frankel maintains that the markets perceived the shift in US policy as soon as Baker arrived at Treasury (Frankel 1994; chapter 6 of this volume). Others, including Baker and Utsumi, then the minister-counselor for finance at the Japanese Embassy, maintain that the markets were caught completely off guard by the surprise of the Plaza. Our own verdict is that policy changed with the move of Baker but became widely apparent only with the Plaza.

The timing of the market reaction matters substantially to the interpretation of the effectiveness of the Plaza Accord, narrowly defined. The key immediate objective was to bring the dollar down to more reasonable levels against the yen and mark, thereby correcting the very large current account imbalances that had developed over the first half of the 1980s. Whether the Plaza deserves its place in history is disputed, as several authors note, by the substantial decline in the dollar's value over several months before the meeting took place.

Frankel's interpretation rescues the Plaza from this inconvenient fact but raises further questions about its interpretation. The Plaza Accord is synonymous with coordinated foreign exchange intervention, but Frankel's theory suggests that the intervention only emphasized, and perhaps at most amplified, a market reaction that was already well under way. John Taylor (chapter 12) argues that the Plaza intervention was ineffectual and that the dollar would have declined anyway. The main mover of exchange rates in 1985 was the widespread realization that the United States no longer wanted a strong dollar and was willing to intervene to weaken it. Was the Plaza, then, really all about the policy shift in the United States? Perhaps the rest of the G-5 only played the role of blessing the US move, assuring markets they would not attempt to oppose or undo the US action?

Two other chapters provide support for this thesis. In chapter 8 Green, Papell, and Prodan note that the literature on the effectiveness of sterilized intervention finds that it is most likely to have an effect when it is consistent with monetary policy. They proxy monetary policy with a real-time Taylor rule to measure whether the Plaza intervention was consistent with monetary policy in the three key countries (the United States, Japan, and Germany) and find that only US monetary policy supported the Plaza intervention, suggesting that markets were primarily responding to US signals.

In chapter 7 Ito provides results from his earlier examination of where market movements occurred in the week after the Plaza announcement (Ito 1987). He finds that most of the movement occurred in New York and that contemporaneous correlation of intradaily price changes was high in all three currencies. Ito interprets this as evidence that the markets were responding to the shift in US policy, not to intervention undertaken in Tokyo or Europe. He describes how the yen calmed and even began to weaken again after the first week, despite US intervention to buy yen.[7] When the Bank of Japan raised the intrabank rate in late October, the yen began to strengthen again; from that point until the reverse interventions began in March 1986, the market moved in response to Japanese policy comments.

In chapter 6 Frankel summarizes the literature on the effectiveness of intervention (including his own important work with coauthors), concluding that the circumstances of intervention greatly affect its likelihood of success. Some of the factors that appear to improve the likelihood of effectiveness include surprise, coordination with other central banks, and public announcement of the intervention. The Plaza fits well into this pattern. Moreover, the dollar had rebounded shortly before the Plaza, and there had been several other "false starts" in launching and especially sustaining the needed dollar decline. But if the dollar decline was driven primarily by the US component of the announcement, with the rest of the G-5 playing supporting roles and the markets having already digested much of the driving impulse, the interpretation of the Plaza requires a bit more nuance.

Joseph Gagnon adds an interesting twist to the debate on intervention effectiveness in chapter 11. He measures the impact of intervention and quasi-intervention on current account balances rather than exchange rates, in order to capture the important feature that intervention often occurs to prevent rather than propel an exchange rate adjustment. If intervention prevents appreciation—a modern version of "competitive depreciation"—the observable outcome would be a higher than otherwise predicted current account. Gagnon finds economically powerful impacts from intervention and notes that the authorities of a number of major countries, most notably China and Japan but

---

7. As Ito notes, the Japanese have not released their daily intervention data for this period, so that side of the story can only be estimated.

probably including a couple of dozen others, believe that it works. He notes, however, that the scale of intervention in the 1980s was puny compared with modern intervention and hence probably too small to have had much effect. His interpretation is that the Plaza's impact on exchange rates derived more from the announcements than from the power of the interventions themselves.

Ito's documentation of the Japanese government's persistently propelling yen appreciation in the months after the Plaza raises the question of why Japan participated so enthusiastically in the Plaza Accord. Utsumi describes Japanese Finance Minister Takeshita's involvement in the planning of the Plaza with Secretary Baker months before it took place. Ito cites Gyohten's (2013) recollection that Takeshita pushed for the Plaza communiqué to include more pro-intervention language.[8] For a country with a trade-based growth model, such a course appears counterintuitive.

The universal view of the authors who address the question is that Japan greatly feared US protectionism, much of which was directed against it. Ito cites Funabashi's (1989) discussion of Prime Minister Nakasone preferring a comprehensive solution to the trade problem via exchange rate adjustment over sector-specific trade negotiations. But no one, in Japan or elsewhere, anticipated the extent of the dollar depreciation and especially the massive appreciation of the yen. Utsumi colorfully relays the urgency of new Finance Minister Kiichi Miyazawa to stop the dollar decline in mid-1986.

Ito also describes how the Bank of Japan came to view the exchange rate coordination begun at the Plaza Accord as contributing to Japan's bubble economy and collapse, a view Utsumi supports. This main "negative result" of the Plaza has emerged from some analyses of that period. Ito strongly rejects that conclusion, as do Fred Bergsten in chapter 14 and Frankel. They note that the strong yen was followed by a boom, not a bust, in Japan. The boom and later bust was caused by the low interest rates put in place to counter the Plaza's feared impact on the Japanese economy, which turned out to be unnecessary, and the absence of effective regulation of the Japanese banking system.

Deservedly or not, the narrow Plaza serves as the benchmark for correcting exchange rate misalignments. Large exchange rate movements can be compared with the misalignments seen in the Plaza period, as Green, Papell, and Prodan (chapter 8) and Bergsten (chapter 14) do (including for the current period), to evaluate their potential to motivate coordinated action. But several authors also point out that it takes more than misalignment to produce agreement on coordinated intervention.

The Japanese case highlights the importance of threats of protectionism to motivate countries with undervalued exchange rates to willingly cooperate to appreciate their currencies. Despite the high value of the dollar today—and the congressional debate over currency "manipulation" in 2015, described in chapter 14—Bergsten, Frankel, and Green, Papell, and Prodan all judge the

---

8. Funabashi (1989) provides anecdotes of similarly aggressive Japanese negotiation during the Plaza meeting.

current situation to lack sufficient risk of protectionist measures to outweigh the harm that surplus countries would expect from promoting a strengthening of their currencies.

Many of the chapters in this volume point out another critical difference between 1985 and today: the relative rates of economic growth in the key countries. In 1985 the German and Japanese economies were expanding comfortably, albeit largely as a result of export booms. Their leadership could afford to take a longer view, accepting that some near-term currency correction would stave off larger protectionist and other problems in the future. By contrast, neither Japan nor the eurozone could probably afford to sacrifice near-term growth today, even if they anticipated future trade friction.

A critical and closely related consideration for undertaking a joint effort like the Plaza is its likelihood of success. In chapter 10 Barry Eichengreen reviews several historical exchange rate agreements to identify key features that have contributed to their results. Governments should have a clear mandate to negotiate, as Baker points out he did at the start of a new presidential term (chapter 2), unlike President Herbert Hoover, who started the failed currency stabilization attempt of 1933 at the end of his term. Modest but specific goals also help; the Plaza aimed primarily and initially only at weakening the dollar with a limited commitment of funds to intervention (which fortunately turned out to be sufficient). Eichengreen attributes the success of the 1936 Tripartite Agreement (signed by France, the United Kingdom, and the United States) to its limited scope. Another of Eichengreen's historical lessons is that all parties must agree on a common diagnosis of the problem. Lack of such consensus contributed to the failure of the 1933 currency stabilization attempt.

Most importantly, Eichengreen finds that coordinated exchange rate policies are much more likely to succeed when the emphasis is on correcting the exchange rate to align with economic fundamentals, not the other way around. He observes this to be the case in the Tripartite Agreement of 1936 and in the narrow sense of the Plaza aiming at near-term correction of misalignment that had strayed far from the underlying economics of the day. Many other authors, including Truman and Frankel, note the same lesson, which applies even more forcefully to the broader meaning of the Plaza Accord as a more ambitious effort at medium-term coordination.

The ultimate judgment on the success of the "narrow Plaza" rests on whether it achieved its two main goals: correcting the large current account imbalances of the middle 1980s and countering the resultant protectionist pressures in the United States, which threatened the continued openness of the global trading system. On both accounts the Plaza was a major if not quite total success.

There was considerable disappointment in the early years after the Plaza that the imbalances remained large, as Truman documents in chapter 9. The US current account deficit continued to grow in nominal terms after 1985, not peaking until 1987. The Institute for International Economics (now the Peterson Institute) convened a major conference in late 1990, entitled

"International Adjustment and Financing: The Lessons of 1985–1991," to assess whether the adjustment process was working as expected and to consider the several theories that were advanced at the time to explain the "failure" of the Plaza. But the three key presentations at that event (Cline 1991, Krugman 1991, and Lawrence 1991), especially the masterful overview by Paul Krugman ("Has the Adjustment Process Worked?"), concluded unequivocally both that the chief imbalances had declined dramatically (if not all the way back to their starting points) and that they had responded to the actual changes in exchange rates in virtually textbook fashion.[9]

The protectionist pressures in the US Congress also largely subsided. The sharp decline of the dollar after the Plaza greatly improved the trade competitiveness of US firms long before the results began to show up in the published data, reducing pleas for import relief or other governmental assistance (Destler 2005). Congress did not pass trade legislation until 1988, and the eventual bill eschewed new trade barriers. It did, however, require Treasury to start making semiannual reports to Congress on exchange rate developments, including the famous (or infamous) mandate to label countries as "currency manipulators" if they violated their IMF commitments to avoid competitive devaluation.

Virtually all of the authors in this volume thus agree that the "narrow Plaza" was a substantial success. An assessment of its overall impact, however, requires consideration of whether it also achieved its broader policy coordination and systemic institutionalization objectives.

The Broader Plaza

The Plaza attempted to coordinate macroeconomic policy adjustment to support and facilitate exchange rate realignment. The United States committed to fiscal consolidation, while Japan and Germany pledged to adopt more stimulative domestic policies. These commitments have faded in the popular memory of the Plaza because they were not memorable—being largely restatements of existing plans—and because the countries themselves largely ignored them or were unable to deliver on them. The authors in this volume unanimously emphasize that altering domestic policies to suit external objectives is rarely successful.

The G-5 nonetheless tried very hard to do so during this period. The Plaza Accord was followed by the G-7 Tokyo Summit of 1986, which represented the most ambitious effort to that time to agree on internationally consistent goals for all the major components of national economic policies, but it also went nowhere. The third step in the process was the Louvre Accord of February 1987, which generated almost a year of concerted effort and instituted target zones (called "reference ranges") for the key currencies; it also eventually ran aground.

---

9. The elimination of the US current account deficit in 1991 was a one-time phenomenon caused by contributions by several Gulf countries to the United States to help finance the First Gulf War, negotiated largely by then Secretary of State James Baker.

Truman attributes this lack of broader success in part to lack of a common diagnosis of the problem, despite a common identification of undesirable exchange rate movements. The United States saw the exchange rate movements and related current account imbalances originating in the lack of domestic demand in Germany and Japan and therefore saw stimulus in the surplus economies as the necessary correction. Germany and Japan viewed the strong (and then weak) dollar as reflecting the large US budget deficit. Because the divergent views by surplus and deficit countries did not suggest adjustment in their own domestic economies, the finance ministers exhibited little appetite to meet their commitments.

One might cynically argue that the Baker team at the Treasury was not particularly devoted to the idea of coordinating policy. Rather, it opportunistically leveraged fear of protectionism by the US Congress to squeeze more macroeconomic commitments from its trading partners. At the outset of the process, and just after the Plaza itself, the United States did try to use its new willingness to intervene as leverage to get the other countries to expand domestic demand. But Japan, and especially the Europeans, quickly realized that the United States wanted to weaken the dollar for its own reasons and that they did not need to concede much to get it to do so.

The evidence presented in this volume suggests that there was indeed a strong and genuine belief within the Baker Treasury about the benefit of deeper international policy coordination. All the Treasury officials from that period say so and still write today of their desire to see greater international coordination to manage problems in the international monetary system. Frankel and Bergsten both recount the early signs of conversion evidenced by Deputy Secretary of the Treasury Richard Darman, and Paul Volcker agrees that there was a change in thinking in favor of more active international coordination of policies.

In the rest of the G-5, French and Japanese support for systematic coordination of exchange rate policies was evident at least as early as the 1983 Jurgensen Report, according to Truman. Ito notes that Miyazawa, who became finance minister in the middle of the Plaza-Louvre period, was also attracted to the idea of target zones for exchange rates. Treasury Deputy Secretary Darman explicitly endorsed the idea in early 1985. The French hoped to leverage US interests to obtain greater domestic stimulus in Germany (Funabashi 1989). The Japanese were so desperate to garner assistance in stopping yen appreciation that they became the most willing participants in making macroeconomic commitments and arguably demonstrated the best follow-through, as described by Ito.

Germany and the United Kingdom exhibited the least enthusiasm for the broader Plaza. Only 8–9 percent of Germany's trade was with the United States in 1985, severely limiting its desire to sacrifice domestic objectives (Funabashi 1989). The British had even greater ideological reservations but were relatively minor players in the Plaza.

Despite the obvious centrality of monetary policy to exchange rate outcomes, the broader Plaza commitments seldom included monetary policy—largely because of the independence of central banks (with the notable exception of Japan), notes Taylor in chapter 12. Japan allowed some monetary policy commitments to be included in the communiqués, reflecting the dominance of its Ministry of Finance at that time. In contrast, the US and German central banks were able to protect their independence from finance ministers' attempts to formally include them in the negotiated packages. Only Japanese monetary policy shows evidence of supporting the broader Plaza efforts. Indeed, Volcker suggests the Fed explicitly avoided the appearance of supporting Finance Ministry–led initiatives. Truman reminds us that Volcker felt the Plaza reduced the likelihood that the Fed would lower rates, which would help weaken the dollar (chapter 9), and Volcker acknowledges that the Fed could have tightened more than it did to help maintain dollar strength after the Louvre and support its reference ranges (chapter 2).

The difficulties encountered with deeper sustained coordination during this period probably play a significant part in explaining the absence of repeat attempts in the subsequent 30 years, despite serious dissatisfaction with the volatility of floating exchange rates. Bergsten notes that a similar process of macroeconomic coordination was attempted in 2007 under the auspices of IMF multilateral consultations, with even less success. Truman and Frankel conclude that episodic coordination may occasionally work but that efforts to achieve sustained coordination are doomed to fail.

The Plaza as Institutional System

In chapter 14, Bergsten reviews the numerous, mostly unsuccessful, efforts at exchange rate and policy coordination that took place before the Plaza. The institutions for such policy coordination, mainly the G-5, gained credibility from the Plaza itself. The G-5 expanded to the G-7 during the Plaza-Louvre period and continues to exist as a caucus for steering the global economy even today.

But the degree of ambition within the system declined sharply in the 1990s: Less than a decade after the Plaza-Louvre, Bergsten and Henning (1996) wrote a book about "the demise of the G-7." The familiar institutions existed, but their legitimacy, authority, and capacity declined sharply. No author in this volume expresses satisfaction with this outcome.

The resulting nonsystem became characterized by heavy use of exchange rate intervention for mercantilist purposes, especially after 2000, which Gagnon carefully links to strong impacts on countries' current account deficits. Frankel documents the history of US accusations of other countries' currency manipulation, which came to the fore again in the congressional debates over trade policy in 2014–15, despite declining evidence of manipulation. Bergsten describes in detail the legislation linked to the pending Trans-

Pacific Partnership in 2015, which revived the issue and led to potentially important changes in US currency policy.

Taylor and Mulford note that the free-for-all environment of discretionary monetary policy—Mulford calls it a Burkian state-of-nature condition—has encouraged competitive monetary expansions. Taylor describes how these expansions can ratchet one another up through feedback loops. Bénassy-Quéré also shows that, for about half the members of the Organization for Economic Cooperation and Development (OECD), monetary policy does not stabilize real exchange rates. Her results raise the question of whether the current system of discretionary monetary policy has indeed facilitated exchange rate instability. Taylor's comments at the Baker Institute conference indicate his concern that monetary policy has effectively become an instrument for currency manipulation.

The chapters by Frankel and Gagnon take the other side on whether loose monetary policy constitutes manipulation, arguing that its expansionary domestic impact should offset for foreigners any exchange rate advantage low interest rates would provide. Frankel further argues that trade partners are free to duplicate, and hence offset, the impact with their own monetary policy. Gagnon points to IMF research that the impact on emerging markets of advanced economy monetary policy is small and generally positive.

In this void of effective governance, the Plaza Accord harkens back to a time when—for better or worse—major economies had the capacity and enthusiasm for changing the system. The practitioners express a good deal of skepticism about the likelihood of a return to a more managed exchange rate system but issue a clarion call for leadership to modify an environment they view as inherently unstable.

Bénassy-Quéré provides a description of why exchange rate stability matters:

> In fact, exchange rate instability is detrimental to the real economy insofar as it (a) results from abrupt changes in exchange rates that do not allow enough time for domestic producers to adjust, (b) takes the form of long-lasting misalignments rather than short-term volatility, (c) induces retaliation from partner countries that could degenerate into trade and/or currency wars, or (d) is a side effect of asymmetric exchange rate adjustments.... However, monetary stability also extends to the smooth provision of international liquidity, as exemplified during the global financial crisis.

One common refrain in this volume from people in office during the Plaza and others, like Bergsten, who held similar positions earlier, was the critical role of leadership in the broader Plaza Accord. Although the ideas behind more active coordination of exchange rate policies—target zones or reference ranges—had been around for a while and had supporters among the G-5, the US Treasury is universally credited with initiating the Plaza process. Only the United States had the political muscle in the G-5 to play the catalyzing role. It still holds that position, though Dallara argues that a small like-minded group could also provide the necessary leadership. Utsumi sees room for the United States to initiate a Plaza II among the advanced economies similar to what occurred in the Plaza-Louvre period. He estimates that another decade remains when the advanced economies can still call the shots—and believes they should.

But many authors point out that the United States no longer carries the economic weight it did 30 years ago, making it a less potent catalyst. Bénassy-Quéré adds that US economic stature has become particularly precarious because the role of the dollar at the center of the international monetary system has not yet declined, creating an uncomfortable imbalance between the system's structure and its governance.

Today it is not clear which would be the appropriate grouping to lead a call for change. Utsumi opts for the traditional G-5. Gagnon and Bergsten call for a new G-3, made up of the United States, the eurozone, and China, or maybe a G-4, which would also include Japan. Dallara posits a new G-5 that includes India.

Most of the authors, however, note the difficulty of coalition building when the major economies have such diverse backgrounds and objectives. China especially evokes concern as the only major economy without a floating exchange rate and the major currency manipulator since the early 2000s. Bergsten notably adds that "there can be no leadership without followership," a point Utsumi echoes. Convincing partners to follow faces the same challenges as building coalitions of leaders. Would China, probably the new target country today, cooperate nearly as extensively as Japan did at the Plaza? Would Germany, now part of a eurozone that includes a number of very weak economies, be able to cooperate to the extent it did then? There is considerable risk of degeneration into a leaderless, "G-0" world economy of the type that Kindleberger (1973) argues was a central cause of the Great Depression in the 1930s.

Baker, Mulford, and Dallara, the Plaza team at Treasury, all call for a renewed institutionalization of something like Plaza-style cooperation in managing exchange rates and indeed national economic policies more broadly. Green, Papell, and Prodan and Bergsten document that the real dollar is very close to Plaza levels of overvaluation against the yen—and almost as strong against the euro—so that any coordination effort would have to begin with a Plaza-like depreciation of the dollar. They doubt the feasibility of any move to a more cooperatively managed exchange rate system, however, despite the strong dollar environment. What would be the incentives to adopt such a system? The effort would need to be consistent with fundamentals, but the fundamentals at the moment all point toward continued dollar strength, as Eichengreen emphasizes. In the current weak growth environment in Europe and Japan, only tremendous pressure would be able to shift monetary policy to tighten to support a stronger euro and yen.

A second observation regards the traditional source of pressure for currency cooperation, trade protectionism in the United States. Bergsten, Frankel, and Green, Papell, and Prodan all judge that, despite the current congressional attention to currency manipulation in the context of new US trade agreements, pressure has not reached a level that significantly concerns other major economies. Several authors worry that the dollar may rise further and the US current account will deteriorate considerably more, so that such sentiment could escalate as Congress addresses several pieces of trade legislation (for the Trans-Pacific Partnership and probably the Transatlantic Trade and Investment Partnership). But all agree that a "Plaza II," in the narrow sense of the term, is not likely any time soon (Frankel concludes that the prospects for such an initiative are minimal).

There remains the question of whether new institutional reforms should be attempted. What sorts of improvements to the current system would the authors in this volume suggest?

Bénassy-Quéré posits that the rise of alternative currencies to the dollar, of which the renminbi is the most likely, could create a more stable multipolar system. Bergsten favors the congressional effort to incorporate enforceable provisions against currency manipulation in trade agreements, if they could be negotiated, and the unilateral US announcement of a readiness to implement "countervailing currency intervention" against aggressive manipulation. His argument—which Gagnon supported during the discussions at the Baker Institute conference—is that the metrics incorporated in new US currency legislation and described in chapter 14 allow clear, uncontroversial identification of manipulation that eliminates the gray areas that have allowed political factors to undermine the credibility of past efforts to fight the practice.

Gagnon goes further, suggesting a new set of international rules to set limits for foreign exchange intervention. Setting and enforcing such rules could be an appropriate task for the IMF rather than any informal G-7 or G-20 arrangement. He suggests adoption of a system of reference rates (à la Williamson 2015) that provides guidelines for when sterilized intervention should be conducted while avoiding any firm limits on exchange rates or changes in monetary policies. Without going nearly as far, Frankel believes that a time will come for renewed efforts at coordinated intervention to reduce currency instability and especially prolonged misalignments.

Based on his conclusion that intervention is fruitless, Taylor prefers a system in which each country follows its own monetary policy, driven by domestic considerations. To avoid instability, he would add one key element to that monetary policy: that its "reaction function" should be spelled out in fairly clear terms, presumably along the lines of the Taylor rule. As long as central banks mostly follow such a rule, he argues, the system can avoid the distortions and instability inherent in discretionary ad hoc monetary policies.

Conclusion

The Plaza was an iconic moment in the history and evolution of international monetary cooperation. It was uniquely successful in achieving all three of its immediate goals: sharply realigning exchange rates, significantly reducing the global imbalances of the day, and providing an effective counter to protectionist pressures in the United States that were threatening to disrupt the international trading system and the world economy.

The Plaza was less successful in pursuing its more ambitious objectives: extensively coordinating the economic policies of the leading economies and institutionalizing the process of international economic cooperation. It nevertheless made some progress in both areas and added significantly to the long-term trajectory of managing globalization more successfully.

Both the more and less successful aspects of the Plaza produced valuable lessons for what to do—and what not to do—when future problems of international adjustment arise. They provide guidance for how to handle both the economics and, even more critically, the domestic and international politics of such issues. The Plaza remains a cardinal point of reference even today, when the world again faces the prospect of a toxic mix of currency disequilibria, growing imbalances, trade policy reactions, and thus uncertainty for both the global economy and world politics.

The Plaza also represents a rare example of international economic cooperation among the major countries of its period. It thus carries broader implications for governance in a globalizing world and for issues that range beyond economics. It embodies an era that we frequently seek to recreate today.

This volume attempts to recapture the essence of the Plaza experience. It blends the recollections of some of the central architects and implementers of the agreement, analysis of its meaning by several leading contemporary observers, and an assessment of its lasting messages by some of the world's top international economists.

We thank the Baker Institute for Public Policy at Rice University, and especially former Secretary of the Treasury (and later Secretary of State) James Baker, III, for making this effort possible. We hope that it will add perspective and insight to our ability to address the many problems of international monetary policy that we face today and will continue to face for the foreseeable future.

References

Bergsten, C. Fred. 1994. Exchange Rate Policy. In *American Economic Policy in the 1980s,* ed. Martin Feldstein. Chicago: University of Chicago Press for the National Bureau of Economic Research.

Bergsten, C. Fred, and C. Randall Henning. 1996. *Global Economic Leadership and the Group of Seven.* Washington: Institute for International Economics.

Cline, William R. 1991. US External Adjustment: Progress, Prognosis, and Interpretation. In *International Adjustment and Financing: The Lessons of 1985–1991*, ed. C. Fred Bergsten. Washington: Institute for International Economics.

Destler, I. M. 2005. *American Trade Politics,* 4th ed. Washington: Institute for International Economics.

Frankel, Jeffrey A. 1994. The Making of Exchange Rate Policy in the 1980s. In *American Economic Policy in the 1980s,* ed. Martin Feldstein. Chicago: University of Chicago Press for the National Bureau of Economic Research.

Funabashi, Yoichi. 1989. *Managing the Dollar: From the Plaza to the Louvre,* 2nd ed. Washington: Institute for International Economics.

Gyohten, Toyoo. 2013. *En no Koubou: Tsu ka Mafia no Dokuhaku* [*The Rise and Fall of the Yen: Monologue of a "Currency Mafia"*]. Tokyo: Asahi Shimbun Publishing Co.

Ito, Takatoshi. 1987. The Intra-Daily Exchange Rate Dynamics and Monetary Policies after the Group of Five Agreement. *Journal of the Japanese and International Economies* 1, no. 3: 275–98.

Kindleberger, Charles P. 1973. *The World in Depression.* Berkeley: University of California Press.

Krugman, Paul R. 1991. Has the Adjustment Process Worked? In *International Adjustment and Financing: The Lessons of 1985–1991*, ed. C. Fred Bergsten. Washington: Institute for International Economics.

Lawrence, Robert Z. 1991. Comments. In *International Adjustment and Financing: The Lessons of 1985–1991*, ed. C. Fred Bergsten. Washington: Institute for International Economics.

Williamson, John. 2015. *International Monetary Reform: A Specific Set of Proposals.* London: Routledge.

I

OFFICIAL RECOLLECTIONS

1

The Architect

JAMES A. BAKER, III

Remarks as prepared for delivery.

First and foremost, I want to recognize a very special person who played a critical role in the Plaza Accord: Paul Volcker. None of what we accomplished at the Plaza Hotel 30 years ago would have happened without the support of a man whom history has shown was a great chairman of the Federal Reserve. His skillful reduction of inflation in the early 1980s—combined with President Ronald Reagan's fiscal policies—helped lead to the fantastic domestic economic growth that followed.

Paul could not be here today, but he will be speaking to us at lunch via a taped interview. It's an honor to have him here in this way, because we all owe him a debt of gratitude for his magnificent service to our nation.

Now before I begin, I want to brag a little bit about the Baker Institute and its founding director, Ambassador Edward P. Djerejian. Ed has led the Institute since it opened in 1993, helping it become the 18th best think tank in the United States and the 9th best university-affiliated think tank in the world, according to a University of Pennsylvania ranking last year. Before then, he was the US ambassador to Syria and then Israel—the only person to hold both positions. I suspect if you press him, Ed will confess that the demand for adroit diplomacy is much greater on college campuses than it is in the Middle East. Fortunately, he's been successful in both arenas.

James A. Baker, III, was the 61st US Secretary of State from January 1989 through August 1992 under President George H. W. Bush. He was the 67th Secretary of the Treasury from 1985 to 1988 under President Ronald Reagan. As Treasury secretary, he was also chairman of the President's Economic Policy Council.

I would also like to recognize several people here today with whom I worked 30 years ago on the Plaza Accord when I was secretary of the Treasury. They include:

- David Mulford, who was then assistant Treasury secretary for international affairs and is now vice chairman international of Credit Suisse;

- Edwin Truman, who was then director of the international finance division of the Federal Reserve Board of Governors and is now a senior fellow at the Peterson Institute for International Economics;

- Charles Dallara, who was then the United States' executive director of the International Monetary Fund and is now the executive vice chairman of Partners Group Holding; and

- Makoto Utsumi, who was then head of the economic section of the Japanese Embassy in Washington and is now the chairman of the global advisory board of Tokai Tokyo Financial Holdings.

I want to talk to you today about the lead-up to the Plaza Accord; what happened when we successfully coordinated macroeconomic policy among the world's principal economies in the 1980s; and finally, the need for greater coordination in today's complex world.

What happened 30 years ago at the Plaza Hotel in New York City was, in many ways, a continuation of the type of international cooperation that had characterized global economics since the end of World War II. During the aftermath of World War I, US policymakers had pulled up the drawbridges and tried to insulate our country from economic problems elsewhere in the world. Essentially, they wanted to keep whatever growth they could generate to themselves.

Those policies did exactly the opposite of what they had hoped. International trade and capital flows dried up, and with them, economic growth. The isolationism and protectionism of that era in part helped cause the Great Depression and arguably set the stage for World War II.

America's decision to stress economic cooperation 70 years ago was also part of our broader strategy to rebuild post–World War II economies and, by so doing, foster stability. Under our leadership, 44 nations signed the Bretton Woods agreement in 1944, setting up the International Monetary Fund and the World Bank. The dollar was pegged to gold, and other world currencies were pegged to the dollar. Soon thereafter, the General Agreement on Tariffs and Trade was put in place to promote free trade. These agreements provided a foundation for postwar global prosperity.

By the time I became secretary of the Treasury, in 1985, we weren't worried about another Great Depression, even though we had gone through a terrible economic downtown only a few years earlier. The Reagan tax cuts and the Fed's successful war on inflation had set the American economy afire. As the US economy grew, so did the global economy.

What concerned us was how to maintain this prosperity in the face of unsustainable, and growing, global economic imbalances. We were confronted with an overvalued dollar (when measured against other currencies) and a trade imbalance that favored the Japanese, the Germans, and other trading partners at the expense of US manufacturers and exporters.

Once again, a protectionist fever was burning in Congress. It was difficult for our Republican administration to beat it back, especially since the House of Representatives was controlled by Democrats. And it grew hotter each time Honda or Mercedes won another customer from the Big Three.

Would we return to the failed go-it-alone policies of the Great Depression? We were determined that this would not happen. We at Treasury concluded that the best—and perhaps the only—way to solve these problems was to work more closely with the finance ministers and central bankers of other major economies.

Item one on our agenda was the dollar. For some years, relative world currency values had been set by the market. Sometimes they fluctuated wildly on foreign exchanges. This made it difficult for governments, companies, and investors to make long-range plans. A business could do everything right, then be ruined by a sudden overnight move in exchange rates. And the disparity between the strong dollar and weak foreign currencies gave foreign competitors a big advantage over companies in the United States. This contributed to our growing trade deficit and sparked demands for high tariffs, import quotas, and other protectionist measures.

Of course, there is no practical way to establish what may be the most effective solution: a global currency. A single global currency would make it easy to buy, sell, and invest in markets from China to Brazil with perfect confidence in the medium of exchange and with no currency risk. But that, of course, couldn't happen. So we decided to try to coordinate the underlying economic fundamentals of the major currency countries. To be effective, we would have to do so with regularity. That process was begun with the Plaza Accord in 1985.

My first stop in this effort at international economic policy coordination was the White House, the home of the only decision maker in the executive branch of the US government. President Reagan liked the idea, and with his approval, we were in a position to go forward without telling anyone else. A leak could have destroyed the effectiveness of what we were planning.

We also needed the support of the Federal Reserve and Chairman Volcker, who had been on record since early 1985 in favor of correcting the problem of the overvalued dollar. He, too, liked the idea.

We then made secret contacts with the finance ministries of the four other major currency countries: Germany, Japan, the United Kingdom, and France. There was predictable skepticism, but as the summer of 1985 wore on, they began to realize that we were indeed serious.

Our leverage with them was that if we didn't act first, the protectionists in Congress would throw up trade barriers. Automakers and other industries were pounding the desks at the White House, Treasury, and Congress, demanding that something be done to save them from foreign competition. And Congress was listening. By late summer, top foreign economic officials had begun to see that we were serious.

Finally, we all met on Sunday September 22, 1985, in the Gold Room of New York's lovely old Plaza Hotel. All participants had managed to arrive secretly for that Sunday afternoon meeting. We picked that day because financial markets would be closed.

We didn't tell the press until the meeting was under way. Once alerted, of course, they showed up in droves. The room was packed.

By the end of the day, we had announced what came to be known as the Plaza Accord.

The results were spectacular. Despite strong resistance from traders, the dollar dropped against other currencies, quickly and substantially, but in an orderly way.

But the Plaza was about more than just currency adjustments. It also established the practice (for a while, at least) of multilateral economic policy coordination. Among other things, the United States undertook to control its fiscal deficit with the Gramm-Rudman-Hollings Act, which slowed the rate of growth of federal spending (although, frankly, it didn't go far enough). Japan agreed to stimulate domestic demand and open its borders to more imports, and Germany said it would reduce the size of its public sector and remove excessive regulations that inhibited labor and capital markets. Importantly, all signatories promised to fight protectionism.

In time concerns grew that the dollar might have fallen too far. This led to the Louvre Accord of February 22, 1987. While the Plaza was a one-time agreement to deal with a specific set of circumstances, the Louvre was more ambitious. It aimed to institutionalize the process of coordination of economic policies to stabilize world currencies within an agreed, but unpublished, set of ranges. Like the Plaza, it also worked for a while.

By 1987 the US current account deficit—which the Plaza communiqué had cited as evidence of trouble in the global economic system—had begun to fall. In 1991 it reached zero. Talk in Congress about erecting trade barriers never completely died away, but it subsided. The Reagan economic boom continued, and the world's economy grew with it.

Of course, multilateral coordination of economic policy is very difficult politically for all countries involved. After I left Treasury, in 1988, the process continued for a short time, then fell dormant. In President Clinton's second term, Robert Rubin briefly revived it to successfully deal with the East Asian economic crises. Otherwise, and sadly, the process largely ended with the Reagan administration.

Admittedly, the circumstances today would make it harder to achieve this goal than it was 30 years ago. When we reached the Plaza Accord, we were dealing with the countries of the G-5: France, Germany, Japan, the United Kingdom, and the United States. Today that group has grown to become the G-20, and China has emerged as a global economic powerhouse.

Still, there are similarities between then and now. The US current account balance today is about 2.7 percent of GNP, a big drop from where we stood in 2005, when it was 6.5 percent. Nevertheless, it is at about the same level as it was in 1985, when we were so worried.

Furthermore, the global economy has not fully recovered from the crash of 2008—much as it had not fully rebounded in 1985. Our growth today is steady but unspectacular. Europe, as a whole, is growing very slowly. And the recent problems with China's stock market—and that government's failed efforts to correct them—foreshadow possible future economic distress.

And so, ladies and gentlemen, I submit that we definitely should embark once again upon a sustained, regular, and comprehensive effort to coordinate international economic policy. Yes, we are living in a new economic world, with more players, more complex markets, and gigantic capital flows. But that is no reason not to make the effort. If we want to maximize long-term growth, minimize the risk of protectionism, and create greater stability in foreign exchange rates, we should learn from our experience with the Plaza Accord and work consistently, vigorously, and in a regularly sustained way to coordinate our macroeconomic policies.

Obviously, that will require leadership from many countries—but most of all from the United States, the world's largest economy and the continuing home of the de facto reserve currency of the world.

2

An Interview with Paul A. Volcker

RUSSELL A. GREEN

Paul Volcker acted as chairman of the Federal Reserve from 1979 to 1987, and in that role participated in the Plaza Hotel meeting and press conference announcing the Accord. The previous chapter by Secretary Baker mentions how essential it was to obtain Volcker's assent to pursuing the Accord. Indeed, a picture from the press conference shows Baker grabbing Volcker to put him in front of the line-up of finance ministers, a light-hearted visual metaphor for how the Federal Reserve's cooperation would be crucial to the aims of the Accord (see photo on the next page).

In the interview, Volcker lays out his support for greater international economic coordination, both three decades ago and today. He explains, however, the concerns central bankers have with exchange rate intervention and coordinated economic policies. He emphasizes that the natural primacy policymakers place on domestic objectives—not just at central banks—disrupts most efforts at coordination. He feels we are likely left with our dollar-centric "messy system" for now.

This interview was conducted on September 28, 2015, shortly after the 30th anniversary of the Plaza Accord and three days before the Baker Institute conference, via teleconference between Houston and New York.

Russell Green: First, Mr. Volcker, let me thank you for talking to me today. It's quite an honor for me to ask some questions about the exchange rate.

Paul Volcker: I regret we have to do this at a distance, but here we are.

Russell A. Green is the Will Clayton Fellow in International Economics at Rice University's Baker Institute and an adjunct assistant professor in the economics department there.

The finance ministers who signed the Plaza Accord: from left, Gerhard Stoltenberg of West Germany, Pierre Bérégovoy of France, James A. Baker, III of the United States, Nigel Lawson of the United Kingdom, and Noboru Takeshita of Japan.

© Bettmann/Corbis. Photographer: Harbus; Rich

Green: Let me ask you first sort of an open-ended question: What do you think made the policy coordination efforts in the 1980s possible, and what made them successful or fall short of their potential?

Volcker: I didn't think of the efforts in the 1980s as being marked by a lot of coordination. There was no coordination in the early part of the 80s, so far as I remember, but you had change in personnel in the US Treasury Department, and the new secretary of the Treasury and his associates were much more activist in achieving coordination with some other countries. So there was a change during that period and it was all kind of symbolized by the so-called Plaza Accord.

Green: After the Plaza Accord got going, would you say that there were factors that made that effort of coordination more successful or factors that made it fall short of its potential?

Volcker: I was not an enthusiastic proponent of the Plaza Accord. I was not against it, but I was a little fearful. I thought the dollar was going to decline, and it was declining on its own. From the central bank standpoint, you're never happy about pushing your own currency down, you think it might get a little out of hand. So we had a lot of discussion as to how we were going to maintain or at least avoid a free fall. In fact, when the program was announced, you had a decline in the dollar, and there was some intervention. But there wasn't much intervention afterward, because the dollar did fall on its own, but against the background, obviously, of intent. So the Plaza Accord certainly contributed toward sizable realignment of currency value, which I do think was necessary.

Green: You mentioned the fear that the dollar might fall in an uncontrolled manner. It seems like central banks in the 1980s were more willing to include exchange rate objectives in their monetary policy decision making than they were in subsequent decades.

Volcker: I'm not sure I agree with that observation. It was a long time ago, but we had a particular problem in the United States. The priority was to deal with inflation. We conducted a restrictive policy, and it resulted, among many other things, in high interest rates and a big appreciation of the dollar. During that period, frankly, the US Treasury was not interested in doing anything to modify that, from the standpoint of intervention or otherwise, which from my standpoint was not very useful or constructive, but nonetheless that was the policy at the time. Then later, beginning in 1985, I guess, conditions changed, the Treasury attitude clearly changed, and it was much more interested in achieving some coordination internationally.

Green: So from the Federal Reserve standpoint, the exchange rate was certainly not the primary objective. Do you think it was the same for your counterparts at, say, the Bundesbank or the Bank of Japan?

Volcker: This was a long time ago, but my memory is that the Bundesbank—which ordinarily was not very pro-intervention during that period—finally in 1984, I suppose, was worried about the relative decline in the mark. They unusually wanted to intervene, and we refused to intervene at the same time to support what they were doing. Now that was an incident that didn't last very long, but it was an example of lack of cooperation internationally.

Green: Once the Plaza Accord took place, and the intervention at least superficially appeared to have been effective, there seemed to be much greater enthusiasm among finance ministries for coordination, at least in the set of meetings that led up to the Louvre Accord.

Volcker: That's true. Of course, Secretary Baker was a leader in that effort.

Green: Did that create complications for domestic monetary policy?

Volcker: I don't recall that creating particular problems in domestic monetary policy at the time the Louvre was put in place. The strictures of the Louvre Accord were violated in a few months. And I can remember from my viewpoint, you might have argued—I don't remember when it was, April or May of 1987—that the Federal Reserve could have tightened more to help maintain the stability of the dollar. We weren't as vigorous as we might have been. But it was a limited area of change or controversy at that point. You didn't get the big change until later in 1987.

Green: So would you say it's sufficient for monetary policy to be focused purely on the domestic set of objectives?

Volcker: It all depends. You can be, in circumstances in which international coordination is important to help reinforce your own objectives over time, even though at the moment it may not be exactly what you would do on domestic grounds. At other times, domestic considerations are probably going to take the foreground, and you have to do what you think is necessary that way. There aren't many central banks that aren't going to subordinate international objectives they think are contrary to their own objectives. In many cases it will be the policy of the central bank to maintain stability in the exchange rate because it's in their domestic interest. So you'll get coordination in those areas because there is no real conflict.

Green: How about other objectives like, say, international financial stability or growth outside of the domestic economy?

Volcker: Well, I happened to be, for a long time, a proponent of a somewhat more activist approach toward stability of exchange rates, and I've often written about that. I must say, it has not been very fashionable through most of the past few decades. When I see what's going on today, maybe we ought to resurrect some of that effort at closer cooperation to achieve—not perfectly fixed exchange rates by any means—but to narrow the range of fluctuation.

Green: I think I noted that in your Bretton Woods Committee speech last year you were lamenting the lack of "an official, rules-based, cooperatively managed monetary system." John Taylor has a paper at this conference [see chapter 12] in which he proposes something similar built around exchange rates, setting clear strategies, perhaps as the Fed did in 1985. Is this sort of similar to the type of reform you are looking for?

Volcker: I haven't seen his paper, so I can't tell you how similar or dissimilar it is. There was an effort two or three years ago to stimulate some interest in a report called the Palais Royal Report.[1] It was pushed particularly by the French, who historically have been on that side. I thought it had useful analysis, but it didn't have much impact.

Green: Do you have a view of what the major impediments to moving in that direction are?

Volcker: I think the major impediments are that it sounds fine in theory, but when the exchange rate objective seems to conflict with domestic urgency,

---

1. Jack Boorman and André Icard, eds., *Reform of the International Monetary System: The Palais Royal Initiative* (Thousand Oaks, CA: SAGE Publications, 2011).

domestic urgency wins out. It's very difficult politically to appear to be subordinating domestic policy to international exchange rate stability, even though in the long run that may be a desirable thing to do.

Green: Let me go back to the Plaza for a second. After the Fed hiked interest rates and then Reagan came in with a very expansionary fiscal policy, it is no wonder that the dollar rose to such heights. One interpretation would be that the Plaza, with its focus on foreign exchange rates and intervention, would be seen in hindsight as sort of a "shoot the messenger" type of strategy, in the sense that the exchange rate was really just indicative of the underlying fundamentals.

Volcker: By 1985 I don't think the exchange rate was indicative of underlying fundamentals. I was convinced it was going in the other direction. But when you look at the early 1980s, I think I should point out that there was a lot of central bank cooperation, not in the exchange rate area particularly, but in dealing with the so-called Latin American debt crisis. That was a truly international effort, in conjunction with the IMF, but the United States was in a leadership position. It sought to try to avoid a breakdown of the banking system at a time when the banks were very heavily exposed to Latin American countries that couldn't pay their debts. It was an interesting incident, because US banks were certainly exposed, but even foreign central banks recognized that this was an international problem. There was just a lot of cooperation during that period.

Green: That's a good point. In discussing the Plaza-Louvre period, you've written that monetary policy can never be a solution to structural problems. When I look at that time, I think the degree of reliance on monetary stimulus in the 1980s seems small now compared to the heavy use of monetary policy today to gloss over structural issues in Europe, in Japan, in the United States, even in emerging-market countries like India. Is there a limit to how far monetary policy can provide cover for structural problems?

Volcker: I think there is a limit. Let me use the United States and China as an example. In the early part of this century, when China was running a big surplus and we were running a big deficit, everybody was kind of happy. They liked the production, they were willing to hold dollars, and we liked to import cheap stuff from China. Prices were very stable. That was a period when, in hindsight but it should have been in foresight, some basic adjustments should have been made in economic policy, apart from anything that the central bank could do to deal with that situation. Things were going smoothly, so there was no particular pressure to do anything. It was not basically, as I see it, a central banking problem. It may have been partly an exchange rate problem, but it was hard to get an agreement on the exchange rate.

Green: One of the motivations for the Plaza was that the United States had, at least at the time, what felt like a heavy reliance on foreign borrowing; with the overvalued dollar, it made us vulnerable to a disorderly drop in the dollar. We've obviously had some large imbalances since then. We've had a downgrading of America's debt rating. But we haven't had a real collapse of the dollar or a big spooking of foreign investors. Is that still a relevant fear?

Volcker: Interesting. In the land of the blind, the one-eyed man is king. The United States is doing better by and large than the rest of the world. In an uncertain, kind of turbulent situation in Europe, and now with respect to China, the dollar doesn't look so bad. I think it is dangerous over a long period of time to have the system so dependent on the dollar. Particularly the indefinite build-up of dollar holdings abroad does leave us vulnerable in different economic circumstances. Right now it doesn't hurt, but I could imagine a time when it would.

Green: Would we be better off moving to more of a multipolar system, with say the euro or the renminbi as alternatives to the dollar?

Volcker: That's a big question, and maybe so. We talk about it quite a lot, but now neither the renminbi nor the euro and the eurozone look stable enough, open enough, or strong enough, financially to carry the load. So it's left with us, and too much so.

Green: Right. It sounds like you would agree, but you know, with the volatility that we had around the time of the Plaza Accord—with the dollar going up and down by 50 percent—this year the dollar is up 20 percent....

Volcker: The big problem, of course, back at the time of the Plaza, which I'm sure Secretary Baker was worried about, was a rise of protectionist pressure in reaction to the seeming lack of competitiveness of American industry. It'll be interesting to see whether that rears its head once again here. Fortunately, I think it's been pretty quiescent.

Green: Is that part of what perhaps explains the lack of ambition to more global approaches to macroeconomics policymaking, that the fear of a negative protectionist outcome is diminished at the moment?

Volcker: I think your observation is probably correct. The sheer political pressure isn't as strong as you might have imagined it to be. But you certainly see it now in the increasing discussion about the problems of competitiveness of American industry, as recently as Caterpillar dropping 20,000 people in the paper today and yesterday and blaming it on competitive difficulties.[2]

---

2. On September 24, 2015, Caterpillar announced major multiyear job cut plans.

Green: Are there other factors, like an intellectual commitment to coordination or lack of leadership, that are part of the reason why we don't see more ambition in terms of coordination?

Volcker: Difficulties in terms of coordination are, I think, evident because of domestic difficulties. If you think of the three partners—the United States, Europe, and China (the United Kingdom is in a slightly different position)—the United States looks the most stable. The others are so preoccupied with their internal problems that I think it will be difficult to work something out.

Green: Where do we go from here?

Volcker: We're going to live with a rather messy system, I think. If people get aggravated enough where they've had enough problems, they go back and think about what could be done to create a more stable system. The question was raised in the middle of the crisis in 2008 and 2009. But as soon as the recovery got under way, people kind of forgot about it again, and it never went very far. That's when the so-called Palais Royal Accord was talked about. I don't see any near-term prospect of a more ordered system. I regret that, but it takes a big commitment on the part of the main actors. I don't think any of the main actors are prepared for it.

Green: If I could ask you one more question. When you speak with Janet Yellen, do you have any particular advice for her in navigating these times?

Volcker: I don't think a current chairman of the Federal Reserve Board needs advice from his or her predecessors, particularly predecessors twice removed! [Laughs.]

Green: Fair enough. Mr. Volcker, thank you very much for taking the time to speak with us.

3

A Personal Account of the Plaza Accord

DAVID C. MULFORD

Secretary Baker was an entirely different personality from Don Regan. He was a skilled and experienced lawyer, an outstanding political operator, and very good with people of all kinds. He was always remarkably well prepared for the many and diverse meetings required of a Treasury secretary and seemed able to read every situation in a way to achieve maximum results. In short, he exercised power judiciously but with maximum effect. The more subtle and thoughtful approach to G-5 issues was apparent immediately.

In February and March 1985, the long-strengthening dollar spiked to its peak against the deutsche mark and the yen. US current account and trade deficits were reported at new historic highs month after month. Strong growth in the US economy and weak growth of domestic demand in Germany and Japan, both of which were enjoying the export benefits of weak currencies, were feeding rising imbalances. Traditional US manufacturing industries were being hit hard by the strong dollar, the term *rust belt* began to appear to describe the destructive pressure of an "overvalued" dollar on the manufacturing industries of the American Midwest, and protectionist forces gathered momentum in the US Congress. Work began in Congress on an omnibus trade bill that promised a comprehensive protectionist trade regime, ostensibly to save US jobs and protect US industry.

These were alarming developments for the administration, especially at Treasury, the keeper over many years of the US commitment to free trade. Secretary Baker, who was sensitive to and well connected with members of

David C. Mulford is vice chairman international of Credit Suisse, rejoining in March 2009 after spending five years as US Ambassador to India. He was undersecretary and assistant secretary of the US Treasury for international affairs during 1984–1992. He served as the senior international economic policy official at the Treasury under Secretaries Regan, Baker, and Brady.

Congress, immediately began to seek an effective means of strengthening macroeconomic policy cooperation with our major trading partners and in particular to bring about a more realistic alignment of global exchange rates to relieve the growing protectionist pressures in Congress.

This was not an easy challenge. Previous overbearing US attitudes within the G-5 had left a residue of resistance and resentment. Continued strong growth in the United States exacerbated the prospect for continuing, if not growing, imbalances, and Treasury's passion for free-floating exchange rates—namely, a policy of no intervention in currency markets—seemed to leave little room for creative ingenuity on the international economic policy front.

This is where knowledge of the functioning of markets, their capacity to read and anticipate changing trends, and finally their susceptibility to unexpected surprise becomes invaluable to a policymaker. With Undersecretary Beryl Sprinkel now removed to the president's Council of Economic Advisers, and a new secretary and deputy secretary of Treasury who were both deeply sensitive to the forces at work in Congress, I brought an understanding of the power of open markets, opening the field for a new US strategy in the international economic policy area. The components of any such strategy aligned themselves in my mind as follows.

It was obvious to me that we had arrived at the point where the emerging global financial market I had seen developing during my years in Saudi Arabia had now fully emerged. Despite this new reality, which could be seen influencing the world around us every day, the realities of a global financial market were not fully understood in Congress or in the political class generally. To put it in terms of stark simplicity, when Americans began a new day they did not check global exchange rate movements overnight before looking at prices in the US stock market or other US economic data.

For reasons beyond my understanding when I arrived in early 1984, the Treasury had closed down its foreign exchange desk. This meant that the Treasury was not a participant in foreign exchange markets. How, I wondered, could we expect to read foreign exchange markets if we were not a participant? How could we communicate with—or even send a message to—the market without the contacts and working knowledge provided by a full-time presence in the market? Even if we were not an active trader and were intent on convincing the market beyond all reasonable doubt that we would never intervene in markets to influence or "manipulate" the value of the dollar, why would we cut ourselves off completely from the market? Within the international area of the Treasury I found that we had neither in-house expertise on foreign exchange markets nor any significant institutional memory of that critical field of activity. Before long I reestablished Treasury's foreign exchange desk and asked Jim Lister, a bright young economist with an interest in the functioning of markets, to open an ongoing dialogue with the market.

In the first quarter of 1985, Europe, especially Germany, suffered one of the coldest winters on record. It was estimated that with construction activity in Germany near standstill in those freezing winter months, Germany would report a significant flattening of its already inadequate domestic demand-driven growth. It was this suppression of growth, which the market seemed to anticipate spilling into the second quarter's economic activity, that had driven the deutsche mark to new lows against the dollar.

The yen peaked (reached a new low against the dollar) in April, a month or so behind the deutsche mark. By May it could be said that the strengthening dollar had "overshot" any reasonable fundamental value, a statement that was based on market feel as much as, if not more than, on fundamental economic analysis. When currency markets "overshoot," just as with any other market, speculative momentum, or herd behavior, may well carry forward for some indeterminate period.

As the second quarter economic data unfolded in Germany, they suggested that a strong rebound was taking place that was not being fully reflected in foreign exchange markets. This was how I read the market situation in early June, when I wrote Secretary Baker a memo outlining a new and dramatically different strategy for the United States to address the overvaluation of the dollar.

US economic policy in the first Reagan administration was strongly driven by the belief that freely functioning markets were the best allocator of resources and the truest determinant of value. I was in general agreement with this market-based approach to economic policy. Following the debilitating years of the Carter administration, this refocus on market-driven activity as opposed to heavy-handed micromanagement by government was a necessary and welcome change, which in its full range of policy adjustment had brought vibrant growth back to the US economy.

I did not, however, share the ideology that markets were perfect and would at all times and in all circumstances bring about correct and sustainable valuations in the shorter run. The Treasury of Don Regan and Beryl Sprinkel maintained a purist commitment to nonintervention in foreign exchange markets. The slightest consideration of market intervention was interpreted as challenging this basic philosophy and revealing a sinister belief that exchange markets, and therefore currency alignments, could and should be manipulated by governments. Intervention in foreign exchange markets by governments would be both damaging and completely ineffective.

I shared the view that markets could not be manipulated by central bank intervention. Daily trading volumes were far too large in modern markets to be manipulated by government intervention with perhaps impressive but essentially inadequate resources. Over time currency values would reflect underlying economic fundamentals. However, the time element was important to me, as was the fact that markets are influenced by short-term developments and reflective of trends often before one can be seen. In my view one could and should communicate with markets and get on the inside of market thinking as a practitioner, as opposed to being simply an analyst. I also believed it was possible to signal markets as to underlying developments, not to manipulate or direct the market but possibly to change its focus and priorities. Sending messages or signals to a market by government is an extremely sensitive matter; if it is to be done, it must be done infrequently, with great skill, and especially with the right timing.

Given these considerations, I developed a proposal for changing the markets' perception of the then high valuation of the dollar. When Europe, and especially Germany, reported their second quarter economic figures and moved into the third quarter with more expansionist expectations, a trend would begin to form. Strong US growth could coexist with strengthening domestic demand growth in Europe and Japan. If this pattern were sustained into the future and currencies began to realign, there would surely begin to be some adjustment of the world's largest imbalances, which were driving the United States toward protectionist policies that would very likely undermine prospects for world growth.

These trends would take time to materialize and become recognized as sustainable by markets. What was needed, in my view, was a message, preferably something of a "shock," to the markets that would significantly and immediately transform market psychology. If the United States was perceived to be in favor of these trends and willing to transform its previous ideologically driven attitudes that had undermined G-5 cooperation efforts, the world would respond in due course to this more favorable prospect. More important, if this "message" could be conveyed in some dramatic form, backed up by firm evidence of this new policy cooperation, the effect might be achieved more quickly. If the message came in the form of a shock or very significant surprise, the effect might well be instantaneous. Changing the US policy of many years' standing not to intervene with other major nations in foreign exchange markets would provide a message that markets could not ignore, especially if we achieved the all-important element of surprise.

This was the game plan for the Plaza Accord of September 22, 1985. Work began among the G-5 deputies in July 1985 to see how much progress we could make with our European and Japanese colleagues in obtaining or encouraging clear policy commitments for stronger growth. If the United States held out the possibility of cooperative action in exchange markets, which the other G-5 countries had been pushing for over the past four years, we might well achieve a credible critical mass of policy commitments from all the G-5 countries. The deputies met repeatedly throughout July, August, and early September. It was long and exhaustive work, but for the first time, thanks to the dedicated efforts, intellectual clarity, and political acumen of my G-5 colleagues, I truly began to understand how complex, important, and hopeful the outlook could be if the United States could exercise its views more judiciously and with greater imagination. The necessary responses were never going to be all we hoped for, but the willingness to put commitments and expectations to paper for eventual public review was impressive.

The discussions were heavily focused on Germany, France, and the United Kingdom, but there was a separate and sustained dialogue between the United States and Japan, in the form of the yen/dollar talks, which began in March

1984 and continued for some eight years. These talks focused on the opening of Japanese markets, the wider international use of the yen for trade and financial transactions, and domestic financial reforms in Japan that would enhance Japanese growth and contribute to a strengthening of the yen. As for the United States, we made a written commitment to reform our tax code, which was accomplished less than one year later in the 1986 Tax Reform Act.

Eventually, in early September of 1985, the critical mass of credible cooperative understandings was judged to be sufficient to lay the plan for a G-5 finance ministers meeting at the Plaza Hotel at the time of the United Nations annual meeting and just prior to the annual meetings in Washington of the International Monetary Fund (IMF) and World Bank. The plan was shared on a need to know basis within the administration (a very small number of officials), and rigorous emphasis was placed on secrecy within the small G-5 group of finance ministry and central bank officials. In the final weeks we negotiated the arrangements between us for intervention operations in the currency markets, setting the amounts each country was to provide as ammunition for these repeated interventions.

The Plaza Accord that September day in New York was the world's best-kept secret. The element of surprise was complete, the market effect immediate and dramatic, and the market judgments of the written policy undertakings and observations were seen as credible evidence of change in the weeks that followed. So stunning was the effect on currency markets that only a modest amount of the war chest resources agreed for market interventions by the central banks were deployed in the days and weeks that followed. The fact that the dollar had begun to move off its peak of the late spring was sharply accelerated in the balance of the year and throughout 1986.

Eventually, the dollar declined by something close to 40 percent from its high against the other major currencies. Cynics and ideologues insisted that the currency adjustment would have happened anyway without the Plaza Accord, but these people did not understand the vital dynamics of markets, the importance and timing of trend identification by markets, and the influence they would have on political attitudes for the prospect of better international policy cooperation. I knew we had administered a successful market shock and that while we would not control foreign exchange markets or manipulate them, we had nevertheless successfully communicated with markets and demonstrated a new direction that strengthened cooperation over the next few years. I was not troubled by the contrary opinions. I had played enough football to recognize Monday morning quarterbacks. Most of them never won a ball game.

Most importantly, in today's context the Plaza Accord was not seen as a beggar-thy-neighbor action, at the time or since. A major realignment of the dollar was achieved by consensus and continuing cooperation on policy issues and established in markets through dialogue and united action. This carried forward in the form of greater trust and closer cooperation among the major nations well into the early 1990s.

The Plaza Accord achieved a big breakthrough for stronger international economic policy cooperation among the major countries and for the global economy as a whole. The dollar continued its downward adjustment for the next year, at which point, as concern grew that perhaps the adjustment had gone far enough, we agreed on a plan to stabilize currencies within certain broadly understood ranges.

This meeting, which became known as the Louvre Accord, took place at the Louvre, in Paris in February 1987. It was memorable for two developments. One was the successful inclusion in the G-5 of two additional members, Canada and Italy. The second was an understanding in the now G-7 that we would establish certain appropriate ranges for our respective currencies in foreign exchange markets. If our currencies moved outside the consensus range, the understanding was that national policies would need to be reviewed.

This could not be a formal agreement announced in detail to the world at large, nor could it be treated as an arrangement to control particular targeted exchange rates. We would be attacked and tested by world markets if we set specific targets for exchange rates. Instead, we had established a general consensus about the value ranges that should be considered by our various central banks to encourage or even defend with joint intervention in markets as we moved forward. The chief value of this accord was that it focused attention on the desired policy objectives of each country, and while implying certain broad value ranges for currencies in markets, it did not provide precise, inflexible guidelines. All markets knew was that at the approximate but unconfirmed edges of these broad and flexible ranges there was a possibility of certain cooperative central bank intervention in markets. Importantly, because of the success of the Plaza Accord and its aftermath in financial markets, G-7 cooperation enjoyed high credibility in world markets.

The exercise in cooperation from the Plaza to the Louvre and beyond contributed greatly to a significant reduction in global imbalances. By 1991 Europe's surplus with the United States had all but been eliminated and Japan's large surplus had been cut by approximately two-thirds. Ministers and central bank governors now listened to one another and took seriously the group effort to recognize that each country's domestic policies had implications for the global economy and world markets that could not be ignored.

Once again, there were many critics of global economic policy cooperation. My own assessment of our success, however, is that we made important progress in a difficult and uncertain world of interdependent sovereign nations and that as a result the global economy was set on a sustainable course, where conditions remained essentially benign for over a decade.

Today we face a similarly threatening situation in the global economy. A cooperative accord such as the Plaza would not be achievable today. We live now in a far more diverse world of global markets that have diffused power generally around the world. In the intervening years the G-7 has atrophied, in part because wider unity in Europe has made such cooperation more complicated. New powers have arisen around the world; the new global forum of the G-20 can in no way replace the cohesion, influence, and confidentiality enjoyed by the G-7 during its peak. Luckily, benign market conditions continued through most of the 1990s.

This is not the case today. We are facing new and potentially dangerous challenges from many directions, with no credible institutional arrangements in place to meet them.

Even the IMF has been weakened, by being drawn heavily into Europe and failing to reform its internal structures to accommodate the rise of new economic powers. At this very moment the IMF is being drawn into expanding the list of Special Drawing Rights countries at a time when there is no assurance of accurate economic or political data from what would be important member countries.

Meanwhile, central bankers have become more collegial and more influential in today's financial system, and finance ministers, who used to lead the G-7, no longer dominate the scene, partly because the traditional importance of fiscal policies and structural reforms has given way to monetary policy as the primary policy source for supposedly stimulating world growth, with what could be said to have been disappointing results since 2010.

These conditions are producing an increasingly threatening scene for world growth and global markets. A bias toward individual country currency depreciation as a deployable policy instrument is now plainly visible. Lower growth is taking hold around much of the world, where capital flows seem to be increasingly unpredictable. Positive, growth-oriented structural policy reform seems to be in decline. The capacity of the banking system to accommodate volatile shifts in fund flows seems to be in question, and in general policy cooperation between countries—whether between the United States and emerging markets or within Europe, as it faces stressful problems with its peripheral countries—is clearly not happening.

It is my view that these are the issues that we need to be discussing today and tomorrow. The Plaza Accord provides a strong example of what can be achieved among nations over an extended period of time, but the reality is that cooperative initiatives like this are simply not being achieved, or even seriously attempted, today. It seems to me that our global markets can be characterized as existing in a "state of nature" condition in the Burkian sense. In my view, it will not be regulators or economists who solve these problems but political leaders in the now-leading world economies that must come forward to restore cooperation and a modicum of order.

Needless to say, the United States will have to play a leading role. Today we have withdrawn; our economy is not robust enough to command world respect. We need to think deeply and creatively about our new financial world and the institutions within it: how greater cohesion, cooperation, and sound order can be restored. In the process we must establish a new and appropriate balance between the relative contributions around the world of fiscal and monetary policies and a new respect for the diversity and potential of our world financial system.

4

Currency Policy Then and Now

The 30th Anniversary of the Plaza Accord

CHARLES H. DALLARA

All of us here today owe a debt of gratitude and should pay tribute to Secretary Baker. Each of us has been in circumstances in which we have seen forces beginning to move, a potential confluence of events, the need for change in direction, strategy, or approach. But until that one person arrives on the scene to guide, lead, authorize, stimulate, and insist upon action, sometimes things don't happen, they don't come together. It was Secretary Baker, arriving at the US Treasury in February 1985, who made the Plaza Accord possible. He provided the leadership that was sorely needed to address global problems of an overvalued dollar and growing protectionist pressures.

I had the privilege to be heavily involved in the conception, development, and implementation of the Plaza Accord under Secretary Baker's direction and leadership. On the day he arrived at the US Treasury Department—Monday, February 4, 1985—the dollar/deutsche mark rate was $3.30. We had a seriously overvalued dollar. Some of us at the Treasury Department thought the exchange rate was nearly out of control.

When Secretary Baker arrived, many of us, including David Mulford and me, were very hopeful that there would be a change in approach toward this issue. David and I, along with other key officials at the Treasury Department at the time, were firm believers in the core tenets of Reaganomics, which emphasized the need to allow the forces of the marketplace to flourish. Many of us also felt, however, that there are times, particularly in financial markets, when

Charles H. Dallara is vice chairman of Partners Group Holding's Board of Directors and chairman of the Americas. He was managing director and CEO of the Institute of International Finance. He also held a variety of senior positions in the US Treasury Department in the Ronald Reagan and George H. W. Bush administrations, including assistant secretary of the Treasury for international affairs, assistant secretary of the Treasury for policy development, and United States executive director of the International Monetary Fund.

market movements can go well beyond fundamentals and become part of the problem rather than part of the solution. That's the way many of us felt looking at the yen/dollar rate and the deutsche mark/dollar rate in late 1984 and early 1985.

David and I had been in touch with Sam Cross, who ran foreign exchange operations at the New York Federal Reserve. We cooperated with him on foreign exchange intervention, to signal that if the upward pressures continued the day Secretary Baker became Treasury secretary we might see if we could follow Yogi Berra's advice and take the fork in the road. Having consulted with David and Sam, I went into the secretary's office at 7:30 the morning he arrived and explained to him that continued upward pressure on the dollar was causing problems in the foreign exchange market. I then sought his authority to intervene. He had been forewarned of the problem and after a brief exchange granted his approval. I was elated. It was probably not more than a couple hundred million that we sold into the marketplace to take some of the pressure off the dollar, but it was the first step that gave us the confidence that we were embarking on a new course.[1]

A few other pieces of the Plaza Accord are relevant for this discussion. First, no matter how important the exchange rate dimension was, for those of us involved in crafting it, the accord was always about much more than just exchange rate policy or intervention in exchange markets. It was an initiative focused on building a broader framework of economic policy coordination.

I consciously use the term *coordination*, not *cooperation*, because in my view the concept of economic policy coordination lasted with energy and vitality for only a few years. The terminology shifted during the late 1980s and early 1990s toward *cooperation*. I'm not saying one is right or wrong, but what we did was coordination as defined in the dictionary: the organization of different elements of a complex body or process so as to enable them to work together more effectively.

That is what Secretary Baker had in mind, and that is certainly what those of us working with him had in mind. We wanted to bring about a framework for coordinating across key policy areas. And if you look at the Plaza Accord, you see that not only is there a crucial paragraph about the exchange markets and willingness to cooperate to align them better with fundamentals, there are also statements in which each country committed to a handful of specific actions to bring about a more orderly and stable global economic and financial system and a system that could promote growth.

Skeptics will say that those particular commitments were, in part, maybe even large part, an embodiment of commitments already made. If you look

---

1. The United States sold nearly $650 million in the deutsche mark and yen markets between January 22 and March 1, 1985, following a January 17 G-5 meeting that produced agreement to support the 1983 Williamsburg Summit. (Jeffrey Frankel notes in chapter 6 of this volume that Baker attended the meeting before he took office as Treasury secretary.) Intervention included a $78 million purchase of marks on Friday, February 8, 1985, according to Federal Reserve data.

at the particulars, there is some truth in that, but it misses the fundamental point that these countries were coming together in a collective action to say "we take ownership of a path to economic and financial stability." It was this sense of ownership that had been missing in those early years of the 1980s and arguably since the collapse of the Bretton Woods system in the early 1970s.

At the same time we sought not only to build a fabric of coordination around fiscal, monetary, and structural tax policies but also to frame a process going forward. We developed a set of economic indicators around which countries were asked to orient their policies, so that there was a mutually compatible set of goals leading toward low, steady, and sustainable inflation growth.

We had endless debates with our friends, particularly from Germany and Japan, about whether those indicators were goals and objectives or just assumptions. We became heavily involved in working with the International Monetary Fund (IMF) at the time. I remember many meetings in David's office with Jacob Frenkel, the chief economist of the IMF at the time, discussing the issue. We never quite resolved it, but at the Tokyo Summit in the spring we were able to articulate what these objectives would be and to use them as a framework for cooperation for the next few years.

In many ways the cooperation and coordination embodied in the Plaza Accord reflected something even more fundamental: the realization of the development of a tightly knit group of key policy officials on both the finance and central banking sides who were increasingly able to work effectively together on a wide range of economic and financial issues, particularly through the remainder of that decade. Those issues included regional development banks, such as the Asian Development Bank and the creation of the European Bank for Reconstruction and Development, and the Brady Plan, which represented a decisive turn in the road in dealing with the Latin American debt problem. The intense cooperation among this overall group, including my good friend Makoto Utsumi, as well as other key officials in the United Kingdom, France, and Germany, was a crucial factor behind the success achieved in these areas.

Those looking for the lessons learned in the Plaza Accord must therefore look deeper than just the particulars of exchange rates, fiscal and monetary policy, or structural policies. They must look to the basic process by which the global economy is guided.

Among the leading countries today, two important features seem to have been lost. The first is exchange rate policy. It has been 23 years since Europe authorized the creation of the euro and more than a decade since the euro was created. However, no one has figured out who is responsible for exchange rate policy. If you ask key European officials, you get different answers. I am not even sure that the US Treasury Department today has an exchange rate policy. I'm not saying exactly what that policy should be, but I do think that the key countries and the key leaders of the world need to reflect on the potential value added in the global economy of having a more articulated set of exchange rate policies.

The second is the existence of a small, tightly knit group of economic and financial leaders that can help guide the world's economies through global turbulence. China recently announced, rather surprisingly to the markets and perhaps even more surprisingly to some other G-5 and G-7 countries, a 3 percent devaluation of its currency. Would it have done so in a world in which the G-5 consisted of the United States, Japan, Germany, China, and India? I'm not sure that it would have. Is that exactly the right grouping? I'm not sure. However, I do know that without a small group of key officials who take collective ownership of the future world economy, we will continue to face the turbulence and volatility that weaken the outlook of the world economy.

In that sense I have a good bit of sympathy for the views provided by Secretary Baker in this volume. Coordination may be more difficult today, as markets are vastly more complex and larger than they were three decades ago; we would be naïve not to understand that. The fundamental need for a small group of policymakers providing a sense of direction remains.

5

The Plaza Accord Viewed from Japan

MAKOTO UTSUMI

The Plaza Accord made history; the precedent it set should not be allowed to fade into history. Exchange rate stability has only become more significant in recent decades, and the dollar is still predominant. Emerging economies are an increasingly important and essential component of international economic stability, but they are not yet ready to participate in the stabilization process. A new Plaza arrangement for the major advanced currencies, undertaken with US leadership, would stabilize the international system and promote global growth.

Historical Significance

In the field of the international monetary system and its functioning, I believe the Plaza Accord has the following historical significance:

1. *The initiative originated in the United States, but it was conducted with the close cooperation of other members of the G-5, including Japan.* During the so-called Nixon shock of August 1971, the United States unilaterally announced the suspension of the direct convertibility of the US dollar to gold as well as other measures. Neither Japan nor other major European countries had even been informed of the change in advance. In sharp contrast to that, the Plaza Accord, also initiated by the United States, was prepared in careful and detailed cooperation with the other G-5 countries.

Makoto Utsumi is chairman of the Global Advisory Board, Tokai Tokyo Financial Holdings, Inc. He held various positions at Japan's Ministry of Finance from 1957 to 1991, including director general of the International Finance Bureau and vice minister of finance for international affairs.

2. *Japan participated willingly.* Chinese leaders often repeat: "We must absolutely refuse to be forced to submit to US pressure on exchange rates like Japan was under the Plaza Accord." But it is not true that Japan submitted to US pressure. Already in June of 1985, Secretary James Baker and Mr. Noboru Takeshita, Japan's finance minister at the time, had been discussing the dollar/yen relation and had agreed on the need to do something about the exchange rate.

3. *The G-5 view of foreign exchange markets became less dogmatic.* The Plaza was the first time after the international monetary system shifted to floating exchange rates that the G-5 ministers of finance and central bank governors admitted that exchange rates do not always fully reflect economic fundamentals.

   One episode not long before the Plaza exemplifies the previous US approach to exchange rates. In 1984 the minister of state of Japan's economic planning agency visited the office of Dr. Beryl Sprinkel, then undersecretary of the US Treasury Department. The minister started to speak: "This overshoot of the dollar..." (the dollar was worth about 250 yen at the time). "No!" interrupted Dr. Sprinkel. "There is no overshoot in the market. The market is always right."

4. *Macroeconomic policy was integrated into exchange rate strategy.* For the purpose of exchange rate adjustment, the G-5 adopted two wheels to work together: cooperation in macroeconomic policies and joint intervention in the exchange markets.

5. *The Plaza Accord was dramatic.* To achieve its goal, the G-5 prepared an imposing theater to address the audience, the global markets. Since then markets have tended to expect some kind of drama at G-5 meetings, but no subsequent meeting, including the Louvre Accord, has been able to create theater comparable to that of the Plaza.

   The Louvre G-6 Accord (January 29–30, 1987) was, in a sense, much more ambitious than the Plaza Accord. It intended to institute a kind of target zone to stabilize exchange rates at "about current levels." But there was neither a detailed and careful consultation well in advance nor any noticeable progress on macroeconomic cooperation. For Japan it was difficult to accept "the current level" (¥153 = $1). Minister Kiichi Miyazawa went back home with a deep sense of disappointment and frustration. However, the Louvre Accord did not last long.

6. *The United States took a long view to developing a coordination process, not just an event.* It is very rare that the US Treasury takes the initiative to institutionalize a process toward improving the stability of foreign exchange markets. The US administration was exposed to the mounting pressure of trade protectionism in Congress and felt the need to do something about exchange rate adjustment. But more important was the fact that Secretary Baker and Richard Darman, his deputy, sought to institutionalize the

process toward both cooperation on macroeconomic policy and stabilization of foreign exchange rates. For them the Plaza meeting was more than a one-time event, it was the beginning of the institutionalization of the process.

Generally speaking, the United States—a large country that can survive in a self-sufficient manner and whose settlements are almost all made in its own currency—tends to take an attitude of benign neglect toward the stability of exchange rates. Countries that depend on international trade are more sensitive to the fluctuation of their currencies. From this viewpoint, the US initiative at the Plaza was epoch-making in the history of international finance. It would prove to have important implications for future discussions in the field of international monetary system, as I describe later.

Impact on the Japanese Economy

Now let us turn to the results of the Plaza Accord, in particular its impact on the Japanese economy.

At the first stage, the key word is *endaka* (strengthening of the yen). The magnitude of the change of the yen rate vis-à-vis the dollar stood out remarkably from the other nondollar currencies. In the 26 months after the Plaza, the yen appreciated from ¥240 yen/dollar to ¥120 yen/dollar. The Japanese manufacturing sector and the Japanese economy itself faced unprecedented challenges. All policy tools were mobilized to slow the *endaka* and mitigate its negative effects.

One episode highlights the urgency of this issue. In the cabinet reshuffle by Prime Minister Nakasone, Mr. Kiichi Miyazawa was appointed minister of finance, replacing Mr. Takeshita. After the attestation ceremony at the Imperial Palace, Mr. Miyazawa took office very late at night on July 22, 1986. The first thing he did at the ministry was to summon me to his office alone. (Just one month before, I had come back to Tokyo from my post in Washington to assume the position of director general of the International Finance Bureau and was hence responsible for the foreign exchange markets.)

The first words out of his mouth were: "Was it not a mistake to have committed to the Plaza Accord without deciding the ceiling of the yen rate vis-à-vis the dollar? Please ask the G-5 countries to gather immediately and to agree on a coordinated remedial action for the excessive strength of the yen."

I answered: "At the time of the Plaza Accord, there was a consensus that the dollar was excessively strong vis-à-vis other currencies. But at this moment, there is no consensus that the yen's strength is excessive. This is why it is currently impossible to realize a coordinated effort for the correction of the yen rate."

Minister Miyazawa replied: "Then what are you going to do to stop the further strengthening of the yen?" I responded by enumerating the list of plans I had been considering. Minister Miyazawa instructed me to carry out these plans immediately.

The second stage after the Plaza Accord regarded the manufacturing sector of Japan. Tremendous efforts were made to rationalize and streamline management through thorough cost-cutting—the only way for Japanese firms to survive under such a radically strengthened yen. These efforts, as well as the drop in the cost of imported raw materials and energy as a result of the strong yen, made Japanese industries very competitive. Exports as well as the current account surplus continued to increase. After suffering a sharp fall in its growth rate in 1986 (to 1.9 percent, down from 6.3 percent in 1985), Japan enjoyed real growth of above 6 percent in 1987–90. A kind of euphoria began to emerge in business circles.

The third stage can be characterized as the period of asset inflation. To counter the strengthening of the yen and its negative effects, the Bank of Japan had to maintain an easy monetary policy. This policy, together with the euphoric sentiment all over the country, brought about substantial asset inflation. Stock prices as well as land prices soared, even causing some serious social problems. On the other hand, consumer prices remained stable, because of the strengthening of the yen.

At stage four the Bank of Japan played a leading role. In an environment without inflation, it dared to assume that the mission of the central bank is to take control of asset inflation. It drastically raised the discount rate, from 2.5 percent to 6 percent, in 15 short months (May 1989– August 1990) and succeeded in bursting the asset bubble. At the same time, it brought about the collapse of the Japanese banking sector and the Japanese economy altogether. (There is still a continued debate among central bankers about the role they should play at the stage of asset inflation.) This was the beginning of Japan's so-called lost decades.

Implications of the Plaza Accord for the Future

At the time of the Plaza, it was still possible that the G-5 or G-7 countries could direct the world economic and financial order. Now there is a new world order, with the emergence of new players. Among the G-7 countries, there are explicit and implicit rules of the game; the new players are not ready to respect these rules. Establishing the G-20 was an attempt to make them adapt to the rules of the game, but it does not seem to be successful at all.

Since the time of the Plaza Accord, cross-border trade and investments have developed dramatically. Therefore, the stability of the foreign exchange markets should be even more crucial now than it was in the 1980s.

Several factors have created an environment that is favorable for successful action by the G-7, especially under the leadership of the United States. First, for the United States, although its dependence on international trade is much more limited than other G-7 countries', the importance of currency stability is rising rapidly, because of the cross-border expansion of corporate sector activities (40 percent of Fortune 500 company profits are generated overseas). The stability of the US dollar is thus becoming much more important even for the United States.

Second, although we frequently hear premature prognoses that the Chinese renminbi is becoming an international currency that might compete with the US dollar, let us look closely at what has happened since June 2015 in China. Heavy direct intervention in the stock markets, drastically strengthened administrative control on foreign exchange transactions, rapidly shrinking exports as well as imports—everything shows a clear retreat of China from the viewpoint of the internationalization of the country and of its currency. Although the International Monetary Fund recently decided to include the renminbi in the Special Drawing Rights (SDR) basket, it is unclear whether China is ready to accept the rules of the game shared by the G-7.

Third, after the Asian financial crisis of 1997–98, the role of the US dollar in Asia paradoxically strengthened. The region is more or less adopting a dollar standard system. The recent retreat of emerging economies will accelerate the revival of the US dollar as a key currency.

Fourth, after experiencing two crises (the Lehman crisis and the Greek crisis), the eurozone has recovered and the European Central Bank has established its reputation as a credible central bank. Japan, after the lost two decades, seems to be recovering its confidence and stability.

Fifth, reflecting these economic fundamentals, the exchange rates among major currencies have been evolving in a relatively stable fashion.

Finally, using the inclusion of the renminbi among the SDR currencies as an opportunity, leaders could persuade China to adopt the G-7's rules of the game in foreign exchange management. If China is not ready to do so, the retreat of emerging-market currencies from the international arena could continue for years. An exchange rate arrangement among the major currencies of the developed world would still be important in encouraging and strengthening cross-border trade and investments, including in emerging economies. It would surely pave the way for a broader international currency mechanism in the future that would include the emerging economies.

II

APPRAISALS OF THE PLAZA

6

The Plaza Accord 30 Years Later

JEFFREY FRANKEL

September 2015 marked the 30th anniversary of the Plaza Accord, probably the most dramatic policy initiative in the dollar foreign exchange market since Richard Nixon floated the currency in 1973. At the Plaza Hotel in New York on September 22, 1985, US officials and their counterparts in the other G-5 countries agreed to act to bring down the value of the dollar. Public statements from the officials were backed up by foreign exchange intervention (the selling of dollars in exchange for other currencies in the foreign exchange market).

The Plaza is justly celebrated as a high-water mark of international policy coordination. The value of the dollar had climbed 44 percent against other major currencies in the five years leading up to 1985 (figure 6.1).[1] Largely as a result of the strong dollar and lost price competitiveness, the US trade balance had sunk to record lows in 1985, spurring congressional support for trade interventions that an economist would have found damaging.

In the two years 1985–87, the value of the dollar fell 40 percent. After the exchange rate turned around, so did the trade balance (with the usual lag). In the end the US Congress refrained from enacting protectionist trade barriers.

Jeffrey Frankel is the Harpel Professor of Capital Formation and Growth at the Harvard Kennedy School. He thanks C. Fred Bergsten, Jin Chen, Russell Green, and Ted Truman for comments.

1. The percentage is expressed in log terms. The Federal Reserve index of the dollar against major currencies rose from 93 in September 1980 to 144 at the February 1985 peak (1973 = 100).

Figure 6.1   Trade-weighted value of the dollar against major currencies, 1973–2015

index, March 1973 = 100

Note: The 1985 peak was far higher than any other point in the last 40 years.

Source: Board of Governors of the Federal Reserve System.

The Plaza Accord made institutional history as well. The group of officials that met in New York developed into the G-7 Finance Ministers Group, which has continued to meet ever since.[2]

Overall, the Plaza was a major public success. It is therefore sobering to realize that the essence of the initiative—a deliberate effort to depreciate a major currency—would be anathema today. In recent years policy actions by a central bank that have the effect of keeping the value of its currency lower than it would otherwise be are likely to be called "currency manipulation" and to be considered an aggressive assault in the "currency wars." In light of these concerns, the G-7 has refrained from intervening in foreign exchange markets in recent years. In February 2013 the G-7 partners even accepted a proposal by the US Treasury to agree to refrain from unilateral foreign exchange intervention, in an insufficiently discussed ministers' agreement that one could call the "anti-Plaza" accord (G-7 2013).

---

2. In 1986 Secretary Baker persuaded the G-7 to agree to monitor a set of "objective indicators," including GDP and other economic variables, hoping to coordinate economic expansion. In February 1987 the G-7 ministers agreed at the Louvre that the dollar had fallen far enough, especially against the yen, and that they would try to prevent it from falling further (Funabashi 1988; Baker 2006, 431–32).

The first section of this chapter reviews what happened at the Plaza in September 1985 and during the months leading up to it.[3] The subsequent two sections consider the effects of foreign exchange intervention and current worries about currency manipulation and currency wars. The last section considers intervention policy and the dollar as of 2015.

History of the Plaza Agreement

A play-by-play review of the events of 30 years ago can help shed light on the interacting roles of politics, personalities, and chance, in addition to the role of economic fundamentals.

Appreciation of the Dollar in the Early 1980s

The 26 percent appreciation of the dollar between 1980 and 1984 was not diffi-cult to explain based on textbook macroeconomic fundamentals. A combi-nation of tight monetary policy associated with Federal Reserve Chairman Paul Volcker during 1980–82 and expansionary fiscal policy associated with President Ronald Reagan during 1981–84 pushed up long-term interest rates, which in turn attracted a capital inflow and appreciated the currency, just as the famous Mundell-Fleming model predicted would happen.

Martin Feldstein, then chairman of the Council of Economic Advisers, popularized the "twin deficits" view of this causal chain. As a result of the fiscal expansion—tax cuts and increased spending—the budget deficit rose (and national saving fell). As a result of the strong dollar, the trade deficit rose. The budget deficit and trade deficit were thus linked. The exchange rate in this view was not the fundamental problem but only the natural symptom of the monetary/fiscal policy mix, the channel through which it was transmitted to the trade deficit (Council of Economic Advisers 1984, Feldstein 1984).

Some trading partners expressed concerns about the magnitude of the dollar appreciation. The French, in particular, favored intervention in the foreign exchange market to dampen such movements. But Treasury Secretary Donald Regan and other administration officials rejected the view that the US trade deficit was a problem, arguing that the strong dollar reflected a global vote of confidence in the US economy, and opposed proposals for interven-tion in the foreign exchange market to bring the dollar down. Their policy was benign neglect of the exchange rate. In the third month of the administration, Under-Secretary for Monetary Affairs Beryl Sprinkel had announced that its intention was not to intervene at all, except in the case of "disorderly markets." For Sprinkel, a long-time member of the monetarist "Shadow Open Market Committee" and follower of Milton Friedman, the matter was a simple case of the virtues of the free market.

---

3. Frankel (1994a) gives a more extensive account of US policy with respect to the exchange rate during the decade of the 1980s. See also Funabashi (1988); Destler and Henning (1989); Baker (2006, 427–33); Mulford (2014, 169–72); and Bordo, Humpage, and Schwartz (2015).

At the Versailles Summit of G-7 leaders in 1982, the United States responded to complaints about excessive exchange rate movements by agreeing to request an expert study of the effectiveness of foreign exchange intervention. When the resulting Jurgensen Report was submitted to the G-7 leaders at the Williamsburg Summit in 1983, the findings of the underlying research were not quite as supportive of intervention as the other countries had hoped (Henderson and Sampson 1983, US Department of Treasury 1983, Obstfeld 1990). The basic argument was that sterilized intervention has no long-lasting effect and unsterilized intervention is just another kind of monetary policy.

Between March 1984 and February 1985, the dollar appreciated another 17 percent. This final phase of the currency's ascent was more rapid than the earlier phases and could not readily be explained on the basis of economic fundamentals. The long-term interest rate differential peaked in June 1984. Its subsequent decline was in the wrong direction to explain the remainder of the upswing. The US GDP growth rate and trade balance were also moving down—the wrong direction to explain the continued dollar appreciation. At the time some economists argued that the foreign exchange market was "misaligned" or had been carried away by an irrational "speculative bubble" (Bergsten 1984, Cooper 1985, Krugman 1985, Frankel 1985). Whatever the cause, the trade deficit reached $112 billion in 1984 and continued to widen. Some who had hitherto supported a freely floating exchange rate for the dollar began to change their minds.

Dating the 1985 Shift in Dollar Policy

Between the first Reagan administration and the second, there was a change in policy with respect to the exchange rate: a shift from a relatively doctrinaire laissez-faire policy during 1981–84 to a more flexible policy of activism during 1985–88. An obvious point from which to date the switch is September 22, 1985, when finance ministers and central bank governors met at the Plaza Hotel and agreed to try to bring the dollar down (Funabashi 1988, 9–41; Mulford 2014, 169–72). The Plaza Accord was certainly the embodiment of the new regime. But I would prefer to date the start of the new era from the beginning of 1985. With the inauguration of the second Reagan administration in January 1985, Don Regan and James Baker decided to trade jobs: Regan became White House chief of staff, and Baker took Regan's job as the secretary of the Treasury (Regan 1988; Baker 2006, 219–20). At the same time, Beryl Sprinkel left Treasury, and Baker's aide Richard Darman became deputy secretary at the department. David Mulford joined the team in January, as the new assistant secretary for international affairs (Mulford 2014, 156).

At the White House Baker had developed a reputation for greater pragmatism than other, more ideological members of the administration. In his January confirmation hearings, he showed signs of departure with respect to exchange rate policy, stating at one point that the Treasury's previous stance against intervention was "obviously something that should be looked at" (Destler and Henning 1989, 41–42).

Another reason to date the change from early in the year is that the dollar peaked in February and had already depreciated by 13 percent by the time of the Plaza meeting. Some observers, such as Feldstein (1986) and Taylor (chapter 12 of this volume), argue that the gap in timing shows that exchange rate "policy" had little connection with the actual decline of the dollar, which was determined in the marketplace regardless of the efforts governments made to influence it.

Notwithstanding that official policy did not change until September, however, there are two persuasive respects in which the bursting of the bubble at the end of February may have been in part caused by policy change. First, it was widely anticipated that Baker and Darman would probably be more receptive to the idea of trying to bring down the dollar than their predecessors had been. If market participants have reason to believe that policy changes to reduce the value of the dollar will be made in the future, they will sell dollars today in order to protect themselves against future losses, which will have the effect of causing the dollar to depreciate today.

Second, some intervention was agreed on at a G-5 meeting on January 17— Baker attended the dinner—and did take place subsequently (Funabashi 1988, 10). Surprisingly, the G-5 public announcement in January used language that, on the surface at least, sounds more pro-intervention than was used later in the Plaza announcement: "In light of recent developments in foreign exchange markets," the G-5 "reaffirmed their commitment made at the Williamsburg Summit to undertake coordinated intervention in the markets as necessary."

The US intervention that winter was small in magnitude.[4] But the German monetary authorities, in particular, intervened heavily, selling dollars in February and March.[5] The February intervention was reported in the newspapers and, by virtue of timing, appears a likely candidate for the instrument that pricked the bubble. Baker's accession to the Treasury in January and the G-5 meeting probably encouraged the Germans to renew their intervention efforts at that time.

One could take a narrow viewpoint and argue that the Plaza Accord should be defined to include only the deliberations made on September 22 at the Plaza Hotel and not other developments in 1985. But my view is that it is appropriate to use the term to include all the elements of the shift in dollar policy that occurred when Baker became Treasury secretary, including other meetings, public statements, perceptions, and—especially—foreign exchange market interventions.

History routinely uses this sort of shorthand: We celebrate 2015 as the 800th anniversary of the Magna Carta, even though the precise paper signed

---

4. The US authorities purchased $659 million in foreign exchange between January 21 and March 1, a fraction of the $10 billion purchased by the major central banks (Federal Reserve Bank of New York 1985a, 1985b).

5. Intervention was particularly strong on February 27. At the time it appeared to have an impact on the market (*Wall Street Journal*, September 23, 1985, 26).

at Runnymede in 1215 had no immediate effect in England and did not even bear that name. Versions were reissued in subsequent years (a 1217 version is the one that was first called Magna Carta) and eventually came to represent the principle that the king was bound by law.

We use "Bretton Woods" to denote the postwar monetary system based on pegged exchange rates facilitated by the International Monetary Fund (IMF) with gold and the dollar as the international reserve assets. But the system that was agreed at Bretton Woods, New Hampshire, in 1944 had been negotiated over the preceding two years and did not really come into full operation until some 15 years later (initially the IMF had little role to play and European countries delayed restoring currency convertibility), by which time it was already beginning to break down (as the convertibility of the dollar into gold was increasingly in question) (Steil 2013). Nevertheless "Bretton Woods" is a useful shorthand, like "Magna Carta." It is similarly useful to apply "Plaza Accord" to the set of changes in policy with respect to the dollar that took place in 1985.

The Plaza Meeting Itself

In April 1985, at an Organization for Economic Cooperation and Development (OECD) meeting, Baker announced, "The US is prepared to consider the possible value of hosting a high-level meeting of the major industrial countries" on the subject of international monetary reform. Similar trial balloons were floated in Congress (Putnam and Bayne 1987, 199). But the other shoe was yet to drop. Monetary and exchange rate issues were not extensively discussed at the Bonn Summit of G-7 leaders in May 1985.[6]

Preparations for the Plaza meeting began soon thereafter but were closely guarded. In June top Treasury officials discussed the possibility of concerted intervention with top officials in Japan's Ministry of Finance (Gao 2001, 175). The G-5 deputies met secretly in July and August, led by Assistant Secretary Mulford (2014, 169–70). Details were worked out in a final preparatory meeting of G-5 deputies in London on September 15.

Finally, on September 22 the G-5 ministers and central bankers met at the Plaza. They agreed on an announcement that "some further orderly appreciation of the nondollar currencies is desirable" and that they stood "ready to cooperate more closely to encourage this when to do so would be helpful." By the standards of such communiqués, this language was considered (at least in retrospect) to have constituted strong support for concerted intervention,

---

6. The G-7 summit of May 1985 was overshadowed by the public relations setback of Bitburg, which arose when President Reagan visited a German cemetery that contained graves of SS soldiers (Putnam and Bayne 1987, 200–201). According to some reports, this mistake on the part of the White House advance team was an indirect consequence of the strong dollar: On the afternoon on which aide Michael Deaver should have been inspecting the Bitburg cemetery, he and other White House aides were reportedly out buying BMWs (Bovard 1991, 316), which at the time could be had in Germany for half the US price as the result of the appreciation of the dollar against the mark. (President Reagan later blessed the Plaza initiative [Baker 2006, 431].)

even though the word *intervention* did not appear. A figure of 10–12 percent depreciation of the dollar over the near term had been specified as the aim in a never-released "nonpaper" drafted by Mulford for the September 15 meeting in London (Funabashi 1988, 16–21). The G-5 ministers at the Plaza accepted those numbers as the aim (according to US government sources).[7] There was, apparently, little discussion among the participants at the Plaza as to whether changes in monetary policy would be required to achieve the aim of depreciating the dollar, suggesting that the agreed intervention should probably be classified as sterilized.

On the Monday that the Plaza announcement was made public, the dollar fell 4 percent against a weighted average of other currencies (slightly more against the mark and the yen). Subsequently, it resumed a gradual depreciation, at a rate similar to that of the preceding seven months.[8]

Is Intervention Effective?

Economists who question whether the Plaza was effective are skeptical about one of two questions regarding the effects of intervention. First, is intervention effective at changing the exchange rate even if it is sterilized (i.e., even if it does not take the form of a change in the money supply)? Second, if it does change the exchange rate, does it change the trade balance? Both questions remain of general interest, well beyond the events of 30 years ago. I consider each in turn.

Is Intervention Effective at Moving the Exchange Rate?

In the decade following the Plaza, the United States and other major governments continued to intervene in the dollar market periodically, sometimes in one direction, sometimes in the other. During most of this period, market participants believed that such interventions were important: Traders would leap for their terminals when reports of central bank sales or purchases came out. In contrast, a majority of American economists and central bankers retained the view of the early 1980s that intervention is ineffective except to the extent that it changes money supplies.[9]

---

7. The "nonpaper" also specified the total scale of intervention to be undertaken over the subsequent six weeks (up to $18 billion) and the allocation among the five countries (Funabashi 1988, 16–21). By the end of October intervention actually undertaken was $3.2 billion by the United States, $5 billion by the other four countries, and more than $2 billion by G-10 countries that were not represented at the Plaza, particularly Italy (Federal Reserve Bank of New York 1985–86).

8. The fact that the rate of depreciation in the six months after the Plaza was no greater than in the six months before the Plaza is the reason why Feldstein (1986) claims that the change in policy had no effect.

9. E.g., Truman (2003). With the advent of quantitative easing, it has become more widely accepted that changes in the balance sheet of the central bank can have effects on interest rates even after controlling for the size of the monetary base, as in the venerable portfolio balance model. If this is the case, why should it not also affect exchange rates? This rehabilitation of the portfolio-balance view is one reason why the effectiveness of sterilized intervention deserves a fresh look.

Using previously unavailable data on daily intervention by the Bundesbank and the Federal Reserve in the 1980s, Kathryn Dominguez and I reexamined the issue (Dominguez and Frankel 1993a, 1993b, 1993c). We found statistically significant effects. For example, in 10 out of 11 major episodes during the period 1985–91, the deutsche mark/dollar rate in the month after the episode moved in the direction in which the monetary authorities were trying to push it. Other researchers have found similar results using broader datasets.[10] Yet others report more negative findings regarding the effectiveness of intervention (e.g., Beine, Bénassy-Quéré, and Lecourt 2002). Edison (1993) and Sarno and Taylor (2001) survey the empirical research.

The econometric part of the Dominguez-Frankel research sought to disentangle two distinct possible effects of intervention. The first is the portfolio effect, which may result from actual purchases and sales of marks and dollars in the marketplace (regardless of whether the central bank's actions are publicly known at the time or kept secret). The second is the additional expectations effect, whereby public reports of intervention may alter expectations of the future exchange rate (regardless of whether the intervention actually takes place), which will feed back to the current equilibrium price. The Dominguez-Frankel study used data that had not been widely used by other researchers, including previously confidential daily intervention data, newspaper reports on intervention, survey data on the expectations of market participants, and a measure of portfolio risk. Results showed significant effects of intervention through both channels, though only in the case of the expectations effect was the impact estimated to be quantitatively large.

Not all attempts at foreign exchange intervention were found to be successful. A number of lessons were drawn as to the circumstances under which intervention is most likely to work (see Dominguez 1990, 2006; Dominguez and Frankel 1993a, 1993b, 1993c; Fratzscher et al. 2015; and research cited in the surveys by Edison 1993 and Sarno and Taylor 2001):

■ Because the foreign exchange market is now so large (several trillion dollars in daily turnover worldwide), purchases and sales on the scale that governments are generally prepared to make will not have much effect if the market is already firmly convinced of the proper value of the currency. If the market is determined to be on the other side, the authorities will lose the battle, particularly if they are trying to support a parity that is no longer justified by macroeconomic fundamentals. Intervention can be successful when the market holds weak views as to the true worth of the currency, particularly in the case of a speculative bubble, and is willing to be led by the authorities, as it was in 1985.

10. For example, Catte, Galli, and Rebecchini (1994) extend the dataset to include intervention operations by other central banks. They claim to find even stronger evidence of effects on the exchange rate. Ito (1987, 2003) found that Japanese intervention to affect the yen/dollar exchange rate was effective, and accompanying US intervention especially so.

- The initial intervention in any given episode during the post-Plaza period (1985–91) had a greater effect than follow-up interventions on subsequent days, suggesting that surprise may be an important element. The effort generally has an effect within the first few days or weeks if it is going to have an effect at all.

- Operations are more likely to be effective if they are coordinated by a number of major central banks, as they were in 1985 and subsequent years. It is particularly important that the United States be one of the countries participating.

- The major effect comes via expectations. The average effect of reports of intervention (by wire services and newspapers) on forecasts of what the rate will be one month ahead was estimated at 0.4 percent, and this effect translated almost one-for-one into the contemporaneous spot exchange rate itself. Intervention should thus be revealed to the public if the authorities want it to have a major effect. Explicit announcements by US officials had greater effects (estimated at about 0.8 percent) than when the New York Fed merely allowed the banks through which it trades to share the information. Examples include the Plaza statement of September 1985, the Louvre statement of February 1987, and the Bush administration's "ambush" to reverse dollar appreciation in July 1991.

- The authorities are not necessarily able to affect the exchange rate for a long period, absent a corresponding change in fundamentals. The effect was usually present one month after the intervention; whether it remained after a year is unclear. Critics of sterilized intervention claim that at most it can have an effect only in the short run. But even short-term effects can be useful. Examples of episodes in which the effect lasted long enough to be useful include the "pricking of the dollar bubble" in 1985, the "bear squeeze" of January 1988 (which supported the dollar as a bridge until expected improvements in the trade balance materialized), and the placing of a floor and ceiling, respectively, on the dollar in February and July 1991.

Occasional intervention continued during the first Clinton administration, in 1992–95, mainly to support the dollar (Frankel 1994b). G-7 intervention in May 1995, after the dollar had depreciated to a record low against the yen, appears to have been successful in turning the trend around, consistent with the mantra of new Treasury Secretary Robert Rubin that "a strong dollar is in the national interest."

Subsequently, however, intervention virtually died out among the G-7. The European Central Bank (ECB) intervened in 2000 to support its then overdepreciated euro (operations in September of that year were undertaken in cooperation with the United States and others). The last time the Bank of Japan intervened in the foreign exchange market was March 2011, in cooperation with the United States and others, to dampen the strong appreciation of the yen that came in the aftermath of the Tohoku earthquake and tsunami.[11] No intervention occurred after that, and in February 2013 the G-7 partners agreed to refrain from foreign exchange intervention altogether.

Updated research on the effectiveness of foreign exchange intervention is needed. Although most large advanced countries no longer intervene in the foreign exchange market, they could do so again in the future. Moreover, major emerging market countries do intervene. Around the time that the G-7 moved to the free-floating corner (i.e., stopped intervening), many emerging-market countries switched to managed floating (having abandoned exchange rate targets after the currency crashes of 1994–2002). Looking at the last 15 years of data for emerging-market countries and some of the smaller advanced countries that still intervene could shed light on policy alternatives routinely faced by emerging markets coping with inflows (as in 2003–08 and 2010–12) or outflows (in the global financial crisis of 2008–09 and perhaps again as the Fed starts to normalize interest rates).

The growing body of empirical literature on intervention in emerging-market countries generally finds effects. Most studies look at the experience of only one or two countries (see Kearns and Rigobon 2005; Disyatat and Galati 2007; Dominguez, Fatum, and Vacek 2013; Menkhoff 2013; and the papers cited therein). The topic is crying out for panel studies. Adler and Tovar (2011); Blanchard, Adler, and de Carvalho Filho (2015); and Fratzscher et al. (2015) are a start, but there is a need for more.

Effects on the Trade Balance

Some skeptics claim that intervention does not move the exchange rate. Others claim that the exchange rate does not move the trade balance. The second sort of skepticism steadily gained adherents in the first two years after the Plaza, when, even though the dollar had depreciated, the US trade deficit continued to increase.[12]

A host of explanations for the lack of trade balance response arose. Many of them (even if not entirely new) gave rise to new areas of academic research. One was the point that pass-through of exchange rate changes to prices of imports in domestic currency is not immediate or complete, especially when the question is passing a dollar depreciation through to higher dollar prices for imports into the large US market.[13]

---

11. That the yen appreciated strongly in response to the disaster was counterintuitive to most. The explanation is that Japan had been taking out insurance against major earthquakes for many years, with the result that money flooded into the country in March 2011.

12. An example of this skepticism is Rose and Yellen (1989). Also relevant is the subsequent "exchange rate disconnect" literature (e.g., Devereux and Engel 2002).

13. Two other explanations for the failure of the depreciation to improve the trade balance in 1986 and 1987 were (a) the idea that the preceding loss of market share from the strong dollar might have become near permanent in some sectors (hysteresis) and (b) the new importance of trade with emerging-market countries whose currencies were not in the traditional exchange rate indices.

In the end the US trade balance did turn around, with a lag of two years. This response was not very different from traditional estimates of the lags. According to the *J*-curve, depreciation worsens the trade balance in the short run, because the rising price of imports outweighs the fall in import quantity or the rise in export quantity. After two years or so, the elasticities have risen enough that the quantity effects begin to outweigh the valuation effect.

The US trade deficit in goods and services peaked in the third quarter of 1987, at $152 billion a year ($38 billion per quarter). By 1991 it was down to $30 billion a year.[14] As Krugman (1991) notes, adjustment in the end turned out to work pretty much as it was supposed to. Observers had been too impatient.

Some similar developments have occurred in recent years. An effect of Abenomics in Japan was the strong depreciation of the yen in 2013, which was as expected. Many observers were disappointed when the Japanese trade balance did not quickly improve. Various explanations were proposed about how "Japan is different" because of its heavy dependence on oil and other imported inputs for which demand is inelastic. Two years later, however, Japan's trade deficit was much reduced. (The 2014–15 global decline in oil prices also helped.)

Did the Plaza Accord Sabotage Japan?

One legacy of the Plaza is a sort of conspiracy theory, which continues to circulate widely in Asia, that the United States deliberately sabotaged the Japanese economy. The most common version is that the effect came via *endaka*, the strong yen, which priced Japanese manufacturing out of world markets (Gao 2001). The claim is that the United States successfully used this weapon against Japan at the Plaza in 1985, then against Korea in 1988–89, and against China in the years since 2004.

In some ways the suspicion is understandable, given the long-time pattern of pressure from the US Treasury on Asian countries to appreciate their currencies. It is true that the yen appreciated sharply against the dollar after the Plaza, rising more than the European currencies. It is also true that Japan's GDP has mostly stagnated since 1990, after decades of strong growth. But the timing is not quite right for the conspiracy theory. In between the 1985–86 appreciation of the yen and the Japanese recessions of the 1990s came the bubble years (1987–89), when exchange rate policy was no longer working to push the yen up but rather to support the dollar.

A variant of the conspiracy theory is the notion that Japanese purchases of dollars during the bubble years led to excessive money growth and the soaring prices of equities and real estate in Japan. The bursting of that bubble then led

---

14. In addition to the depreciation, a US recession was also an important reason for reduced imports in the years 1990–91. The record US trade deficits of the mid-1980s were exceeded in the mid-2000s, even as a share of GDP.

to the Japanese recession. This idea is virtually the opposite of the theory that the Plaza was responsible for the end of strong growth in Japan: Buying dollars is the opposite of selling dollars (Corbett and Ito 2010).

Currency Manipulation

In 1985 G-7 coordination meant joint intervention in the foreign exchange market. Today G-7 coordination means refraining from intervention, which is called currency manipulation if pursued unilaterally. Some observers, such as Gagnon (2012, 2013), specify that foreign exchange intervention is a necessary criterion in the definition of currency manipulation. Others believe that monetary stimulus even without intervention can qualify as currency manipulation.

The first sentence of the 2013 G-7 communiqué delegitimizes foreign exchange intervention: "We, the G-7 Ministers and Governors, reaffirm our long-standing commitment to market-determined exchange rates...." The second sentence seems to accept the broadening of the definition of manipulation to other policies that can affect the exchange rate: "We reaffirm that our fiscal and monetary policies have been and will remain oriented towards meeting our respective domestic objectives using domestic instruments, and that we will not target exchange rates." The implication is that monetary stimulus is valid as long as the authorities are not aware that it is likely to depreciate their currency—or at least as long as doing so is not their purpose. In the absence of mind-reading skills, the communiqué in practice rules out intervention as well as statements by officials to influence currencies but it does not rule out monetary stimulus.

Beggar-Thy-Neighbor Policies

Is currency depreciation a beggar-thy-neighbor policy that calls for enforced rules against currency manipulation? Let us stipulate that because a depreciation of the currency raises a country's price competitiveness on world markets, it stimulates the country's net exports—perhaps with a delay of a year or two—and thus achieves a switching of world spending toward the goods and services of the originating country at the expense of spending on goods and services of other countries. (Notice that I assume here that the switching effects that the exchange rate has via the trade balance dominate any other effects it may have.[15])

It is then easy to see why such an exchange rate policy is often viewed as

---

15. In some countries, especially emerging markets and developing countries, depreciation of the currency has contractionary effects, which may be large enough to offset the expansionary switching effect on the trade balance. These effects include balance sheet effects (if the depreciating country has a large stock of debt denominated in foreign currency) and the effect on the local-currency price of oil or other imported inputs. If these contractionary effects of depreciation were important, it would seem to follow that an appreciation of other currencies—because the dollar is depreciating—would have expansionary effects on their economies. Beggar-thy-neighbor would be converted to enrich-thy-neighbor.

a classic beggar-thy-neighbor policy, analogous to erecting tariffs. It might seem a short step from there to the view that everyone would be better off in a cooperative regime in which all countries agreed to refrain from deliberate intervention to depreciate their currencies (just as all countries benefit if they all remove protectionist trade barriers). But the analogy may be misplaced. A noncoordinated world in which each country chooses its monetary policy independently, subject to the choices of other countries, is very different from the problems of a noncoordinated world in which each country chooses its tariffs independently.

The classic examples of both kinds of beggar-thy-neighbor policies came in the 1930s. The Smoot-Hawley Tariff, enacted by the United States in 1930, was emulated by other countries, causing global trade to collapse. Britain, the United States, France, and other countries pursued competitive devaluations in the early 1930s, as each in turn took its currency off the gold standard (Eichengreen 2015). The disasters of the 1930s motivated the architects of the postwar system who met at Bretton Woods in 1944 to adopt both the principle of free trade and the principle of pegged exchange rates. The dollar could not be devalued. Other exchange rates were adjustable in the event of fundamental disequilibrium, but to devalue otherwise would be considered unfair currency manipulation under IMF Article IV.

Eichengreen and Sachs (1985, 1986) offer a powerful revisionist interpretation of the exchange rate developments of the 1930s. They argue that (unlike tariffs) the devaluations were not collectively damaging but may actually have been beneficial. Each devaluation was a reduction in the value of the currency not just in terms of other currencies but also in terms of gold. When each country had taken its turn, the net effects on exchange rates largely canceled out, but the net effects vis-à-vis gold did not. Each country was left with a currency that was worth less in terms of gold (the price of gold was higher in terms of their currency). As a result, the nominal value of gold reserves rose. As gold reserves were the ultimate backing for the money supply, the rise in their value allowed an expanded money supply in each country and lower interest rates, which is just what the world needed at the time.

The Bretton Woods system came crashing down in the early 1970s. After the members of the IMF ratified the move to floating exchange rates in the Jamaica Communiqué of January 1976, they agreed to a framework for mutual surveillance under the 1977 Decision on Surveillance over Exchange Rate Policies; in 1978 they amended Article IV. Both Principle (A) of the 1977 Decision and Clause 3 of Section 1 of Article IV require that each member "avoid manipulating exchange rates or the international monetary system in order to prevent effective balance of payments adjustment or to gain an unfair competitive advantage over other members." It is almost as if they shifted from interpreting manipulation as failure to intervene sufficiently in the foreign exchange market to interpreting it as excessive intervention in the foreign exchange market.

US Complaints about Currency Manipulation by Others

Congressional concerns about US trade in the mid-1980s did result in one major piece of currency legislation. In the Omnibus Trade and Competitiveness Act of 1988, Congress mandated biannual reports from the US Treasury regarding whether trading partners were manipulating currencies. Section 3004 requires the Treasury to "consider whether countries manipulate the rate of exchange between their currency and the United States dollar for purposes of preventing effective balance of payments adjustments or gaining unfair competitive advantage in international trade." Under the law the United States must hold talks with governments deemed to be breaking the rules.

In the first of the Reports to Congress on International Economics and Exchange Rate Policy, filed in October 1988, Korea and Taiwan were found guilty of manipulation; Singapore and Hong Kong got off with warnings (policy changes were recommended). In the years that followed, all countries deemed to be manipulators or given warnings were Asian.

In 2003 the United States began to put increasing pressure on China to appreciate its currency.[16] There were good arguments why China should have moved in the direction of increasing exchange rate flexibility and allowed its currency to appreciate (whether the criterion was China's own economic interest or the need to facilitate an orderly unwinding of record global current account imbalances). But especially in US election years, such as 2004, much of the political pressure was tied to the bilateral US-China trade deficits and loss of American jobs in manufacturing, criteria that have little basis in IMF agreements or economic logic. Much of the pressure on the Treasury to name China a manipulator came from Capitol Hill. The Schumer-Graham bill, originally proposed in February 2005, would have imposed (WTO-illegal) tariffs of 27.5 percent on all Chinese goods if China did not substantially revalue its currency. The bill did not pass, but other versions were subsequently proposed.

Many in Congress in 2015 opposed giving trade promotion authority (TPA) to President Obama because the legislation did not include language to enforce prohibition of currency manipulation by other countries.[17] TPA is the same "fast-track" authority that every president since Nixon has been granted to allow international trade negotiations to proceed. Obama wanted it in particular to be able to complete negotiations over the Trans-Pacific Partnership (TPP) with Asian countries and the Transatlantic Trade and Investment Partnership (TTIP) with Europe.

Currency manipulation is best addressed in other forums, including bilateral and G-20 talks and IMF surveillance. Critics believe those venues are too

---

16. For more extensive analysis of this history and other relevant references, see Frankel and Wei (2007).

17. Some economists (e.g., Bergsten 2013, 2015; Gagnon 2012, 2013) support such provisions regarding currency manipulation, enforced by trade sanctions; many others are opposed (e.g., Bénassy-Quéré et al. 2014, Frankel 2015).

weak and want to be able to apply the penalty of trade sanctions. My view is that if the United States had insisted that strong currency manipulation language go into the TPP, other countries would have refused—and with good reason. There is too much disagreement over what constitutes unfair currency manipulation. Some US interest groups and members of Congress, for example, think that China and Japan are manipulating their currencies right now even though they are not. The provision would thus likely have been misused.

An analogy could be made with antidumping legislation. The original intellectual rationale for such legislation was predatory pricing. But the way the laws ended up being written and enforced, cases seldom involve predatory pricing. In practice antidumping countermeasures are usually a disguised form of protectionism. Currency manipulation rules could be misused in the same way.

There are times when a country's currency can be judged undervalued or overvalued and times when its trading partners have a legitimate interest in raising the question with its government. But even in those rare cases when currency misalignment is relatively clear, trade agreements are not the right venue for addressing it, in my view. The undervalued renminbi was addressed in bilateral China-US discussions in 2004-11, with success: China allowed the currency to appreciate 35 percent over time. Today the renminbi is well within a normal range (Kessler and Subramanian 2014, Cline 2015, IMF 2015). Although the People's Bank of China did indeed buy up huge quantities of dollars in exchange for renminbi between 2004 and 2014, thereby keeping its currency from appreciating as fast as it otherwise would have, it stopped doing so in 2014.[18]

China isn't in the TPP or the TTIP. Japan is in the TPP, and the yen depreciated greatly over 2014-15. Some US economic interests, particularly the auto industry, accuse Japan of manipulation to keep the yen undervalued. Many congressional critics cite Japan as the target of their proposals to insist that currency manipulation language be part of the TPP. But the Bank of Japan has stopped intervening in the foreign exchange market, beyond one episode in 2011. In 2013 Japan joined the other G-7 countries in agreeing to refrain from foreign exchange intervention.

Members of the eurozone are in the TTIP negotiations, and the euro has depreciated significantly over the last year. But the ECB has not intervened to push down the euro. It is party to the 2013 agreement not to intervene.

Does Monetary Stimulus Constitute Currency Manipulation?

Both Japan and the ECB have undertaken substantial monetary easing since 2013, which explains some of the depreciation of their currencies. It is presumably these actions that US critics of TPA, TPP, and TTIP have in mind when

---

18. If anything, the Chinese sold dollars in exchange for renminbi during 2014-15, keeping the value of the currency *higher* than it would otherwise would have been. China's reserves peaked at $3.99 trillion in July 2014 before declining to $3.23 trillion by January 2016.

they accuse Japan and Europe of currency manipulation. But monetary expansion is not currency manipulation. For one thing, countries can hardly be blamed for undertaking monetary stimulus when domestic economic conditions require it. As the US Treasury explains to domestic critics, that is what the United States did with its quantitative easing of 2008–12, the context in which Brazilian Minister Guido Mantega, backed by President Dilma Rousseff, originally coined the term "currency war."

Furthermore, when monetary stimulus is the cause of currency manipulation, as opposed to sterilized foreign exchange intervention, the presumption of a negative impact on other countries via the trade balance disappears. Counteracting the effect via the exchange rate and consequent expenditure switching is the intended increase in income and consequent boost to imports.

Finally, even if the expenditure-switching effect of monetary stimulus dominates the expenditure-increasing effect, so that there is an overall loss of demand to trading partner countries, countries need not be passive. They can respond to a loss in demand with macroeconomic stimulus of their own.

There is an argument for our time that is analogous to the Eichengreen-Sachs (1985, 1986) reinterpretation of the 1930s (Eichengreen 2013). Yes, US developments have major impacts on other countries, even when exchange rates are floating (see, e.g., Rey 2015). But if trading partners don't like the implications of a dollar depreciation such as the one that resulted in 2010–11 from the second round of US quantitative easing, their central banks are free to ease their own monetary policies (buying domestic assets) or even intervene in the foreign exchange market (buying dollars) to prevent the unwanted appreciation of their own currencies—as China and many other emerging-market countries did during that period. The currency war critique is right in the indisputable respect that, by definition, not every country can depreciate its currency. But it does not follow that a system in which every central bank is buying assets (domestic or foreign) is a system in which everybody is worse off. To the contrary, the result may even be the sort of global monetary expansion that the world needs during a time such as the 1930s or the aftermath of the 2008–09 global recession.

Conclusion: Is It Time for Another Plaza?

Although the G-7 countries have not found the need to intervene in their foreign exchange markets in recent years, it would be shortsighted to think that this state of affairs will continue forever. Coordinated intervention should be a legitimate option. Almost by definition, if a group of major countries jointly agree to intervention operations, they must believe it is in their interests. No set of rigid multilateral rules either prohibiting or requiring intervention should be sought, particularly in the context of trade rules.

Intervention is most likely to make sense on those infrequent occasions when the exchange rate wanders far from macroeconomic fundamentals, as it had by early 1985. The weakness of the euro in 2000–01 and the strength of the yen in 2011 were two such "misalignments."[19] They are also the most recent occasions on which the United States joined with partners in concerted foreign exchange intervention. One might have argued that the euro was again getting close to meeting the criterion when it strengthened in early 2014 despite very low growth in the eurozone.[20] But on that occasion ECB plans for quantitative easing, which eventually went into effect in January 2015, soon succeeded in depreciating the euro to a more appropriate level.

The dollar appreciated 18 percent between mid-2014 and mid-2015. The US trade balance is expected to deteriorate as a result. Congressional worries over trade have been strong enough in recent years to seriously endanger President Obama's efforts to negotiate trade agreements. Some observers, such as C. Fred Bergsten (in chapter 14), have asked whether the dollar might be getting close to the level at which "another Plaza" is called for.

The answer is no. The situation today is different from the situation in 1985.[21] For one thing the dollar's recent appreciation is nowhere near as great as it was leading up to 1985. For another, unlike then, the macroeconomic fundamentals of textbook theories explain the recent appreciation episode unusually well. The US economy performed relatively strongly from mid-2014 to mid-2015, both compared with the preceding six years and compared with other countries. For this reason the Fed ended quantitative easing in 2014 and is getting ready to raise interest rates—in contrast to other countries, where central banks have moved toward monetary stimulus. Both US economic performance and the change in monetary policy are explanations for the strong dollar. These developments should be welcomed, taken as a whole, notwithstanding the effect on exports.

Wouldn't a rising trade deficit have a negative effect on US growth? Not really. The dollar appreciation is probably one of the major reasons why the Fed held off until after June 2015 on its long-anticipated decision to raise short-term interest rates, to avoid a growth slowdown or even a descent into deflation. Precisely because the Fed can be relied on to target the overall economy, the dollar and trade balance primarily affect the composition of GDP, not the total.

The Plaza should remain the classic precedent for coordinated G-7 intervention in the foreign exchange market when one or more of their currencies is very far out of line. Those conditions do not apply today. But the pendulum will swing back. The day will come when Plaza-style intervention is again appropriate.

---

19. Misalignments can arise from unwarranted exchange rate movements when the currency is floating and from the absence of warranted movements when the currency is pegged.

20. The ECB could have decided to buy dollars, if it had not agreed the year before to refrain (Jeffrey Frankel, "Why the ECB Should Buy US Treasuries," keynote speech delivered at the Federal Reserve Bank of Dallas and Southern Methodist University, Dallas, April 4, 2014).

21. Green, Papell, and Prodan (chapter 8 of this volume) conclude that the present differs from the pre-Plaza period in several key dimensions.

References

Adler, Gustavo, and Camilo Tovar Mora. 2011. *Foreign Exchange Intervention: A Shield against Appreciation Winds?* IMF Working Paper 11/165. Washington: International Monetary Fund.

Baker, James A., III. 2006. *Work Hard, Study... and Keep Out of Politics! Adventures and Lessons from an Unexpected Public Life.* New York: Penguin Group.

Beine, Michel, Agnès Bénassy-Quéré, and Christelle Lecourt. 2002. Central Bank Intervention and Foreign Exchange Rates: New Evidence from FIGARCH Estimation. *Journal of International Money and Finance* 21, no. 1: 115–44.

Bénassy-Quéré, Agnès, Pierre-Olivier Gourinchas, Philippe Martin, and Guillaume Plantin. 2014. The Euro in the "Currency War." *Les notes du conseil d'analyse économique* 11.

Bergsten, C. Fred. 1984. The United States Trade Deficit and the Dollar. Statement before the Senate Committe on Banking, Housing and Urban Affairs, Subcommitte on International Finance and Monetary Policy. Washington. June 6.

Bergsten, C. Fred. 2013. Currency Wars, the Economy of the United States and Reform of the International Monetary System. Twelfth Annual Stavros Niarchos Foundation Lecture at the Peterson Institute for International Economics, Washington, May 16.

Bergsten, C. Fred. 2015. The Truth About Currency Manipulation. *Foreign Affairs,* January 18.

Blanchard, Olivier, Gustavo Adler, and Irineu de Carvalho Filho. 2015. *Can Foreign Exchange Intervention Stem Exchange Rate Pressures from Global Capital Flow Shocks?* IMF Working Paper 15/159. Washington: International Monetary Fund.

Bordo, Michael, Owen Humpage, and Anna Schwartz. 2012. *Foreign-Exchange-Market Operations in the Twenty-First Century.* NBER Working Paper 17984. Cambridge, MA: National Bureau of Economic Research.

Bordo, Michael, Owen Humpage, and Anna Schwartz. 2015. *US Foreign-Exchange Operations and Monetary Policy in the Twentieth Century.* Chicago: University of Chicago Press.

Bovard, James. 1991. *The Fair Trade Fraud.* New York: St. Martin's.

Catte, Pietro, Giampaolo Galli, and Salvatore Rebecchini. 1994. Concerted Interventions and the Dollar: An Analysis of Daily Data. *In The International Monetary System,* ed. Peter B. Kenen, Francesco Papadia, and Fabrizio Saccomanni. Cambridge: Cambridge University Press.

Cline, William. 2015. *Estimates of Fundamental Equilibrium Exchange Rates, May 2015.* PIIE Policy Brief 15-8. Washington: Peterson Institute of International Economics.

Cooper, Richard. 1985. The U.S. Payments Deficit and the Strong Dollar: Policy Options. In *The U.S. Dollar: Recent Developments, Outook, and Policy Options.* Kansas City, MO: Federal Reserve Bank of Kansas City.

Corbett, Jenny, and Takatoshi Ito. 2010. What Should the US and China Learn from the Past US-Japan conflict? *VoxEU,* April 30.

Council of Economic Advisers. 1984. The United States in the World Economy: Challenges of Recovery. Chapter 2 in *1984 Economic Report of the President.* Washington: Government Printing Office.

Destler, I. Mac, and C. Randall Henning. 1989. *Dollar Politics: Exchange Rate Policymaking in the United States.* Washington: Institute for International Economics.

Devereux, Michael, and Charles Engel. 2002. Exchange Rate Pass-Through, Exchange Rate Volatility, and Exchange Rate Disconnect. *Journal of Monetary Economics* 49, no. 5: 913–40.

Disyatat, Piti, and Gabriele Galati. 2007. The Effectiveness of Foreign Exchange Intervention in Emerging Market Countries: Evidence from the Czech Koruna. *Journal of International Money and Finance* 26, no. 3: 383–402.

Dominguez, Kathryn. 1990. Market Responses to Coordinated Central Bank Intervention. *Carnegie-Rochester Conference Series on Public Policy* 32.

Dominguez, Kathryn. 2006. When Do Central Bank Interventions Influence Intra-Daily and Longer-Term Exchange Rate Movements? *Journal of International Money and Finance* 25: 1051-71.

Dominguez, Kathryn, Rasmus Fatum, and Pavel Vacek. 2013. Do Sales of Foreign Exchange Reserves Lead to Currency Appreciation? *Journal of Money, Credit and Banking* 45, no. 5: 867-90.

Dominguez, Kathryn, and Jeffrey Frankel. 1993a. Does Foreign Exchange Intervention Matter? The Portfolio Effect. *American Economic Review* 83, no. 5: 1356-69.

Dominguez, Kathryn, and Jeffrey Frankel. 1993b. *Does Foreign Exchange Intervention Work?* Washington: Institute for International Economics.

Dominguez, Kathryn, and Jeffrey Frankel. 1993c. Foreign Exchange Intervention: An Empirical Assessment. In *On Exchange Rates*, ed. Jeffrey Frankel. Cambridge, MA: MIT Press.

Edison, Hali. 1993. The Effectiveness of Central Bank Intervention: A Survey of the Post-1982 Literature. *Special Papers on International Economics*. Princeton, NJ: Princeton University.

Eichengreen, Barry. 2013. Currency War or International Policy Coordination? *Journal of Policy Modeling* 35, no. 3: 425-33.

Eichengreen, Barry. 2015. *Hall of Mirrors: The Great Depression, The Great Recession, and the Uses—and Misuses—of History*. New York: Oxford University Press.

Eichengreen, Barry, and Jeffrey Sachs. 1985. Exchange Rates and Economic Recovery in the 1930s. *Journal of Economic History* 45, no. 4: 925-46.

Eichengreen, Barry, and Jeffrey Sachs. 1986. Competitive Devaluation and the Great Depression: A Theoretical Reassessment. *Economic Letters* 22, no. 1: 67-71.

Federal Reserve Bank of New York. 1985a. *Quarterly Review* 10 (Spring): 60.

Federal Reserve Bank of New York. 1985b. *Quarterly Review* 10 (Autumn): 52.

Federal Reserve Bank of New York. 1985-86. *Quarterly Review* 10 (Winter): 47.

Feldstein, Martin. 1984. The Dollar Exchange Rate. Remarks before the World Affairs Council of Philadelphia, February 29.

Feldstein, Martin. 1986. *New Evidence on the Effects of Exchange Rate Intervention*. Cambridge, MA: National Bureau of Economic Research.

Frankel, Jeffrey. 1985. The Dazzling Dollar. *Brookings Papers on Economic Activity* 1: 199-217.

Frankel, Jeffrey. 1994a. The Making of Exchange Rate Policy in the 1980s. In *American Economic Policy in the 1980s*, ed. Martin Feldstein. Cambridge: University of Chicago.

Frankel, Jeffrey. 1994b. Clinton's Dollar Policy and the Effectiveness of Foreign Exchange Intervention. *Revue d'économie financière* (December).

Frankel, Jeffrey. 2015. *The Chimera of Currency Manipulation*. Project Syndicate, June 10. Available at www.project-syndicate.org/commentary/trade-negotiations-currency-manipulation-by-jeffrey-frankel-2015-06.

Frankel, Jeffrey, and Shang-Jin Wei. 2007. *Assessing China's Exchange Rate Regimes*. Economic Policy 51. London: Center for Economic and Policy Research.

Fratzscher, Marcel, Oliver Gloede, Lukas Menkhoff, Lucio Sarno, and Tobias Stohr. 2015. *When Is Foreign Exchange Intervention Effective? Evidence from 33 Countries*. Discussion Papers of DIW Berlin 1518 (November). Berlin: German Institute for Economic Research.

Funabashi, Yoichi. 1988. *Managing the Dollar: From the Plaza to the Louvre*. Washington: Institute for International Economics.

G-7. 2013. Statement by G7 Finance Ministers and Central Bank Governors, February 12. Available at www.g8.utoronto.ca/finance/fm130212.htm.

Gagnon, Joseph E. 2012. *Combating Widespread Currency Manipulation*. PIIE Policy Brief 12-19. Washington: Peterson Institute for International Economics.

Gagnon, Joseph E. 2013. Currency Wars. *Milken Institute Review* 15, no. 1: 47–55.

Gao, Bai. 2001. *Japan's Economic Dilemma: The Institutional Origins of Prosperity and Stagnation*. Cambridge: Cambridge University Press.

Henderson, Dale, and Stephanie Sampson. 1983. Intervention in Foreign Exchange Markets: A Summary of Ten Staff Studies. *Federal Reserve Bulletin* 69: 830–36.

IMF (International Monetary Fund). 2015. *IMF Completes the 2015 Article IV Consultation Mission to China*. Press Release 15/237, May 26. Washington.

Ito, Takatoshi. 1987. The Intradaily Exchange Rate Dynamics and Monetary Policies after the Group of Five Agreement. *Journal of the Japanese and International Economies* 1, no. 3: 275–98.

Ito, Takatoshi. 2003. Is Foreign Exchange Intervention Effective? The Japanese Experience in the 1990s. In *Monetary History, Exchange Rates and Financial Markets, Essays in Honour of Charles Goodhart*, Volume 2, ed. Paul Mizen. Cheltenham, UK: Edward Elgar Publishers.

Kearns, Jonathan, and Roberto Rigobon. 2005. Identifying the Efficacy of Central Bank Interventions: Evidence from Australia and Japan. *Journal of International Economics* 66: 31–48.

Kessler, Martin, and Arvind Subramanian. 2014. *Is the Renminbi Still Undervalued? Not According to New PPP Estimates*. RealTime Economic Issues Watch, May 1. Washington: Peterson Institute for International Economics.

Krugman, Paul. 1985. Is the Strong Dollar Sustainable? In *The U.S. Dollar: Recent Developments, Outlook, and Policy Options*. Kansas City: Federal Reserve Bank of Kansas City.

Krugman, Paul. 1991. Introduction. In *International Adjustment and Financing: The Lessons of 1985–1991*, ed. C. Fred Bergsten. Washington: Institute for International Economics.

Menkhoff, Lukas. 2013. Foreign Exchange Intervention in Emerging Markets: A Survey of Empirical Studies. *World Economy* 36, no. 9: 1187–208.

Mulford, David. 2014. *Packing for India: A Life of Action in Global Finance and Diplomacy*. Lincoln, NE: Potomac Books.

Obstfeld, Maurice. 1990. The Effectiveness of Foreign-Exchange Intervention: Recent Experience. In *International Policy Coordination and Exchange Rate Fluctuations*, ed. J. Frenkel, M. Goldstein, and W. Branson. Chicago: University of Chicago Press.

Putnam, Robert, and Nicholas Bayne. 1987. *Hanging Together: The Seven-Power Summits*. Cambridge, MA: Harvard University Press.

Regan, Donald. 1988. *For the Record: From Wall Street to Washington*. New York: St. Martin's.

Rey, Hélène. 2015. *Dilemma not Trilemma: The Global Financial Cycle and Monetary Policy Independence*. NBER Working Paper 21162. Cambridge, MA: National Bureau of Economic Research.

Rose, Andrew, and Janet Yellen. 1989. Is There a J-Curve? *Journal of Monetary Economics* 24, no. 1: 53–68.

Sarno, Lucio, and Mark Taylor. 2001. Official Intervention in the Foreign Exchange Market: Is It Effective and, If So, How Does It Work? *Journal of Economic Literature* 39: 839–68.

Steil, Benn. 2013. *The Battle of Bretton Woods*. Princeton, NJ: Princeton University Press.

Truman, Edwin M. 2003. The Limits of Exchange Market Intervention. In *Dollar Overvaluation and the World Economy*, ed. C. Fred Bergsten and John Williamson. Special Report 16. Washington: Institute for International Economics.

US Department of Treasury. 1983. *Report of the Working Group on Exchange Market Intervention* (Jurgensen Report). Washington.

7

The Plaza Accord and Japan
Reflections on the 30th Anniversary

TAKATOSHI ITO

The Plaza Accord, followed by the Louvre Accord, is one of the most significant events in the history of international finance in the post–World War II era. For Japanese policymakers, economists, and journalists, the Plaza Accord is as important as fixing the yen to 360/dollar in 1949, the breakdown of the Bretton Woods regime in 1971, and the breakdown of the Smithsonian Agreement in 1973. However, there are widely different views among policymakers and academics in Japan about the impacts the Plaza-Louvre Accords had on the Japanese economy. Some regard it as a symbolic event that marks the moment in which Japan firmly secured a role in international economic policy coordination that would be led by the Group of Five (G-5) countries. Others regard it as a trigger for the long-run trend of yen appreciation for the next 10 years. Some look back to the Plaza as a bad example of international policy coordination that distorted domestic monetary policy. There is a bit of a Rashomon effect.

As time has passed and some of the people involved in the negotiations in 1985–88 have told stories and written memoirs, it is now possible to reconstruct what really happened behind closed doors and evaluate, with the benefit of hindsight, the policy actions taken at the time. An early account of the Plaza-Louvre period is by Yoichi Funabashi (1988), who interviewed key policymakers at both meetings. Paul Volcker and Toyoo Gyohten (1992, chapters

Takatoshi Ito is professor of international and public affairs at Columbia University and a research associate at the National Bureau of Economic Research. He is grateful to Toyoo Gyohten and Haruhiko Kuroda for comments on an earlier version of this chapter and to Fred Bergsten, David Mulford, Makoto Utsumi, Russell Green, and other participants at the conference on October 1 for their comments.

8 and 9) have provided their own accounts and views.[1] In his memoirs (written in Japanese), Gyohten (2013) provides a revealing account of economic and political developments during this period, part of which is based on his diary. Takita (2006, chapters 4–6) is based on interviews with Makoto Utsumi, who retained memorandums and records of various meetings with counterparts.[2]

This chapter is organized as follows. The next section describes exactly what was agreed to at the Plaza Hotel in September 1985. The second section frames the issue of exchange rate policy in a broader context of policy coordination that continued as the Louvre Accord in February 1987. Section three examines lessons learned by different institutions in Japan. The last section draws some conclusions.

What Was Agreed to in the Plaza Accord?

The meeting of G-5 finance ministers and central bank governors (G-5M) was called primarily to rectify the overvaluation of the US dollar. In terms of the real effective exchange rate (REER), the dollar appreciated by about 40 percent between January 1981 and March 1985. The United States was running fiscal and trade deficits. The administration blamed the overvalued dollar for the latter and took the initiative to call a G-5M meeting. The date was set for September 22, but the prospective meeting was kept confidential.[3] Per usual practice, the G-5 deputies (G-5D) met in London several days before the meeting and hammered out a draft of the agreement, putting in brackets issues to be decided by ministers and governors.

At the outset of the meeting, Treasury Secretary James A. Baker, III, proposed issuing a communiqué to maximize the impact of actions that were about to be taken.[4] It stated the following:

The Ministers and Governors agreed that exchange rates should play a role in adjusting external imbalances. In order to do this, exchange rates should better reflect

---

1. Gyohten was director general of the international finance bureau at the Ministry of Finance (the number three position in international finance policy in Japan) at the time of the Plaza Accord and vice minister of international affairs at the Ministry of Finance (the number two position in the field after the minister of finance) at the time of the Louvre Accord.

2. Utsumi was minister at the Japanese Embassy in Washington at the time of the Plaza Accord and director general of the International Finance Bureau at the Ministry of Finance at the time of the Louvre Accord.

3. Until the Plaza meeting, the existence of the G-5M was kept confidential. Finance Minister Noburo Takeshita played nine holes of golf before going to the airport to catch a PanAm (not JAL) flight, so that the press and businesspeople would not suspect that he was going abroad.

4. At the 2015 Rice University conference, those people involved in the Plaza meeting told the author that the core preparation team had agreed that a surprise announcement would be made during the Plaza meeting. The media were gathered, but reporters were not informed of the nature of the forthcoming announcement; some speculated that it would have to do with matters related to Iran Contra. The surprise announcement was planned in light of only moderate success at the confidential G-5 meeting in January 1985.

fundamental economic conditions than has been the case. They believed that agreed policy actions must be implemented and reinforced to improve the fundamentals further, and that, in view of the present and prospective changes in fundamentals, some further orderly appreciation of the main nondollar currencies against the dollar is desirable. They stand ready to cooperate more closely to encourage this when to do so would be helpful.[5] [Emphasis added]

The communiqué did not mention "intervention" or a targeted level of appreciation of nondollar currencies; these issues were kept confidential. The press and academics tried to guess whether there were target exchange rates. It was not known at the time that the G-5D produced a nonpaper that stated that "a 10–12 percent downward adjustment of the dollar from present levels would be manageable over the near term." The existence of the nonpaper was revealed to the press later (see Funabashi 1988 and Gyohten 2013).

The G-5D also discussed the obligation to intervene to achieve the exchange rate goals. According to Gyohten (2013), the total amount of intervention was set at $18 billion in six weeks. Countries would be relieved of their intervention obligation if the necessary currency adjustment was achieved. According to Funabashi (1988), the nonpaper draft identified intervention shares of 25 percent each for the United States, Japan, and Germany and 12.5 percent each for the United Kingdom and France. Following German objections, the United States revised the ratios to 30 percent each for the United States and Japan, 25 percent for Germany, 10 percent for France, and 5 percent for the United Kingdom.

In the meeting at the Plaza Hotel, Japan was very open to policy coordination, and willing to accept greater appreciation of the yen. Gyohten (2013, 68) recalls that Finance Minister Takeshita proposed removing the word *some* from the phrase "some further orderly appreciation" in the communiqué so that the intention would become clearer. He also proposed using the word *justified* (a bracketed alternative in the G-5D draft) instead of *desirable* in that sentence. Others opposed both proposals. Minister Takeshita also proposed taking out the phrase *when to do so* (bracketed in the G-5D draft), but the Europeans opposed the deletion. Federal Reserve Chairman Paul Volcker added the word *orderly*, which was not in the G-5D draft, in the same phrase. He must have had concern about disorderly behavior of exchange rates, which turned out to be warranted.

The communiqué was issued on Sunday, September 22, 1985. The Tokyo market was closed on Monday, September 23, for a national holiday. Interventions were conducted in European and US markets that day and in Tokyo on September 24.[6] Ito (1987) reported that on September 24, "the Tokyo

5. The statement is available at http://warp.ndl.go.jp/info:ndljp/pid/8779816/www.mof.go.jp/english/international_policy/convention/g7/g7_850922.pdf.

6. One market participant, Takao Sako, recalls being in the office despite the national holiday and selling dollars on behalf of the Bank of Japan on Monday September 23 (see www.gaitame.com/

market opened at 229.7 and closed at 230.1, while the Bank of Japan reportedly sold $1.3 billion. It was only after the big jump had already taken place that the Bank of Japan started heavy intervention; and the intervention did not seem to cause yen appreciation. (It is possible, however, to say that it prevented a sharp rebound.)" In the seven days that followed the Plaza announcement, Japan sold $1.25 billion, surpassing the $635 million by France, the $480 million by the United States, the $247 million by Germany, and the $174 million by the United Kingdom, according to Gyohten (2013, 77).

Both the announcement of the communiqué and the interventions that followed it surprised the market. The dollar weakened against the other four currencies. Within a week the yen appreciated vis-à-vis the dollar by 11.8 percent; both the German mark and the French franc rose 7.8 percent, and the British pound appreciated by 2.9 percent. These outcomes represented a great success for the G-5, almost achieving the policy goal.

Interventions and the depreciation of the dollar continued. G-10 countries that do not belong to the G-5 joined in interventions to sell dollars. By the end of October, the United States had sold $3.2 billion; Japan $3.0 billion; Germany, France, and the United Kingdom collectively $2 billion; and the other G-10 countries $2 billion. Yet the total G-10 interventions ($10.2 billion) were much smaller than the interventions that had been perceived as necessary to achieve the goal of dollar depreciation ($18 billion), according to Gyohten (2013).

Daily intervention data released by the United States and the Bundesbank years later indicate that the United States purchased $1.4 billion of yen and $1.9 billion of deutsche marks during this period (table 7.1). Germany purchased $3 billion of US dollars.

Many observers emphasized the role of interventions in moving the exchange rates so quickly after the Plaza Accord; anecdotal evidence was mounting that interventions by the monetary authorities had large impacts on the dollar depreciation. The amounts of interventions by G-5 countries were not officially announced at the time but guessed by market participants. Research on the effectiveness of official interventions became popular in the months, if not years, following the Plaza Accord. The problem at the time was that daily intervention figures were not disclosed. Academics competed to find data for research purposes (see Dominguez and Frankel 1993a, 1993b). When the daily official intervention data did become available, in the 1990s and 2000s, the quality of research advanced (see Sarno and Taylor 2001; Ito 2003, 2007). Unfortunately, data on intervention by Japan before April 1991 have not been disclosed, making precise analysis of the Plaza interventions impossible.

Success in depreciating the dollar can be attributed to the announcement effect, intervention effects, and associated monetary policy changes. The Bank of Japan raised its short-term interest rate to help the yen appreciate.

---

blog/sakoh_weekly/2015/09/20150923125106.html [in Japanese]). Bank of Japan intervention that day is not officially confirmed or mentioned in any memoirs.

Table 7.1 Daily interventions in the foreign exchange markets by the United States and Germany, September 23–December 11, 1985

Date	US intervention (millions of US dollars)		German intervention (millions of deutsche marks)	Exchange rate	
	Purchases/sales of yen with US dollar	Purchases/sales of deutsche marks with US dollars	Purchases/sales of deutsche marks with US dollar	Yen/dollar	Deutsche mark/ US dollar
September 23, 1985	-70.00	-79.00	-22	231.90	2.732
September 24, 1985	-127.00	0.00	-126	229.80	2.716
September 25, 1985	0.00	0.00	-223	226.90	2.680
September 26, 1985	-10.00	0.00	-148	220.30	2.662
September 27, 1985	-17.00	-15.00	-59	220.10	2.678
September 30, 1985	0.00	-90.00	-86	216.50	2.679
October 1, 1985	0.00	0.00	0	215.00	2.652
October 2, 1985	0.00	0.00	-112	214.10	2.649
October 3, 1985	-3.00	0.00	-78	212.79	2.620
October 4, 1985	-35.00	-15.00	0	213.45	2.634
October 7, 1985	-132.20	-75.00	-64	215.45	2.651
October 8, 1985	-20.00	0.00	-101	216.00	2.647
October 9, 1985	-153.10	-166.50	0	214.80	2.648
October 10, 1985	-10.00	-255.10	0	215.40	2.656

(table continues)

Table 7.1   Daily interventions in the foreign exchange markets by the United States and Germany, September 23–December 11, 1985 *(continued)*

Date	US intervention (millions of US dollars)		German intervention (millions of deutsche marks)	Exchange rate	
	Purchases/sales of yen with US dollar	Purchases/sales of deutsche marks with US dollars	Purchases/sales of deutsche marks with US dollar	Yen/dollar	Deutsche mark/ US dollar
October 11, 1985	–100.00	0.00	–201	214.65	2.658
October 14, 1985	0.00	0.00	–109	n.a.	n.a.
October 15, 1985	–25.00	–196.65	–197	215.45	2.662
October 16, 1985	–67.00	–797.00	–465	217.30	2.685
October 17, 1985	–110.25	–60.00	–345	215.15	2.648
October 18, 1985	0.00	0.00	0	215.15	2.638
October 21, 1985	–151.20	0.00	–45	215.70	2.638
October 22, 1985	0.00	0.00	–114	216.10	2.645
October 23, 1985	–20.00	0.00	–30	215.90	2.638
October 24, 1985	–211.70	–50.00	–171	216.70	2.650
October 25, 1985	–50.00	0.00	0	214.90	2.654
October 28, 1985	0.00	0.00	0	213.50	2.643
October 29, 1985	0.00	0.00	–5	212.43	2.622
October 30, 1985	–50.00	–10.00	0	211.50	2.623

October 31, 1985	0.00	−27.00	0	211.55	2.619
November 1, 1985	0.00	0.00	0	209.00	2.602
November 4, 1985	0.00	0.00	0	207.90	2.598
November 5, 1985	0.00	0.00	0	208.00	2.614
November 6, 1985	0.00	0.00	0	205.25	2.600
November 7, 1985	−77.20	−25.00	0	205.60	2.628
November 8, 1985	0.00	0.00	−246	205.85	2.623
November 11, 1985	0.00	0.00	0	n.a.	n.a.
November 12, 1985	0.00	0.00	−42	205.85	2.623
November 13–December 10, 1985	0.00	0.00	0		
December 11, 1985	0.00	0.00	−129	203.90	2.543
Total	−1,439.65	−1,861.25	−3,118.00		

n.a. = not available due to bank holiday

Note: US interventions in market transactions in yen/dollar (millions of US dollars) and in deutsche mark/dollar (millions of US dollars). German intervention in Bundesbank purchases on dollar/deutsche mark (millions of deutsche mark). Japanese monetary authorities have not disclosed daily intervention data prior to April 1, 1991.

Source: Federal Reserve Economic Data (FRED) at Federal Reserve Bank of St. Louis.

Figure 7.1 Daily yen/dollar and deutsche mark/dollar exchange rates, January 1, 1985–December 31, 1987

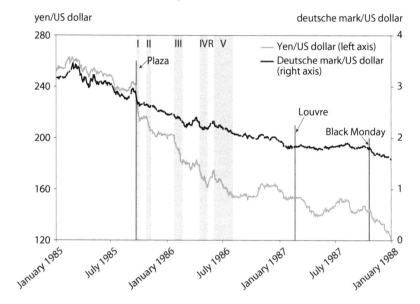

I, II, III, and IV = waves of yen appreciation; R = reversing period

Sources: Federal Reserve Economic Data (FRED) at Federal Reserve Bank of St. Louis; Pacific Exchange Rate Service at the University of British Columbia.

How Was the Goal Achieved?

The goal was to appreciate the value of nondollar currencies by 10–12 percent, according to the G-5D nonpaper. The yen was 240/dollar the Friday before the Plaza Accord. A 10 percent appreciation (to 216/dollar) was achieved on September 30. However, the yen appreciation did not stop there. By the end of 1985, the yen approached 200 yen/dollar (figure 7.1).

Ito (1987) divided 24 hours into three business-hour segments (Tokyo, Europe, and New York) and compares the yen/dollar movements of different periods following the Plaza Accord. Table 7.2 shows the intraday yen/dollar changes for each segment (cumulative within the period).

Ito (1987) also presented the intraday (cumulative) changes in the yen, the deutsche mark, and the pound vis-à-vis the dollar in each of the three major markets. High correlation among the three countries suggests that that the origin of news that moved the exchange rates was the United States. Low correlation suggests idiosyncratic shocks. If, for example, the yen appreciation was large but the correlation with the deutsche mark or the pound was low, then the change represented yen appreciation vis-à-vis all other currencies.

The rapid appreciation of the yen immediately following the Plaza Accord occurred mostly in markets other than Tokyo, partly because the day after the accord was signed was a national holiday in Japan. As Ito (1987) noted:

When the first market, New Zealand's Wellington market, opened on Monday, September 23, the yen appreciated by 5 yen to 234 yen/$. The Tokyo market, which would have opened next, was closed for a national holiday. The London market put 232 yen/$, and appreciation continued during the New York market session, opening at 231 and closing at 225.5 yen/$. By the time the Tokyo market opened on September 24, the yen had already appreciated by more than 10 yen. The Tokyo market opened at 229.7 and closed at 230.1, while the Bank of Japan reportedly sold $1.3 billion. It was only after the big jump had already taken place that the Bank of Japan started heavy intervention; and the intervention did not seem to cause yen appreciation. (It is possible, however, to say that it prevented a sharp rebound.) Thus, the Bank of Japan's role in the yen appreciation was minimal at this stage. It is safe to say that the initial jump was caused by the "announcement" itself.

The week after the Plaza Accord was the first wave of yen appreciation (regime I in table 7.2). Most of the yen appreciation took place in the New York market, where all nondollar currencies rose. The market was surprised by the change in US policy to "international coordination" for correcting the over-valued dollar. The volume of intervention by the Bank of Japan surpassed that of the Federal Reserve (Gyohten 2013). It is possible that the Bank of Japan asked the Federal Reserve to intervene on its behalf in the New York market, but some of the interventions must have been done in Tokyo. Somehow resistance to yen appreciation was stronger in the Tokyo market.

The second wave of yen appreciation (regime II in figure 7.1 and table 7.2) occurred between October 25 and November 7. After the first wave, the exchange rate markets became calm, and market participants started to suspect that the aim of the Plaza had been achieved. The G-5 finance ministers meeting in Seoul on the margin of the annual meeting of the International Monetary Fund (IMF) in October did not produce a follow-up statement to the Plaza, adding weight to the view that the dollar had hit bottom. "In fact, the exchange rate expectation survey taken among the market participants on October 16 in the Tokyo market confirms this point. The means of the survey show that the yen rate would be 214 in 1 month, 217 in 3 months, and 222 in 6 months" (Ito 1987). I inferred that "the Japanese authorities judged that the amount of yen appreciation was not enough and feared that the dollar might creep up to its previous level. Faced with a conflicting market expectation, the Bank of Japan decided to take a stronger action" (Ito 1987). On Thursday, October 24, 1985, the governor of the Bank of Japan, Satoshi Sumita, announced in a regular press conference that the bank would adopt a high interest rate policy, aimed at appreciating the yen from the macro fundamental side. The yen started to appreciate the day after and continued to appreciate for two weeks, as more market participants became convinced of the new monetary policy.[7] The second wave of yen appreciation occurred

---

7. However, the foreign exchange market was not impressed by that announcement alone for the rest of the day or overnight. On Friday, October 25, the exchange rate was 216.55 yen/dollar when

Table 7.2 Decomposition of changes in the yen/dollar exchange rate (yen)

| Regime[a] | Dates | Total change[b] | Accumulated yen changes by market[c] | | |
			Tokyo	Europe	New York
G-5	September 20–23, 1985	–7.75	(Closed)	(not defined)	–7.75
I	September 23–30, 1985	–14.95	–0.85	–1.425	–12.675
Q	October 1–24, 1985	0.12	4.225	–1.525	–2.005
II	October 25–November 7, 1985	–10.745	–7.70	–1.80	0.055
Q	November 8–December 17, 1985	–3.675	–0.12	–0.305	–4.30
Q	December 18, 1985–January 23, 1986	–0.30	–0.41	–0.78	–0.825
III	January 24–February 19, 1986	–21.10	–7.775	–6.84	–7.415
Q	February 20–April 15, 1986	–2.40	0.64	–4.125	1.21
IV	April 16–May 12, 1986	–17.45	–6.91	–1.385	–6.095
R	May 13–June 2, 1986	11.70	5.50	2.92	5.90
V	June 3–July 31, 1986	–21.25	–6.78	–5.665	–7.155
Q	August 1–September 26, 1986	0.985	2.135	–5.85	3.28

a. Regime names I, II, III, IV, and V = waves of yen appreciation; R = reversing period; Q = relatively calm spell.
b. Total change is defined as the change from the New York (NY) closing of the last day of the preceding regime to the last day of the current regime with two exceptions: The G-5 regime is the change from the NY closing on September 20, Friday, to the NY opening of September 23, Monday. Note that the Tokyo market was closed on September 23, due to a bank holiday. The total change in the first regime is defined as the change from the opening of the NY market on September 23 to the NY close of September 30.
c. The daily change in the Tokyo market is defined as the yen/dollar change from the NY close of the preceding business day to the Tokyo close of the day. The daily change in the European market is defined as the yen/dollar change from the Tokyo close to the NY opening of the day. The daily change in the NY market is defined as the yen/dollar change from the NY opening to the NY close of the day. The accumulated changes in a regime are the sum of the daily changes in the respective regime. Due to country-specific bank holidays, the three-market changes do not add up to the total change of the regime.

Source: Ito (1987).

in the Tokyo market, suggesting that the market-moving news originated in Tokyo. This episode represented yen appreciation rather than dollar depreciation.

With regard to the market during the second wave, in Ito (1987) I was under the impression that the interest rate hike was coordinated by the Bank of Japan and the Ministry of Finance, because narrowing the interest rate spread between Japan and the United States would, and did, make the yen appreciate. Paul Volcker and his European counterparts in the G-5 criticized the increase in the interest rate (Gyohten 2013, 84; Volcker and Gyohten 1992, 247; and Takita 2006, 211–12). The spirit of the Plaza was to correct external imbal-

---

the Tokyo market opened. As the short-term interest rate soared in the morning session, the yen appreciated to 214.90 by the close of the Tokyo market. The market missed a cue or did not believe the words but waited for interest rate action overnight.

ances, so stimulating the domestic economy by the interest rate cut was the right decision. Apparently, the Bank of Japan did not consult with the Ministry of Finance or the US Federal Reserve before it hiked its interest rate. From the point of view of appreciating the yen, raising the interest rate was a powerful action: The second wave of exchange rate movement saw yen appreciation (not dollar depreciation), and the coefficient of the interest rate spread is statistically significant (Ito 1987).

Why was Japan so eager to appreciate the yen beyond the secretly agreed upon goal of 10 percent appreciation? According to Gyohten (2013, 69–70), "as far as [nondollar] currency appreciation, Japan was most forthcoming. [During the Plaza meeting] Finance Minister Takeshita expressed that Japan could accept yen appreciation up to 200 yen/dollar. Germany stated its position that it does not consider a goal of 10–12 percent depreciation of the US dollar as its obligation."

Why, then, was Finance Minister Takeshita so eager to accept yen appreciation? Gyohten (2013, 58–59) notes that Finance Minister Takeshita and Secretary Baker hit it off in the bilateral meetings that took place months before the Plaza: "In June 1985, Secretary Baker visited Tokyo for the G-10 Finance Ministers meeting. He laid out his action plan on the exchange rate and macroeconomic policies [to Takeshita]. The bilateral negotiation continued in July in Paris, in August in Hawaii and became a conclusion in G-5D in London."

The second wave of yen appreciation brought the yen to just above 200/dollar, where it stayed for the next two and half months. Based on Gyohten's account of Takeshita's intention, this level must have been a comfortable one.

Even during the calm period, many events took place. The high interest rate policy was abandoned on December 17. The discount rate cut by the Bank of Japan (a reversal of its policy), which would not occur until January 30, 1986, was rumored as early as December 20. Another piece of big news during this period was the drop in oil prices and OPEC's decision on December 8 not to cut supply but to instead tolerate low prices. As expected, the currencies of oil-importing countries (including Japan and Germany) appreciated and the currencies of oil-exporting countries (including the United Kingdom) depreciated. Appreciation of the deutsche mark started in early November and continued into late January. Perhaps during the calm yen period of November and December the reversal of the interest rate policy by the Bank of Japan, which was to put pressure for yen depreciation, was met with the oil price decline, which created pressure for yen appreciation. Another possible explanation is that the monetary authorities of Japan made an implicit decision that 200 yen/dollar would be the target and adjusted the interest rate and communication.

Was Intervention Effective?

Did concerted interventions or market forces account for the success in depreciating the dollar in the first and second waves? Feldstein (1986), Volcker and Gyohten (1992, chapter 8), and Gyohten (2013) note that the dollar had been depreciating because of market forces since February; interventions may have accelerated movement, but the fundamental force was the market. The Plaza Accord only maintained and accelerated an already moving ball (the US dollar), an analogy Volcker made. The yen peaked against the dollar on February 20, at 262.80, and the deutsche mark peaked against the dollar at 3.4526 on February 25. The dollar was down to 240 yen just before the Plaza meeting. So in a sense, the trend of yen appreciation continued, at much faster speed, after the meeting.

A fact that is implicitly overlooked by the Feldstein-Volcker-Gyohten view is that the turnaround in January was also helped, if not caused, by interventions. Although it is often overlooked, the G-5 met on January 17, 1985, eight months before the Plaza G-5, and agreed to drive down the US dollar. The move signifies a change in the laissez-faire strategy of then Secretary Don Regan (see Bordo, Humpage, and Schwartz 2015, 280). The Federal Reserve intervened on February 1, selling $48.8 million against the yen; it sold $594 million in interventions on eight days between January 22 and March 1. The Federal Reserve did not intervene after March 2 until the Plaza interventions. The Bundesbank bought DM 11.5 billion against the US dollar in interventions on 24 days between January 11 and March 4. It did not intervene after March 5 until the Plaza interventions. The Japanese monetary authorities sold about $550 million in their interventions between January and March (Ito and Yabu 2015). The Japanese authorities did not intervene from April until the Plaza meeting in September. I would argue that these interventions by the G-3 contributed to the turning around and sliding of the US dollar from late February onward.

In Ito (1987) I gave more credit to the role of interventions, which ensured that the markets understood the intent of the central banks and the resolve of the monetary authorities. In fact, interventions were conducted so that the dollar would not return to an appreciation trend, if not push to depreciate. A case in point was the intervention by the Bank of Japan on September 24, 1985, when it conducted a massive intervention but the exchange rate did not move in the Tokyo market (see table 7.3). Put differently, the massive intervention was needed to prevent the dollar from appreciating from the depreciated level of the day before.

Ito (1987) stressesd that the monetary authorities' communication was important in defending and eventually letting go of the 200 yen/dollar barrier. In his first press conference of the year, the governor of the Bank of Japan indicated that the yen should be kept at about 200; the announcement had the effect of raising the yen from 198.55 on January 2 to above 200 on January 3. The move defended the 200 barrier. It was contradicted by Finance Minister

Table 7.3 Contemporaneous correlation of intradaily changes in exchange rates (correlation coefficient between −1 and 1)

Regime	Dates	Currency	Tokyo		Europe		New York	
			Yen	Deutsche mark	Yen	Deutsche mark	Yen	Deutsche mark
I	September 23–30, 1985	Deutsche mark	0.84		0.93		0.72	
		Pound	0.36	0.55	−0.51	−0.33	0.74	0.97
Q	October 1–24, 1985	Deutsche mark	0.75		0.61		0.96	
		Pound	0.65	0.80	0.27	0.65	0.56	0.63
II	October 25–November 7, 1985	Deutsche mark	0.52		0.69		0.92	
		Pound	0.20	0.70	0.63	0.72	0.85	0.94
Q	November 8–December 17, 1985	Deutsche mark	0.42		0.59		0.76	
		Pound	0.41	0.32	0.48	0.57	0.70	0.83
Q	December 18, 1985–January 23, 1986	Deutsche mark	0.44		0.63		0.93	
		Pound	0.34	0.69	0.34	0.27	0.74	0.87
III	January 24–February 19, 1986	Deutsche mark	0.81		0.71		0.78	
		Pound	0.28	0.07	0.06	0.32	0.31	0.43
Q	February 20–April 15, 1986	Deutsche mark	0.40		0.76		0.50	
		Pound	0.29	0.33	0.52	0.53	0.40	0.50
IV	April 16–May 12, 1986	Deutsche mark	0.82		0.84		0.88	
		Pound	0.81	0.85	0.58	0.84	0.70	0.88
R	May 13–June 2, 1986	Deutsche mark	0.73		0.77		0.87	
		Pound	0.11	0.61	0.72	0.82	0.78	0.87
V	June 3–July 31, 1986	Deutsche mark	0.47		0.76		0.58	
		Pound	0.28	0.05	0.11	0.10	0.85	0.36
Q	August 1–September 26, 1986	Deutsche mark	0.85		0.82		0.75	
		Pound	0.31	0.30	0.41	0.47	0.37	0.39

Notes: Changes in yen/dollar, deutsche mark/dollar, and pound/dollar in the specific market everyday are measured in the same manner as in table 7.2. The correlation matrix is then calculated for each regime and each market. See also note on regimes below table 7.2.

Source: Ito (1987).

Takeshita later in January. Ito (1987) reconstructed news and events from newspaper accounts at the time:

> Finance Minister Takeshita was in Washington, DC, on his way home from the London G-5 meeting of January 18 and 19. At a press conference in the United States, he reportedly said that he would allow the yen to go below the 200 level. The Tokyo market was informed of Takeshita's remark by a news wire at around 3 p.m., 30 minutes before the closing of the market. The yen jumped from 201 to 198 in a matter of 20 minutes; then profit-taking brought it back to 199.50 at the closing (3.30 p.m.). Finance Minister Takeshita came home that evening, long after the Tokyo market was closed, and gave another news conference in Tokyo. He said that "if the exchange rate becomes in the 190s as a natural result of the market movement, it should not be artificially brought back [to more than 200]. Though it varies depending on sectors, the 190s would be acceptable by the industries." [Literal translation from *Nihon Keizai Shinbun*, January 25, 1986.] This news conference in Tokyo was in turn reported in the European and New York markets, which were still open. The yen jumped to 198 in the London market and then declined to 196.60 by the closing of the New York market.

Funabashi (1988, 18) reports that Minister Takeshita had already mentioned that 190 could be possible during the Plaza meeting. Takeshita's embracing of yen appreciation comports with Gyohten's account of the Japanese position in the meeting.

Thus the third wave of yen appreciation (regime III in figure 7.1 and table 7.2) started. The yen appreciated 10 percent in the four-week period after the Takeshita statement. In Ito (1987) I believed that this appreciation was not policy driven but that by letting go of the artificial 200 yen/dollar barrier, the fundamentals of the oil price decline appreciated the yen. This appreciation occurred evenly in Tokyo, London, and New York, with the yen continuously appreciating as the oil price declined.

Overachievement and Reverse Intervention

The third wave of appreciation brought the yen to the 180s. Breaching 190 alarmed the Japanese monetary authorities. The possibility of reversing the direction of intervention (that is, buying dollars by selling yen) was mentioned, but "reverse intervention" did not occur until March 18 when the yen appreciated to 175/dollar. Leading up to the intervention there was one major policy coordination event: On March 6 and 7, France, Germany, Japan, and the United States cut their discount rates by 0.5 percent in concert. This first "coordinated" discount rate cut would theoretically expand aggregate demand without affecting the exchange rate. However, right after the coordinated interest rate cut, the yen appreciated suddenly, which led to the reverse intervention of March 18 by the Bank of Japan. The yen appreciated from 179 (on the day of the discount rate cut announcement) to 174.90 in 11 days. It was turned around quickly, however, returning to the 180 level in a week. In this sense a coordinated interest rate cut was successful in keeping the exchange rate stable, albeit with a quick fall and rise immediately following the rate cut.

The fourth wave of the yen appreciation occurred from April 16 to May 12. The yen appreciated by more than 17 yen/dollar during this period. One of the triggers was the G-5 Summit Agreement, which did not appear to endorse Japan's reverse intervention (to stop yen appreciation).[8] On April 21 the yen broke the post–World War II record high, set at about the time of President Carter's dollar defense in 1978. The short-term interest rate was lowered, and reverse interventions continued. Yen appreciation during this period took place in the Tokyo and New York markets. Appreciation of the currency occurred in Germany as well as Japan during this period. This period is thus marked by dollar depreciation vis-à-vis the yen and the mark. The low interest rate in the United States became obvious. The market decided that the implications for long-term interest decline in the United States was greater than in other countries, despite the appearance of a coordinated discount rate cut.

By mid-May the yen was approaching 160/dollar, a level that prompted more interventions. However, the yen quickly turned around, depreciating to the level that prevailed before the summit and before the fourth wave of the appreciation. From May 13 to June 2, the yen depreciated by more than 11 yen. According to Ito (1987), "Some people attribute this turnaround to Treasury Secretary Baker's testimony in Congress on May 13 stating that the yen had appreciated enough." Gyohten (2013, 81) corroborates the view: "Secretary Baker tried to lend support to Japan. In his testimony in Congress he said, 'The decline of the dollar vis-à-vis the yen has already offset the dollar appreciation that had occurred earlier.'" The yen depreciated to 174/dollar at the end of May (the R-regime in figure 7.1 and table 7.2).

This yen depreciation turned out to be short-lived, however: By-mid June the yen was again approaching 160/dollar. Politicians and exporters started to worry. Gyohten (2013, 80) recalls that Prime Minister Nakasone told him that the yen should be brought back to the level of 170 before the Lower House–Upper House double elections on July 6. Reverse interventions were conducted in vain. However, the ruling party won the election by a large margin.

After the landslide victory of the double elections, Prime Minister Nakasone shuffled the cabinet, and Kiichi Miyazawa replaced Takeshita as finance minister on July 22, 1986. Miyazawa, who had been outside the cabinet, had

---

8. The Tokyo Summit of the G-5 was held on May 4–6, 1986. During the summit, the media reported that Japan sought coordinated intervention to prevent further dollar depreciation (or yen appreciation), a move the United States rejected. In the final agreement, the G-5 was expanded to include Canada and Italy; finance ministers and central bank governors of the G-7 countries would conduct "multilateral surveillance to make their best efforts to reach an understanding on appropriate remedial measures whenever there are significant deviations from the intended course and recommend that remedial efforts focus first and foremost on underlying policy fundamentals, while reaffirming the 1983 Williamsburg commitment to intervene in exchange markets when to do so would be helpful" (see www.mofa.go.jp/policy/economy/summit/2000/past_summit/12/e12_a. html). Tokyo perceived the agreement as not particularly helpful in stopping yen appreciation.

been more critical of yen appreciation. He met Secretary Baker on September 6 in San Francisco to ask the United States to end its dollar depreciation policy. The United States demanded that Japan adopt a tax cut as economic stimulus.

After two months of negotiations, the Miyazawa-Baker agreement was announced on October 31. The Bank of Japan agreed to lower the discount rate from 3.5 to 3.0 percent; the government submitted a supplementary budget including public works spending of ¥3.6 trillion; it also considered a tax cut (no details about which were provided); and agreed to maintain the current yen/dollar rate, consistent with economic fundamentals. The last item was new and instrumental in maintaining the stability of the yen/dollar rate until the end of the year.

This agreement was a prelude to the target zone of the exchange rate. Gyohten (2013, 91) recalls that "the finance minister himself was supportive of the target zone idea." In his memoirs he recalls that on January 21, 1987, he and Finance Minister Miyazawa visited Secretary Baker, Deputy Secretary Richard Darman, and Assistant Secretary David Mulford. The idea of a target zone was confidentially agreed upon at that meeting. The problem was that Japan and the United States had different ranges in mind. The target zone range was supposed to be established as 145–165 or 150–165. In either case when the yen appreciated to 150, there was a commitment of concerted interventions. The level of 150 yen/dollar was the absolute extreme (yen depreciation) for Miyazawa. The zone for the deutsche mark was proposed to be 1.70 to 1.90. The United States and Japan agreed that the range would not be revealed until the G-5 in Paris.

The Louvre Accord

The United States had looked for ways to reduce its current account deficits. The Plaza Accord was engineered to weaken the dollar to make a necessary adjustment. The effects of the exchange rate realignment did not come swiftly, however. The United States then pressured Japan and Germany to stimulate domestic demand in their economies (through expansionary fiscal policy and monetary policy) to boost US exports to those countries. Funabashi (1988) characterizes the Louvre Accord as the product of the efforts of Secretary Baker to win from Miyazawa and German finance minister Gerhard Stoltenberg "substantive stimulus measures in return for a US agreement to stabilize the dollar."

On February 21–22, the Louvre meeting of G-5/G-7 Finance Ministers and Central Bank Governors was held. Some meetings were for the G-5 only, Canada and Italy joined in others. The most famous part of the communiqué read as follows:[9]

> The Ministers and Governors agreed that the substantial exchange rate changes since the Plaza Accord will increasingly contribute to reducing

---

9. The statement is available at http://warp.ndl.go.jp/info:ndljp/pid/8779816/www.mof.go.jp/english/international_policy/convention/g7/g7_870222.pdf.

external imbalances and have now brought *their currencies within ranges broadly consistent with underlying economic fundamentals*, given the policy commitments summarized in this statement. Further substantial exchange rate shifts among their currencies could damage growth and adjustment prospects in their countries. In current circumstances, therefore, *they agreed to cooperate closely to foster stability of exchange rates around current levels.* [Emphasis added]

Gyohten (2013, 106–27) was responsible for some the preparation for what later became known as the Louvre Accord. The accord—and insistence that exchange rates be managed in a target zone—were Secretary Baker's idea. Minister Miyazawa and Vice Minister Gyohten negotiated with their counterparts with increasing frequency between January 27 and February 21–22. Many discussions took place regarding the paragraphs containing Japanese policy commitments as well as the exchange rate management. The target zone idea was led by Secretary Baker, supported by France and Japan, and opposed by Germany and the United Kingdom. The United States was demanding a clear commitment on domestic demand expansion—something the Japanese side could not commit to, because a commitment cannot be made prior to the Diet passing the budget bill, which was still under the discussion at the time.

During the preparation for the G-5M in Paris (later known as the Louvre meeting), the Japanese position was that the target zone should be 150–165 (Gyohten 2013, 114). The Europeans insisted the Japanese authorities agree to 145–165.[10] The Japanese rejection of the 145–165 range frustrated the US negotiating team. Without an agreement in the G-5D with clear language for the level or the range, the G-5M meeting would start without a script.

The G-5M took place at the Louvre Museum on Saturday, February 21, 1987. France, Germany, the United Kingdom, and the United States proposed to "foster stability of exchange rates around present levels." Japan opposed the language of "present," and it was changed to "around current levels." The Japanese side did not like the implication that the word *present* referred to be the closing rate of the previous day (153.50 yen/dollar). It believed that the word *current* made the time frame a bit more ambiguous.

Gyohten (2013, 94) recalls that the idea of the target zone of +/–2.5 percent (and 5.0 percent) was discussed at the dinner but that nothing to that effect was signed. There was no examination of whether the closing rate of the day before was at equilibrium either.

The press and academics were very interested as to whether the target zone was agreed or not and if so what the range was. The French authorities tended to call it a "reference range." Both Gyohten (2013) and Funabashi (1988) recall that Japan resisted any expression that might have brought the yen/dollar rate below the 150 threshold. The Japanese position was to defend the 150 yen/dollar as a maximum for yen appreciation. If the "present" level meant 153.50, then –2.5 percent meant 150 yen/dollar and –5.0 percent meant 145.825, which

---

10. The Japanese side would have been happier had the implied zone been 150–170, the range Prime Minister Nakasone preferred, according to Gyohten (2013).

was not acceptable to the Japanese negotiation team. So in a sense the Japanese side was rejecting the 5 percent range. Its position represented a disappointment for the Europeans and the United States.

The final text did not include any number for the target level. But it was agreed implicitly that the yen would have the central rate of 153.50/dollar and the deutsche mark 1.825/dollar, the closing rates on February 20, the day before the Louvre meeting. There was no announcement on the range, whether a target zone (or reference range, as the French called it) of +/−2.5 percent or 5 percent existed. The G-5M dinner adjourned without making these points explicit, according to Gyohten (2013).

The Louvre Accord was supposed to be signed by the G-7, but the Italians did not sign the documents, so it was the G-6.[11]

The Defense Line, the Target Zone, and Its Rebasing

Substantial yen appreciation had taken place by the time Miyazawa became finance minister. Under the Plaza Accord, the yen target was 10 percent appreciation from 240 yen/dollar (i.e., 216 yen/dollar). However, Minister Takeshita said that Japan would voluntarily accept appreciation of up to 200 and possibly into the 190s. Indeed, the yen broke the 200 barrier in late January 1986. It appreciated into the 180s in February and the 170s in March. Heavy intervention by the Japanese authorities started in March in a failed attempt to defend the line of 180.

The yen quickly appreciated to 170 in a two-week period in April—despite $2.7 billion of Japanese intervention in April, the largest monthly intervention in the floating period since March 1978. It moved into the 160s in late April. It fluctuated between 163 and 175 in May and June, when intervention amounts were $1.1 billion in each of the two months. The yen resumed its appreciation trend in July and August. It moved into the 150s in mid-July and stayed in the narrow range of 153–155, except for a few days, until the end of September. Interventions amounted to $3.9 billion in July and $3.0 billion dollars in August. A level just above 150 was a serious defense line at this point. Heavy interventions in July and August seemed to prevent the yen from rising beyond 153.

There was no intervention from September to December, during which time the yen fluctuated between 153 and 164. Revealed preference suggests that the Japanese authorities were comfortable with the range at the time. In January 1987 the yen appreciated from 160 to 151, despite interventions of $8.7 billion, a much higher level of interventions than in 1986.

Miyazawa had secured an agreement from Baker that 150 was the defense line for Japan. The albeit small intervention by the United States on January 28, when the exchange rate was about 151 yen/dollar, was a token in honor of this confidential agreement. It stopped the yen appreciation for the moment.

---

11. The Italian delegation protested that the substantive G-5 took place before the planned G-7, and pulled out from the planned meeting.

Going into the Louvre meeting, there was no intervention by the Japanese authorities in February. The yen stayed in a very narrow range of 152.50–154. Japan refused to accept a target zone in which the yen/dollar rate went below the critical 150 level. Miyazawa was also hesitant to accept a target zone that obliged Japan to intervene in the other direction (stopping yen depreciation below the 160 level).

The Louvre communiqué mentioned the "stability of the exchange rates around current levels." Interpreted as the exchange rate of the day before, the "current level" was 153.50 yen/dollar. The first defense line of 2.5 percent appreciation meant 150 yen/dollar; the second defense line of 5 percent (145.825 yen/dollar) was the level Miyazawa regarded as too much appreciated. These numbers were discussed over the G-5 dinner on February 21, 1987, at the Louvre, without clear conclusions (Gyohten 2013, 125).

The Japanese and US authorities intervened heavily in March and April to halt the yen appreciation, based on what was orally agreed to during the Louvre dinner. The yen crossed the defense line to reach 149.32 on March 24 and 145.68 on March 31.

The United States intervened with $720.20 million to halt the yen appreciation on March 24. The move represented the first significant US intervention to resist yen appreciation since November 1978, when President Carter defended the dollar, and by far the largest one-day intervention ever.

In November 1978 the United States intervened to sell yen, buying $194 million over eight days. In a separate episode, it sold yen and bought $50.2 million on January 5, 1981. In response to the Miyazawa-Baker meeting of January 1987, the United States intervened to sell yen for the first time since 1981, buying $50 million worth. The day before the massive March 24 intervention, the United States bought $3 million of yen. The intervention on March 24—by far the most significant event—can be attributed to the Louvre Accord.

Large US interventions continued for the rest of March. The US authorities intervened with $2.4 billion in March. The Japanese authorities bought $6.1 billion in March. In a sense, for the month of March, the US and Japanese authorities jointly held up the promise of the 5 percent target zone (or reference range) defense line.

In the first week of April, the yen stayed at about 146/dollar. During the G-7 meeting in Washington during the IMF meeting, Miyazawa tried to push the yen back inside the original 5 percent range, a move the Europeans opposed. Secretary Baker proposed "rebasing" the target range around 146, setting the 2.5 percent range at 142.43–149.65 and the 5 percent range at 139.04–153.30 (Funabashi 1988, 189). It is not clear (from accounts or memoirs) that the Japanese accepted the rebasing; neither Gyohten (2013) nor Takita (2006) mentions it. The G-7 communiqué of April 8 noted the following:

2. The Ministers and Governors reaffirmed the commitment to the cooperative approach agreed at the recent Paris meeting, and noted the progress achieved

in implementing the undertakings embodied in the Louvre Agreement. They agreed, however, that further

3. The Ministers and Governors reaffirmed the view that around current levels their currencies are within ranges broadly consistent with economic fundamentals and the basic policy intentions outlined at the Louvre meeting. In that connection, they welcomed a statement provided a basis for continuing close cooperation to foster the stability of exchange rates.[12]

Could market participants read from these paragraphs that the finance ministers and central bank governors agreed to rebasing? Perhaps. The yen quickly appreciated, from just below 145 on April 9 to just below 139, touching the defense line of the newly "rebased" target range on April 27.

The United States intervened with only small amounts ($208 million on April 22 and $189 million on April 23), but not in the last week of April. The Japanese side intervened heavily in April. During that month, the US authorities intervened with $1.5 billion and the Japanese authorities with $9.7 billion.

What happened next was interesting. The yen stayed between 141 and 152 from May to the end of July, with limited interventions. The rebased range held. During these months Japan intervened less than the United States—a rare event. This intervention behavior suggests that Japan accepted the "rebasing" reality, however reluctantly. Another factor that could explain a tacit acceptance of the rebased range was that by the spring of 1987, the Japanese economy was showing strong growth, partly as a result of declining oil prices and partly as a result of fiscal and monetary stimulus measures taken as part of the Louvre Accord. Japanese politicians, including Miyazawa, could be a bit relaxed about yen appreciation to 140s in the spring–summer of 1987 compared with January–February of 1987, when Miyazawa was so desperate to defend the absolute maximum of 150.

In the second half of August 1987, there was a sudden appreciation of the yen from 150 to 141/dollar. In September the yen stayed in the range of 141–145. This sudden appreciation invited heavy intervention again by the Japanese and US authorities; the 140 defense line was well protected. This behavior suggests that there was a rebasing of the range that was agreed to by the United States and Japan, if not all of the G-7.

Black Monday and the End of Policy Coordination

The yen/dollar rate stayed in the 140–150 range, with interventions, until Black Monday (October 19, 1987). As the US stock market crashed, the US monetary authorities shifted attention to domestic financial stability and started monetary easing. The yen/dollar rate moved below 140 on October 29 and below 130 on December 10. The yen appreciated to 121 on December 31 before reversing its trend in 1988.

---

12. The text is available at www.g8.utoronto.ca/finance/fm870408.htm.

Although efforts were not totally rewarded, interventions continued in an attempt to stop, or at least slow, the appreciation of the yen and the fall of the dollar. In October the Japanese authorities intervened with $234 million and the US authorities with $65 million. In November Japan intervened with $4.7 billion and the United States with $428 million; in December Japan intervened with $2.8 billion and the United States with $1.1 billion. The authorities resisted but were losing the battle, as the yen appreciated from 140 to 121.

In 1988 the yen fluctuated between 121 and 130 between January and April and between 125 and 136 between May and October. There was no intervention by the Japanese or US authorities between May and September 1988.

Was 120–135 the second rebased range? To my knowledge, no such discussion is recorded. The yen appreciated again between late October and December. It reached 121/dollar again at the beginning of December. The Japanese and US authorities conducted large interventions in November and December. The Japanese authorities intervened with $2.9 billion in November and $100 million in December. The US authorities intervened with $1.6 billion in November and $200 million in December. In December 1988 both countries bought dollars, selling yen. The following year the two countries reversed the direction of intervention. The US authorities started to buy yen in an attempt to halt the yen depreciation at 132/dollar. The Japanese authorities also bought yen, selling dollars in April 1989. These events suggest that the two countries had substantially moved the target range to 120–132 by 1989. However, it is probably a stretch to call it a revised Louvre Accord.

There was no announcement about terminating the Louvre Accord. How long did it last? People who were involved in the Plaza-Louvre policy coordination have different views regarding how long the Louvre Accord had impacts on policy. Observers who emphasize the target zone (reference range) in the Louvre Accord believe the Louvre was de facto terminated in a few months, when the yen/dollar rate dipped below 150, the defense line for Japan. Gyohten (2013, 96) writes: "The target rate of the Louvre was defeated by the market. The dollar depreciated precipitously and the yen appreciated to 138 yen/dollar on April 27. The Louvre Accord did not function after all. Deputy Secretary Richard Darman left the Treasury in frustration in April, and Chairman Volcker resigned from the position in August."

Others suspect that the Louvre Accord worked until Black Monday, in October 1987, with the rebasing of the range that would include 140 yen/dollar at the April 8 meeting of the G-7, as the yen/dollar rate stayed at 140–150 until Black Monday. Funabashi (1988, 211) writes: "The stock market crash in October had exposed underlying weaknesses in the structure of the policy coordination process. Overwhelmed by the stock market meltdown, the Reagan administration held down interest rates and let the dollar fall once again, in apparent disregard of the spirit of the Louvre Accord."

If coordinated interventions are taken as evidence of exchange rate policy coordination, coordination can be said to have continued well into 1988. Figure 7.2 shows monthly interventions by the Japanese and US authorities in the

Figure 7.2 Volume of monthly interventions in exchange rate market and exchange rate, January 1985–December 1988

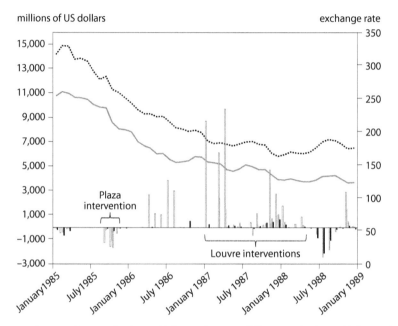

millions of US dollars   exchange rate

▭ Japanese intervention in yen/dollar market   ▨ US intervention in yen/dollar market
▨ US intervention in deutsche mark/dollar market   ⋯⋯ Deutsche mark/dollar * 100 (right axis)
■ German intervention in deutsche mark/dollar market —— Yen/dollar (right axis)

Sources: Ito and Yabu (2015); Federal Reserve Economic Data (FRED) at Federal Reserve Bank of St. Louis.

dollar/yen market and the US and German authorities in the dollar/deutsche mark market. Joint interventions related to the Louvre Accord seem to have continued through April 1988 and resumed in November and December 1988 for the yen market to prevent too much appreciation of the yen.[13]

Several actors exited from the stage. James Baker's last day as treasury secretary was August 17, 1988. Kiichi Miyazawa's last day as finance minister was December 9, 1988. Interventions to support the dollar (or prevent too much yen appreciation) continued sporadically until December 12, 1988, according to the intervention data disclosed by the Federal Reserve. Between January and December 1988, the US authorities sold yen to buy $2.783 billion. These actions helped hold the 120 yen/dollar defense line.

---

13. The United States and Germany disclosed the daily intervention amounts for this period. Japan disclosed daily intervention for the period starting in April 1991. Ito and Yabu (2015) estimate the monthly intervention by the Japanese Ministry of Finance using a reliable proxy variable in the budget.

In 1988 the United States and Japan intervened in the same months: March, April, October, November, and December. Remarkably, US intervention exceeded Japanese intervention in October and December 1988. I believe these interventions were based on the United States' own policy initiatives as well as coordinated intervention based on the Louvre Accord. By this time, the United States was concerned that the dollar might depreciate too much. In 1989 the yen started a depreciation phase, so there was no need for intervention. Moreover, the most important actors, Secretary Baker and Finance Minister Miyazawa, had stepped down by the end of 1988.

Figure 7.3 shows the nominal yen/dollar rate (dotted line) and the REER of the yen (solid line) for a longer time series. It reveals several sustained yen appreciation spells in the post–Bretton Woods period. The appreciation in 1978 took the yen/dollar rate from 240 in January to 176 in October (27 percent in nine months). The appreciation in 1985 took the yen/dollar rate from 260 in February 1985 to 153 in July 1986 (41 percent in 18 months).

Three Lessons from the Plaza-Louvre Accords

The Plaza-Louvre experiences had profound and long-lasting impacts on Japanese policymakers and economic relations between the United States and Japan. Economic conditions in Japan changed drastically in the 1990s, but memory of the Plaza remained—and still remains, 30 years later—for all policymakers.

Three lessons stand out as to what the United States and Japan learned from the Plaza-Louvre currency/policy coordination exercises. First, the Bank of Japan learned that pressure to lower the interest rate in the name of international coordination may force an error in monetary policy. Second, the Japanese government collectively learned that accepting appreciation does not prevent trade conflicts; trade conflicts have to be fought with or without currency policy coordination. The market learned that the United States can use the threat of yen appreciation as a weapon against Japan in trade negotiations. Third, the Ministry of Finance learned that international currency coordination of any kind, including a target zone, is not possible.

Lowering the Interest Rate in the Name of International Coordination May Have Led to a Bubble

As stock prices and land prices in Japan plummeted in the 1990s, growth declined and business activities slowed. The average growth rate was about 5 percent in the second half of the 1980s, despite the yen appreciation after the Plaza Accord and the eventual failure of policy coordination around the exchange rates and macroeconomic policies after Black Monday. Stock and land prices in Japan rose by a factor of three to four between 1985 and 1989. The country was experiencing a typical financial bubble, in which asset prices continued to rise because investors believed that prices would continue to rise. Transaction prices deviated from their fundamental values.

Figure 7.3 Nominal yen/dollar exchange rate and real effective exchange rate of the yen, January 1973–December 1999

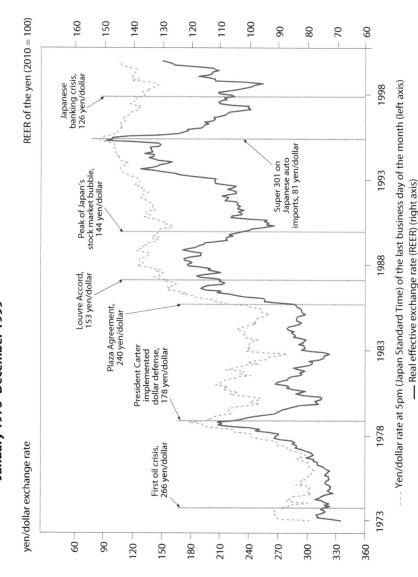

Source: Bank of Japan.

Stock and land prices started to decline in 1990. The growth rate dropped to about 1–2 percent after 1992. Construction companies, developers, and nonbank financial institutions started to suffer from lower real estate prices and stopped interest payments to larger banks. The financial system suffered from the decline in asset values, the increase in nonperforming loans, and capital deterioration. Financial institutions were losing capital quickly, but the loss was hidden by many tactical moves during the mid-1990s. However, smaller financial institutions started to fail in 1995. In November 1997 Hokkaido Takushoku Bank, one of the 20 "city banks," which is the category of large banks with nationwide branch networks; Yamaichi Securities, a Big Four securities firm; and a few other smaller financial institutions failed, setting of a full-fledged banking crisis.

From 1997 to 2003, the Japanese government and the Bank of Japan were busy managing crises. Priority was given to preventing the crisis in the financial sector from spreading to the rest of the economy, rehabilitating weakened financial institutions, and strengthening the system. The Financial Supervisory Agency was created to manage the ongoing crisis and strengthen financial sector supervision. It arranged the first and second rounds of capital injection to major banks to mitigate bank vulnerability. The financial crisis eroded confidence in the Japanese economy at large. Growth slowed further (resulting in a recession in 1998), and deflation set in.

The Bank of Japan learned from the 1985–89 episode that the domestic interest rate policy was distorted by the Ministry of Finance, which put a higher priority on international policy coordination—first to accept yen appreciation, then to prevent yen appreciation—than domestic price stability. Forcing the Bank of Japan to keep the interest rate low to prevent yen appreciation caused high inflation in 1973–74 (see Ito 2013) and an asset price bubble in 1985–89. Policy coordination with the Ministry of Finance, not to mention international coordination, spelled disaster. When the Bank of Japan gained legal independence in 1998, it quickly dissociated itself from the Ministry of Finance. It regarded any outside suggestion on monetary policy, including the suggestion of adopting inflation targeting, as a threat to its independence (Ito 2004). The Bank of Japan thought that adopting inflation targeting of 2 percent would require strong unconventional policy, which in turn might produce a financial bubble, which would not be accompanied by consumer price inflation—just like in the second half of the 1980s. The memory of the Plaza made the Bank of Japan reject such a proposal.

Currency Appreciation Does Not Prevent Trade Conflicts

The Plaza Accord can also be framed in terms of trade conflicts between the United States and Japan, which started to flare up in the first half of the 1980s. Japan's voluntary restraint of automobile exports to the United States started in 1981. Market-oriented sector-specific (MOSS) talks started in 1985. The United States demanded that Japan open its markets in electronics, telecommunications, medical equipment and pharmaceuticals, and forestry products. The US Trade Representative (USTR) used Section 301 against Japanese semiconductor makers. In June 1985 the Semiconductor Industry Association (SIA) filed a Section 301 petition with the Office of the USTR. The Japanese government and semiconductor makers thought the basis of SIA complaints was weak, but it still had to deal with the complaint and the threat of trade sanctions. It is likely that one of the reasons for Japan's acceptance of yen appreciation was its desire to reduce trade conflicts.

According to Funabashi (1988, 88–89), Prime Minister Nakasone decided to accept yen appreciation in order to address the trade imbalance. Unless trade was tackled comprehensively, including through the exchange rate (rather than through a sector-specific approach), the conflict would not be resolved. Accepting the exchange rate was expected to reduce the importance of sector-specific issues and lead to a harmonious relationship with the United States.

Yen appreciation beyond the agreed upon target in the Plaza, and later the Louvre, Accords eliminated some of the competitive edge of Japanese exporters. Exchange rate policy to avoid trade conflicts then became the conflict itself. The United States began to use yen appreciation as a threat to force Japan to swallow US demands on Japanese imports of US products. It demanded first "market access" for government and quasi-government procurement in the 1980s and then "voluntary imports" of US automobiles in the early 1990s. Japan and many economists on both sides of the Pacific regarded US demands and its unilateral approach, culminating in Super 301, as a violation of the General Agreement on Tariffs and Trade (GATT)/World Trade Organization (WTO). Japan started to say no to unreasonable US demands. At the height of US-Japan trade conflict—roughly 1988–94—US frustration led the market to believe that the United States would engineer yen appreciation as a weapon. Whenever negotiations deadlocked or broke off, the currency market pushed the yen higher.

As seen in figure 7.3, the peak of the yen (in nominal yen/dollar) before 2010 was 81 (in April 1995). The yen appreciated very quickly from 90/dollar on March 30 to 81/dollar on April 19 (10 percent in 20 days), and stayed between 81 and 87 until the end of June. This episode of yen appreciation is often associated with the ongoing automobile conflict between the United States and Japan. During this period the USTR announced that it would impose a 100 percent tariff on Japanese exports of luxury cars to the United States if Japan did not agree to numerical targets of US-made auto parts, increased use of US-made auto parts in production in the United States, and increased US auto imports to Japan. Japan refused to accept numerical targets but agreed to expand production and the use of US-made auto parts in the United States.

McKinnon and Ohno (1997) authored a thesis that trade disputes between the United States and Japan played a large role in the yen's appreciation since 1971. Yen appreciation did not correct the bilateral trade imbalance, but it did produce the Japanese stagnation and deflation of the 1990s. What they call a policy trap is a circular argument that yen appreciation causes deflation in Japan, which shrinks imports, resulting in a widening of the US-Japan trade imbalance. The trade imbalance infuriates the United States, which then puts pressure on the yen to appreciate. They believe that a floating exchange rate tends to produce inflation and deflation. Japan is a case in point.

International Currency Coordination Is Not Possible

Japan's Ministry of Finance is in charge of exchange rate policy and foreign exchange intervention. It holds the special account in which almost all official foreign reserves are held. The ministry issues short-term treasury bills to obtain yen liquidity and intervenes to obtain foreign assets, presumably overwhelmingly in dollars (see Ito 2007 for details). The special account for foreign reserves holds foreign currency as assets and domestic treasury bills as liabilities.

What officials at the Ministry of Finance learned from the Plaza and Louvre Accords was the impossibility of international coordination to target a specific level or narrow range in management of the yen/dollar exchange rate. Different officials have different opinions, of course, but I would summarize the current conventional wisdom as follows. First, international coordination is difficult. Second, the market tends to overshoot exchange rate policies by the monetary authorities. In a deep market like the yen/dollar market, private capital flows are much larger than the volumes monetary authorities can mobilize. Third, when markets overshoot or misalign by a wide margin with some herd behavior or speculative long/short positions, there may be a role for intervention and announcement of ad hoc policy coordination to correct the situation. The Plaza Accord was such a case in depreciating the US dollar. Other examples include interventions to reverse the yen appreciation trend at about 120 in December 1988 and again at about 81 yen in April 1995.

The Europeans succeeded in introducing the euro in 1999, fixing the intra–European Monetary System (EMS) exchange rates. The stability of the EMS became top priority; the exchange rate vis-à-vis the dollar or yen became less important. In 1992 the pound dropped out of the EMS and did not return. Thus from the mid-1990s, the yen, along with the pound, came to be the major currencies after the dollar and the euro. These four currencies may fluctuate freely for the indefinite future.

Assessment

Analysis of both the political and the economic aspects of the attempted policy coordination during the 1985–88 period raises several policy questions.

Was It a Mistake for the Japanese Authorities to Have Accepted the US Demand for Sharp Appreciation at the Plaza Meeting?

Was the long process of yen appreciation that started with the Plaza agreement responsible for eventually pushing the Japanese economy off the cliff into stagnation for two decades? My answer is a resounding "no," for several reasons. First, at the Plaza meeting, Finance Minister Takeshita was much more open than the Europeans toward the objective of appreciating nondollar currencies. The United States did not have to force Japan to agree to these conditions; the Plaza agreement of aiming for 200 yen/dollar was acceptable to Minister Takeshita. Second, at the Louvre meeting, Japan was indeed reluctant to accept further yen appreciation beyond 150. Massive joint interventions by Japan and the United States took place to defend the Louvre target zone, but the Louvre range was not held. The range was "rebased" in April, but even that range could not be maintained. Japan intervened by buying $21 billion between March 1986 and January 1987 and $28 billion from March 1987 to April 1988. From May to September 1988, the yen stayed in the range of 124–135, without interventions, another 10–15 percent appreciation from Miyazawa's defense line of 150.

Did the failure to halt yen appreciation hurt the Japanese economy? No. With the benefit of hindsight, yen appreciation was not a problem in 1987–88. The "yen appreciation recession" was over in late 1986; the Japanese economy was actually booming toward an asset price bubble. Japanese fundamentals were strong, and oil prices had dropped. Declining oil prices in late 1985 to 1986 implied that yen appreciation would be more natural than something adverse to the economy.

If policy erred in 1987–88, it was not because the yen appreciated beyond the Louvre target but because the Japanese resisted yen appreciation too much. Resisting appreciation caused the bubble of 1985–89, which later burst, creating nonperforming loans, the banking crisis, and stagnation. Policies that fought strong yen appreciation had kept the interest rate lower than otherwise, which fueled asset price inflation. A counterfactual is to allow yen appreciation in the environment of strong growth and asset price inflation but devote political attention and capital to reducing the vulnerability of the financial sector. Three decades later, China was repeating the same mistake in the late 2000s until the early 2010s by resisting a rapid appreciation, which resulted in a real estate boom.

Did the Plaza-Louvre Accords Help Defuse Protectionism and Correct External Imbalances?

Japan's Ministry of International Trade and Industry (MITI) learned the lesson that exchange rate adjustment does not defuse trade tensions: Relations between Japan and the United States deteriorated in 1987, after the United States found Japan in violation of the US-Japan Semiconductor Agreement of July 1986. It is understandable that MITI officials felt that whatever the Japanese Ministry of Finance and US Treasury agreed on about currency did not defuse the tension. Of course, one can pose the following counterfactual question: If the Plaza Accord had not been struck, would the US-Japan trade war have been worse than it was? The memory of the trade war, which climaxed in 1994–95, is so painful that Japanese trade officials do not recognize any easing of tension by the currency adjustment of the Plaza; the exchange rate and macroeconomic adjustment did little with respect to disputes over individual products, according to them. US officials and economists tend to argue that the Plaza and Louvre Accords did ease tension. The fact that after the Louvre Accord took effect Secretary Baker started to emphasize that the dollar had adjusted enough must have contributed to calming Congress.

What about the macro adjustment? The external imbalances—US trade deficits, Japanese trade surpluses, and the US-Japan bilateral imbalance—did not start shrinking until 1987, two years after the dollar peaked against the deutsche mark and the yen. Although it took 18–24 months, the J-curve effect did work (see Ito 1993). At least in the macroeconomic aspects, yen appreciation by policy coordination vis-à-vis the Plaza and Louvre Accords contributed to correcting the imbalances. A question remains as to whether correcting macro imbalances made a difference in the US Congress, which was excited about trade sanctions against Japan.

Did the Yen Appreciation in 1985–88 Haunt Japan for Decades to Come?

Some economists believe that the yen appreciation episode of 1985–88 convinced Japan, the United States, and the markets that the yen was on an ever-appreciating trend.[14] Japan's economic fundamentals were strong, and the yen deserved appreciation. The Japanese monetary authorities feared yen appreciation because of its potential damage to exporting industries, which were the backbone of the economy. Knowing that the Japanese government feared yen appreciation, some US officials used "talking up the yen" to gain trade concessions. This interpretation points to the 1985–88 episode as a source of the political economy damages of the 1990s, 2000s, and 2011–12. This "fear of yen appreciation" has a certain validity, at least in the 1990s, as many policies have been employed to avoid yen appreciation.

Conclusion

The Plaza Accord of September 1985 was the beginning of a brief period of policy coordination by the G-5. Treasury Secretary Baker led the initiative, but Japan was a very willing participant. Finance Minister Takeshita was willing to commit to appreciation of more than 10–12 percent. The objective of depreciating the dollar by 10–12 percent, from 240 yen/dollar, was achieved, with less intervention than expected. However, the appreciation did not stop at 10–12 percent. The yen appreciated to 200/dollar by the end of 1985, to 190 by January 1986, and to 160 by the summer of 1986. At that point Japan was eager to stop further yen appreciation. The United States also thought the exchange adjustment had been achieved, but it wanted Japan and Germany to stimulate

---

14. McKinnon and Ohno (1997) argue that market expectation of further yen appreciation made the Japanese interest rate lower, via interest rate parity and deflationary pressure.

their domestic economies so that US-Japan and US-Germany trade imbalances would be reduced.

The Louvre Accord set a reference range (or target zone) in which G-7 currencies were to be stabilized. Finance Minister Miyazawa was attracted to the idea of a target zone, but the United States and Japan could not agree to the ceiling (maximum appreciation) of the Japanese yen. Hence, the communiqué did not reflect strong language or commitment for keeping the exchange rate within the range.

For many reasons—including Black Monday, rotations of actors, and the market overwhelming the reference range—the Louvre Accord was short-lived. By the spring of 1988, any commitment to intervene, if it ever existed, had disappeared.

The lessons of the Plaza and Louvre Accords differ from one country to another and one institution to another. In Japan, the Bank of Japan, MITI, and Ministry of Finance have different institutional memories about the Plaza-Louvre attempt to stabilize the exchange rate and stimulate the domestic economy. The Bank of Japan began to oppose coordination with the Ministry of Finance, let alone international coordination. It believed that the low interest rate was forced upon it to prevent too much yen appreciation and that it spawned the bubble in the second half of the 1980s. MITI grew stronger and opposed US demands for numerical targets for imports from the United States. It delinked the trade dispute from currency policy. The Ministry of Finance abandoned hope for exchange rate coordination among the major currencies. It started to accelerate liberalization of domestic and external finance to internationalize the yen.

References

Bordo, Michael D., Owen F. Humpage, and Anna J. Schwartz. 2015. *Strained Relations: US Foreign-Exchange Operations and Monetary Policy in the Twentieth Century*. Chicago: University of Chicago Press.

Dominguez, Kathryn M., and Jeffrey A. Frankel. 1993a. *Does Foreign Exchange Intervention Work?* Washington: Institute for International Economics.

Dominguez, Kathryn M., and Jeffrey A. Frankel. 1993b. Does Foreign Exchange Intervention Matter? The Portfolio Effect. *American Economic Review* 83, no. 5: 1356-69.

Feldstein, Martin. 1986. *New Evidence on the Effects of Exchange Rate Intervention*. NBER Working Paper 2052. Cambridge, MA: National Bureau of Economic Research.

Funabashi, Yoichi. 1988. *Managing the Dollar from the Plaza to the Louvre*. Washington: Institute for International Economics.

Gyohten, Toyoo. 2013. *En no Koubou: Tsu ka mafia no Dokuhaku*. [*The Rise and Fall of the Yen: Monologue of a "Currency Mafia"*]. Tokyo: Asahi Shimbun Publishing Co.

Ito, Takatoshi. 1987. The Intra-Daily Exchange Rate Dynamics and Monetary Policies after the Group of Five Agreement. *Journal of the Japanese and International Economies* 1: 275-98.

Ito, Takatoshi. 1993. The Yen and the International Monetary System. In *Pacific Dynamism and the International Economic System*, ed. C. Fred Bergsten and Marcus Noland. Washington: Institute for International Economics in association with the Pacific Trade and Development Conference Secretariat, Australian National University.

Ito, Takatoshi. 2003. Is Foreign Exchange Intervention Effective? The Japanese Experiences in the 1990s. In *Monetary History, Exchange Rates and Financial Markets: Essays in Honour of Charles Goodhart*, vol. 2, ed. Paul Mizen. Cheltenham, UK: Edward Elgar.

Ito, Takatoshi. 2004. Inflation Targeting and Japan: Why Has the Bank of Japan Not Adopted Inflation Targeting? In *The Future of Inflation Targeting*, ed. Christopher Kent and Simon Guttmann. Sydney: Reserve Bank of Australia.

Ito, Takatoshi. 2007. Myths and Reality of Foreign Exchange Interventions: An Application to Japan. *International Journal of Finance & Economics* 12, no. 2: 133–54.

Ito, Takatoshi. 2013. Great Inflation and Central Bank Independence in Japan. In *The Great Inflation: The Rebirth of Modern Central Banking*, ed. M. D. Bordo and A. Orphanides. Chicago: University of Chicago Press for the National Bureau of Economic Research.

Ito, Takatoshi, and Tomoyoshi Yabu. 2015 (forthcoming). *Kawase Kainyu to Gaika Junbi: Unyo soneki no Choki Tokei* [Forex Intervention and Foreign Reserves: Long-term Estimate of Profits/Losses from Interventions], submitted and under review. Available upon request.

McKinnon, Ronald I., and Kenichi Ohno. 1997. *Dollar and Yen: Resolving Economic Conflict between the United States and Japan*. Cambridge, MA: MIT Press.

Sarno, Lucio, and Mark P. Taylor. 2001. Official Intervention in the Foreign Exchange Market: Is It Effective and, If So, How Does It Work? *Journal of Economic Literature* 39, no. 3: 839-68.

Takita, Yoichi. 2006. *Nichibei Tsuka Kosho: Nijunenmeno Shinjitus* [Japan-US Currency Negotiations: Truth after 20 Years]. Tokyo: Nihon Keizai Publishing.

Volcker, Paul, and Toyoo Gyohten. 1992. *Changing Fortunes: The World's Money and the Threat to American Leadership*. New York: Three Rivers Press.

8

Why Was the Plaza Accord Unique?

RUSSELL A. GREEN, DAVID H. PAPELL, AND RUXANDRA PRODAN

The attention given to the 30th anniversary of the Plaza Accord—reached by the United States, Japan, Germany, France, and the United Kingdom on September 22, 1985—is testament to the fact that it was a watershed moment in exchange rate policy. It initiated a new paradigm of cooperation among the major economies outside of a currency crisis, leading to more ambitious, though arguably less successful, efforts like the Louvre Accord (Baker 2006, 431–32; Mulford 2014, 171). It appears to be the most effective example of coordinated exchange rate policy in the post–Bretton Woods period, with the dollar appreciating far more against the yen and mark than anticipated.[1]

What made the Plaza so unique, combining both strong cooperation among major countries and effectiveness at impacting exchange rates? The uniqueness of the Plaza relates at least partly to the rarity of simultaneous motivation by the major economies to engage in potentially costly intervention. Several explanations could play a role in dissuading countries from attempting intervention.

This chapter explores two potential explanations of why the Plaza has not been repeated. The first is that 1985 was an outlier in post–Bretton Woods experience in the degree of currency misalignment present. Using a measure of real overvaluation relative to real interest differentials, we show that in the

Russell A. Green is the Will Clayton Fellow in International Economics at Rice University's Baker Institute and adjunct assistant professor in the economics department there. David H. Papell is the Joel W. Sailors Endowed Professor and chair of the Department of Economics at the University of Houston. Ruxandra Prodan is clinical assistant professor of economics at the University of Houston. The authors thank C. Fred Bergsten, Charles Engel, John Taylor, and Ted Truman for helpful comments.

1. Agreement on the effectiveness of the Plaza is not universal. See Feldstein (1986) and Bordo, Humpage, and Schwartz (2010).

first quarter of 1985 the US dollar was more overvalued against all other G-7 currencies except the Canadian dollar than at any other time. The potential disruption from such large overvaluation may have provided an overwhelming motivation for intervention.

The size of overvaluation may also have amplified the effectiveness of intervention via a "coordination channel." By pointing out that the market had deviated from fundamentals, sterilized intervention coordinates the beliefs of traders that the market needs to correct toward fundamentals-determined values.[2] After the Plaza intervention, when the market finally began to realign with fundamentals, it had a large correction to make. The size of the correction made the Plaza anomalously effective.

The second explanation we investigate is whether the intervention was consistent with the direction of monetary policy implied by domestic economic conditions for the three key countries (the United States, Germany, and Japan) in 1985. Since at least the 1983 Jurgensen Report, it has been recognized that sterilized exchange rate intervention is most likely to be effective when it is consistent with the direction of monetary policy (see, for instance, Jurgensen 1983, Sarno and Taylor 2001, and Menkhoff 2010).[3] The need for policy consistency relates to the need for credibility with markets for intervention to work through signaling or coordination channels. Signaling involves sterilized intervention indicating the direction of monetary policy to markets. For the coordination channel, the direction of monetary policy is one critical fundamental.

In 1985 inflation had stabilized in all three countries (at below 4 percent in the United States, at 2 percent in Japan and Germany). However, growth rates were moving in opposite directions. According to real-time data available to policymakers, in the first half of 1985 the United States was experiencing slower economic growth whereas growth was trending upward in Germany and Japan. The Plaza intervention may have been effective partly because it was consistent with looser monetary policy in the United States and tightening in Germany and Japan. If intervention credibly signaled future monetary policy consistent with the intervention, any coordination effect would have been amplified, because the fundamentals themselves would be moving in favor of a weaker dollar.

There are other explanations for the Plaza's uniqueness. For instance, the strong depreciation of the dollar may have been assisted by expectations of shifts in fiscal policy. The Gramm-Rudman-Hollings Balanced Budget Act passed the US House of Representatives on August 1, 1985, and the Senate on October 1, 1985, becoming law in December 1985.

---

2. The "coordination channel" does not necessarily imply coordinated intervention by multiple monetary authorities. Coordination in this case involves coordinating the beliefs among traders about fundamentals-based exchange rate values. Researchers have provided evidence for the coordination channel operating in the dollar-mark (Reitz and Taylor 2008) and dollar-yen (Reitz and Taylor 2012) markets.

3. The intervention undertaken by these countries at the Plaza, in accord with essentially all intervention by major economies, was sterilized.

Contributing to the uniqueness of the Plaza is the fact that coordinated intervention in general has been rare; major shifts in exchange rate policy of the magnitude announced at the Plaza have been even rarer. Ideology contributes to this rarity, as key players in office at other times, such as Treasury secretaries Donald Regan and Robert Rubin, preferred to trust the market to determine the exchange rate rather than attempt to influence market outcomes.

Experience matters, as empirical evidence of the effectiveness of sterilized intervention is not strong. Whether measured using instrumental variables, event study methods, or high-frequency data, sterilized intervention by major economies has no impact on exchange rates beyond a period of a few weeks, according to more than 30 years of empirical work.[4] Monetary authorities may believe intervention is effective (Neely 2001, 2008), but they likely subscribe to Truman's (2003) view that short-term impacts are the best that can be achieved.

Economic theory may have discouraged efforts to coordinate intervention. New Keynesian open economy models typically suggest that optimal monetary policy can ignore the exchange rate and focus exclusively on domestic inflation, using a Taylor rule. Since the turn of this century, researchers have developed dynamic stochastic general equilibrium models that include nominal rigidities, monopolistic competition, and producer-currency pricing (Obstfeld and Rogoff 2002, Benigno and Benigno 2006, Clarida 2014). These models demonstrate that domestic inflation–targeting regimes constitute optimal monetary policy or come trivially close. In other words, the exchange rate need not enter the objective function of the central bank. Exchange rate intervention—or, equivalently, altering domestic interest rates to achieve an exchange rate target—is not necessary for optimal monetary policy. Allowing coordination of policies does not alter this theoretical result. A floating exchange rate with the central bank remaining focused on domestic targets remains optimal, so coordinated exchange rate intervention cannot improve welfare.[5]

In exploring our first potential explanation for the uniqueness of the Plaza accord, we define overvaluation as the residual between the actual and predicted real exchange rate from a simple short-term real interest rate differential model. We calculate dollar overvaluation against the mark, lira, franc, euro, yen, pound, and Canadian dollar for the entire post–Bretton Woods period. The period just before the Plaza demonstrates the greatest historical overvaluation of the dollar against every European currency. Against the yen,

---

4. For surveys of the literature on intervention effectiveness at various points in time, see Jurgensen (1983), Edison (1993), Sarno and Taylor (2001), and Menkhoff (2010).

5. John Taylor discusses the policy implications of these results in chapter 12. A model developed by Engel (2011) suggests that monetary policy should target the real exchange rate. His model is similar to others reviewed by Clarida (2014), except that it makes the more realistic assumption of local-currency pricing. This assumption allows something akin to differential pricing, creating welfare losses that are better minimized by including a real exchange rate term in the Taylor rule. Although domestic interest rates provide sufficient tools to hit the target, his model opens the door to exchange rate intervention consistent with the optimal monetary policy target when large deviations of the real exchange rate occur.

the dollar overvaluation peaked in the third quarter of 1982, but it remained high and nearly matched the peak in the first quarter of 1985. The Canadian dollar, in contrast, was only mildly undervalued in 1985.

For examining the second potential explanation, we propose that the deviation of policy rates from the rate implied by the Taylor rule indicates policy space for credible, consistent, sterilized intervention. For instance, if the policy rate is above the Taylor rule–implied rate, markets would be likely to believe a central bank signal that it wants to loosen monetary policy. Intervention to depreciate the domestic currency would be consistent with movement toward the Taylor rule–implied rate and hence more likely to be credible.

Clarida, Gali, and Gertler (1998) indicate that Taylor rules do a reasonable job of describing monetary policy for most G-7 countries, at least since the 1980s. Studies like Orphanides (2003) establish the importance of using real-time data when evaluating historical policy scenarios. Survey data show that Taylor rules provide close approximations to professional forecasts of policy interest rates across the G-7 countries since at least the Greenspan era (Mitchell and Pearce 2010; Fendel, Frenkel, and Rülke 2011; Pierdzioch, Rülke, and Stadtmann 2012). Engel, Mark, and West (2008) and Molodtsova and Papell (2009) show that Taylor rule models provide more evidence of out-of-sample exchange rate predictability than monetary, interest rate, or purchasing power parity models. Consistent with the theory that foreign exchange market participants pay attention to Taylor rule deviations, Wilde (2012) finds that real exchange rates correlate with bilateral Taylor rule deviations (deviations of the interest differential from the Taylor rule–implied differential) in the expected direction in both the dollar-mark and dollar-yen markets. One interpretation of Wilde's evidence, however, is that markets respond to Taylor rule deviations regardless of whether intervention occurs. Ito and Mishkin (2006) caution against using Taylor rules for Japan because of the sensitivity of results to the estimation period and measure of the output gap.

There are many ways to specify policy rules. We focus on the original Taylor (1993) rule, where the federal fund rate equals 1.0 plus 1.5 times inflation plus 0.5 times the output gap, assuming that the target inflation rate and the equilibrium real interest rate both equal 2.0 percent. We use real-time data available to policymakers when interest rate decisions were made: real-time GDP (or GNP) and GDP (or GNP) deflator data. We compute Taylor rule deviations as the difference between the central bank's policy rate and the interest rate implied by the Taylor rule in the United States, Germany, and Japan.

By our metric, foreign exchange intervention to depreciate the dollar in the third quarter of 1985 was consistent with monetary policy for the United States. Intervention by Germany and Japan was not consistent. However, it was consistent with the Taylor rule–implied interest rate differentials between the United States and both Germany and Japan. We consider this evidence of weak consistency for Japan and Germany. The overall pattern of consistency suggests that, to the extent consistency with monetary policy mattered, the effectiveness of the Plaza derived from the fact that markets were focused on the United States.

The next section focuses on the real overvaluation explanation, laying out the empirical approach, describing the data, and presenting the results. The following section does the same for the monetary policy consistency explanation. The last section discusses the results in order to interpret the historical record and considers the current context.

Overvaluation of the Real Exchange Rate

Nominal exchange rates receive the bulk of attention from policymakers, primarily because of their high-frequency availability. They matter for inflation because of the impact on imported goods. These considerations should play into policymakers' inflation-targeting rules, according to most variations of the models mentioned above.

In practice the impact of nominal exchange rates on inflation rises to the fore. Truman (2014 and chapter 9 of this volume) documents that concern outside the United States about the impact of dollar appreciation on domestic inflation was one impetus for commissioning the Jurgensen Report on the effectiveness of foreign exchange intervention. Germany in particular was concerned about the inflationary impact of the depreciation of the mark against the dollar in the pre-Plaza period (Funabashi 1989). For these reasons most evaluations of exchange rate misalignment during the Plaza period have examined nominal values.[6]

Real exchange rates are the preferred unit of observation for understanding incentives to intervene. They matter for trade balances and hence for most of the political pressure related to exchange rates.

There are many metrics for measuring the overvaluation of real exchange rates, the development of which remains an active area of research. For instance, as part of its exchange rate surveillance, the International Monetary Fund uses the residual of a panel regression of real effective exchange rates on a substantial battery of explanatory variables, including real short-term interest rate differentials (Phillips et al. 2013).

Because it is concerned with monetary policy, this chapter uses a benchmark for overvaluation that relies exclusively on the short-term real interest rate differential. Central banks primarily target short-term nominal interest rates and inflation, which yield the real interest rate. Real interest parity theoretically indicates that real exchange rate movements can be explained entirely by the expected short-term real interest rate differential. Compared with uncovered interest parity in nominal terms, real interest parity has more—if not conclusive—evidence of validity (Edison and Melick 1999, MacDonald and Nagayasu 2000, Mark and Moh 2005, Hoffmann and MacDonald 2009, Byrne and Nagayasu 2010), although it is generally found to hold only at long-run (business cycle) frequencies.

---

6. For instance, Feldstein (1994) informally assesses the dollar to be overvalued relative to interest rate differentials in nominal terms by the end of 1984.

From a theoretical perspective, real interest parity derives from combining the uncovered interest parity condition $E_t \Delta s_{t+1} = i_t - i_t^*$ with the Fisher equation $r_t = i_t - E_t \pi_{t+1}$ to get

$$E_t \Delta q_{t+1} = r_t - r_t^* \tag{8.1}$$

where s_t is the log of the nominal exchange rate at time t (foreign currency/ US dollar), i_t is the nominal short-term interest rate, r_t is the real interest rate, $\pi_t \equiv p_t - p_{t-1}$ is the inflation rate, p_t is the log of the price level, and q_t is the log of the real exchange rate, defined as $q_t \equiv s_t + p_t - p_t^*$. The operator $E_t(\cdot_{t+j})$ indicates expectations at time t of the value of $(\cdot)$ for time $t + j$, Δ is the first-difference operator, and * indicates a foreign variable.

Equation 8.1 requires specification of the future value of the real exchange rate, so we make what Edison and Melick (1999) describe as the "standard" assumption that relative purchasing power parity (PPP) holds (that is, the expected real exchange rate is constant). Hence the relationship we estimate is

$$q_t = \alpha + \beta(r_t - r_t^*). \tag{8.2}$$

This specification, which we use to explain short-run movements of the real exchange rate, admittedly plays a little loose by using a long-run PPP relationship. For identifying overvaluation, however, this assumption is unlikely to materially change the results.[7] We assume, from Engel (2015), that the real exchange rate is stationary and therefore estimate the equations using ordinary least squares (OLS).

We examine the misalignment of the dollar against the mark, franc, lira, pound, yen, and Canadian dollar using quarterly data from the second quarter of 1973 through the second quarter of 2015.[8] The nominal exchange rates from the Pacific Exchange Rate Service are the average of the daily rates in the last month of the quarter.

Consumer price indexes and short-term interest rates come from the OECD database, using the last month of the quarter. Because of missing short-term interest rate data, for interest differentials in Japan and the United Kingdom (including the counterpart US rate) we use T-bill data from the International Financial Statistics database. The real interest rate is constructed as the nominal interest rate for the quarter minus the percentage change of the consumer price index on the same quarter one year earlier.[9]

---

7. Many more sophisticated approaches to estimating this equation have been performed. See, for example, Campbell and Clarida (1987), Edison and Pauls (1993), Mark and Moh (2005), Hoffmann and MacDonald (2009), and Engel (2015).

8. The data for Italy begin only in the fourth quarter of 1978. Before adoption of the euro, these series are historical. Following the euro adoption, the mark, franc and lira are pseudo rates imputed by applying the euro locking rate to the current euro exchange rate.

9. Although π_t is not a sophisticated proxy for $E_t \pi_{t+1}$ it is not uncommon to use it as such (see, for instance, Edison and Pauls 1993 and Edison and Melick 1999).

Table 8.1 Regression results for real exchange rates and real interest differentials in the G-6 countries

Country	β	Standard error	t-statistic	P-value
Canada	0.005	0.002	2.206	0.028
France	0.007	0.002	3.445	0.000
Germany	0.014	0.002	6.428	0.000
Italy	0.009	0.002	4.711	0.000
Japan	0.012	0.002	5.633	0.000
United Kingdom	0.003	0.001	2.867	0.004

Note: The regression for each country reflects the equation $q_t = \alpha + \beta(r_t - r_t^*)$. Results are based on quarterly data for the period between 1973Q2 and 2015Q2. The data for Italy begin only in 1978Q4.

Source: Authors' calculations.

We begin with nominal exchange rates, because they frame the public perception of currency values. Panel a in figures 8.1 to 8.6 depicts the nominal exchange rate for the other G-6 currencies against the dollar. For all of the European currencies, March 1985 is a very clear peak of dollar strength, with no comparable episodes within 10 years before or after.[10] Of course, the franc, mark, and lira were joined in the exchange rate mechanism (ERM) at the time and so did not float independently. For Japan the dollar had been strong for some time, having reached comparable values in the late 1970s, 1980, and 1982; it never saw comparable strength against the yen after February 1985. Even Canada, which was not part of the Plaza narrative, faced a historically strong dollar that year, although the Canadian dollar would remain weak for another year, before declining in March 1986.

Adjusting for prices makes 1985 stand out more prominently. Panel b in figures 8.1 to 8.6 presents the log of the real exchange rates. For the European countries, even extending the euro countries forward in a composite series for France, Germany, and Italy, March 1985 is an absolute maximum in the post–Bretton Woods era. For Japan February 1985 becomes an absolute maximum, although the real yen had been weak since 1982. In real terms the second quarter of 1995 also stands out for an extremely strong yen, almost of the magnitude of 10 years earlier.

Panel b also includes the predicted exchange rates from the real interest differential models. The predicted values derive from the results of the regressions of equation 8.2, presented in table 8.1. The coefficients for the real interest differential have the proper sign at high levels of significance, indicating that higher relative interest rates strengthen a country's exchange rate. The coef-

---

10. There may be some discrepancy between the peaks for monthly average and daily data. For instance, Germany's daily peak occurred on February 25.

Figure 8.1 Nominal, actual real, and predicted real deutsche mark/US dollar exchange rates, 1973Q2–2015Q2

a. Nominal deutsche mark/US dollar exchange rate (log)

Source: Pacific Exchange Rate Service.

b. Actual and predicted real deutsche mark/US dollar exchange rate (log)

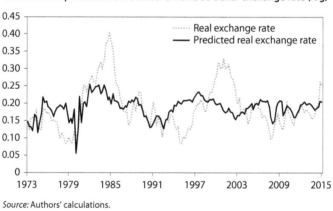

Source: Authors' calculations.

(figure continues)

ficients are consistent with the ones Engel (2015) finds using a vector error correction model and forecasted future inflation rates. The explanatory power of our model is low, however, with the possible exception of Germany. This is apparent in figures 8.1 to 8.6, as real exchange rates display much greater volatility than real interest differentials would predict.

The wide difference in volatility means that our key indicator, the regression residuals, or the deviation of the real exchange rate from the rate predicted by real interest differentials, broadly reflects the same pattern as the real interest rate. Panel c in figures 8.1 to 8.6 presents this measure. Once again March 1985 stands out as having the largest dollar overvaluation relative to the European countries in the post–Bretton Woods period. For Germany, France, and Italy,

Figure 8.1   Nominal, actual real, and predicted real deutsche mark/US dollar exchange rates, 1973Q2–2015Q2 *(continued)*

c. Deviations of actual from predicted real deutsche mark/US dollar exchange rate (log)

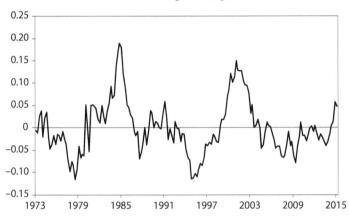

Source: Authors' calculations.

however, the euro weakness in 2000–2001 presents another period of similar dollar strength, with a peak in the second quarter of 2000 of comparable magnitude to that seen in the days before the Plaza. For the United Kingdom the 2000–2001 period of dollar strength is visible but not especially pronounced.

Outside Europe the deviations continue to show that 1985 was an outlier, though perhaps not as unique as for the Europeans. The dollar had experienced episodes of strength against the yen for a decade, with February 1985 representing only a local maximum within an episode that had begun in 1982. The dollar weakness 10 years later, in the second quarter of 1995, emerges as the largest single episode of dollar-yen misalignment. In Canada the deviations draw out the strength of the dollar in the pre-Plaza period, with a local maximum in the first quarter of 1985 and a decline beginning in the fourth quarter of 1985. Although the maximum is not an all-time high for the US dollar against the Canadian dollar—and Canada is not conventionally part of the Plaza-Louvre narrative—at the time it was the highest point in the post–Bretton Woods period.

Unmentioned thus far is the obvious fact that the Plaza meeting took place six to seven months after the peak of dollar overvaluation. The beginning of the decline coincided with Secretary Baker taking office at the Treasury in early February; Frankel (1994) dates the policy switch to that time. Nevertheless, it seems unlikely that markets would have anticipated the Plaza. Surprise was central to the planning of the Plaza (see chapter 3). It remains an open question whether the entire post-Plaza decline of the dollar resulted from the Plaza, whether the Plaza only accelerated the decline for a brief period, or something in between.

**Figure 8.2   Nominal, actual real, and predicted real franc/
US dollar exchange rate, 1973Q2–2015Q2**

a. Nominal franc/US dollar exchange rate (log)

Source: Pacific Exchange Rate Service.

b. Actual and predicted real franc/US dollar exchange rate (log)

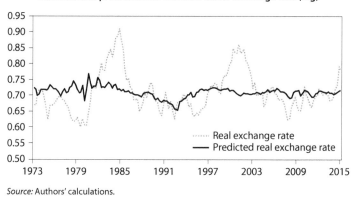

Source: Authors' calculations.

(figure continues)

Consistency of Intervention with Monetary Policy

We now turn from the question of why the G-5 intervened in 1985 to the question of why that intervention appeared effective. For this exercise we narrow our focus to the G-3 (the United States, Germany, and Japan), in whose currencies the Plaza intervention was planned. The intention is to identify the signaling or coordination channel content of intervention, as perceived in real time by the monetary authorities, central bankers, and market participants. We focus on the question of whether intervention was consistent with the intentions of the central bank, a factor critical for the effectiveness of sterilized intervention.[11]

---

11. There is a difference between sterilized intervention consistent with monetary policy and unsterilized intervention. In practice nearly all intervention by major economies is immediately

**Figure 8.2   Nominal, actual real, and predicted real franc/
US dollar exchange rate, 1973Q2–2015Q2**
(continued)

c. Deviations of actual from predicted real franc/US dollar exchange rate (log)

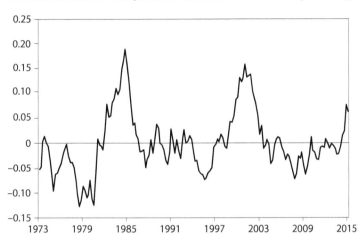

Source: Authors' calculations.

The need for policy consistency relates to the need for credibility of sterilization, pointed out in King's (2003) survey of intervention effectiveness. For intervention to work through signaling or coordination channels, the message about future monetary policy or a broader set of fundamentals that influence exchange rate values must be credible. Consistency of intervention with monetary policy provides credibility.

Furthermore, although they have done so, central banks do not like intervening when doing so is inconsistent with their monetary policy objectives. Truman (2003) calls the risk that inconsistent intervention will damage central bank credibility on the inflation front "signal risk." He and Bordo, Humpage, and Schwartz (2010) document how this concern led the Federal Reserve in 1990 to unilaterally stop the practice of joining the US Treasury Department in US intervention. The desire to avoid signal risk is another reason why monetary policy consistency provides a useful indicator of policy space for intervention.

For this purpose we need a measure of consistency with monetary policy available in real time with at least quarterly frequency. A target policy rate predicted by a Taylor rule using real-time data meets this requirement. Although the Taylor rule does not perfectly predict policy rates—many more subtle factors influence central banks' decisions than the arguments of the Taylor rule—

---

sterilized, leaving open the question at the time of intervention of whether monetary policy will move consistently with the intervention. In contrast, unsterilized intervention is a form of monetary policy that should be immediately recognizable by the lack of central bank action to sterilize.

Figure 8.3 Nominal, actual real, and predicted real lira/US dollar exchange rate, 1978Q4–2015Q2

a. Nominal lira/US dollar exchange rate (log)

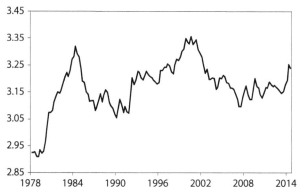

Source: Pacific Exchange Rate Service.

b. Actual and predicted real lira/US dollar exchange rate (log)

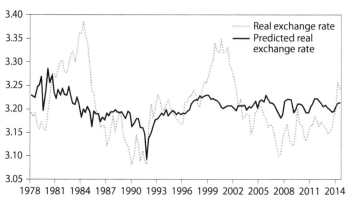

Source: Authors' calculations.

(figure continues)

the rule's broad success at predicting policy rates makes it a reasonable proxy. In this section we shift the analysis back to nominal measures, as is standard for Taylor rule analysis.

Taylor (1993) originally proposed the following monetary policy rule:

$$i_t^* = \pi_t + \delta(\pi_t - \pi_t^*) + \gamma y_t + r^* \tag{8.3}$$

where i_t^* is the central bank's target level of the short-term nominal interest rate, π_t is the inflation rate, π_t^* is the central bank's target level of inflation, y_t is the output gap (the percent deviation of actual real GDP from an estimate of

**Figure 8.3 Nominal, actual real, and predicted real lira/
US dollar exchange rate, 1978Q4–2015Q2**
(continued)

c. Deviations of actual from predicted real lira/US dollar exchange rate (log)

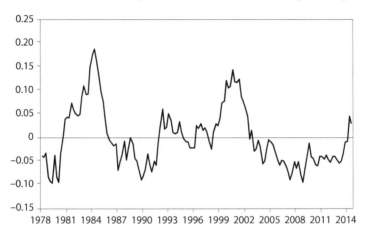

Source: Authors' calculations.

its potential level), and r^* is the equilibrium level of the real interest rate. Taylor postulated that the output and inflation gaps enter the central bank's reaction function with equal weights of 0.5 ($\delta = \gamma = 0.5$) and that the equilibrium level of the real interest rate and the inflation target were both equal to 2 percent, producing the following equation:

$$i_t^* = 1.0 + 1.5\pi_t + 0.5y_t. \tag{8.4}$$

We define deviations as the difference between the actual federal funds rate and the interest target implied by the Taylor rule with the above coefficients. A positive deviation of the observed federal funds rate from the Taylor rule rate can be interpreted as providing the central bank with policy space to raise the interest rate if it wanted to appreciate its currency. In this case sterilized intervention to appreciate the currency (sales of foreign exchange reserves in exchange for domestic currency, combined with using the domestic currency for offsetting open market purchases of domestic assets) would be viewed as consistent with domestic monetary policy objectives.

We apply this specification of the Taylor rule to the G-3 economies (figures 8.7–8.9). Taylor originally proposed the parameters with the Federal Reserve in mind. Gerberding, Seitz, and Worms (2005) and Clausen and Meier (2005) use real-time data to establish the rule's suitability for Germany as well. For Japan Bernanke and Gertler (1999) and Ito and Mishkin (2006) support an inflation target of 2 percent. Kamada (2005) prefers a Taylor rule with an inflation target of zero, which effectively shifts the implied interest rate up by

**Figure 8.4 Nominal, actual real, and predicted real pound/
US dollar exchange rate, 1973Q2–2015Q2**

a. Nominal pound/US dollar exchange rate (log)

Source: Pacific Exchange Rate Service.

b. Actual and predicted real pound/US dollar exchange rate (log)

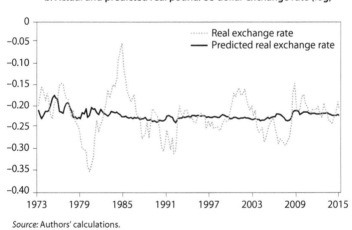

Source: Authors' calculations.

(figure continues)

1 percentage point relative to the standard parameterization. For the purposes of analyzing the Plaza period, the choice of inflation target makes no difference, as we show that the deviation exceeds 1 percentage point in 1985.[12]

---

12. In their benchmark work using revised data, Clarida, Gali, and Gertler (1998) find a significant coefficient for the real exchange rate in the German and Japanese Taylor rules, potentially complicating the relationship between misalignment and monetary policy–consistent intervention. However, the coefficient is small. Adding a comparable term to our Taylor rule does not affect the implied interest rates.

Figure 8.4   Nominal, actual real, and predicted real pound/ US dollar exchange rate, 1973Q2–2015Q2 *(continued)*

c. Deviations of actual from predicted real pound/US dollar exchange rate (log)

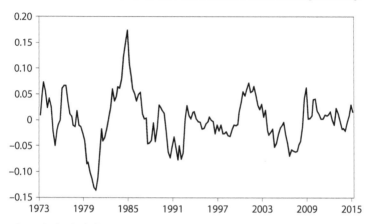

Source: Authors' calculations.

The implied Taylor rule interest rate is calculated from data on inflation and the output gap. We limit our analysis to data from the first quarter of 1980 to the fourth quarter of 1989, the period surrounding the time of the Plaza-Louvre Accords. For the United States, we use the Real-Time Data Set for Macroeconomists, originated by Croushore and Stark (2001) and maintained by the Philadelphia Fed. It contains vintages of nominal and real GDP (GNP before December 1991) from the fourth quarter of 1965, with the data in each vintage extending back to the first quarter of 1947. For Japan we use the international real-time dataset compiled by Fernandez, Koenig, and Nikolsko-Rzhevskyy (2011), which contains vintages of nominal and real GNP with the data in each vintage extending back to the first quarter of 1968.[13] For Germany we use the real-time dataset compiled by Gerberding, Seitz, and Worms (2005), which includes real and nominal output, the Bundesbank's own estimates of potential output, and the GDP deflator.[14]

To construct the output gap (the percentage deviation of real GDP from potential GDP) for the United States and Japan, we must detrend the real GDP data. We use real-time detrending, where the trend is calculated from the first quarter of 1947 through the vintage date for the United States and from the first quarter of 1968 for Japan. The three leading methods of detrending are linear, quadratic, and Hodrick-Prescott (HP). For the United States, Nikolsko-

---

13. Their dataset was assembled from the original OECD Main Economic Indicators, available for 1962–98, which was merged with the current OECD real-time dataset, which starts in 1999.

14. For details about this dataset, see Molodtsova, Nikolsko-Rzhevskyy, and Papell (2008).

Figure 8.5   Nominal, actual real, and predicted real yen/US dollar exchange rate, 1973Q2–2015Q2

a. Nominal yen/US dollar exchange rate (log)

Source: Pacific Exchange Rate Service.

b. Actual and predicted real yen/US dollar exchange rate (log)

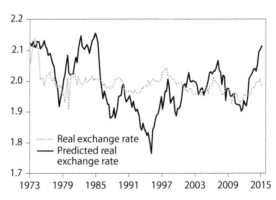

Source: Authors' calculations.

(figure continues)

Rzhevskyy, Papell, and Prodan (2014) find that quadratic detrended output gaps provide a closer approximation to benchmark real-time output gaps calculated using Okun's Law and a better representation of the recovery from the Great Recession than the alternatives. On this basis they suggest that quadratic detrending is the preferred method.

For Japan we also compute the quadratic detrended output gaps from the fourth quarter of 1980 through the fourth quarter of 1989. During this period the measure corresponds with all three of Japan's official business cycle turning points, as determined by the Cabinet Office. Most important for this chapter, it corresponds well with the peak of the Japanese business cycle in the second quarter of 1985, when we find a real-time output gap of 3.3 percent. Previous

**Figure 8.5   Nominal, actual real, and predicted real
yen/US dollar exchange rate,
1973Q2–2015Q2** *(continued)*

c. Deviations of actual from predicted real yen/US dollar exchange rate (log)

Source: Authors' calculations.

studies, using real-time and revised data and an HP filter, find an output gap
that falls between 0 and 1 for the same period.[15] Such low output gap values
at the peak of the cycle suggest that the quadratic detrending method is more
accurate than the HP detrending method for Japan. For Germany the output
gap is simply the difference between real and potential GDP, so no detrending
is necessary. For all countries we construct inflation rates as the year-on-year
change in the GDP deflator, the ratio of nominal to real GDP.

Figure 8.7 displays the actual federal funds rate and the original Taylor
rule–implied interest rates for the United States, as well as the deviations from
the original Taylor rule, for 1980–89. It shows that Taylor rule deviations were
positive throughout the Plaza-Louvre period. Positive deviations at that time
are consistent with other Taylor rule findings using revised (Clarida, Gali,
and Gertler 1998) or real-time (Orphanides 2003) data. The positive deviations during the Volcker disinflation period preceding the Plaza Accord were
atypical of the US historical experience of negative deviations during most of
the 1970s and 2000s and small deviations during the Great Moderation of
the late 1980s and 1990s, as Nikolsko-Rzhevskyy, Papell, and Prodan (2015)
show.

We can also look in detail at what happened with rates around the Plaza
Accord. The Federal Reserve had been easing interest rates back into the single
digits since 1984, but it stopped easing in mid-1985. The target rate edged up

---

15. Kamada (2005), using an HP filter, finds a real-time output gap of 1 percent. Using an HP
filter with revised data, Haltmaier (2001), Hirose and Kamada (2003), Kamada (2005), Urasawa
and Seitani (2008), Hirose and Naganuma (2010), and Yamada and Jin (2012) find values for the
output gap that fall between 0 and 1 percent. The only exception to this pattern is the *World
Economic Outlook* estimate of –0.5 percent (IMF 2015).

Figure 8.6   Nominal, actual real, and predicted real Canadian dollar/US dollar exchange rate, 1973Q2–2015Q2

a. Nominal Canadian dollar/US dollar exchange rate (log)

Source: Pacific Exchange Rate Service.

b. Actual and predicted real Canadian dollar/US dollar exchange rate (log)

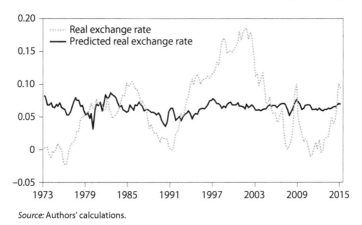

Source: Authors' calculations.

(figure continues)

slightly from 7.75 percent on May 20, 1985, to 8.0 on September 6, and the effective federal funds rate rose from 7.5 to 7.9 percent.[16] The Taylor rule suggests loosening rates by 0.4 percent over this period because of a drop in the output gap and a minor decline in inflation.

By December the effective federal funds rate had tightened to 8.3 percent, despite the fact that the federal funds target had edged back to 7.75 percent

---

16. At this time the Federal Open Market Committee established 4–percentage point bands for the federal funds rate, so the target rate comes from the Federal Reserve Bank of New York that administered the band (see www.newyorkfed.org/markets/statistics/dlyrates/fedrate.html).

Figure 8.6   Nominal, actual real, and predicted real Canadian dollar/US dollar exchange rate, 1973Q2–2015Q2 *(continued)*

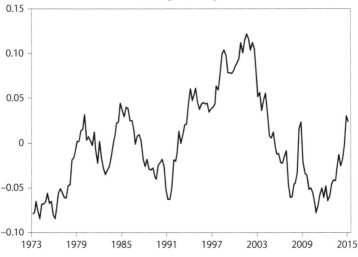

c. Deviations of actual from predicted real Canadian dollar/US dollar exchange rate (log)

Source: Authors' calculations.

on December 18. The decline in the policy rate matches the suggestion of the Taylor rule to reduce rates by 0.2 percent. Indeed, the Fed went on to continuously lower target rates until the rate reached 5.875 percent at the end of 1986. So while the Taylor rule was suggesting interest rates 1.5–2.0 percentage points below the effective rate in 1985, US intervention during the fourth quarter of 1985 forecast a resumption of monetary policy loosening as it moved closer to the rate implied by the Taylor rule.

The results for Germany do not comport as nicely with the hypothesis. The Taylor rule–implied rate and the money market rate track fairly closely, but they reveal large, sustained positive deviations in the early 1980s, similar to the United States (figure 8.8). Where the rate does deviate, such as in the early 1980s, it roughly matches previous results using revised (Clarida, Gali, and Gertler 1998) or real-time (Gerberding, Seitz, and Worms 2005) data.

Most important for this study, the Taylor rule lies below the money market rate, which we interpret to mean that the Bundesbank did not have policy space for intervention to weaken the dollar. Indeed, the Lombard rate was cut by half a percentage point in August 1985 and not moved until the start of 1987. However, the Bundesbank reduced the deviations between the key money market interest rates and the Taylor rule–implied rate to zero between the fourth quarter of 1984 and the second quarter of 1986, with money market rates falling until the first quarter of 1988. Rates moved consistently with the

**Figure 8.7   Deviations from the Taylor rule in
the United States, 1980–89**

a. Federal funds rate and rate implied by Taylor rule

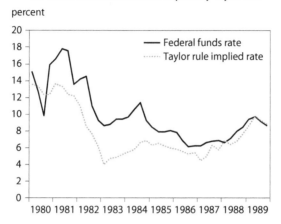

Source: Federal Reserve Economic Data (FRED) at the Federal Reserve
Bank of St. Louis.

b. Deviation of actual rate from rate implied by Taylor rule

Source: Authors' calculations.

Taylor rule, helping validate its use as an indicator of the direction of monetary policy at this time.

The interest rate differential is an important factor determining the exchange rate, as discussed in the previous section. If the foreign Taylor rule suggests that foreign rates would fall more slowly than US rates, foreign monetary policy could still be interpreted as consistent with dollar weakening. In 1985 overnight money market rates in Germany were below the federal funds rate, with the differential growing steadily over the year, from 2.75 to 3.5 percentage points. Because of lower inflation and a much more negative output

Figure 8.8 Deviations from the Taylor rule in Germany, 1980–89

a. Money market rate and rate implied by Taylor rule

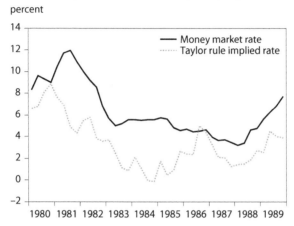

percent

Source: IMF, *International Financial Statistics* database (line 60B).

b. Deviation of actual rate from rate implied by Taylor rule

percent

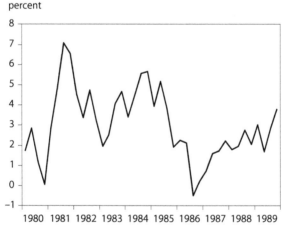

Source: Authors' calculations.

gap in Germany, the differential in the Taylor rule–implied rates was much larger than the observed differential, hitting 6.1 percentage points in the second quarter of 1985.

In the third quarter of 1985, however, output improved in Germany and softened in the United States, shrinking the Taylor rule–implied differential. In the next four quarters, the Taylor rule–implied differential continued to fall on the back of strengthening German growth and inflation and persistent softening of US inflation. The change was not a mere blip; the actual nominal interest rate differential fell as well throughout 1986.

For Japan the Taylor rule–implied rate presents a fairly tight fit after 1980 to the overnight call rate targeted by the Bank of Japan, though it too exhibits a large, sustained positive deviation in the early 1980s (figure 8.9). The Taylor rule rates correspond with previous results using real-time data (Kamada 2005).[17] For our period of interest, the deviation of the call rate and the Taylor rule rates declines from the first quarter of 1984 through the second quarter of 1985, suggesting that the Taylor rule provides some guidance for the direction of monetary policy during the Plaza.

As with the United States and Germany, Japanese interest rates were well above the Taylor rule–implied rates throughout 1985. Positive deviations suggest that Japanese participation in the Plaza intervention was not consistent with the presence of policy space for monetary policy. The Bank of Japan did not heed the Taylor rule, however, allowing the call rate to rise through the second half of 1985, perhaps in support of the intervention. Real-time data showed inflation falling in the final quarter, however, so the Taylor rule–implied interest rate dropped, causing the deviation to grow in the fourth quarter of 1985. The next move of the official discount rate did not come until January 1986, when it was lowered by half a percentage point. Inflation picked up in Japan that year, but the Bank of Japan continued to ease rates. As a result, for 1986 and most of 1987 the call rate converged to the Taylor rule.

In the third quarter of 1985, as the G-5 began intervening, rates in Japan were lower than in the United States. As Japanese call rates rose that quarter, the nominal rate differential moved to support the direction of intervention. Inflation ticked up in Japan that quarter while US output softened, so the Taylor rule–implied interest rate differential moved in the same direction as the nominal differential. However, as intervention continued into the fourth quarter, the two differentials diverged. The nominal differential supported the intervention, but the Taylor rule–implied differential moved in favor of dollar strengthening. For the next five quarters, the Taylor rule–implied differential suggests growing policy space in support of a weakening dollar, but with the Bank of Japan cutting rates the observed nominal differential did not favor a weakening dollar.

---

17. As Ito and Mishkin (2006) point out, there is disturbingly little consistency in the Taylor rule–implied interest rates estimated for Japan in the mid-1980s. Findings vary significantly, depending on the estimation period, the measure of output gap, and the estimation method (Kamada 2005 and Miyazawa 2011 illustrate the variety of results). Looking only at 1985, Clarida, Gali, and Gertler (1998) find no significant gap. Several studies that attempt to follow the Clarida, Gali, and Gertler methodology find positive gaps in 1985 (Bernanke and Gertler 1999, Okina and Shiratsuka 2002, Miyazawa 2011, Wilde 2012).

Figure 8.9   Deviations from the Taylor rule in Japan, 1980–89

a. Money market rate and rate implied by Taylor rule

percent

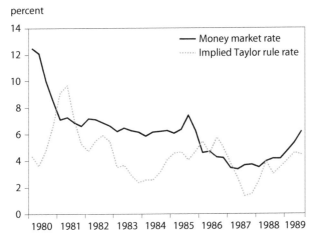

Source: Data from the Organization for Economic Cooperation and Development.

b. Deviation of actual rate from rate implied by Taylor rule

percent

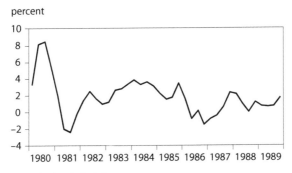

Source: Authors' calculations.

Discussion

It is uncontroversial to observe that the overvaluation of the dollar at its peak in the first quarter of 1985 was unprecedented in the post-Bretton Woods era. We document the overvaluation by examining the real exchange rate relative to a rate implied by the real interest rate differential. Other chapters in this volume provide more detail on the general point we aim to make: that such a large overvaluation provides the necessary motivation for policymakers to attempt a difficult act like coordinated exchange rate intervention. Fortunately, such large misalignments of the dollar against other major currencies are rare. Against the European currencies examined here, 1985 was the largest single episode of real misalignment seen under floating exchange rates, with or without adjusting for interest rate differentials. The degree of misalignment helps explain the uniqueness of the Plaza Accord.

Of course, the dollar turned around in the first quarter of 1985; the US real exchange rate adjusted for interest rate differentials had depreciated by almost 20 percent in September relative to its peak. Why was the urgency not gone by then? As noted by others in this volume, the US Congress was actively considering protectionist trade measures. While the depreciation would certainly have helped their constituents, the J-curve effect imposes a long lag between movements in the real exchange rate and the political pressure to help producers of tradable goods. Not until a year after the Plaza did US industry begin to feel the impact of the dramatic reversal in the exchange rate (Feldstein 1994); not until the time of the Louvre Accord would it have started to make a difference. Funabashi (1989) documents that political pressure from Congress supported US Treasury negotiations on exchange rate policy throughout this period.[18]

Examination of Taylor rule–implied interest rates reveals one potential source of impact. The chapters in this volume by David Mulford (chapter 3), Jeffrey Frankel (chapter 6), Joseph Gagnon (chapter 11), and Fred Bergsten (chapter 14) note that the major policy change that affected the foreign exchange market came from the United States. In chapter 7 Takatoshi Ito cites findings from his research (Ito 1987) that most of the exchange rate movement in the first month after the Plaza Accord occurred in New York, which he interprets as evidence that markets were responding primarily to the US policy change. Our evidence is consistent with this interpretation. The United States was the only G-3 country with policy space to intervene consistently with monetary policy, as measured by the deviation of target short-term rates from the Taylor rule–implied interest rate, as both Germany and Japan shared the large, sustained positive Taylor rule deviation with the United States throughout most of the early 1980s.

It can be argued, however, that the Taylor rule–implied interest differential was consistent with the Plaza intervention for both currency pairs. Both declined going into the third quarter of 1985, suggesting greater policy space for the Bundesbank and the Bank of Japan to cut rates more slowly than the Fed. This type of policy space is a weaker standard for monetary policy consistency, as it does not resolve the purely domestic policy inconsistency. (Unsterilized sales of dollars by foreign central banks would move foreign interest rates upward, while the Taylor rule indicates policy space for cutting rates.) In fact, the Bundesbank did subsequently reduce rates slowly enough to close the interest differential, though the Bank of Japan did not.

To the extent that there was a signaling or coordination channel propelling the dollar downward after the Plaza, it was primarily a US story. The coor-

---

18. In nominal terms the dollar fell until the end of 1988, depreciating another 37 percent against the mark and 48 percent against the yen beyond the decline it experienced before the Plaza.

dinated nature of the Plaza helped amplify the signal from the United States, making it appear more credible and durable. In addition, the US Treasury wanted to leverage its policy change to extract concessions from Japan and Germany (Funabashi 1989). The combination of fiscal stimulus in Germany and Japan and discipline in the United States noted in the Plaza communiqué were also consistent with a weaker dollar. One can speculate about whether the impact would have been similar if the United States had made a Plaza-type announcement unilaterally.

The synchrony of large positive deviations from the Taylor rule in all three countries in this period may be no coincidence. Presumably, the large US deviation at this time reflected Paul Volcker's effort to rebuild the Federal Reserve's inflation-fighting credibility. Rates in the other two economies may have been pulled above Taylor rule–implied rates in order to resist the pace of dollar appreciation. Hutchison (1988) and Glick and Hutchison (1994) show empirically that attempts to stabilize the exchange rate against the dollar influenced Bank of Japan monetary policy from 1975 until the Plaza. Clarida, Gali, and Gertler (1998) and Molodtsova, Nikolsko-Rzhevskyy, and Papell (2008) find the same result for the Bundesbank starting in 1979; Bundesbank data show consistent intervention to weaken the dollar from the first quarter of 1981 until the first quarter of 1985.

After the Plaza Accord provided assurance of the direction of the dollar, both the Bundesbank and the Bank of Japan appeared to take advantage of their policy space to lower rates, despite the fact that doing so worked against continued dollar weakness. The Taylor rule deviation closed for both economies by the middle of 1986.

As the Taylor rule deviations for all three countries moved closer to zero in 1986 and 1987, the language of various communiqués shifted emphasis toward currency stability. The Louvre Accord of February 1987 exemplifies this shift most effectively. The negotiating tactic of the US Treasury was to elicit more economic stimulus from Germany and Japan in exchange for US support for putting a floor beneath the falling dollar. In terms of policy consistency, however, the United States' push for economic stimulus sent mixed messages about how exchange rates should move.

The US Treasury wanted lower rates in all three countries. To the extent that all three lowered equally, differentials would not change, so monetary policy would not be inconsistent with (but also not supportive of) stopping the dollar's fall. The central banks paid significant attention to moving rates in step together, though synchrony did not always happen (Funabashi 1989, Volcker and Gyohten 1992).

In contrast, fiscal policy goals were explicitly inconsistent with exchange rate objectives. They had remained unchanged from the Plaza Accord: fiscal stimulus in Germany and Japan and greater discipline in the United States. Textbook macroeconomic models indicate that this pattern of fiscal policy change should cause the dollar to fall further. Had the G-3 countries been more successful at implementing their fiscal commitments, fiscal policy might have been a reasonable explanation for why the Louvre Accord was not more effective at halting the decline of the dollar. Funabashi's (1989) interpretation of contemporary market reports indicates the opposite. The lack of progress on the fiscal agenda helped cause the dollar to fall during this period.

The dollar is, of course, strong again. Our measure of overvaluation indicates that it rose about 10 percent in real terms against the euro and Canadian dollar and 15 percent against the yen through the second quarter of 2015. Against the euro, the pace of real appreciation implies that the dollar will hit the 1985 peak within 2.5 years. The level of dollar overvaluation against the yen is already approaching the peaks witnessed in 1985. The pace of nominal yen appreciation slowed in the second half of 2015, but the previous pace of appreciation was rapid.

A strong dollar at the 30th anniversary of the Plaza naturally raises questions about the desirability of a similar agreement today. All three G-3 central banks (with the European Central Bank [ECB] now replacing the Bundesbank) have hit the zero lower bound for short-term interest rates. In order to be consistent with monetary policy, a coordinated intervention to weaken the dollar would require the ECB and Bank of Japan to raise interest rates; it is inconceivable that either institution would agree to higher interest rates in order to strengthen their currencies. By the end of 2015, monetary policy in the United States was moving, albeit slowly, toward tightening; intervention to take the steam out of the dollar would not be consistent with monetary policy. Furthermore, the prospects for enacting fiscal policy changes consistent with a weakening dollar appear similar to what they were 30 years ago, with a lack of fiscal space in Japan, gridlock in the United States, and conservative fiscal preferences in Germany. For the moment, at least, we should not expect another Plaza Accord.

References

Baker, James A., III. 2006. *Work Hard, Study... and Keep out of Politics! Adventures and Lessons from an Unexpected Public Life*. New York: Penguin Group.

Benigno, Gianluca, and Pierpaolo Benigno. 2006. Designing Targeting Rules for International Monetary Policy Cooperation. *Journal of Monetary Economics* 53, no. 3: 473–506.

Bernanke, Ben, and Mark Gertler. 1999. Monetary Policy and Asset Price Volatility. *Economic Review* 84, no. 4: 17–51. Federal Reserve Bank of Kansas City.

Bordo, Michael D., Owen F. Humpage, and Anna J. Schwartz. 2010. *U.S. Foreign-Exchange-Market Intervention during the Volcker-Greenspan Era*. Working Paper 16345. Cambridge, MA: National Bureau of Economic Research.

Byrne, Joseph P., and Jun Nagayasu. 2010. Structural Breaks in the Real Exchange Rate and Real Interest Rate Relationship. *Global Finance Journal* 21, no. 2: 138–51.

Campbell, John Y., and Richard H. Clarida. 1987. The Dollar and Real Interest Rates. *Carnegie-Rochester Conference Series on Public Policy* 27, no. 1: 103–39.

Clarida, Richard. 2014. *Monetary Policy in Open Economies: Practical Perspectives for Pragmatic Central Bankers*. Working Paper 20545. Cambridge, MA: National Bureau of Economic Research.

Clarida, Richard, Jordi Gali, and Mark Gertler. 1998. Monetary Policy Rules in Practice: Some International Evidence. *European Economic Review* 42, no. 6: 1033–67.

Clausen, Jens Richard, and Carsten-Patrick Meier. 2005. Did the Bundesbank Follow a Taylor Rule? An Analysis Based on Real-Time Data. *Swiss Journal of Economics and Statistics* 141, no. II: 213–46.

Croushore, Dean, and Tom Stark. 2001. A Real-Time Data Set for Macroeconomists. *Journal of Econometrics* 105: 111–30.

Edison, Hali J. 1993. *The Effectiveness of Central-Bank Intervention: A Survey of the Literature after 1982.* Princeton Studies in International Economics 18. Princeton, NJ: Department of Economics, Princeton University.

Edison, Hali J., and William R. Melick. 1999. Alternative Approaches to Real Exchange Rates and Real Interest Rates: Three Up and Three Down. *International Journal of Finance & Economics* 4, no. 2: 93–111.

Edison, Hali J., and B. Dianne Pauls. 1993. A Re-Assessment of the Relationship between Real Exchange Rates and Real Interest Rates: 1974–1990. *Journal of Monetary Economics* 31, no. 2: 165–87.

Engel, Charles. 2011. Currency Misalignments and Optimal Monetary Policy: A Reexamination. *American Economic Review* 101, no. 6: 2796–822.

Engel, Charles. 2015. *Exchange Rates, Interest Rates, and the Risk Premium.* Working Paper 21042. Cambridge, MA: National Bureau of Economic Research.

Engel, Charles, Nelson C. Mark, and Kenneth D. West. 2008. *Exchange Rate Models Are Not as Bad as You Think.* NBER Chapters. Cambridge, MA: National Bureau of Economic Research.

Feldstein, Martin. 1986. *New Evidence on the Effects of Exchange Rate Intervention.* Working Paper 2052. Cambridge, MA: National Bureau of Economic Research.

Feldstein, Martin. 1994. American Economic Policy in the 1980s: A Personal View. In *American Economic Policy in the 1980s,* ed. Martin S. Feldstein. Chicago: University of Chicago Press.

Fendel, Ralf, Michael Frenkel, and Jan-Christoph Rülke. 2011. "Ex-Ante" Taylor Rules: Newly Discovered Evidence from the G7 Countries. *Journal of Macroeconomics* 33, no. 2: 224–32.

Fernandez, Adriana, Evan Koenig, and Alex Nikolsko-Rzhevskyy. 2012. *A Real-Time Historical Database for the OECD.* Globalization and Monetary Policy Institute Working Paper no. 96. Federal Reserve Bank of Dallas.

Frankel, Jeffrey A. 1994. Exchange Rate Policy: 1. In *American Economic Policy in the 1980s,* ed. Martin S. Feldstein. Chicago: University of Chicago Press.

Funabashi, Yoichi. 1989. *Managing the Dollar: From the Plaza to the Louvre,* 2nd ed. Washington: Institute for International Economics.

Gerberding, Christina, Franz Seitz, and Andreas Worms. 2005. How the Bundesbank Really Conducted Monetary Policy. *North American Journal of Economics and Finance* 16, no. 3: 277–92.

Glick, Reuven, and Michael Hutchison. 1994. Monetary Policy, Intervention, and Exchange Rates in Japan. In *Exchange Rate Policy and Interdependence: Perspectives from the Pacific Basin,* ed. Reuven Glick and Michael M. Hutchison. Cambridge: Cambridge University Press.

Haltmaier, Jane. 2001. *The Use of Cyclical Indicators in Estimating the Output Gap in Japan.* International Finance Discussion Paper 701. Washington: Board of Governors of the Federal Reserve System.

Hirose, Yasuo, and Koichiro Kamada. 2003. A New Technique for Simultaneous Estimation of Potential Output and the Phillips Curve. *Monetary and Economic Studies* 21, no. 2: 93–112.

Hirose, Yasuo, and Saori Naganuma. 2010. Structural Estimation of the Output Gap: A Bayesian DSGE Approach. *Economic Inquiry* 48, no. 4: 864–79.

Hoffmann, Mathias, and Ronald MacDonald. 2009. Real Exchange Rates and Real Interest Rate Differentials: A Present Value Interpretation. *European Economic Review* 53, no. 8: 952–70.

Hutchison, Michael M. 1988. Monetary Control with an Exchange Rate Objective: The Bank of Japan, 1973-86. *Journal of International Money and Finance* 7, no. 3: 261-71.

IMF (International Monetary Fund). 2015. *World Economic Outlook* (April). Washington.

Ito, Takatoshi. 1987. The Intradaily Exchange Rate Dynamics and Monetary Policies after the Group of Five Agreement. *Journal of the Japanese and International Economies* 1, no. 3: 275-98.

Ito, Takatoshi, and Frederic S. Mishkin. 2006. Two *Decades of Japanese Monetary Policy and the Deflation Problem*. NBER Chapters. Cambridge, MA: National Bureau of Economic Research.

Jurgensen, Philippe. 1983. *Report of the Working Group on Exchange Market Intervention*. Washington: US Treasury Department.

Kamada, Koichiro. 2005. Real-Time Estimation of the Output Gap in Japan and Its Usefulness for Inflation Forecasting and Policymaking. *North American Journal of Economics and Finance* 16, no. 3: 309-32.

King, Michael R. 2003. Effective Foreign Exchange Intervention: Matching Strategies with Objectives. *International Finance* 6, no. 2: 249-71.

MacDonald, Ronald, and Jun Nagayasu. 2000. The Long-Run Relationship between Real Exchange Rates and Real Interest Rate Differentials: A Panel Study. *IMF Staff Paper* 47, no. 1.

Mark, Nelson C., and Young-Kyu Moh. 2005. The Real Exchange Rate and Real Interest Differentials: The Role of Nonlinearities. *International Journal of Finance & Economics* 10, no. 4: 323-35.

Menkhoff, Lukas. 2010. High-Frequency Analysis of Foreign Exchange Interventions: What Do We Learn? *Journal of Economic Surveys* 24, no. 1: 85-112.

Mitchell, Karlyn, and Douglas Pearce. 2010. Do Wall Street Economists Believe in Okun's Law and the Taylor Rule? *Journal of Economics and Finance* 34, no. 2: 196-217.

Miyazawa, Kensuke. 2011. The Taylor Rule in Japan. *Japanese Economy* 38, no. 2: 79-104.

Molodtsova, Tanya, Alex Nikolsko-Rzhevskyy, and David H. Papell. 2008. Taylor Rules with Real-Time Data: A Tale of Two Countries and One Exchange Rate. *Journal of Monetary Economics* 55, Supplement 1: S63-S79.

Molodtsova, Tanya, and David H. Papell. 2009. Out-of-Sample Exchange Rate Predictability with Taylor Rule Fundamentals. *Journal of International Economics* 77, no. 2: 167-80.

Mulford, David. 2014. *Packing for India: A Life of Action in Global Finance and Diplomacy*. Lincoln, NE: Potomac Books.

Neely, Christopher J. 2001. The Practice of Central Bank Intervention: Looking under the Hood. *Federal Reserve Bank of St. Louis Review* 83, no. 2: 1-10.

Neely, Christopher J. 2008. Central Bank Authorities' Beliefs about Foreign Exchange Intervention. *Journal of International Money and Finance* 27, no. 1: 1-25.

Nikolsko-Rzhevskyy, Alex, David H. Papell, and Ruxandra Prodan. 2014. Deviations from Rules-Based Policy and Their Effects. *Journal of Economic Dynamics and Control* 49 (December): 4-17.

Nikolsko-Rzhevskyy, Alex, David H. Papell, and Ruxandra Prodan. 2015. The Taylor Principles. Department of Economics, University of Houston. Photocopy.

Obstfeld, Maurice, and Kenneth Rogoff. 2002. Global Implications of Self-Oriented National Monetary Rules. *Quarterly Journal of Economics* 117, no. 2: 503-35.

Okina, Kunio, and Shigenori Shiratsuka. 2002. Asset Price Bubbles, Price Stability, and Monetary Policy: Japan's Experience. *Monetary and Economic Studies* 20, no. 3: 35-76.

Orphanides, Athanasios. 2003. Historical Monetary Policy Analysis and the Taylor Rule. *Journal of Monetary Economics* 50, no. 5: 983-1022.

Phillips, Steven, Luis Catão, Luca Ricci, Rudolfs Bems, Mitali Das, Julian Di Giovanni, D. Filiz Unsal, Marola Castillo, Jungjin Lee, Jair Rodriguez, and Mauricio Vargas. 2013. *The External Balance Assessment (EBA Methodology)*. IMF Working Paper 13/272. Washington: International Monetary Fund.

Pierdzioch, Christian, Jan-Christoph Rülke, and Georg Stadtmann. 2012. Who Believes in the Taylor Principle? Evidence from the Livingston Survey. *Economics Letters* 117, no. 1: 96–98.

Reitz, Stefan, and Mark P. Taylor. 2008. The Coordination Channel of Foreign Exchange Intervention: A Nonlinear Microstructural Analysis. *European Economic Review* 52, no. 1: 55–76.

Reitz, Stefan, and Mark P. Taylor. 2012. FX Intervention in the Yen-US Dollar Market: A Coordination Channel Perspective. *International Economics and Economic Policy* 9, no. 2: 111–28.

Sarno, Lucio, and Mark P. Taylor. 2001. Official Intervention in the Foreign Exchange Market: Is It Effective and, If So, How Does It Work? *Journal of Economic Literature* 39, no. 3: 839–68.

Taylor, John B. 1993. Discretion versus Policy Rules in Practice. *Carnegie-Rochester Conference Series on Public Policy* 39, no. 1: 195–214.

Truman, Edwin. 2003. The Limits of Exchange Market Intervention. In *Dollar Overvaluation and the World Economy*, ed. C. Fred Bergsten and John Williamson. Special Report 16. Washington: Institute for International Economics.

Truman, Edwin. 2014. *The Federal Reserve Engages the World (1970–2000): An Insider's Narrative of the Transition to Managed Floating and Financial Turbulence*. PIIE Working Paper 14-5. Washington: Peterson Institute for International Economics.

Urasawa, Satoshi, and Haruki Seitani. 2008. *Accuracy of Measuring Business Cycle Components: Constructing Confidence Intervals for Output Gap in Japan Based on Simulation Technique*. ESRI Discussion Paper 194. Tokyo: Economic and Social Research Institute.

Volcker, Paul, and Toyoo Gyohten. 1992. *Changing Fortunes: The World's Money and the Threat to American Leadership*. New York: Crown.

Wilde, Wolfram. 2012. The Influence of Taylor Rule Deviations on the Real Exchange Rate. *International Review of Economics & Finance* 24, no. 1: 51–61.

Yamada, Hiroshi, and Lan Jin. 2012. Japan's Output Gap Estimation and ℓ_1 Trend Filtering. *Empirical Economics* 45, no. 1: 81–88.

9

The Plaza Accord

Exchange Rates and Policy Coordination

EDWIN M. TRUMAN

The Ministers and Governors, noting the recent developments in the exchange markets, expressed their commitment to work toward greater exchange market stability. Toward this end, the Ministers and Governors:

- *Reaffirmed their commitment to pursue monetary and fiscal policies that promote a convergence of economic performance at non-inflationary, steady growth;*

- *Stressed the importance of removing structural rigidities in their economies to achieving the objectives of non-inflationary steady growth and exchange market stability, and expressed their intent to intensify efforts in this area; and*

- *In light of recent developments in foreign exchange markets, reaffirmed their commitment made at the Williamsburg Summit to undertake coordinated intervention in the markets as necessary.*

The Ministers and Governors believe that this approach will provide a solid framework for sustaining recovery, reducing inflation, increasing employment, and achieving greater exchange rate stability.

—Announcement of G-5 Ministers and Governors, January 17, 1985[1]

In the 1980s and early 1990s, international coordination of macroeconomic policies focused primarily on three interrelated topics: exchange rates, current

Edwin M. Truman is nonresident senior fellow at the Peterson Institute for International Economics. From 1977 to 1998 he directed the Division of International Finance at the Federal Reserve System. He thanks Tyler Moran for technical assistance and James Boughton, Sam Cross, Joseph Gagnon, Russell Green, C. Randall Henning, Larry Promisel, Catherine Schenk, Peter Sturm, and Paul A. Volcker for comments and encouragement.

1. Announcement by G-5 Ministers and Governors, Washington, DC, January 17, 1985, www.g8.utoronto.ca/finance/fm850117.htm (accessed on July 9, 2015).

account positions, and promotion of noninflationary growth (growth with low inflation or rates that did not increase).[2] The meeting of the G-5 ministers and governors on January 17, 1985, marked the start of a new period of activism for the group and later for the G-7 ministers and governors. For the first time they issued a statement. The G-7 leaders had met annually since November 1975, issuing statements, communiqués, and associated annexes and reports after each meeting. The G-5 finance ministers and central bank governors had met several times a year starting earlier in the 1970s, but they did not issue statements, and there was often no publicity about their meetings.

The January 1985 announcement mentioned exchange markets and exchange market stability five times.[3] This was no accident. The statement was motivated by a desire to signal a willingness to support the pound, which had depreciated about 10 percent against the dollar over the previous three months. Despite the Reagan administration's general disapproval of foreign exchange market intervention, outgoing Treasury Secretary Donald Regan and incoming Secretary James Baker were prepared to help President Reagan's good friend Prime Minister Margaret Thatcher with at least some verbal intervention in the context of continued concerns about global growth.[4] Concerns about current account imbalances were soon to emerge as well.[5]

This chapter covers three episodes of international economic policy coordination, each focused on exchange rates and exchange market intervention: the 1983 report to the G-7 leaders of the working group on exchange market intervention known as the Jurgensen Report; the Plaza Accord of September 1985; and the closely linked Louvre Accord of 1987, which built on a surveillance framework established at the 1986 Tokyo G-7 leaders' meeting. For each episode I discuss the problem and the extent of consensus on its identification and diagnosis; examine how the problem was treated and show the extent to which the parties followed through on their commitments and understandings, sometimes with adjustments; and evaluate the short- and longer-term results. The chapter concludes with a coda summarizing developments with respect to policy coordination on exchange rates from the late 1980s through the first 15 years of the 21st century.

To preview my conclusions: With respect to identification of the problem and its shared diagnosis in the Jurgensen episode, the issue of the effectiveness and appropriateness of exchange market intervention was identified early in the US dollar's ascent. The diagnosis, insofar as recognizing the possibility of commissioning a study is concerned, was generally shared by all involved. In

---

2. During the 1980s international economic policy coordination also focused on the global debt crises in Latin America and elsewhere.

3. The announcement also included an introductory paragraph describing the meeting.

4. Sometimes personal chemistry trumps ideology. Although sterling stabilized against the dollar after the announcement, it later resumed its decline.

5. In 1984 the US current account deficit more than doubled from its 1983 level to reach $94 billion, a record 2.3 percent of US nominal GDP.

the Plaza episode, identification of the dollar's super strength was recognized late, and the diagnosis of its causes was not widely shared. The same was true in the Louvre episode; by early 1987, the dollar had already depreciated too far and too fast for some.

On treatment, in the Jurgensen episode the treatment was only the report of the working group, which in the immediate aftermath went nowhere. In the Plaza episode, some intervention treatment was applied, but that was all. In the Louvre episode, greater intervention was applied over a period of almost 12 months, and in the end the United States made an ad hoc adjustment in its budget plans.

My evaluation of the Jurgensen episode is that it had little short-run impact but subsequently shaped thinking about intervention as a useful tool, in particular if coordinated and linked to support of or supporting policy measures. The Plaza Accord was successful in accelerating the decline of the dollar and forestalling protectionist US legislation, but it overachieved on the former, requiring subsequent efforts to try to stop the dollar's decline in the Louvre Accord. Little was accomplished in terms of changes in G-7 macroeconomic policies. The accord failed in its short-term objective to stabilize the dollar in the short run, though the intervention may have slowed the adjustment. With respect to macroeconomic policies, coordination pressures can be credited with eventually inducing a modest adjustment in the US budget deficit and contributing positively to that multiyear process.

The Jurgensen Report

The relevance of the Jurgensen Report to international economic policy coordination during the 1980s is not in its immediate impact on policy but rather as the basis for what ultimately became the G-7 approach to foreign exchange operations.[6] With a lag, the report opened the door to a resumption of larger-scale US cooperation with its partners on exchange rate management. The episode differs from the others examined here in that although it started and ended with the G-7 leaders and involved their finance ministries and central banks, the substance of the report was produced by lower-level officials.[7] Later the G-7 ministers, their deputies, central bank governors, and leaders put their own glosses on the report.

Problem Identification and Diagnosis

Treasury Undersecretary Beryl Sprinkel announced on April 17, 1981, that the Reagan administration would follow an approach of minimal exchange market intervention, operating only when necessary to counter conditions of disorder in the exchange market. In congressional testimony on May 4, he presented the

---

6. For an elaboration on some of the material in this and the following sections with respect to the role of the Federal Reserve System, see Truman (2014).

7. I was one of them, representing the Federal Reserve.

rationale for the new policy. It was based in part on a belief in markets and their appropriate responses to sound (and unsound) economic fundamentals and in part on the view that exchange rates should respond to domestic economic policies of individual countries—the keep-your-own-house-in-order approach to international economic policy cooperation.[8] Sprinkel did not define "disorderly market conditions," the rubric that had governed US intervention policy since the late 1970s. The phrase was taken from the principles associated with International Monetary Fund (IMF) oversight of members' adherence to their obligations under the new Article IV of the Articles of Agreement (IMF 2013).[9] He said the Reagan administration would adopt a stricter definition of disorderly market conditions than had been the policy of the Carter administration, with its frequent large-scale intervention operations starting in November 1978.[10]

Between December 1980 (shortly before President Reagan took office) and early June 1982, the dollar appreciated 18 percent against the major currencies in nominal terms (figure 9.1) and 14 percent in price-adjusted terms (figure 9.2).[11] After the dollar's weakness in the late 1970s, its recovery was welcomed by many. Its rise began with a lag after the Federal Reserve's determined attack on inflation in 1979. That posture continued to produce high nominal and real interest rates in the early 1980s.

Some officials in other major countries thought the dollar's rise had gone too far, in part because its strength tended to undercut their own efforts to reduce inflation and in part because the rise was viewed as too rapid. Even though the dollar's appreciation contributed to a sharp movement of the

---

8. Testimony of Beryl Sprinkel before the Joint Economic Committee, May 4, 1981, www.jec.senate.gov (accessed on July 8, 2015). See also Destler and Henning (1989, 18–26).

9. Principle B for bilateral surveillance of a member's exchange rate policy, which was put in place with the 1978 revision of the Articles, states: "A member should intervene in the exchange market if necessary to counter disorderly conditions, which may be characterized inter alia by disruptive short-term movements in the exchange rate of its currency."

10. After April 17, 1981, and during the first Reagan administration, the United States intervened on 19 days, selling a total of $1.013 trillion, half of it during 1984. During the entire eight years of the Clinton administration it intervened on just 20 days, purchasing dollars on 18 days and selling dollars on 2. However, during the Clinton years the average daily operation was slightly more than $750 million, whereas during the first Reagan administration it was slightly more than $50 million. Between August 1978 and January 1979, the United States sold $9.4 billion in foreign currencies, buying back $8.1 billion through early June 1979 before selling an additional $5.4 billion through July of that year. See Holmes and Pardee (1979) and Pardee (1979) for information on intervention during the Carter years.

11. The nominal appreciation against the major currencies was larger than the price-adjusted appreciation because the US inflation rate was lower than the inflation rates of its major trading partners on average. The dollar's nominal appreciation with respect to a broader group of currencies was about 18 percent. Against the German mark and the Japanese yen, the nominal appreciation was 20 percent (www.federalreserve.gov/releases/h10/hist/). Real effective exchange rates (also known as price-adjusted exchange rates) are indexes of the foreign exchange value of the dollar deflated by the relative levels of consumer prices.

Figure 9.1 Nominal exchange rate index, 1980–89

index, December 1980 = 100

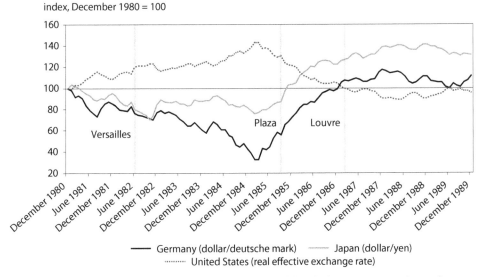

Source: Federal Reserve Bank of St. Louis, https://research.stlouisfed.org/fred2/categories/32145 (accessed on July 10, 2015).

Figure 9.2 Real effective exchange rate index, 1980–89

index, December 1980 = 100

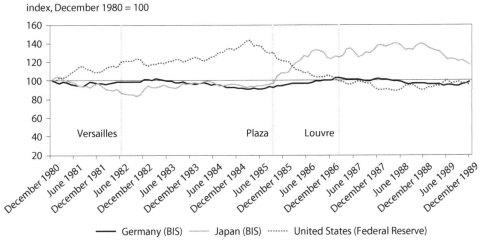

BIS = Bank for International Settlements

Source: Federal Reserve Bank of St. Louis, https://research.stlouisfed.org/fred2/categories/32145 (accessed on July 10, 2015).

US current account back into deficit following surpluses in 1980 and 1981, foreign finance ministers and central bank governors bemoaned the lack of cooperation by the United States in managing exchange rate movements. Led by Germany, they were also critical of the US mix of macroeconomic policies—a federal fiscal deficit that reached 4 percent of GDP in FY1982 and a federal funds rate averaging 14 percent during the first half of the calendar year as consumer price index (CPI) inflation decelerated from a 12-month increase of 8.6 percent at the end of 1981 to 4.0 percent at the end of 1982.

The central issue identified at the Versailles G-7 summit on June 6, 1982, was the lack of consensus on the effectiveness and appropriateness of official intervention in foreign exchange markets. US unwillingness to coordinate (in other words, participate) in exchange market operations was based on a view that such operations were ineffective and inappropriate. Other countries did not share this view. The G-7 leaders agreed to establish a working group to study the impacts of foreign exchange market intervention—reaching consensus about addressing the differences in view underlying the lack of consensus on the broader topic.[12]

Treatment

The Working Group on Exchange Market Intervention was chaired by Philippe Jurgensen of the French Treasury. Participants were officials of the G-7 finance ministries and central banks as well as the European Economic Communities (EEC) and the representatives of the EEC presidency (Denmark and later Belgium). The group met 10 times over the subsequent 8 months and considered some 2,000 pages of documentation. That documentation included written material supplied by each participant and more than a dozen research studies.[13] Participants refrained from drawing policy implications until the last meeting of the working group, something that facilitated a free give and take in discussions of the material.

The working group's report contributed to a better understanding in official circles of the distinction between sterilized and unsterilized intervention and examined the issues associated with foreign exchange market intervention from a number of perspectives.[14] In academic and some central bank circles, economists generally understood the distinction, but the distinction

---

12. The study was not mentioned in the summit declaration. The declaration's only mention of intervention was in a statement on international monetary undertakings. It merely reiterated the current reality: "We are ready, if necessary, to use intervention in exchange markets to counter disorderly conditions, as provided for under Article IV of the IMF Articles of Agreement" (Declaration of the Seven Heads of State and Government and Representatives of the European Communities, Versailles Summit, June 6, 1982).

13. Ten US studies were later published as Federal Reserve Board Staff Studies. Henderson and Sampson (1983) summarize them.

14. Sterilized intervention affects the currency composition of the asset side of a central bank's balance sheet but does not affect the size of the liability side. Unsterilized intervention affects the liability side.

had not penetrated finance ministries to any substantial degree. The working group devoted a significant amount of time to discussing this distinction and associated issues of measurement based on a paper by Adams and Henderson (1983).[15] The working group's report devoted three paragraphs to this issue.

Bordo, Humpage, and Schwartz (2015, 275) claim that the report's wording was imprecise and that "the imprecision seemed, and probably was, intentional." This criticism is unjustified. The intention in setting out the distinction in the first few pages of the report was precisely to signal its importance. Some central bankers and other observers, however, feel that the distinction was too stark and oversimplified in trying to isolate intervention from other policy actions at the time (see, for example, Volcker and Gyohten 1992, 236–37). Bordo, Humpage, and Schwartz (2015, 276) are also mistaken to criticize the report for failing "to discuss the potential conflict with domestic monetary policy objectives that unsterilized [or sterilized for that matter] intervention could create." The report, written in 1983, does not use the language Bordo, Humpage, and Schwartz used more than 30 years later, but paragraph 20 clearly flags the issues involved:

> Intervention is only one of several factors that influence the monetary authorities' monetary liabilities (monetary base). As long as monetary targets are being met (whether or not these relate to the monetary base), the monetary effects of intervention can be considered in some sense as having been neutralized. When objectives are not met, it is a matter of judgement, in each case, whether it is intervention or some other factors (or both) that must be considered to have contributed to the outcome. (Jurgensen 1983, 6–7)

On the effectiveness of intervention, the working group concluded:

> Intervention had been an effective tool in the pursuit of certain exchange rate objectives—notably those oriented toward influencing the behaviour of the exchange rate in the short run. Effectiveness was found to have been greater when intervention was unsterilized than when its monetary effects were offset.... [S]terilized intervention did not generally have a lasting effect, but... intervention in conjunction with domestic policy changes did have more durable impact.... [A]ttempts to pursue exchange rate objectives which were inconsistent with fundamentals through intervention alone tended to be counterproductive. (Jurgensen 1983, 17)

Much of the research effort was directed at trying to determine whether sterilized intervention had been effective during the floating rate period. That

---

15. Even today there is not full agreement on issues of definition and measurement. The narrowest definition is the one in the text. An expanded definition would focus on bank reserves and allow intervention to be "sterilized" by the sale of central bank notes or bonds to offset any increase in reserve liabilities. A still broader definition focuses on "monetary conditions," which could include a variety of measures, including one or more interest rates. Essentially all intervention operations in the major currencies discussed in this chapter were sterilized on one definition or another. In other words, they were intended to be sterilized as the authorities understood that term.

research was based primarily on a portfolio balance model that assumes that securities denominated in different currencies are not perfect substitutes.[16] Its results provided weak support for the effectiveness of intervention via the portfolio balance channel but also identified the possibility of a signaling channel.

The working group expressed the view that "closely coordinated action had at times been more effective than intervention by only one central bank because it gave a signal to the market that the authorities were working to the same purpose" (Jurgensen 1983, 26). The group discussed, but did not report on, proposals from the French and the Japanese to move toward a regime in which there was systematic coordination of exchange rate management policies. Discussion of these proposals was repeated in meetings of the G-7 deputies reviewing the Jurgensen report. Japan put forward a rather complete plan for target zones based on real exchange rates linking the dollar, yen, and mark.

The report of the working group went next to the summit finance ministers, central bank governors, and representatives of the European Community. Based on a draft by the deputies, on April 29, 1983, they issued the following statement:[17]

> The achievement of greater exchange rate stability, which does not imply rigidity, is a major objective and commitment of our countries.... Under present circumstances, the role of intervention can only be limited. Intervention can be useful to counter disorderly market conditions and to reduce short-term volatility. Intervention may also on occasion express an attitude toward exchange markets. Intervention will normally be useful only when complementing and supporting other policies. We are agreed on the need for closer consultations on policies and market conditions; and, while retaining our freedom to operate independently, are willing to undertake coordinated intervention in instances where it is agreed that such intervention would be helpful.

My hope in participating in the intervention study was that the group would be able to carve out an agreed role for sterilized intervention as a supporting tool of economic, including monetary, policy. In that we were moderately successful. Although the results of our empirical research were disappointing, contrary to some interpretations, the report was not anti-intervention.

The release of the working group's report and the associated statement on April 29 did not attract much attention in the markets. Sam Cross, at the time the manager of foreign exchange operations at the Federal Reserve Bank of New York (on behalf of the US Treasury's Exchange Stabilization Fund [ESF] and the account of the Federal Open Market Committee [FOMC]),

---

16. The effectiveness of large-scale asset purchases (quantitative easing) by the Federal Reserve and other central banks relies on the same basic assumption. Researchers, in some cases using more modern techniques, have found substantial impacts of such operations on interest rates. However, recent central bank operations in domestic securities have been on a wholly different scale from operations in foreign currencies in the 1970s and early 1980s.

17. G-7 Statement on the Intervention Study, April 29, 1983.

commented that the nonreaction may have been because immediately after the April 29 meeting Secretary Regan said that US policy had not changed.[18] It did not change for another 21 months.

When G-7 leaders subsequently met in Williamsburg on May 28–30, 1983, they added little to what the ministers and governors had said other than a reference to the Jurgensen Report itself: "We will improve consultations, policy convergence, and international cooperation to help stabilize exchange markets, bearing in mind our conclusions on the Exchange Market Intervention Study."[19] The Williamsburg Declaration also failed to produce a ripple in foreign exchange markets. The treatment was prepared but application was delayed (see the G-5 statement quoted at the beginning of this chapter).

Evaluation

Although the Jurgensen Report did not lead to immediate changes in policies, it enhanced the participating finance ministries' and central banks' understanding of the possibilities of and constraints on foreign exchange market intervention and affected the attitudes of other officials. The report laid the ground for future cooperation on exchange rates, in particular with respect to coordinated operations, the need to support or receive support from other policies, and the signaling of official attitudes to the market.

The Plaza Accord

Paul Volcker was concerned about the adverse implications of the strong dollar and associated fiscal and current account deficits for the domestic and international economy in the period before 1985. His concerns were expressed in a note he wrote in early 1984 in which he advocated a fresh approach that included a rare endorsement of US intervention to limit the dollar's appreciation in cooperation with other countries, in particular the Bundesbank, which had begun to intervene heavily. The note—which he never sent to Secretary Regan—also raised his concerns about the combination of a large US budget deficit, growing US current account deficit, and reliance on a net inflow of foreign capital (Volcker and Gyohten 1992, 238–39). He was already sharing these concerns privately with the Treasury and chose to avoid a more public brawl.

During late 1984 and the first half of 1985, the G-10 as well as the G-24 group of developing countries drafted separate reports on the functioning of the international monetary system. These reports were motivated in part by ruminations, including from the US administration, about a "new Bretton Woods" conference. In the G-10 discussions, the French delegation raised the possibility of a system of target zones for exchange rates in which countries

---

18. Sam Y. Cross, Notes for FOMC Meeting, May 24, 1983, www.federalreserve.gov/monetary-policy/files/FOMC19830524material.pdf (accessed on July 8, 2015).

19. Declaration on Economic Recovery, Williamsburg Summit, May 30, 1983, www.g8.utoronto.ca/summit/1983williamsburg/communique.html (accessed on July 8, 2015).

would be under some obligation to act to keep their exchange rates within those zones. The initiative did not generate much traction, in part because of opposition from the US Treasury and the Bundesbank. The G-24 report endorsed target zones. An IMF staff proposal for the use of objective indicators to guide policies, in particular policies toward exchange rates, also resurfaced, echoing US proposals during the monetary reform discussions by the Committee of Twenty in the first half of the 1970s (Boughton 2001, 203–206).

By the end of 1984, the dollar had strengthened substantially. Compared with four years earlier, it had risen 37 percent against the currencies of major trading partners in terms of the Federal Reserve Board staff's price-adjusted index and 41 percent in nominal terms, a whopping 60 percent against the mark, and 24 percent against the yen (the mark's appreciation was substantially smaller than that of the yen in real effective terms [compare figures 9.1 and 9.2]). This was the context in which the G-5 finance ministers and central bank governors met on January 17, 1985, and made the announcement quoted at the beginning of this chapter.

The action signified a new type of exchange market intervention: coordinated verbal as well as market intervention. The public statement was followed immediately by substantial dollar sales by European central banks and Japan. The US monetary authorities sold dollars two days later as well as on February 1, the last day Regan was US Treasury secretary. They also bought deutsche marks from customers on February 4, the first day James Baker was US Treasury secretary. The US authorities' market sales between the G-5 meeting and March 1 (a total of $659 million, according to Cross 1985b) were substantial compared with the scale of operations in the previous three years, but the amounts were small relative to those of the other G-5 and G-10 authorities.[20] Cross reported to the FOMC on February 13: "The current attitude of other G-10 countries toward our intervention seems to range from frustration to irritation. They acknowledge US concerns about our not bashing our own currency.... Very broadly there is concern that the element of uncertainty introduced by the January G-5 agreement may be fizzling out unless there are some new initiatives."[21]

The foreign exchange value of the dollar dipped following the January G-5 statement, but after recovering it peaked within a month or two in terms of the various indexes and against the mark and the yen. By early September 1985, the dollar was down, but only slightly, from its level at the end of 1984, less than 4 percent on the nominal index against the major currencies.

---

20. US dollar sales included $16.8 million to purchase sterling on February 19.

21. Sam Y. Cross, Notes for FOMC Meeting, February 13, 1985, www.federalreserve.gov/monetary-policy/files/FOMC19850213material.pdf (accessed on July 9, 2015).

Figure 9.3   Current account balance in Germany, Japan, and the United States, 1981–90

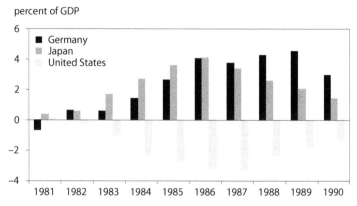

Source: IMF, *World Economic Outlook*.

Problem Identification and Diagnosis

Until the agreement announced at the Plaza Hotel in New York on September 22, 1985, US officials tended to applaud the dollar's strength.[22] They saw it as international investors' show of support for US economic policies and response to the positive performance of the US economy, which was welcoming and encouraging the inflow of foreign investment, the counterpart to the expanding US current account deficit (Destler and Henning 1989, 26–30) (figure 9.3). In the eyes of some (Bergsten 1994), the administration tolerated the widening of the US current account deficit because it facilitated economic expansion while limiting inflation.

The political and economic environment was changing. The strength of the dollar was becoming a problem for the United States as well as for its foreign partners. The challenge was to establish a consensus diagnosis of the problem. In Truman (2006) I argue that developments in advance of the Plaza meeting conveyed three messages to policymakers: the US fiscal/monetary mix was flawed, protectionism could be on the horizon, and a bubble in the dollar's foreign exchange value in 1984 and early 1985 could be about to burst. All three messages eventually contributed to a weak international consensus on the problem of the dollar's high value and what to do about it. Conspicuously, in terms of debates today, foreign exchange market intervention by other countries to drive down their currencies against the dollar was not one of the candidate causes.

---

22. A partial exception was the 1983-84 yen-dollar talks, which aimed at liberalizing Japan's domestic and external financial markets and promoting the internationalization and apprecia-tion of the yen (see Frankel 1984).

Many economists, including Volcker and others at the Federal Reserve, focused on the US fiscal deficit and the associated mix of monetary and fiscal policies in the United States as the cause of the dollar's strength. Drawing on a briefing of the Federal Reserve Board by Peter Isard that illustrated the statistical connection between the high federal budget deficit (about 5 percent of GDP), rising net private investment in the context of the recovery, other sources of net private saving, and net inflows of saving from abroad (the counterpart to the current account deficit), Volcker hammered on the need to address the budget deficit in testimony before the Joint Economic Committee and Senate Budget Committee.[23] Volcker attached Isard's tables to his testimonies. He knew that there was no simple causal link between budget deficits and current account deficits, but in the circumstances he believed both were serious problems.

Economic and financial officials in other countries were more attracted to the notion of a causal link because it conveniently took their own policies off the hook. If only the United States would reduce its budget deficit, they would not have to change their policies, experience an appreciation of their currencies, or face lower external surpluses. This pseudo-analysis of miraculous global adjustment was wrong, convenient, and not limited to this period. No country, including the United States, can achieve adjustment of its current account position via fiscal restraint or expansion and also maintain full employment and price stability without changes in other policies or variables (e.g., monetary policy and/or the exchange rate). Moreover, if it is large enough, the external adjustment will affect the national accounts of other countries.

For their part, US politicians, when they were not supporting protection legislation, argued for a lower dollar in order to take them off the hook of having to address the US fiscal deficit as part of a solution. Scores of legislative proposals were introduced in Congress. Many explicitly advocated protection against imports, and some mandated a more activist US foreign exchange policy (Destler and Henning 1989, 90–112). The Midwestern Rust Belt, where traditional US manufacturing was concentrated and a large share of US exports originated, was badly hurt by the 1980–82 recessions and high interest rates, did not receive much benefit from the Reagan expansion, and suffered from the strong dollar. Manufacturing tends to be more interest sensitive than other sectors, and real interest rates remained high, because of a combination of the pressure of large fiscal deficits and the Federal Reserve's continuing effort to reduce US inflation, which also contributed to the strength of the dollar.

Central bankers in the United States and the other G-5 countries were concerned that the soaring dollar was being fueled by speculation rather than fundamental forces and would end in an uncontrollable bust, with serious

---

23. Testimony by Paul A. Volcker before the Joint Economic Committee, February 5, 1985, http://fraser.stlouisfed.org/docs/historical/volcker/Volcker_19850205.pdf (accessed on July 9, 2015). Testimony by Paul A. Volcker before the Senate Budget Committee, February 8, 1985, http://fraser.stlouisfed.org/docs/historical/volcker/Volcker_19850208.pdf (accessed on July 9, 2015).

global economic and financial consequences.[24] In May 1984, when the dollar's nominal value in terms of its major trading partners was only 30 percent above its level in December 1980, my colleagues at the Federal Reserve made a presentation to the FOMC on the US external position.[25] They concluded that with an unchanged value of the dollar, the US external position was unsustainable, because US net external debt would be rising faster than US nominal GDP, reaching close to 15 percent of GDP by 1990. They investigated the implications of a rapid depreciation of the dollar by 45 percent over two years, concluding that it would boost growth and inflation over the first two and half years but produce a lower level of economic activity after that, as monetary policy responded to the growth and inflation and continuing fiscal deficits crowded out investment. They also investigated a smoother adjustment, which combined fiscal tightening and compensatory monetary adjustment.

Volcker testified on February 20, 1985, that the Federal Reserve had cut the discount rate and eased pressures on bank reserves in November and December 1984 in part because of the potential disruptive situation of the continuing dollar strength (Obstfeld 1990, 205). Concerns about a sharp decline of the dollar, if not a disorderly bursting of the dollar's bubble, were not unfounded.[26]

The three diagnoses and concerns about the dollar (the US monetary/fiscal mix, rising protectionism, and a bubble that would burst) were not mutually exclusive. Each contributed to establishing a weak consensus that collective action was needed. For one reason or another, by the summer of 1985, not only US Treasury officials and US Secretary of State George Shultz but also officials of the other G-5 countries were persuaded that something had to be done to bring the dollar down, even though it had already begun to decline (Volcker and Gyohten 1992, 242; Funabashi 1988, 76–79). As David Mulford (2014, 170) reports, "Eventually, in September the critical mass of credible cooperative understandings was judged to be sufficient to lay the plan for a G-5 finance ministers meeting at the Plaza Hotel."

---

24. Marris (1985) delivered the strongest alarms about a hard landing for the global economy. Boughton (2001, 202) cites an IMF Staff study for the 1985 US Article IV review that concluded that "a substantial portion of the real appreciation of the dollar, particularly in the second half of 1984, remains unexplained."

25. Board of Governors of the Federal Reserve System, "The US External Position, May 21, 1984," www.federalreserve.gov/monetarypolicy/files/FOMC19840522material.pdf (accessed on June 24, 2014).

26. At the February 1985 FOMC, the staff projected that the price-adjusted foreign exchange value of the dollar against the major currencies would depreciate by about 15 percent over the next two years under the weight of the rising US current account deficit. The dollar peaked in March 1985 before declining 38 percent over the next three years.

Treatment

Under Secretary Baker, Deputy Secretary Richard Darman, and Assistant Secretary for International Affairs David Mulford, the US Treasury began to develop a strategy to deal with the problem based on a June 1985 memorandum by Mulford (2014, 167). According to Funabashi (1988, chapter 1), in July 1985 preliminary policy discussions began with Japanese officials leading up to the agreement unveiled by the G-5 finance ministers and central bank governors on September 22 at the Plaza Hotel. As Secretary Baker (2006, 429) reports, "Our leverage with them was that if we didn't act first, the protectionists in Congress would throw up trade barriers." The Federal Reserve was not brought into the planning until quite late, when issues of intervention tactics had to be discussed.[27] This approach may have been a mistake, because it meant that the Federal Reserve, along with other central banks, did not have ownership of, and therefore commitment to, the substance of the Plaza Accord.

Market forces alone might have continued the dollar's decline beyond the summer of 1985, but they were reinforced by the Plaza Accord:[28]

> [T]hat exchange rates should play a role in adjusting external imbalances... [E]xchange rates should better reflect fundamental economic conditions than has been the case... [A]greed policy actions must be implemented and reinforced to improve the fundamentals further... [and] some further orderly appreciation of the main non-dollar currencies against the dollar is desirable. They stand ready to cooperate more closely to encourage this when to do so would be helpful.

Volcker, supported by Bundesbank President Karl Otto Pöhl, expressed concerns about the dollar's moving too far too fast and insisted on inserting the word "orderly" before "appreciation" in the G-5 statement. Although the press release did not mention coordinated foreign exchange operations, they were implied by the last sentence and were the center of discussion at the meeting in New York. Some degree of consensus was reached on the basis of a nonpaper that set out the proposed scale and sharing of intervention operations over the next six weeks in order to achieve a further decline of the dollar of 10-12 percent (Funabashi 1988, chapter 1). The Plaza Accord was noteworthy in that it involved quantitative goals and measures, even though they were not fully agreed upon.

The intervention operations proceeded roughly as discussed by G-5 officials on September 21-22. The small amounts were coordinated and sterilized, as implicitly recommended in the Jurgensen Report. But contrary to the

---

27. What I, at the Federal Reserve Board, knew about Treasury's thinking came from my close friend and counterpart at the Bundesbank, Wolfgang Reieke, who was privy to the Treasury's conversations in Europe.

28. Announcement of the Ministers of Finance and Central Bank Governors of France, Germany, Japan, the United Kingdom, and the United States, New York, September 22, 1985, www.library. utoronto.ca/g7/finance/fm850922.htm (accessed on July 9, 2015).

recommendation in the Jurgensen Report, they were not supported by other economic policies. The dollar quickly declined 10.5 percent against the mark and 14 percent against the yen. The G-5 authorities sold only $8.1 billion during the period, compared with a notional war chest of $18 billion laid out in the nonpaper. The US share of the $8.1 billion was about 40 percent.[29]

Funabashi reports some US disappointment over the scale of Bundesbank intervention and the German counterargument that they were coordinating and financing intervention in dollars within the European Monetary System (EMS), in particular by the Italians. Funabashi also reports that the Bundesbank had been annoyed by the lack of intervention follow-through by the US authorities following the January 1985 G-5 meeting. Bundesbank purchases of marks during the six weeks after January 17 were DM 10.9 billion, down from DM 2.7 billion during the six weeks after the Plaza meeting.[30]

By the end of 1985, the dollar was down 14 percent against the mark and 17 percent against the yen. Cross (1985a, 2) commented on some of the reasons for the apparent success:

> In part, the exchange market reaction reflected the fact that the announcement was unexpected. More importantly, market participants noted that the initiative had come from the United States and was viewed as a change in the US government's previously perceived attitude of accepting or even welcoming a strong dollar. In addition, the agreement was interpreted as eliminating the likelihood that the Federal Reserve would tighten reserve conditions in response to rapid US monetary growth.

The G-5 ministers and governors also included in the Plaza Accord three pages of text concerning their countries' other policy intentions, five to seven commitments per country. All were statements of current policies rather than changes in those policies. The United States included in its commitments a restatement of its intention to reduce government expenditures as a share of GDP and to reduce the budget deficit in FY1986 by more than 1 percent of GDP. Each country included resisting protectionism in its list. Indeed, one of the more forceful paragraphs in the Plaza statement pointed to the risks from protectionist pressures:[31]

---

29. Sam Y. Cross, Notes for FOMC Meeting, November 4–5, 1985, www.federalreserve.gov/monetarypolicy/files/FOMC19851105material.pdf (accessed on July 9, 2015). Funabashi (1988) describes the notional budget agreed at the Plaza and suggests that the notional US share according to the nonpaper, which was never completely agreed to, was to be 35 percent. At the Federal Reserve, those of us who knew about the nonpaper did not pay much attention to it because it applied only to a six-week period and was quickly overtaken by events.

30. Of course, during early 1985 the deutsche mark was still weakening, and during the second half of the year it was strengthening. See https://research.stlouisfed.org/fred2/categories/32145 for these and other data on Bundesbank intervention.

31. Announcement of the Ministers of Finance and Central Bank Governors of France, Germany, Japan, the United Kingdom, and the United States, New York, September 22, 1985, www.library.utoronto.ca/g7/finance/fm850922.htm (accessed on July 9, 2015). Baker (2006, 433) points

The US current account deficit, together with other factors, is now contributing to protectionist pressures which, if not resisted, could lead to mutually destructive retaliation with serious damage to the world economy: world trade would shrink, real growth rates could even turn negative, unemployment would rise still higher, and debt-burdened developing countries would be unable to secure the export earnings they vitally need.

The dollar's descent following the Plaza Accord was not welcomed by all parties as it extended into 1986. The new year did feature a remarkable amount of policy coordination among the major central banks, however, albeit not initially. At a meeting of the G-5 ministers and governors in London in January, Secretary Baker and some other finance ministers pressed for coordinated cuts in central bank interest rates (Baker 2006, 431). Volcker and Pöhl successfully resisted this proposal. They blocked including any mention of monetary policy in a proposed communiqué, which was scrapped as a result. The central bankers were not attracted by the publicity that would have been associated with that degree of cooperation with finance ministries. However, on January 30, 1986, after the London meeting, the Bank of Japan cut its discount rate.

In late February, Volcker stared down a unilateral cut in the Federal Reserve's discount rate favored by a majority of the Board of Governors. Subsequently, in early March, first the Bundesbank and, the next day, the Bank of Japan and the Federal Reserve cut their discount rates (Funabashi 1988, Volcker and Gyohten 1992, Boughton 2001). Both the Bank of Japan and the Federal Reserve cut their discount rates again on April 21, and the Federal Reserve cut its rate again in July and in August.[32] The Bank of Japan cut its rate again on October 31, in the context of Baker's meeting with Japanese finance minister Kiichi Miyazawa (see below) and again on the eve of the Louvre meeting.[33] The central banks had two concerns: slowing if not stopping the dollar's depreciation and, in particular on the part of the Federal Reserve, encouraging foreign growth.

Meanwhile, building on discussions at the IMF, the US Treasury embraced the idea of developing a set of economic indicators to guide international economic and monetary cooperation. The leaders at the G-7 summit in Tokyo in May somewhat reluctantly endorsed this ambitious approach:[34]

---

proudly to this sentence as motivating his emphasis on the importance of international economic policy coordination.

32. Over the course of 1986, the federal funds rate declined by about 200 basis points. The interest rate on 10-year US Treasury securities declined about 70 basis points in the first half of the year but subsequently increased about 150 basis points. Judgments about inflation were complicated by the collapse in the price of petroleum and related products.

33. At the time the Bank of Japan did not enjoy the degree of independence from its finance ministry that the Bundesbank and Federal Reserve enjoyed.

34. Statement of the Group of Seven Finance Ministers, September 27, 1986, www.g8.utoronto.ca/finance/fm860927.htm (accessed on August 12, 2015).

[T]o cooperate with the IMF in strengthening multilateral surveillance, particularly among the countries whose currencies constitute the SDR [Special Drawing Rights], and request that, in conducting such surveillance and in conjunction with the Managing Director of the IMF, their individual economic forecasts should be reviewed, taking into account indicators such as GNP growth rates, inflation rates, interest rates, unemployment rates, fiscal deficit ratios, current account and trade balances, monetary growth rates, reserves, and exchange rates.

This initiative was resisted by the Japanese and Germans (Funabashi 1988, 142), who—correctly—anticipated that the process would focus on their external surpluses. It harkened back to US proposals to the Committee of Twenty in the early-1970s and presaged a similar initiative launched by the G-20 almost 30 years later in the form of the mutual assessment process in support of the G-20 commitment to strong, sustainable, and balanced growth.[35] As Volcker predicted, these structures are well intentioned but generally fail to overcome political resistance to policy change (Volcker and Gyohten 1992, 278–79). As a byproduct, the 1986 initiative opened the door for the IMF to play a more central role in the G-7 policy consultation and coordination process that persists in the G-7 and G-20 to this day.

As 1986 drew to a close, officials of other countries expressed concern about the perception that US officials were talking down the dollar (Volcker and Gyohten 1992). Obstfeld (1990, 227) quotes the 1986 annual report of the Bundesbank:

These [pre-Louvre intervention] efforts were in vain, not least because statements by US officials repeatedly aroused suspicion on the markets that the U.S. authorities wanted the dollar to depreciate further. Moreover, until then [late January 1987] the Americans hardly participated in the operations to support their currency. Nor did the Federal Reserve counteract the downward trend of the dollar through monetary policy measures, despite the risks to price stability which it clearly perceived.

Evaluation

The Plaza Accord was an immediate success with respect to achieving a further depreciation of the dollar. One can disagree about the role that official foreign exchange market intervention played in this episode, but the depreciation of the dollar did accelerate for a while. Both surprise and novelty were important ingredients.

After the Plaza announcement, foreign exchange markets began to react to unexpected movements in the US external accounts (Klein, Mizrach, and Murphy 1991). The dollar tended to decline against the mark and the yen when

---

35. International Monetary Fund, *Factsheet: The G20 Mutual Assessment Process (MAP)*, March 15, 2015, www.imf.org/external/np/exr/facts/g20map.htm (accessed on July 17, 2015).

the monthly US trade balance was lower than expected and vice versa. This pattern had not existed previously. Klein, Mizrach, and Murphy conclude that the Plaza Accord marked a change in regime as viewed by market participants. The US authorities had abandoned their hands-off approach to the dollar and were concerned about a widening of the US trade and current account deficits.

With respect to the impact of G-5/G-7 pronouncements on exchange rates from 1975 to 2008, Fratzscher (2009) distinguishes between two counterfactual alternatives. In the first, a random walk approach, changes in exchange rates in the wake of G-7 meetings are measured over successive intervals up to 12 months from the date of the meeting to test whether there was what he calls "perceived" success or impact. In the second, success is based on the difference between the actual path of the exchange rate and the path of the exchange rate in which the starting point is derived from a four-factor projection as of the day before the G-7 announcement; one of the factors is the deviation of the exchange rate from its average over the previous five years—a measure of underlying misalignment.

Not surprisingly, Fratzscher finds more evidence of perceived than actual success.[36] With respect to perceived success, the post-Plaza movements of the dollar conformed to what might well have happened without the extensive exchange market operations in the fall of 1985, because the dollar was clearly overvalued and a bubble had developed. Fratzscher's results support the view that exchange market intervention is not just about changes in the supply of or demand for a currency or about signaling future changes in monetary or other policies, including fiscal and structural policies, consistent with improvements in the fundamental determinants of exchange rates; intervention and official statements may also serve to coordinate market views on the level or direction of exchange rates (Sarno and Taylor 2001, Truman 2003).[37]

More recent research tests the portfolio balance model cited earlier in connection with research underlying the Jurgensen Report. Using instrumental variables in panel regressions, Adler, Lisack, and Mano (2015) find robust evidence that intervention in foreign exchange markets affects the level

---

36. This is a more sophisticated finding than my (Truman 1994) post hoc ergo propter hoc criticism of the results of Catte, Galli, and Rebecchini (1994).

37. The signaling channel was hinted at, without using the current terminology, in the Jurgensen Report. Critics of exchange market intervention—for example, Bordo, Humpage, and Schwartz (2015, 9-15 and 302)—state incorrectly that any signals are only about monetary policy. In fact, signals can be about fiscal and other policies, such as banking, which are often designed to support the intervention, or the intervention may provide a bridge to implementing those other policies. Writing about the Plaza-Louvre period, Obstfeld (1990, 223) discusses the signaling channel, including why actual intervention, rather than just words in a communiqué, can reinforce policy credibility and time consistency. He concludes that "on several occasions, however, intervention seems to have been effective in signaling to exchange markets the major governments' resolve to adjust other macroeconomic policies, if necessary, to achieve exchange rate goals." Mulford (2014, 168) articulates his view in the context of the Plaza Accord: "It was possible to signal markets as to underlying developments, not to manipulate or direct the market, but possibly to change its focus and priorities."

Table 9.1   Nature of media treatment of the G-5 and G-7, 1982–88

Type and date of meeting	Before meeting	After meeting	Change	Average of before and after the meeting
Leaders meetings				
June 6, 1982	−0.01	0.00	0.01	0.00
May 30, 1983	0.03	0.05	0.01	0.04
June 9, 1984	0.00	0.05	0.05	0.03
Meetings of finance ministers and central bank governors				
January 17, 1985	−0.09	−0.01	0.09	−0.05
September 22, 1985	−0.14	−0.03	0.11	−0.09
September 27, 1986	−0.12	−0.05	0.07	−0.09
February 22, 1987	−0.15	−0.02	0.13	−0.09
April 8, 1987	−0.05	−0.01	0.05	−0.03
September 26, 1987	0.02	0.13	0.11	0.07
December 22, 1987	0.13	0.14	0.01	0.13
April 13, 1988	0.22	0.11	−0.11	0.16
September 24, 1988	0.25	0.11	−0.14	0.18

Note: Analysis covers only meetings in which the postmeeting statements addressed exchange rates.
– indicates negative press coverage.

Source: Fratzscher (2009) and supporting data supplied by the author.

of exchange rates, with impacts that persist for some time. However, the size of the effects is small relative to the scale of intervention in the 1980s. Sterilized intervention of 1 percentage point of GDP depreciates/appreciates a nominal exchange rate by as much as 2.0 percent, with a half-life of one to two years. In the wake of the Plaza Accord, with US GDP of $4,213 billion, US intervention of $3.3 billion would have produced a depreciation of 0.16 percent (0.38 percent based on the combined G-5 intervention of $8.1 billion). Gagnon and collaborators (Bayoumi, Gagnon, and Saborowski 2015; chapter 11 of this volume) resuscitate the portfolio balance model in the wake of its success in explaining the effects of quantitative easing by central banks after the global financial crisis hit.[38]

Judging by data on the media treatment of G-5/G-7 meetings assembled by Fratzscher (2009), attitudes toward these gatherings gradually changed from the time of the summit meeting in June 1982 through the Plaza meeting of finance ministers and central bank governors in September 1985 (table 9.1). Before the meeting in January 1985, the media treated the G-5 negatively.

---

38. The intervention data I cite are actual purchases and sales, not net changes in foreign assets on the balance sheets of the monetary authorities (or related measures), the measure employed by Adler, Lisack, and Mano and Gagnon and his collaborators.

Following the surprise announcement, press treatment was close to neutral, leaving the average treatment before and after the meeting still negative. Before the Plaza meeting, which was unscheduled, press treatment was even more negative; after the meeting it was less so. This pattern (negative before the meetings, less so after the meetings, but on average negative) continued through April 1987. The higher profile of the G-5/G-7 reinforces, from a different perspective, the findings of Klein, Mizrach, and Murphy (1991) of a regime change.

The debate about the effectiveness of foreign exchange market intervention in general and as part of the Plaza Accord in particular will never be resolved definitively. The relevant point with respect to policy coordination and the Plaza Accord is that the stated or implicit short-run objective was achieved. It is more difficult to establish whether this apparent success reflects causation (by verbal or actual intervention), simple correlation, or some combination of the two.

The Plaza Accord can be said to have overperformed—a concern at the Federal Reserve almost from the start. At the October 1, 1985, FOMC meeting, only nine days after the G-5 meeting, concerns were raised about the implications of a "precipitous decline of the dollar," and a request was made for a special briefing on the topic. On the way to the IMF meetings in Seoul later in the week, Volcker, in what should have been treated as an off-the-record comment to *Washington Post* columnist Hobart Rowen but ended up in the paper a few weeks later, commented that "one could have too much of a good thing."

At the November 4 FOMC meeting, the staff made a presentation on the economic and policy consequences of exchange rate adjustment.[39] It outlined the possible paths of external adjustment, the implications for the real economy, the dynamics of possible interest rate and price changes, and associated monetary policy issues in terms of the risks to inflation and/or growth. In his conclusion, Stephen Axilrod, the staff director and secretary of the FOMC, said that he favored engineering a gradual adjustment of the dollar.

Gradual adjustment was not in the cards, but neither was US recession or inflation. Aided by the collapse of energy prices in 1986, US inflation did not rise appreciably until late in the decade. Real interest rates, in particular long-term rates, did not increase much either. However, similar concerns about excessive or excessively rapid dollar depreciation were expressed at a meeting of the G-10 governors at the Bank for International Settlements (BIS) that I attended in early December 1985. During congressional testimony, Volcker was frequently asked about the risks associated with a sharp dollar decline. On February 19, 1986, according to my notes, he responded to a question from then Congressman Charles Schumer that he was not interested in seeing the

---

39. Board of Governors of the Federal Reserve System, Staff Presentation to the FOMC on Economic and Policy Implications of Exchange Rate Adjustments, November 4, 1985, www.federalreserve.gov/monetarypolicy/files/FOMC19851105material.pdf (accessed on July 9, 2015).

dollar falling further. At that point the dollar had declined 14 percent against the major currencies since the day before the Plaza meeting.

With respect to supporting policies, Volcker reports that there was no agreement with respect to interest rates at the Plaza or with the US Treasury, though he notes, "it is hardly unusual for secretaries of the Treasury to want easier monetary policy; from that viewpoint there would have been nothing new in the Plaza Accord. But the real effect, at the margin, was to reduce the size and likelihood of any easing of [US] monetary policy" (Volcker and Gyohten 1992, 247). In this context he was shocked and dismayed that on October 24 the Bank of Japan allowed a substantial increase in Japanese short-term interest rates in the context of a slight rebound by the dollar.[40]

On US fiscal commitments in the Plaza Accord, expenditures did decline as a share of GDP in FY1986, but revenues declined as well; as a result, the deficit declined only 0.1 percentage points, to 5.0 percent of GDP.[41] Baker (2006) acknowledges that critics claim that the United States reneged on its fiscal commitments, but he adds that they were made in good faith. The US administration and Congress were by that time wrestling with the fiscal deficit but having difficulty reaching consensus on how to deal with it. The first Gramm-Rudman-Hollings Balanced Budget Act was signed into law on December 12, 1985.[42]

Mulford (2014, 169) points to "clear policy commitments for stronger growth" from US partners at the Plaza as key to the deal. Unfortunately, the commitments of other countries to promote growth or structural change in their economies were not fulfilled. In the face of small output gaps in Germany and Japan in 1985—now estimated at –0.5 and –0.3 percent of potential GDP, respectively[43]—one would have wished that these countries had sought to offset the potential negative impact of currency appreciation. Instead, their output gaps increased in 1986 and 1987. In both countries the increase in domestic demand exceeded the increase in GDP in both years, suggesting the negative influence of currency appreciation on GDP. In Japan the increase in domestic demand slowed to 3.7 percent in 1986, down from 4.1 percent in 1985, but picked up to 5.1 percent in 1987. In Germany domestic demand increased to 3.3 in 1986, up from 0.9 percent in 1985, but dropped off to an increase of 2.6 percent in 1987 (IMF 1993).

In summary, the short-term effects of the policy coordination in the Plaza episode were impressive in terms of the subsequent correction in the dollar's

---

40. According to Takagi (2015, 154), neither the Japanese Ministry of Finance nor the US authorities were consulted or informed in advance. An increase in the discount rate would have required approval from the Ministry of Finance.

41. The deficit did drop to 3.2 percent of GDP in FY1987, followed by 3.1 percent in FY1988 and 2.8 percent in FY1989 before rising back to 4.7 percent in FY1992.

42. The procedures in the act were subsequently declared to be unconstitutional in 1986 and replaced in September 1987 with a second act.

43. IMF, *World Economic Outlook* database, April 2015.

foreign exchange value, even if the small amount of foreign exchange market intervention in the immediate aftermath had little directly to do with it. It is true that, with the further decline of the dollar despite the effort to stabilize currencies via the Louvre Accord, the US current account deficit ultimately began to shrink. In terms of economic policy coordination, however, the longer-term effects were between minimal and nugatory, for two reasons. First, the G-7 never reached full consensus on the diagnosis of the immediate problem they were trying to address. Yes, they were trying to depreciate the dollar, partly in response to the threat of protectionist threats derived again in part from the growing US current account deficit and drag of net exports on the US expansion. But the other parties saw the US fiscal deficit as the principal cause of the US current account deficit.

Second, partly because of this difference in diagnoses, no country took fiscal or structural policy actions designed to support the exchange rate changes that occurred, to increase domestic demand growth in the countries whose currencies were appreciating and reduce it in the United States, in part by reducing the fiscal deficit. A weaker dollar to blunt US protectionism was consistent with domestic politics in the United States and elsewhere; more fundamental changes in other policies were not.

The Louvre Accord

The conventional view is that the Plaza Accord was aimed solely at bringing down the super-dollar. By that metric it was widely perceived as successful. Indeed, many officials viewed the effort to bring down the dollar as too successful. They began to press for words and then actions to halt the dollar's decline.

In their statement following their meeting on September 27, 1986, the G-7 finance ministers addressed the issue of global imbalances, recited various steps being taken, and observed that "these actions should help to stabilize exchange rates, and all are necessary so that imbalances can be reduced sufficiently without further significant exchange rate adjustment."[44] They were disappointed.

As the dollar continued to decline, in particular, against the yen, the Japanese authorities beseeched the US Treasury to do something. Ultimately, on October 31 Baker and Miyazawa agreed to a joint statement. From the standpoint of the Japanese, the most important sentence was this one: "They expressed their mutual understanding that, with the actions and commitments mentioned above, the *exchange rate realignment achieved between the yen and the dollar since the Plaza Agreement is now broadly consistent with the present underlying fundamentals*, and reaffirmed their willingness to cooperate on exchange market issues" (emphasis added). Contrary to market expectations fed by the

---

44. Statement of the G-7 Finance Ministers, September 27, 1986, www.g8.utoronto.ca/finance/fm860927.htm (accessed on August 12, 2015).

Japanese authorities following the Baker-Miyazawa meeting, the US authorities did not intervene to support the dollar as it subsequently weakened further.

From the standpoint of the US authorities, the most important points in the Baker-Miyazawa statement were the commitment by the Japanese to a fiscal stimulus package, a tax reform, and another cut in the Bank of Japan's discount rate, which was announced as part of the statement. The US authorities had adopted the view that exchange rate adjustments alone would not correct the US current account deficit. At the December 10–11, 1986, meeting of Working Party Three (WP-3) of the Economic Policy Committee of the Organization for Economic Cooperation and Development (OECD), which I attended, Mulford lectured other delegates on the importance of policies to stimulate growth. They could either adopt such policies, he said, or expect further depreciation of the dollar. In the fall of 1986, Volcker and the staff of the Federal Reserve had a similar view, pressing central bank partners to relax their monetary policies further, although the Fed's approach was less forceful than Mulford's. In mid-December Baker and Mulford met with German Finance Minister Gerhard Stoltenberg and his deputy, Hans Tietmeyer, in an effort to build on the agreement with the Japanese and to obtain a commitment from the Germans to promote growth (Funabashi 1988, 172–73; Boughton 2001, 218). They made only limited progress, but talks continued. In September 1986 not only the Japanese authorities but also the Bundesbank had begun to resist the dollar's decline via exchange market purchases of dollars.

By the end of 1986, 15 months after the Plaza Accord, the dollar had declined by an average of about 20 percent against the major currencies in both nominal and price-adjusted terms. The nominal decline was more than 30 percent against both the mark and the yen.

By January 20, 1987, the dollar had depreciated against the yen by another 3.5 percent since the end of 1985. On January 21 Baker and Miyazawa met again. They issued a statement reiterating that the bilateral exchange rate "has been broadly consistent with fundamentals" and "reaffirmed their willingness to cooperate on exchange market issues" (Funabashi 1988, 276). The US authorities did not "cooperate" in the form of intervention until seven days later, when they bought $50 million of yen. As of that day, the dollar had declined a further 7 percent against the mark from the end of 1986. During January 1987, the Bundesbank sold marks on six days; the US authorities did not operate in marks, because they were not yet fully committed to the Louvre strategy. But the stage was almost set ("almost" because the meetings of the G-5 and G-7 were not set until February 18).

Problem Identification and Diagnosis

In February 1987 the United States and its principal partners finally agreed to identify the dollar's persistent decline as a problem. The diagnosis of the problem was shared to some extent, but once again it was not a full operational consensus. The candidate diagnoses bore some relation to those before the Plaza meeting: (1) macroeconomic policies (now fiscal stimulus in other countries in addition to a tightening of US fiscal policy); (2) trade (except that now the issue was not only the risk of US protectionism but also the stubborn continued expansion of the US external deficit); and (3) the possibility that the decline of the dollar would accelerate and contribute to a hard landing for the global economy.

With respect to macroeconomic policies, the debate was no longer entirely one-sided, concentrating on the US fiscal deficit. Other countries still saw the US budget deficit as a major, if not the principal, cause of the US external imbalance. For their part the US authorities had been pressing other countries for months to stimulate growth in their economies, both to compensate for the effects of changes in exchange rates and to reinforce the impact on the US current account balance (see figure 9.3). Volcker recalls his view that "without more expansionary action abroad, I was afraid the momentum of world expansion would falter, that the [US] trade and current account would remain in deep deficit, and that the dollar would eventually and unnecessarily weaken further" (Volcker and Gyohten 1992, 275).

With respect to external adjustment, the US current account deficit in 1986 was $147 billion (3.2 percent of GDP), up from $118 billion (2.7 percent of GDP) in 1985 and headed for $161 billion (3.3 percent of GDP) in 1987. In 1986 the current account surpluses of both Germany and Japan were more than 4 percent of their respective GDPs.

On the exchange rate front, the movements of the dollar in 1986 and 1987 against the mark had contributed to the need for exchange rate realignments within the exchange rate mechanism (ERM) of the European Monetary System in April of 1986 and again in January of 1987. The Japanese authorities were "desperate for exchange rate stability," according to Takagi (2015, 158). Arguably, a rapid US fiscal adjustment might weaken the dollar, in particular if US monetary policy eased at the same time. Those calling for the US fiscal adjustment to abort the dollar's decline had to appeal to positive effects on confidence to make their argument hang together.

The Federal Reserve was more involved in the pre-Louvre discussions than with the pre-Plaza discussions. The concern, shared by Volcker and G-7 officials, was that a continued decline of the dollar would further undermine global growth and at best complicate and postpone the necessary adjustment process.[45] Baker had an additional motivation: He did not want the Federal Reserve to have to hike interest rates to combat inflation and resist further dollar depreciation during the run-up to a presidential election year. I and others on the Federal Reserve Board staff thought that it was a mistake to try to cut short the dollar's depreciation, in part because the depreciation to date was not sufficient to eliminate the US current deficit and in part because we anticipated that downward pressures on the dollar would continue to be

---

45. World growth was 4.9 percent in 1984, 3.9 percent in 1985, and 3.2 percent in 1986 (IMF, *World Economic Outlook* database, April 2015, www.imf.org/external/pubs/ft/weo/2015/01/weodata/index.aspx [accessed on July 10, 2015]).

intense.[46] We sent a memorandum to Volcker outlining our arguments. He did not buy them.

Treatment

On February 22 the ministers and governors of the G-6 countries[47] met in Paris and announced the Louvre Accord.[48]

> The Ministers and Governors agreed that the substantial exchange rate changes since the Plaza Agreement will increasingly contribute to reducing external imbalances and have now brought their currencies within ranges broadly consistent with underlying economic fundamentals, given the policy commitments summarized in this statement. Further substantial exchange rate shifts among their currencies could damage growth and adjustment prospects in their countries. In current circumstances, therefore, they agreed to cooperate closely to foster stability of exchange rates around current levels.[49]

This announcement inaugurated a brief real-world experiment with target zones, reference ranges, or reference zones for exchange rates among the major currencies (the precise terminology was never agreed upon).[50] Mulford (2014, 171) recalls that the G-6/G-7 "agreed on a plan to stabilize currencies within certain broadly understood ranges.… If our currencies moved outside the consensus ranges, the understanding was that national policies would need to be reviewed."

The reference (base) levels and their associated ranges were not announced. However, it has been accurately reported that the reference rates were 1.8250

---

46. The February 4, 1987, staff forecast for the FOMC (FRB 1987) incorporated a moderate continued decline of the dollar through 1988, less than the 10 percent that occurred mostly in 1987, and foresaw the US current account narrowing only to $127 billion in 1988 (the deficit turned out to be $121 billion that year). By the end of 1986, the dollar's depreciation was already contributing to an improvement in US real net exports of goods and services in the GDP accounts, which we recognized.

47. The Italian officials were invited, but they went home when they learned that the G-5 had met the day before.

48. Statement of the G-6 Finance Ministers and Central Bank Governors, February 22, 1987, www.g8.utoronto.ca/finance/fm870222.htm (accessed on July 17, 2015).

49. The Louvre communiqué also stated: "It is important that the newly industrialized developing economies should assume greater responsibility for preserving an open world trading system by reducing trade barriers and pursuing policies that allow their currencies to reflect more fully underlying economic fundamentals." Similar concerns led to the enactment of the Omnibus Trade and Competitiveness Act of 1988, which mandated that the US Treasury report twice a year on developments in international economic and exchange rate policies in consultation with the Board of Governors of the Federal Reserve System and the IMF. The Treasury's report continues to attract both market and political attention.

50. It can be argued that the ERM of the European Monetary System was a target zone system and that some countries have used this type of system unilaterally (Williamson 2007), but the Louvre Accord is the only example involving the major currencies.

marks and 153.50 yen per dollar (Boughton 2001, 219 and associated references). The scheme involved an inner range of +/–2.5 percent, after which action, implicitly intervention, should be considered, and an outer range of +/–5.0 percent, after which there would be a greater presumption (but no requirement) of action/intervention.

The scheme was not entirely accepted, in particular by Pöhl on behalf of Germany and the Bundesbank, who was supported by Volcker in being unwilling to embrace any automaticity about intervention. In addition, the Japanese authorities did not want the yen to strengthen above 150 yen to the dollar and even 2.5 percent would take the yen there. A notional budget of $4 billion, divided one-third each among Europe, Japan, and the United States, was intended to support the scheme until early April, when the group would next meet. As with the Plaza Accord, the quantitative precision in the Louvre Accord was a plus, even though it was not fully agreed to and not part of the public record.

Within the Federal Reserve, few were privy to the details of the accord. Cross reported to the FOMC on March 31:

> On March 11, as the dollar moved up through the DM 1.8700 level, the Desk sold $30 million against marks *in accordance with the agreements reached in Paris.* This operation, though limited in size, was visible and taken by market operators as a signal that the Paris agreement would seek to limit any significant rise of the dollar, as well as any significant decline. As a result, the dollar's recovery was, in a sense, capped and the dollar subsequently began to move lower.[51] [Emphasis added]

The inner point of the upper range for weakness in the mark was DM 1.8706. On March 11 the United States chose to buy marks, as that rate was pierced in New York. The Bundesbank did not operate that day.

The pace of coordinated intervention purchases of dollars and sales of yen accelerated in April. Between March 31 and May 19, total dollar purchases were $24 billion, of which the United States purchased $3 billion, bringing the US total since the Paris meeting to $4.2 billion. Only $200 million were purchases against the mark.[52]

At the April 8 G-5/G-7 meeting, the midpoint of the indicative range for the yen against the dollar was raised to 146, with the same +/–2.5 and +/–5 percent ranges, despite Japanese concern about a yen stronger than 150. By May 5 the yen was again above the 5 percent top of the range. The mark was within the 5 percent range but above the 2.5 percent range. The dollar recovered somewhat over the summer but subsequently declined.[53]

---

51. Sam Y. Cross, Notes for FOMC Meeting Held on March 31, 1987, www.federalreserve.gov/monetarypolicy/files/FOMC19870331material.pdf (accessed on July 17, 2015).

52. Sam Y. Cross, Notes for FOMC Meeting Held on May 19, 1987, www.federalreserve.gov/monetarypolicy/files/FOMC19870519material.pdf (accessed on July 17, 2015).

53. The Bundesbank's first post-Louvre intervention was purchases of dollars on May 5, following US sales of marks for dollars on the two previous business days.

After the flurry of yen strength in March–May 1987, at meetings at the OECD and BIS, international officials and national representatives were generally satisfied with the results of the Louvre Accord. Participants at the June 10 G-7 summit in Venice were characteristically upbeat about prospects while also noting that "exchange rate changes alone will not solve the problem of correcting... imbalances while sustaining growth. Surplus countries [must] design their policies to strengthen domestic demand.... Deficit countries... [must] reduce their fiscal and external imbalances."[54]

By the time of the meeting of the WP-3 on July 9–10, which I attended, doubts were being expressed about how long exchange rates would hold at current levels and whether the commitments of Germany and Japan to stimulate their economies and by the United States to address its fiscal issues would be met.

On September 4, 1987, in response to a resumption of dollar weakness triggered by the release of poor US trade numbers on August 14 and to signs of an uptick in inflation, the Federal Reserve raised the discount rate to 6 percent and tightened the provision of reserves, which served to push up the federal funds rate by about 75 basis points between then and the stock market break on October 19.[55] The ministers and governors remained upbeat in their statement following their meeting on September 26, but at the same meeting IMF managing director Michel Camdessus told them that even with improved macroeconomic policies more exchange rate movement would be necessary to eliminate global imbalances (Boughton 2001, 221).[56]

In late September short-term interest rates began to rise in Japan and in particular in Germany, ostensibly because of an increase in inflation. (The inflation pickup was hardly provocative. In Germany the increase in the consumer price index in 1987 was 0.2 percent, after a decline of 0.1 percent in 1987 and before a rise of 1.3 percent in 1988. The pattern in Japan was similar.) The interest rate on 10-year German government bonds rose by 70 basis points over the summer to about 6.7 percent in September and 6.9 percent in October. The comparable US rate dipped by about 100 basis points over the summer but in the fall backed up 70 basis points toward 9 percent. US consumer price inflation was about 4 percent and rose less than half a percent in the fall. The high real long-term rates were a puzzle in several countries.

---

54. G-7 Venezia Economic Declaration, June 10, 1987, www.g8.utoronto.ca/summit/1987venice/communique/index.html (accessed on July 17, 2015).

55. September was the first month of Alan Greenspan's tenure. He was about to travel to his first meeting with his central bank colleagues at the BIS. Volcker had also snugged short-term rates in April in response to dollar weakness, but conditions were later relaxed. He recently told me that in retrospect he wished Federal Reserve policy had been tightened before he left office in August 1987 but that he had not wanted to complicate life for his successor.

56. Camdessus was present because at the Venice summit the leaders invited the IMF managing director to participate in the development of mutually consistent medium-term objectives and projections. Boughton cites this invitation as the high point of this round of efforts to improve multilateral surveillance with the involvement of the IMF.

Another set of disappointing US trade data was released on October 14, upsetting foreign exchange and financial markets. On Sunday, October 18, Baker criticized the Bundesbank: "We will not sit back in this country and watch surplus countries jack up interest rates and squeeze growth worldwide in the expectation that the United States somehow will follow by raising its interest rates" (2006, 440). These comments were negatively received by the press and markets and put further downward pressures on the dollar (Cross 1987).

What role these developments played in the stock market break on October 19 is both disputed and beyond the scope of this account. What is clear is that the Federal Reserve responded by adding liquidity and letting the federal funds rate ease at a time when other central banks did so only grudgingly and with a lag.[57] The lack of parallel action helped spell the end of the Louvre Accord.[58]

On October 16, the Friday before Black Monday and the US stock market break, the dollar was again in the lower half of its ranges against both the yen and the mark. By October 29, it had passed through the outer points; by the end of the year, the dollar had depreciated 21 percent against the yen and 14 percent against the mark and the major currencies as a group from the levels at the time of the Louvre Accord.

International cooperation did not dry up entirely. The relevant authorities consulted with their counterparts almost daily, but they did not agree about whether or how to respond to the stock market break. Funabashi (1988) argues that after the stock market break, US officials ignored the Louvre Accord, or at least its spirit, in their choice of policies, in particular monetary policy.

The Louvre Accord was somewhat more explicit than the Plaza Accord in terms of macroeconomic policy commitments. The G-6 statement called for countries with current account surpluses to strengthen domestic demand and reduce their external surpluses.[59] The specific commitment by Germany, which was less than dramatic, was to follow through with "comprehensive tax reform" and other structural supply-side measures. Japan signed on to the principle of stimulating domestic demand but pledged to complete its "comprehensive tax reform" and put forward a "comprehensive program" to stimulate domestic demand in Japan only after the 1987 budget was approved. The United States pledged to pursue policies to reduce the 1988 deficit to 2.3 percent of GNP

---

57. The federal funds rate rose by about 75 basis points between the end of August and mid-October, and it declined by a like amount between October and the end of the year. However, FOMC policy at that time was framed in terms of pressures on reserve positions and did not involve an explicit target for the federal funds rate.

58. Henning (1994) argues—incorrectly in my view (Truman 2006, 194)—that the reference ranges continued through Baker's departure from the Treasury in August 1988 and gradually unraveled in 1989-90. It is possible that the framework persisted in the minds of some US Treasury officials, but that was never communicated to me.

59. Statement of the G-6 Finance Ministers and Central Bank Governors, February 22, 1987, www.g8.utoronto.ca/finance/fm870222.htm (accessed on July 17, 2015).

from a then-estimated 3.9 percent in 1987 and hold the growth of government expenditures to less than 1 percent.[60]

The US authorities were disturbed by the further rapid depreciation of the dollar in the fourth quarter of 1987. For their part, the G-7 partners were unwilling to act or even make a collective statement in support of the dollar until the United States produced more on the fiscal front. After an intense set of negotiations, the administration and the bipartisan leadership of the Congress reached agreement on a budget package that promised to cut the 1988 and 1989 budget deficits by a combined $76 billion through both spending restraint and tax increases. The package was passed on December 21 and signed by President Reagan on December 22, 1987. The agreement took so long to complete that the G-7 did not have time to meet before Christmas. The result was the first issuance, on December 22, of a statement by the G-7 ministers and governors without a face-to-face meeting, often called the Christmas or Telephone Communiqué.[61]

Curiously, on exchange rates the communiqué stated: "The Ministers and Governors agreed that either excessive fluctuation of exchange rates, a further decline of the dollar, or a rise in the dollar to an extent that becomes destabilizing to the adjustment process, could be counter-productive by damaging growth prospects in the world economy." The United States was not eager to recoup the dollar's depreciation since September. The market appeared to be unmoved by the G-7 statement, and the dollar declined by another 3 percent against the major currencies on average over the remaining trading days of the year.

The end-of-year market was apparently oversold on the dollar. Immediately after the turn of the year, the authorities successfully mounted a concerted, aggressive counterattack. Over the first nine trading days of 1988, the US authorities bought only $685 million through sales of marks and yen, less than half the amount they bought between December 22 and the end of the year, but with greater visibility and public commentary. The same was true for the Bundesbank in the size of its operations before and after the new year. However, the operations were conducted in such a manner that they helped reverse market sentiment. Several European central banks cut interest rates (Cross 1988). By mid-January the dollar had risen 11 percent against the mark, 2 percent against the yen, and 4 percent against the major currencies on average from the end of 1987.

Evaluation

Like the Plaza Accord, the Louvre Accord had two basic objectives: stabilizing exchange rates and, with greater urgency than in the Plaza case, promoting external adjustment through proactive macroeconomic policies. On the

---

60. The deficit target was not achieved; see footnote 41.

61. Statement of the G-7 Finance Ministers and Central Bank Governors, December 22, 1987, www.g8.utoronto.ca/finance/fm871222.htm (accessed on July 17, 2015).

first the Louvre was a qualified failure even in the short run. On the second participants did not deliver the promised changes in policies, at least not in the required time frame. One consequence for the longer term was the de facto collapse of the structure of economic policy coordination that had been constructed on a range of indicators, not just exchange rate policies. It failed because of a lack of sufficient substantive policy actions outside of the intervention realm.

With respect to exchange rates, the dollar continued to depreciate unevenly throughout 1987, despite heavy intervention, with a final period of weakness leading up to and, in particular, after the US stock market break. The yen was formally rebased once and de facto rebased a second time. The mark was also de facto rebased in the fall. These rebasings are sufficient evidence that the Louvre Accord failed to deliver on its promise that exchange rates should remain around the levels observed in February 1987.

This harsh judgment can be qualified in two respects. First, without the accord, with its soothing statements by policymakers and the associated, largely coordinated, heavy (by the standards of the day) foreign exchange intervention, the decline of the dollar during 1987 might have been larger. However, again applying the results of Adler, Lisack, and Mano (2015) to the case of the Louvre Accord with its much larger-scale intervention than following the Plaza Accord does not suggest that the intervention should have been expected to be very successful. US net intervention of $8.8 billion (0.19 percent of 1987 GDP) translates into support for the dollar of 0.4 percent; the combined intervention of the United States, Germany, and Japan of approximately $50 billion (including German intervention of an estimated $3.8 billion and allowing for Japanese intervention for the rest, as estimated by Ito, in chapter 7 of this volume) would have produced an effect supporting the dollar of only 2 percent at most—a tiny offset to the dollar's nominal depreciation against major currencies of 14 percent that occurred between the Louvre and the end of 1987. The political economy in neither the United States nor any other G-7 country, except possibly Japan, would have supported the monetary authorities in operations seven times larger ($350 billion) to offset the depreciation that occurred.

Second, as an attempt to implement a system of target zones or reference ranges for exchange rates, the system was too tight, with inner margins of +/-2.5 percent and outer margins of +/-5 percent. These margins were half as wide as those suggested by Daniel Lebegue in 1985 and 1986 (Funabashi 1988, 198–99) or by John Williamson and Marcus Miller (1987) in their blueprint on the topic.[62]

Wider margins would have implied less intervention, less need for rebasing, and perhaps more buy-in from some of the governments and central banks.

---

62. Bergsten and Williamson (1983 but delivered at a conference in 1982) as well as Williamson and Miller were influential and active in interesting the US Treasury, as well as others, in the concept of target zones. See also Williamson (2007).

Volcker, for example, was never a fan of freely floating exchange rates and was broadly receptive to restraints on wide swings in major exchange rates. The Bundesbank and the German government never really embraced the Louvre Accord intervention understandings. The technical provisions on the presumption of intervention were also not taken seriously at the Federal Reserve after the first six months or so.

Funabashi (1988, 203) makes other technical criticisms. According to him, the initial central values were arbitrary rather than based on analysis to select values that would have been consistent with external and internal balance in the economies of the participants—so-called fundamental equilibrium exchange rates. The ranges were not published, suggesting that participants were not serious and limiting the scope for stabilizing speculation from the market. The arrangements were provisional, because that was all that could be agreed. And intervention was not required; the edges of the ranges merely signaled an obligation to consult.

As a structure to guide exchange rate policy, the Louvre scheme was deficient in placing sole emphasis on nominal bilateral exchange rates rather than effective (average) rates, preferably real effective rates (see the contrasting behavior of the yen and the mark in figures 9.1 and 9.2; see also Williamson 1985 and Williamson and Miller 1987).

On external adjustment, the participants did not agree on the basic analytical framework involving compensating, progrowth policies on the part of the countries with surpluses whose currencies were to stop appreciating and more aggressive action on the part of the United States to address its fiscal deficit. Although the United States was struggling with its fiscal challenges, it was not able to put enough on the table as a quid pro quo to induce the other countries to act as well.

Volcker attests to both problems (Volcker and Gyohten 1992, 272 and 283). On the latter, he reports questioning Secretary Baker's candor in his fiscal promises at the Louvre meeting to reduce the 1988 fiscal deficit to 2.3 percent of GDP from its 1987 estimated level of 3.9 percent and to hold the growth of government expenditures to less than 1 percent. Baker replied that he was bound by the administration's recent budget. The comment reinforces one of the critiques of the Plaza-Louvre period: that the domestic policy and political institutions in the participating countries constrained the international coordination process. In the event, the US federal budget deficit fell by only 0.1 percent of GDP in FY1988.[63] Outlays rose 6.4 percent in nominal terms, declining by only 0.4 percentage points of GDP. But in the aftermath of the Louvre, pressures for policy coordination can be credited with promoting the US budget adjustments agreed between the US administration and Congress at the end of 1987.

The impulse from fiscal policies in countries with current account surpluses was negative for Japan in 1986, 1987, and 1988; for Germany it was negative

---

63. See footnote 41.

Figure 9.4 GDP growth in Germany, Japan, and the United States, 1980–90

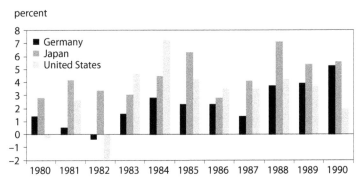

percent

Source: World Bank, *World Development Indicators.*

in 1985 and 1986 and neutral in 1987 and 1988, according to the IMF (1993). The response of growth rates was disappointing (figure 9.4). Germany's GDP rose by only 1.5 percent in 1987, down from 2.4 percent in 1986 and an average of 2.5 percent the two previous years. Japan's GDP rose 4.1 percent in 1987, up from 2.8 percent in 1986 but well below the average of 5.4 percent the two previous years. Growth picked up smartly in both countries in 1988, perhaps in response to a short period of monetary easing following the stock market break.

Given the domestic policy process and political institutions of the day, which are not all that different from today, were the Louvre and the associated system of indicators too ambitious? Did any of the participants really take seriously the new structure of multilateral surveillance, in the sense that they were prepared to act on its implicit recommendations? Given that the participants were unable to match talk with action, it is fair to say that the Louvre Accord was too ambitious and that the framework on which it was constructed lacked the substantive political and, therefore, policy support to make it effective.

The G-7 was riding quite high in media opinion, however. After the February meeting the chatter was only slightly negative (see table 9.1). Media coverage turned positive before the September G-7 meeting and was more positive after it. The same was true around the time of the December 1987 statement, but this time the G-7 got little bounce from its announcement. In 1988 the G-7 received its most favorable pre-meeting reviews, but its post-meeting press treatment, while still positive, waned in intensity.

Coda

Coordinated attempts to deal with global imbalances did not end in 1987 with the Louvre Accord. Coordination of intervention operations by the major countries also was not abandoned, but operations became more ad hoc (see

Truman 2014 for more on this later period). The US current account reached a then-record deficit in 1987 at $161 billion (3.3 percent of GDP). The German and Japanese surpluses that year were slightly smaller as a percent of GDP than they had been the year before, but the absolute size of the German surplus was larger, and it expanded in 1988 and 1989 in dollar terms and as a percent of GDP (see figure 9.3). Policymakers and analysts expressed doubts about whether the external imbalances would ever be reduced, and concerns persisted that the global economy risked a hard landing if the United States did not curb its external and internal deficits.

The United States current account deficit finally began to narrow in 1988; that process continued until it recorded a small surplus in 1991, accompanied by large transfer payments in connection with the financing of the First Gulf War and a brief US recession. As a share of GDP, the deficit stayed below its record levels of the 1980s until 2000. Its initial narrowing was accompanied by persistent US intervention from mid-1988 to early 1990 that was designed to resist dollar appreciation and was generally coordinated with partners. The US authorities built up large holdings of foreign exchange reserves. Whether because of the intervention or not, the broad index for the real foreign exchange value of the dollar on a monthly average basis fluctuated in a narrow range of +4 percent and –6 percent of its value between December 1987 and December 1991.

At the same time, the United States continued to plug away at reducing its fiscal deficit. The Omnibus Budget Reconciliation Act of 1990 contained the pay-as-you-go provisions of the Budget Enforcement Act of 1990 as well as President George H. W. Bush's step back from his pledge of no new taxes; the Clinton administration passed the Omnibus Budget Reconciliation Act of 1993; and the US economy recovered in the middle and late 1990s. Early in the Clinton administration, the G-7 ministers and governors in their statement of April 29, 1993, praised US fiscal plans.[64] The administration used that praise by appealing to those international commitments in its efforts to gain congressional passage of its fiscal program.

The dollar began to weaken in the early months of the Clinton administration. That weakness was accompanied from time to time by US foreign exchange market intervention in coordination with its major partners. The operations were on a larger scale than during the late 1980s.[65] In July 1994 the US Treasury publicly articulated a desire to see a stronger dollar. In early 1995 this posture morphed into a statement that a strong US dollar was in the national interest. That policy formulation is controversial among people who believe the United States can and should have a proactive exchange rate policy, but it has been

---

64. Statement of the G-7 Finance Ministers and Central Bank Governors, April 29, 1993, www. library.utoronto.ca/g7/finance/fm930429.htm (accessed on August 26, 2015).

65. During the post-Louvre period, US authorities purchased an average of $179 million on 60 days. Through October 1995 under the Clinton administration, total purchases rose to an average of $696 million on 18 days.

articulated by Treasury secretaries for the past 20 years with respect to the dollar's value in terms of the major currencies. US policy with respect to the currencies of emerging-market countries has been another matter.

Since August 1995 the United States has operated only occasionally in the foreign exchange markets, always in coordination with its major partners. Support for the yen in June 1998 was explicitly linked to Japan's taking action on its banking problems. The same restraint has been true for the other G-7 countries; Japan was the last member of the group to embrace a policy of limited exchange market operations in 2004.[66]

In February 2013 the G-7 ministers and governors issued a statement that ritually reiterated their commitment to consult closely on exchange markets and cooperate as appropriate. In the context of discussions of the use of other policies to influence exchange rates, such as large-scale asset purchases by central banks (quantitative easing), it declared "our fiscal and monetary policies have been and will remain oriented towards meeting our respective domestic objectives using domestic instruments, and that we will not target exchange rates."[67] This statement was motivated by concerns about suggestions that the policies of Prime Minister Shinzo Abe should target the yen's exchange rate, in particular through large-scale purchases of foreign currency assets. The statement is important as a benchmark for policy because not only did participants commit not to use foreign exchange market intervention as part of their quantitative easing, they also implicitly endorsed a policy of limited, transparent, and generally coordinated intervention. The G-7 ministers and governors have taken this policy perspective to meetings with representatives of the larger group of G-20 countries, with some success judging by the reduced intervention in foreign exchange markets in recent years.

With respect to global external imbalances, the lesson of the Plaza-Louvre period is that a substantial degree of coordination on exchange rate policies is relatively easy (perhaps because those policies principally involve only finance ministries and central banks); coordination of macroeconomic policies is more challenging, in part because they involve a broader array of domestic political actions and interests. This lesson is not new. In the early 1970s, the Committee of Twenty was unable to agree on the use of one or more indicators to guide the global macroeconomic adjustment process. The lesson would be repeated in the 2006-07 IMF-sponsored multilateral consultation on global imbalances.[68]

---

66. The Japanese authorities acted unilaterally to sell yen on September 15, 2010, and jointly with the United States and other partners on March 18, 2011, to sell yen as it rose in volatile markets following the Tohoku earthquake.

67. Statement of G-7 Finance Ministers and Central Bank Governors, February 12, 2013, www.g8.utoronto.ca/finance/fm130212.htm (accessed on July 20, 2015).

68. "IMF's International Monetary and Financial Committee Reviews Multilateral Consultation," Press Release No. 07/72, April 14, 2007, www.imf.org/external/np/sec/pr/2007/pr0772.htm (accessed on July 20, 2015). See Truman (2014, 31) for some observations by Karen Johnson on this exercise that mirror the 1985-87 lack of consensus.

It appears that this lesson is being relearned in the G-20's mutual assessment process, in which the IMF staff play a supportive role, providing indicators and analyses.[69]

In the wake of the 2008–09 global financial crisis and recession, global imbalances have receded somewhat as a matter of high-level policy concern, but they could well reemerge. The foreign exchange market intervention of some emerging-market and developing countries in the context of their large current account surpluses remains a matter of some concern (see chapter 11 of this volume). It cannot be excluded that the United States and other G-7 countries will resume large-scale foreign exchange market intervention, but at the moment their doing so appears unlikely.

International economic policy coordination is largely episodic, because it is directed not at fine-tuning policies but at making gross policy adjustments in response to common problems. The sine qua non for success is that the problem or problems are promptly identified and that consensus on their diagnoses is strong. The stronger the consensus, the more likely treatment will be well defined, comprehensive, and forceful, including through an openness to alterations as participants gather experience. Episodic international policy coordination has a reasonable chance of achieving some degree of short-term success. Longer-term success is likely to founder on the weakness of the diagnostic consensus and the challenges of domestic political economy, which undercut thorough treatment. Policymakers and students of policymaking can, however, learn from experience.

References

Adams, Donald B., and Dale W. Henderson. 1983. *Definition and Measurement of Exchange Market Intervention*. Staff Study 126. Washington: Board of Governors of the Federal Reserve System.

Adler, Gustavo, Noemie Lisack, and Rui C. Mano. 2015. *Unveiling the Effects of Foreign Exchange Intervention: A Panel Approach*. IMF Working Paper 15/130. Washington: International Monetary Fund.

Baker, James A., III. 2006. *Work Hard, Study... and Keep Out of Politics! Adventures and Lessons from an Unexpected Public Life*. New York: Penguin Group.

Bayoumi, Tamim, Joseph E. Gagnon, and Christian Saborowski. 2015. Official Financial Flows, Capital Mobility, and Global Imbalances. *Journal of International Money and Finance* 52 (April): 146–74.

Bergsten, C. Fred. 1994. Exchange Rate Policy. In *American Economic Policy in the 1980s*, ed. Martin Feldstein. Chicago: Chicago University Press.

Bergsten, C. Fred, and John Williamson. 1983. Exchange Rates and Trade Policy. In *Trade Policy in the 1980s*, ed. William R. Cline. Washington: Institute for International Economics.

Bordo, Michael D., Owen F. Humpage, and Anna J. Schwartz. 2015. *Strained Relations: US Foreign Exchange Operations and Monetary Policy in the Twentieth Century*. Chicago: University of Chicago Press.

---

69. International Monetary Fund, *Factsheet: The G20 Mutual Assessment Process (MAP)*, March 15, 2015, www.imf.org/external/np/exr/facts/g20map.htm (accessed on July 17, 2015).

Boughton, James M. 2001. *Silent Revolution: The International Monetary Fund 1979–1989*. Washington: International Monetary Fund.

Catte, Pietro, Giampaolo Galli, and Salvatore Rebecchini. 1994. Concerted Interventions and the Dollar: An Analysis of Daily Data. In *The International Monetary System*, ed. Peter B. Kenen, Francesco Papadia, and Fabrizio Saccomanni. Cambridge: Cambridge University Press.

Cross, Sam Y. 1985a. Treasury and Federal Reserve Foreign Exchange Operations: August–October 1985. *FRBNY Quarterly Review* (Winter): 1–8.

Cross, Sam Y. 1985b. Treasury and Federal Reserve Foreign Exchange Operations: February–July 1985. *FRBNY Quarterly Review* (Autumn): 1–18.

Cross, Sam Y. 1987. Treasury and Federal Reserve Foreign Exchange Operations: August–October 1987. *FRBNY Quarterly Review* (Winter): 48–53.

Cross, Sam Y. 1988. Treasury and Federal Reserve Foreign Exchange Operations: November1987–January 1988. *FRBNY Quarterly Review* (Winter): 54–59.

Destler, I. M., and C. Randall Henning. 1989. *Dollar Politics: Exchange Rate Policymaking in the United States*. Washington: Institute for International Economics.

Frankel, Jeffrey A. 1984. *The Yen-Dollar Agreement: Liberalizing Japanese Capital Markets*. Policy Analyses in International Economics 9. Washington: Institute for International Economics.

Fratzscher, Marcel. 2009. How Successful Is the G-7 in Managing Exchange Rates? *Journal of International Economics* 79, no. 1: 78–88.

FRB (Board of Governors of the Federal Reserve System). 1987. *Greenbook* (February). Available at www.federalreserve.gov/monetarypolicy/files/fomc19870211gbpt119870204.pdf (accessed on August 26, 2015).

Funabashi, Yoichi. 1988. *Managing the Dollar: From the Plaza to the Louvre*. Washington: Institute for International Economics.

Henderson, Dale W., and Stephanie Sampson. 1983. Intervention in Foreign Exchange Markets: A Summary of Ten Staff Studies. *Federal Reserve Bulletin* 69, no. 11 (November): 830–36.

Henning, C. Randall. 1994. *Currencies and Politics in the United States, Germany, and Japan*. Washington: Institute for International Economics.

Holmes, Alan R., and Scott E. Pardee. 1979. Treasury and Federal Reserve Foreign Exchange Operations: August 1978–January 1979. *FRBNY Quarterly Review* (Spring): 67–87.

IMF (International Monetary Fund). 1993. *World Economic Outlook*, May. Washington. Available at www.imf.org/external/pubs/ft/weo/weo0593/ (accessed on August 11, 2015).

IMF (International Monetary Fund). 2013. Decision on Bilateral and Multilateral Surveillance, July 24, 2012. In *Selected Decisions and Selected Documents of the International Monetary Fund*. Washington. Available at www.imf.org/external/pubs/ft/sd/2013/123113.pdf (accessed on August 10, 2015).

Jurgensen, Philippe. 1983. *Report of the Working Group on Exchange Market Intervention* (March). Washington: US Treasury Department.

Klein, Michael, Bruce Mizrach, and Robert G. Murphy. 1991. Managing the Dollar: Has the Plaza Agreement Mattered? *Journal of Money, Credit, and Banking* 23, no. 4: 742–51.

Marris, Stephen. 1985. *Deficits and the Dollar: The World Economy at Risk*. Policy Analyses in International Economics 14. Washington: Institute for International Economics.

Mulford, David. 2014. *Packing for India: A Life of Action in Global Finance and Diplomacy*. Lincoln, NE: Potomac Books.

Obstfeld, Maurice. 1990. Effectiveness of Foreign-Exchange Market Intervention. In *International Policy Coordination and Exchange Rate Fluctuations*, ed. William H. Branson, Jacob A. Frenkel, and Morris Goldstein. Chicago: University of Chicago Press for the National Bureau of Economic Research.

Pardee, Scott E. 1979. Treasury and Federal Reserve Foreign Exchange Operations: February 1979–July 1979. *FRBNY Quarterly Review* (Autumn): 47–63.

Sarno, Lucio, and Mark P. Taylor. 2001. Official Intervention in the Foreign Exchange Market: Is It Effective and, If So, How Does It Work? *Journal of Economic Literature* 39 (September): 839–68.

Takagi, Shinji. 2015. *Conquering the Fear of Freedom: Japanese Exchange Rate Policy since 1945.* Oxford: Oxford University Press.

Truman, Edwin M. 1994. Comment on "Concerted Interventions and the Dollar: An Analysis of Daily Data," by Pietro Catte, Giampaolo Galli, and Salvatore Rebecchini. In *The International Monetary System,* ed. Peter B. Kenen, Francesco Papadia, and Fabrizio Saccomanni. Cambridge: Cambridge University Press.

Truman, Edwin M. 2003. The Limits of Exchange Market Intervention. In *Dollar Overvaluation and the World Economy*, ed. C. Fred Bergsten and John Williamson. Washington: Institute for International Economics.

Truman, Edwin M. 2006. What Can Exchange Rates Tell Us? In *C. Fred Bergsten and the World Economy*, ed. Michael Mussa. Washington: Peterson Institute for International Economics.

Truman, Edwin M. 2014. *The Federal Reserve Engages the World (1970–2000): An Insider's Narrative of the Transition to Managed Floating and Financial Turbulence*. Working Paper 14–5. Washington: Peterson Institute for International Economics.

Volcker, Paul A., and Toyoo Gyohten. 1992. *Changing Fortunes: The World's Money and the Threat to American Leadership*. New York: Crown.

Williamson, John. 1985. *The Exchange Rate System*. Policy Analyses in International Economics 5. Washington: Institute for International Economics.

Williamson, John. 2007. *Reference Rates and the International Monetary System*. Policy Analyses in International Economics 82. Washington: Peterson Institute for International Economics.

Williamson, John, and Marcus H. Miller. 1987. *Targets and Indicators: A Blueprint for the International Coordination of Economic Policy*. Policy Analyses in International Economics 22 (September). Washington: Institute for International Economics.

10

Before the Plaza

The Exchange Rate Stabilization Attempts of 1925, 1933, 1936, and 1971

BARRY EICHENGREEN

The Plaza Accord is controversial.[1] On the one hand, it is hailed as "perhaps the high-water mark of international economic cooperation over the past 40 years."[2] On the other, it is impugned as having had little effect on currency values, as having heightened rather than reduced instability (by causing the dollar to overshoot in the opposite direction), and even as having been indirectly responsible for Japan's lost decade (as recounted if not necessarily endorsed in IMF 2011).

Negotiations over exchange rates are always controversial. They are economically complex and politically fraught, since rhetoric is easy to offer while commitments are hard to keep. They tap into deep-seated beliefs about whether markets produce desirable outcomes and, if not, whether intervention can improve them. They prompt the question, debated by academics if not also practitioners, of whether international cooperation on monetary and financial matters is more likely to be productive or counterproductive.

One episode from 1985 is not exactly sufficient evidence for resolving these disputes. In this chapter I therefore consider a number of earlier episodes

Barry Eichengreen is professor of economics and political science at the University of California, Berkeley.

1. The Plaza Accord was an agreement between the French, German, Japanese, British, and US governments, signed on September 22, 1985, at the Plaza Hotel in New York, that sought to reverse the sharp appreciation of the dollar and stabilize currencies, broadly speaking, at more suitable levels.

2. Alan Beattie, "Steep Path to Modern-Day Plaza Accord," *Financial Times*, September 16, 2010.

when officials sought to implement agreements to move exchange rates to desired levels and stabilize them there.[3]

In 1925 the United States, with leadership from the Federal Reserve Bank of New York, sought to cooperate with the United Kingdom in reversing the postwar depreciation of sterling and stabilizing the bilateral sterling/dollar exchange rate at pre–World War I levels. In 1933 the major countries of the world, led by the United States, the United Kingdom, and France, sought to stabilize exchange rates and avoid another round of competitive devaluations following earlier depreciation of sterling and then the dollar against the gold bloc currencies. In 1936 the Americans, British, and French sought to facilitate depreciation and adjustment of the franc against the dollar and sterling while preventing the American and British currencies from becoming severely over-valued and at the same time avoiding another round of competitive devaluations that might neutralize efforts to realign the franc. And in 1971 the United States and its foreign partners sought a stabilization agreement under which the dollar would be adjusted downward by an amount adequate to correct US balance of payments weakness while at the same time limiting the adverse impact on foreign economies that found themselves with a stronger dollar exchange rate as a result.

My analysis of these episodes can be thought of as an effort to put the Plaza Accord into a broader historical context. In each case I ask a series of questions about these agreements. First, what was the problem in foreign exchange markets that governments were trying to solve, to what extent was there a common diagnosis of that problem, and how widely was it shared? Second, what were the obstacles to cooperation? Third, how successful were the representatives of different countries in achieving their goals? Fourth, were there unintended consequences, positive or negative, of their agreement? In the conclusion I explore what light this historical analysis sheds on the Plaza Accord.

Sterling/Dollar Stabilization in 1925

The year 1925 saw the culmination of efforts by the United States to intervene in international financial markets with the goal of stabilizing the sterling/dollar exchange rate at prewar levels. Its intervention was successful but had unintended consequences.

World War I was more expensive for Great Britain than the United States, Britain having, among other things, entered the war three years earlier. When gold exports were embargoed in 1914, sterling depreciated against the dollar, but it was held at a relatively modest discount for the duration of the war, through a combination of intervention and controls. With the abandon-

---

3. The definitions of *appropriate* and *stabilize* were not consistent over time—not surprisingly, perhaps, since there is no agreement on such terms and concepts among negotiators.

ment of controls in 1919, sterling depreciated further, reaching a low of $3.60 against the dollar, down from a prewar parity of $4.86.

This floating exchange rate was widely viewed as suboptimal, given favorable perceptions of the performance of the prewar gold standard. The United States had become a greater international commercial and financial power as a result of the war, and American officials saw restoring stable exchange rates as essential for promoting US exports of commodities, merchandise, and finance. Sterling being one of the two leading international currencies, along with the dollar, US officials viewed stabilization of the sterling/dollar rate as a key event that would lead other countries to follow. British officials, as the stewards of an even more outward-oriented economy, shared these concerns. They saw restoration of the bilateral sterling/dollar rate to prewar parity as desirable for enhancing the position of London as an international financial center and maintaining Britain's prestige (although there were a few prominent dissenters from this view).

Starting in 1921, sterling was gradually pushed up in the direction of the prewar dollar parity through the maintenance of high interest rates in the United Kingdom. But restrictive policies limited investment and made for slower growth, which raised questions about the sustainability of high interest rates. Sterling's appreciation weakened the balance of payments and limited the Bank of England's accumulation of free gold reserves, which could be used as a buffer against shocks. The hope was that once the prewar parity was reached, positive credibility effects might allow these constraints to be relaxed. The problem was getting there.

Anglo-American cooperation was facilitated by the fact that key policymakers in the two countries shared these priorities and concerns. It was eased by the fact that there were only two countries involved in negotiations.[4] A complication was that the main proponent of coordinated intervention was the Federal Reserve and not the US Treasury (in the United States as in other countries, it is customary for treasuries to take the lead in exchange rate management and agreements) and, in particular, that the motive force was the Federal Reserve Bank of New York and not the Board of Governors, with which the New York Fed had difficult relations.

The main mover was Benjamin Strong, the influential governor of the New York Fed. Strong was an internationalist by temperament. With experience on Wall Street, he appreciated the advantages to New York as a financial center of successful restoration of an international system of stable exchange rates. He was also on close personal terms with Montagu Norman, the governor of the Bank of England. Herbert Hoover, a critic, later called Strong "a mental annex to Europe" (Hoover 1941).

---

4. The reality was more complicated, but only a bit, what with negotiations over the Dawes Loan for Germany and stabilization loans for other European countries (the latter mainly through the League of Nations, of which the United States was not a member).

By 1924 more than five years had passed since the conclusion of the war. Germany had stabilized the mark, and other countries had stabilized their currencies at various levels, suggesting that, in the absence of early action to restore parity against the dollar, sterling and London might lose their traditional positions.

Strong and Norman therefore negotiated over how to engineer the final push. Norman agreed to keep interest rates high. Strong got his Fed colleagues to agree to a series of discount rate cuts. With leadership from New York, the reserve banks reduced their discount rates from the 4½ percent levels prevailing since early 1923 to 3–4 percent between May and October of 1924. In a 1924 statement prepared for the House of Representatives Committee on Banking and Currency, Strong cited international considerations as a rationale for lower discount rates and expansionary open market operations. These initiatives were designed "to render what assistance was possible by our market policy toward the recovery of sterling and resumption of gold payment by Great Britain."[5]

In addition, the Open Market Investment Committee authorized the New York Fed to purchase $300 million of US Treasury bonds, pushing down yields and encouraging capital and gold to flow across the Atlantic toward Britain. But there was still the immediate need on the part of the Bank of England for an additional cushion of reserves.[6] To meet it, in early 1925 the Federal Reserve Bank of New York provided a $200 million line of credit to the Bank of England in exchange for an equivalent amount of sterling deposit credit, while Strong encouraged J. P. Morgan & Co., with which he was on friendly terms, to provide a supplementary $100 million credit to the British government.[7] Sterling continued to strengthen; with this US support in place, it was stabilized at the prewar parity in April 1925.

These decisions were controversial at the time and became even more controversial subsequently. John Maynard Keynes, among others, criticized the $4.86 rate as dangerously overvalued. Commerce Secretary Hoover objected that Strong's internationally motivated policies were fueling financial ex-

---

5. Hearings on HR 7895 before the Committee on Banking and Currency of the US House of Representatives, 69th Congress, First Session, part 1, p. 336.

6. There was some disagreement within British circles about whether a cushion was needed for the return to gold. Norman was strongly of the view that a cushion of at least an additional $300 million was needed. Otto Neimeyer (then still at Treasury, not yet at the Bank of England) disagreed, on the grounds that the conditions attached to the American support (that the Bank of England might be asked to raise interest rates) either implicitly or explicitly were undesirable. Neimeyer also doubted that $300 million would make much difference or alleviate the need for the Bank to raise interest rates in response to market pressure. Sir Warren Fisher (permanent secretary to the Treasury, the most senior civil servant at Treasury) disliked the cushion because it meant that Britain would become indebted and subordinate to another country (Moggridge 1972, 79–81).

7. Morgan had been an agent for the British government during the war. It had an interest in rebuilding international financial business between London and New York, in which the bank hoped to play a leading role.

cesses in the United States.[8] In his memoirs Hoover (1941, 9) pointed to the rapid growth of loans to stockbrokers and dealers and sharp appreciation of share prices as early as 1925. In November he protested to the nominal head of the Federal Reserve Board, Daniel Crissinger, that Strong's policies were fueling speculation. He wrote members of the Senate Banking and Currency Committee, which had oversight of the Federal Reserve, making the same objection and, extraordinarily for a sitting commerce secretary, even drafted a letter for a prominent senator to sign and send to the Fed. He enlisted two allies on the Board of Governors, Adolph Miller, formerly a professor at the University of California, Berkeley, and Charles Hamlin, a founding governor of the board, to register his objections. But none of these efforts reversed policy.

The consequences of the agreement were not entirely as hoped. The British balance of payments failed to magically strengthen, forcing another negotiation among central bankers in 1927, this one involving not just Strong and Norman but also Hjalmar Schacht of the Reichsbank and Charles Rist of the Banque de France. In a renewed effort to prop up sterling, Strong and Norman asked the German and French banks to cut interest rates (which they refused to do) and to refrain from converting their sterling securities into gold in London (which they agreed to do, but only temporarily). Consequently, the burden of adjustment fell on Norman and Strong. Norman agreed "to do whatever it takes" (in Mario Draghi terms) to maintain the sterling parity, while Strong once more cut interest rates and purchased securities to induce gold and capital to flow toward London.

Together their actions bought four more years of currency stability. But none of these steps addressed sterling's underlying weakness. When the Great Depression hit and, in 1931, the pound came crashing down, the dollar fell, too (more on this in the next section).

The internationally motivated decision to cut interest rates in 1927 was resisted by other reserve banks, which, for the first time in the history of the Federal Reserve System, the Board forced to go along. This led to bad feeling and recrimination between New York and the other Federal Reserve banks. This tension undermined their ability and willingness to work together to contain the spreading financial crisis in 1931–33.[9] That the agreement between Norman and Strong was made at a private meeting between the governor of the New York Fed and foreign central bankers and then presented to the Board as a fait accompli was criticized in House of Representatives hearings in 1928.[10]

In addition, there was the fillip to stock market speculation (although economists differ, as always, on how important monetary policy as opposed

---

8. Hoover served as commerce secretary from 1921 to 1928 before becoming president.

9. I describe these consequences in Eichengreen (2015).

10. Hearings on HR 11806 before the Committee on Banking and Currency of the US House of Representatives, 17th Congress, First Session.

to other factors was for events on Wall Street).[11] Strong had gaily told Charles Rist that he was going to give "a little coup de whiskey" to the stock market. He ended up providing more. Adolph Miller, in a 1935 address, argued that the decision gave "a further great and dangerous impetus to an already over-expanded credit situation, notably to the volume of credit used on the stock exchanges" (Miller 1935, 449). In his memoirs, Hoover essentially blamed the decision for not just the Wall Street boom but also the Great Crash and the Great Depression. This, clearly, is going a bit far (Hoover had an obvious interest in deflecting blame).

Still, the successful 1925 stabilization agreement is a cautionary tale. It shows how policymakers, once they commit to moving the exchange rate and holding it at a certain level, may be forced to double down on their bets. It cautions against elevating exchange rate stabilization to a primary goal of policy, especially when its pursuit causes policy to be diverted from more fundamental domestic goals, like the maintenance of price and financial stability (the argument that the 1927 interest rate cut helped fuel the Wall Street bubble points to the potential for this kind of conflict between exchange rate stability and financial stability). The debate over the US decision to loosen monetary policy as a way of supporting the currency of an important foreign partner is eerily reminiscent of the debate over whether Japanese decisions to adjust policy at the Plaza in 1985 and at the Louvre in 1987 helped set the stage for the Japanese crisis and lost decade.

The Failed Stabilization Effort of 1933

Britain's abandonment of the gold standard in September 1931 induced a score and more of countries to follow. It then took more than six months for monetary policy to be reoriented toward the needs of internal stability. Sterling fell as low as $3.40 before recovering to the $3.80–$4.00 range. Over the first half of 1932, the Bank of England cut interest rates from 6 to 2 percent. At midyear H. M. Treasury established the Exchange Equalisation Account to intervene in the foreign exchange market (officially to prevent undue fluctuations, in the American view to keep the floating pound down), and the Chancellor of the Exchequer, Neville Chamberlain, assumed effective control of monetary policy.

The depreciation of sterling, as a reminder that the commitment to the prevailing set of exchange rates was not irrevocable, ratcheted up the pressure on the United States. Expectations that the new president, Franklin Delano Roosevelt, would devalue led to a run on the dollar during the interregnum between the election in November 1932 and the inauguration in March 1933 (see Wigmore 1987). That run in turn forced the bank holiday as Roosevelt's first act on assuming office and led to the decision to "temporarily" embargo gold exports.

---

11. The case is perhaps most strongly made by Rothbard (1963).

Against this chaotic backdrop, the leaders of the principal countries sought to reach an agreement on currency stabilization. The idea of an international conference to address currency, trade, and related issues had been in the air since at least 1930 and arose repeatedly in bilateral meetings among leaders. An international conference in Lausanne in July 1932 concluded with agreement to call another conference to consider currency stabilization and related issues. It was eventually scheduled for London in June 1933 (Kindleberger 1973, 200–01).

The perception that exchange rate instability was a problem that contributed to the collapse of international trade and lending was broadly, if not universally, shared. French officials, many of whom had experienced exchange rate volatility, inflation, and financial instability at first hand in the 1920s, argued strongly for the restoration of fixed rates. Not incidentally, France was suffering growing problems of overvaluation and deflation as a result of the depreciation of sterling and now the dollar. The other gold bloc countries shared its concern.

British officials also worried about exchange rate instability. More specifically, they worried that FDR might aggressively devalue the dollar and push the sterling/dollar rate back to $4.86 or even higher. Agreement by the United States not to intervene too aggressively in gold and foreign exchange markets was desirable from their point of view. At the same time, British policymakers, having seen the advantages of increased policy space, refused to limit their own monetary room for maneuver. In effect, they were happy to encourage an exchange rate stabilization agreement if it left their own hands untied.

Roosevelt's views were unclear to others because they were unclear to the president himself. As Herbert Feis, economic advisor to the State Department, later wrote, "His ideas veered and waffled. Even now, with many records opened, it is not easy to trace their gyrations" (Feis 1966, 144).[12] In April FDR seemed favorably predisposed toward the gold standard and exchange rate stabilization, assuming that countries could agree to cooperate on the necessary reflationary measures. But by May he had become impressed by the very positive impact of depreciation of the dollar on commodity prices and the stock market.[13] As a result of his bilateral meetings with European officials, he had also grown more pessimistic about the scope for cooperative reflationary action.[14]

---

12. Rauchway (2015) elaborates the point. Edwards (2015) presents a different view.

13. Kindleberger (1973, 206) writes, "As the dollar fell on international exchanges in May—going from $3.85 to the pound on April 29 to $4.00 on May 31—Roosevelt became less and less interested in stabilization.... He was prepared to agree on the dates of the conference—in mid-June. Nothing else was decided."

14. Other advisors to the administration, such as James Warburg of the State Department, Oliver Sprague of Treasury, and George Harrison of the New York Fed, continued to favor reestablishment of fixed rates and the gold standard, but they did not convince the president.

When the American delegates to the London conference unexpectedly produced a temporary stabilization agreement and then promised a proposal for stabilizing exchange rates on a permanent basis, FDR transmitted his famous "bombshell message" of July 3 denigrating fixed exchange rates as "old fetishes of so-called international bankers" and blowing the American delegation and the conference out of the water.[15] This unilateral declaration was criticized as signaling US isolationism and encouraging Italian ambitions in Ethiopia, Japanese ambitions in China, and German ambitions in Europe. Roosevelt followed the example of Britain and Chamberlain, using his powers under the Thomas Amendment to the Farm Relief Act to seize direct control of the monetary reins. Starting in October, through the agency of the Reconstruction Finance Corporation, he purchased gold on the open market, pushing down the dollar and pushing the sterling/dollar rate back to roughly pre-1931 levels.

But the fatal mistake—committed by Hoover and not Roosevelt—had been to call the conference in the first place. Doing so raised expectations, which were bound to be disappointed given the very different diagnoses and prescriptions of the representatives of different countries. The priority and solution in the eyes of the French was stabilizing exchange rates, ideally at predevaluation levels; the problem was the reluctance of other governments to pursue the deflation necessary to meet those exchange rate commitments. For the British, in contrast, deflation was the problem, not the solution, and the role of the exchange rate was to adjust so as to allow Chamberlain to carry out his pledge to return prices to their 1929 levels.[16]

---

15. Kindleberger (1973, 214) writes, "The deal worked out among the financial representatives called for the dollar to be stabilized at $4.00 to the pound and $0.04662 to the franc, with a 3 percent spread on either side…. Each of the three central banks would support its currency by selling gold, up to a limit of 4 or 5 million ounces, equivalent to $80–$100 million. When this was used up, the agreement would be reexamined." Compounding the problem was the fact that the American delegation in London had failed to keep the president and his advisors informed of its progress. This lapse led FDR and his circle to misinterpret a temporary agreement to stabilize exchange rates for the duration of the conference as a permanent exchange rate accord. According to Kindleberger, "The news of the [temporary] stabilization leaked to the press, and the exchange market firmed from $4.12 to $4.02; the commodity and stock markets declined. The Committee for the Nation sent President Roosevelt a telegraph calling for the dollar to be cut 43 percent, based on calculations for restoring US prices, which implied a pound rate of $5.70. Roosevelt sent the delegation telegrams on June 17… saying that $4.00 was unacceptable…."

16. Meltzer (2003) offers a different interpretation, with which I do not agree. According to him, the British, French, and Americans all agreed on the desirability in principle of the gold standard and fixed exchange rates but disagreed fundamentally on their appropriate level. The United States and the United Kingdom wanted currencies that were devalued against foreign currencies, including against one another, while the French wanted to see predevaluation exchange rates restored or at least the extent of US and British devaluation severely limited. My view is that the parties disagreed fundamentally on the importance of exchange rate stability. The French and FDR early on viewed it as a priority, to which price levels and internal conditions generally should be forced to adjust; the British and FDR later attached priority to price stability (to returning prices to 1929 levels) and saw the exchange rate as a variable that should be adjusted as needed to make this possible.

Hoover essentially agreed with the French and failed to comprehend that any president, including FDR, might fail to share his view. He made the mistake of agreeing to the conference before an election, which he lost, which meant that he could not commit the United States to the conference agenda. FDR, on assuming the presidency, was compelled to appoint a delegation; that he sent a diverse delegation with varied and conflicting views on monetary stabilization was not inadvertent. When those delegates unexpectedly indicated that they were on the verge of producing a stabilization agreement, he was forced to issue his bombshell message. All participants in some sense lost credibility as a result of these events.

The lesson of the stabilization effort of 1933 is to avoid convening ambitious exchange rate stabilization negotiations in the absence of a reasonable degree of agreement on the nature of the problem and what needs to be done. Agreement should encompass the relevant countries but also extend within governments. It should be shared by the relevant branches of government, and there should be reason to expect that it will be shared not just by current policymakers but also by their successors.

The Tripartite Agreement of 1936

Having successfully exerted upward pressure on commodity prices, in January 1934 Roosevelt repegged the dollar to gold at $35 an ounce (up from the $21 prevailing before 1933), although the United States stood ready to pay out gold on demand only to official foreign holders that also maintained convertibility. FDR having pushed down the exchange rate against other currencies still pegged to gold at an unchanged domestic-currency price, the sterling/dollar rate recovered to $4.86 and even a bit higher (appropriately, it can be argued, given that the US depression and deflation were even more serious than the British).

Devaluation by the United States and the other members of the dollar area intensified the pressure on the currencies of the gold bloc that still maintained convertibility at an unchanged gold price. The Belgian franc was the first gold bloc currency to fall, in 1935.

Markets then trained their sights on France, not without reason: The country had an increasingly overvalued currency as a result of exchange rate developments abroad. Successive French governments and the Banque de France had shunned all significant reflationary monetary policies, consigning the country to a deepening deflation. As unemployment mounted, support for the parties of the center-right and their orthodox policies crumbled. The result, predictable in hindsight, was the electoral victory of the Socialist-led Popular Front, headed by Léon Blum.

The situation was not unlike that in the United States three years earlier. Given the condition of the economy and the promise of the opposition party, soon to assume office, to take whatever steps were needed to stabilize prices and restart economic growth, it was not hard to see devaluation coming. At the same time, a considerable segment of the French political and financial establishment remained wedded to the gold standard, given the country's traumatic experience with a floating exchange rate a decade earlier. Blum himself, while possessing many admirable qualities, was no financial expert. Not unlike Roosevelt, he wanted to satisfy the demands of those who saw merit in maintenance of the gold standard and an unchanged franc exchange rate as well as those who urged economic stabilization and reflation, both at the same time. It was not clear, when faced by the incompatibility of the two objectives, which way he would jump.

Once Blum formed his government, in June 1936, and devaluation came to appear increasingly imminent, French policymakers were animated by two further considerations. First, they were concerned that any change in the franc exchange rate should be dressed up as an international agreement rather than constituting an admission of failure by a new government that had effectively made a campaign pledge not to devalue. As part of that agreement they might even secure commitments of support from the British and US authorities, or so it was hoped. Second, the French sought assurances that if they did devalue, the needed improvement in international competitiveness would not be neutralized by further competitive devaluations by the British and Americans or by their imposition of retaliatory tariffs.

The British and Americans, for their part, were concerned that the French devaluation not be excessive, undercutting their own competitiveness. Harry Dexter White, newly appointed to the Treasury, warned in May 1935 that France was apt to devalue by too much, creating new maladjustments. He recommended negotiating an international agreement to prevent them from doing so (Clarke 1977, 15). At the same time, the British and Americans were also concerned that France devalue by an adequate margin, since a small devaluation that did not restore competitiveness might do more to undermine confidence than restore it and be followed by a second devaluation, roiling financial markets.

In addition, the Americans and British again wanted to keep their options open: Britain had the Exchange Equalisation Account to intervene in the foreign exchange market if sterling's strength looked excessive, the US administration now possessed a similar account—the Exchange Stabilization Fund, established by the Gold Reserve Act of 1934—and FDR retained the option of devaluing the dollar further under the provisions of that act. Drummond (2008, 201) describes how the British view under Chamberlain evolved: "The pound would not be [competitively] devalued, but neither would it be pegged to gold or the dollar until the world had been freed of the trading and financial barriers that had made the old gold standard unworkable."

To be sure, others, such as Frederick Leith-Ross (chief economic advisor to the British government and architect of the Treasury View) and various officials of the Bank of England, continued to hanker after pegged rates, but to no avail. Similarly, others concerned with US policy (such as Jacob Viner, who served as an advisor to Treasury Secretary Henry Morgenthau, and Alvin Hansen, who wrote a paper as a consultant to the State Department in

1935) saw exchange rate uncertainty as a major factor discouraging trade and hindering recovery; they were more inclined toward a meaningful exchange rate arrangement. But as had been the case with proposals for such an agreement in 1933, the president was not convinced. FDR's reaction to Hansen's proposal for a stabilization agreement was that "the man should absolutely be fired" (Clarke 1977, 12).

By June 1936 Morgenthau was convinced that the French should devalue before being forced into doing so by the markets. But the Blum government needed the act to be dressed up in a diplomatic cloak and consequently resisted until September. The French pushed for a formal agreement by the three governments specifying new central rates surrounded by fluctuation bands, a bit wider than before, and commitments of bilateral support between the participating exchange equalization funds.[17] This was more than the US and British governments could accept: Both now saw the exchange rate as properly subordinate to domestic price stability and were not willing to tie their policies to France.[18]

In the end the French got not a joint declaration but three separate, loosely harmonized statements by the three governments. The three statements, dated September 26, implicitly recognized the new exchange rate of 105 French francs to the pound (where the pound was at roughly $5.00) as broadly appropriate. But the statements contained no numbers, instead speaking in general terms of "consultation" and "cooperation."

Morgenthau hailed the agreement as the "greatest move taken for peace in the world since the World War," anticipating Richard Nixon's characterization of the Smithsonian Agreement as "the greatest monetary agreement in the history of the world" (Clarke 1977, 12). The reality was more limited. Although the statements spoke of consultation and cooperation, there was no commitment to cooperate in holding exchange rates at their newly established levels. Over the winter of 1936–37, the French intervened to prevent the franc from falling farther, while the British intervened to prevent sterling from

---

17. On September 9, just before devaluing, the French submitted a text to Washington and London proposing an agreement whereby the three currencies would be stabilized against one another. It proposed that the specified limits "shall not be modified except by common agreement or subject to notifying the contracting powers in the case of exceptional and unforeseen circumstances, the final objective of the contracting parties being the general return to the international gold standard when the conditions necessary are found to be realized" (Drummond 2008, 206).

18. Negotiations started with a visit to Washington, in June 1936, by Emmanuel Monick, France's financial attaché in London. Monick told the United States that France would devalue, and FDR agreed that the United States would not retaliate as long as the French devaluation was not excessive and US prices did not fall. The problem, Monick conveyed to the Americans, was that the British were unwilling to make a similar commitment. The British sought a formula whereby they could bless the French devaluation and encourage the French not to make it excessive while maintaining their room for maneuver. In July they promised not to retaliate by devaluing the pound or by imposing discriminating duties as long as France chose a rate of not more than 100 francs to the pound. At the same time, in a letter to the French at the end of July, Chamberlain stated in no uncertain terms that he was not providing a guarantee that sterling would be stabilized at any particular level (Clarke 1977).

strengthening excessively. The US Treasury sterilized gold inflows starting in December 1936 to prevent the US price level from rising faster (to prevent the US real exchange rate from becoming overvalued).[19] But there was no formal cooperation between governments; each country was on its own. Ultimately, the weak currency country, France, was forced into a further devaluation in 1937, as a result of the negative supply shock imparted by the other policies of the French government in 1936–37.[20]

Of the few systematic assessments of the effects of the Tripartite Agreement, Eichengreen and James (1991) finds that exchange rates were somewhat less volatile after the Tripartite Agreement than before.[21] Their interpretation is that exchange rates had been restored to more appropriate levels as a result of the agreement, obviating the need for sharp changes in levels like those affecting sterling in 1931, the dollar in 1933, and the franc in 1936 (with the renewed depreciation of the franc in 1937 constituting a partial exception).

The lesson of the Tripartite Agreement is to avoid excessively ambitious commitments that may be impossible to meet. The agreement was possible because the three countries concerned had an interest in seeing the franc devalued by enough to correct the French economy's problem of overvaluation but not by so much as might significantly damage the competitiveness of its partners, and they had similar views of what constituted enough but not too much. The agreement avoided an excessive devaluation, which might have elicited currency or tariff retaliation. It moved exchange rates in more sustainable directions and had a modestly stabilizing impact on foreign exchange markets. It helped make realignment palatable to the French by allowing them to package it, for domestic consumption, as part of an international agreement while not committing the governments involved to subordinate their domestic objectives to cooperation on exchange rates in any meaningful sense. In currency stabilization agreements, sometimes less is more.

The 1971 Smithsonian Agreement

The story of the Smithsonian negotiations of December 17–18, 1971, is sufficiently well known that it can be recounted selectively here. The situation was not unlike that in 1936. The problem then was that the French franc was overvalued. The challenge for negotiators was to agree on a realignment that was sufficient to correct this problem but not so large as to create serious problems for the country's partners. It was to prevent other countries from taking offsetting steps that might neutralize the improvement in French competitiveness

---

19. US gold sterilization policies are discussed in Irwin (2012).

20. A recent assessment of those policies is Cohen-Setton, Hausman, and Weiland (2015).

21. Lewis (1949) agrees with this assessment. Drummond (1979) and Sauvy (1967) disagree, concluding in favor of no discernible impact. In addition, international real interest rate differentials were smaller, as a result of the decline in covered interest differentials, exchange risk premia, and real exchange rate variability.

and to agree on the structure of the exchange rate system now that the currency formerly at its center (in this case the franc) was no longer tied to gold.

In 1971 the problem was that the dollar was overvalued, as evident from the fact that the United States was hemorrhaging gold reserves.[22] The challenge was to get foreign countries to accede to dollar devaluation sufficient to stem US gold losses and not to offset any increase in the dollar price of gold by depreciating their currencies commensurately.[23] It was to prevent Congress from imposing new import duties if other governments failed to go along. And it was to agree on the structure of the new system once the dollar was no longer freely convertible into gold at a fixed price.

The recognition that dollar devaluation was needed was widely shared, although engineering the devaluation had to surmount a collective action problem: Fearing a loss of competitiveness, other countries generally preferred that the dollar be devalued against someone else's currency rather than their own. This created an argument for an international conference at which a set of new parities against the dollar could be collectively agreed upon. The United States employed good-cop, bad-cop tactics to elicit agreement from other countries to convene the meeting at the Smithsonian. The bad cops, President Nixon and Treasury Secretary John Connolly, closed the gold window in August and imposed a 10 percent import surcharge, signaling that they would use trade policy as a sanction against countries that hesitated to negotiate.[24] The good cop, Undersecretary of the Treasury for International Monetary Affairs Paul Volcker, traveled to Europe to reassure foreign leaders that the United States was interested in a negotiated solution.

The Smithsonian Agreement included the necessary realignment of the dollar. Countries other than the United States saw a collective 10 percent appreciation of their currencies, although some (like Germany and Japan) contributed more than others, depending on the perceived strength of their economies and their dependence on US foreign policy protection.[25] The dollar

---

22. The source of those gold losses need not detain us here. One interpretation was that expansive US monetary and fiscal policy was responsible for dollar overvaluation and the US balance of payments deficit. Another view, known as the Triffin Dilemma, was that US deficits were intrinsic to the operation of the system, given the growing demand of other countries for international reserves, which could be met only by their accumulation of US dollars and/or conversion of dollars into gold. The second view pointed to the need for an increase in the dollar price of gold, while the first highlighted the need for a change in dollar exchange rates and, to maintain them, appropriate adjustments in US monetary and fiscal policies.

23. "There were strong doubts," as Volcker later put it, "about the willingness of other countries to permit a sizable adjustment, however initiated" (1978–79, 6).

24. Johnson (1973) refers to the use of US "muscle power to force the others to make exchange rate adjustments that the United States considered necessary for its own interests but the others were reluctant to make."

25. The French franc was revalued against the dollar by 8.57 percent, the deutsche mark by 13.57 percent, the yen by 17.9 percent. The exact numbers reflected a compromise between Nixon and French President Georges Pompidou, who met in the Azores to hammer out their differences before the Smithsonian conference.

was realigned to more appropriate levels. Its adjustment was not offset by other countries. The United States did not have to resort to tariffs or other undesirable expedients to achieve this goal; the import surcharge imposed in August was lifted following the successful conclusion of negotiations. It was "no mean feat to manage a devaluation of the proud dollar in a way that did not turn American opinion and policy inward," as Volcker (1978–79, 6) later put it.[26]

The new system was a compromise between the champions of fixed and adjustable exchange rates. Other currencies were again linked to the dollar but surrounded now by wider fluctuation bands (+/-2¼ percent versus +/-1 percent). The dollar was no longer freely convertible for official foreign holders of dollars as had been the case before August (reflected in the fact that the market price was now significantly higher than the official price). This compromise reflected the fact that there was less than full agreement on how the post-Bretton Woods system should be structured. There was strong disagreement within the US administration between the proponents of fixed and floating exchange rates, with Fed Chairman Arthur Burns and Volcker supporting fixed rates and Director of the Office of Management and Budget and future Treasury Secretary George Schultz supporting floating rates. As a result, the United States was unable to firmly commit to either fixed or flexible rates.

Similarly, there were significant differences between other countries over how much exchange rate flexibility was appropriate. West Germany had already adjusted the deutsche mark/dollar exchange rate more than once to maintain price stability; increasingly, it saw exchange rate stability as a lower priority than internal stability.[27] Canada, reflecting its positive experience with floating exchange rates, recommended wider adoption of a flexible system. France, in contrast, remained wedded to fixed exchange rates and gold convertibility, in part reflecting the enduring influence of the interwar experience recounted above.[28] Japan saw itself as an export economy; while it was prepared to revalue the yen as much for political as economic reasons, it was reluctant to see generalized floating, for fear that it would interfere with the growth of international trade (see Angel 1991).[29]

The Smithsonian Agreement did not include a commitment on the part of the United States to run a particular set of monetary and fiscal policies to

---

26. Volcker later argued that the weakness of the Smithsonian Agreement was that other countries were reluctant to see larger revaluations against the dollar (Feldstein 2013, 106). Others argue that even had it been feasible, a larger realignment would not have resolved the underlying contradictions of the system and would only have put off the day of reckoning (see Eichengreen 1993).

27. Germany revalued the deutsche mark in October 1969 and floated it against the dollar in May 1971. Austria moved all but simultaneously, revaluing by 5 percent. Switzerland revalued by 7 percent; the Netherlands floated.

28. In the immediate aftermath of Nixon's closing of the gold window, Germany proposed a joint float of European Community currencies, which France opposed.

29. In the end the Japanese government was converted by the import surcharge and threats of more of the same (Irwin 2013).

defend the new system of parities. It did not entail a commitment to keep inflation within a specified range. It focused on ends rather than means (to paraphrase the assessment in Sachs 1986). In this respect it was not unlike the 1936 Tripartite Agreement—and it ultimately met the same fate.

Already in 1972 there were complaints that US inflation was excessive (reflecting the pressure Nixon was placing on the Federal Reserve in an election year) and that it was infecting other countries. US capital outflows resumed. Under the circumstances, it is not surprising that "the greatest monetary agreement in the history of the world" proved ephemeral. On February 12, 1973, the new Treasury secretary, George Schultz, announced a 10 percent devaluation of the dollar (an increase in the price of gold from $35 to $42.22 an ounce). The move only encouraged speculation against what remained of the parities negotiated in December 1971.

By the summer of 1973, after a bit more than a year, the new system of parities had collapsed. The Smithsonian Agreement left little in the way of an enduring legacy.

Implications for the Plaza Accord

Other chapters in this volume analyze the Plaza Accord in detail. Here I merely suggest how it should be viewed in light of the history of exchange rate stabilization agreements.

A first implication of that history is that exchange rate agreements are helpful when they bring exchange rates in line with appropriate monetary and fiscal policies but not when they force appropriate monetary and fiscal policies to be modified in order to support arbitrary exchange rate targets. Put another way, policymakers privilege exchange rate targets, subordinating their pursuit of more fundamental goals of policy like price stability and high employment, at their peril. In 1985 the high dollar was associated in the popular mind—and, more specifically, in the minds of US business leaders—with the Federal Reserve's relatively tight anti-inflationary monetary policy. There was pressure on the Fed to relax its stance in order to bring down the dollar and avoid further hollowing out US industry. Given the country's recent experience of inflation and the sacrifice made to reduce the inflation rate to more tolerable levels, relaxing Fed policy in order to facilitate dollar realignment was undesirable. Public statements and limited foreign exchange market intervention in January followed by the Plaza Accord in September facilitated that realignment without requiring an adjustment in Federal Reserve policy.[30] German negotiators similarly resisted a rigid agreement that might have required them to divert monetary policy from the fundamental goal of low inflation, preferring to rely, appropriately under the circumstances, on public statements and sterilized foreign exchange market intervention. Intervention was used to support

30. I leave to other chapters the task of analyzing the relative importance of these and other developments in exchange rate movements, though I am broadly in agreement with the assessment in Frankel (1994).

the continued pursuit of appropriate monetary policies by moderating their uneven impact and dissipating incipient protectionist pressures that, had the exchange rate not adjusted, might have created irresistible pressure for the Fed's disinflationary stance to be relaxed. This was an example of an agreement designed to bring exchange rates in line with appropriate monetary policies. Anglo-American agreements in the 1920s, when hitherto appropriate monetary policies were modified to bring them in line with arbitrary exchange rate targets, were a prominent counterexample.

A second implication for the Plaza is that it was wise to defer convening an international meeting to discuss the exchange rate issue until there was broad agreement among the principal countries involved on the desirability of facilitating further adjustment in the dollar exchange rate.[31] There had to be a change in US international economic policy leadership, from Donald Regan to James Baker, before this precondition was met. The experience of 1933 cautions against prematurely raising expectations and engaging in unproductive negotiations if internal divisions are likely to prevent their successful conclusion. It also points to the wisdom of convening such negotiations after, as opposed to immediately before, an election, so that policy continuity can be ensured.

A third implication is that a productive outcome at the Plaza was facilitated by the fact that agreement among governments encompassed not just principles but specific magnitudes, as it had, for example, in 1936 and to a lesser extent in 1971. At the Plaza the United States, Germany, and Japan all agreed, accounts suggest, on a 10–12 percent depreciation of the dollar against the deutsche mark and the yen relative to September 1985 levels.[32] But while there was broad agreement on the desirability of exchange rates in that range, there was little appetite for an ambitious stabilization agreement of a sort that governments were unlikely to successfully maintain, given divergent conditions in the three economies. The Plaza communiqué therefore omitted, appropriately, mention of specific levels or ranges for exchange rates. As in 1936 (and unlike 1971), less was more.

A fourth implication is that there could be constructive negotiations at the Plaza because there was broad agreement within—as well as between—governments about the desirability of exchange rate adjustment. This had not been the case in the United States, in particular, before 1985, when the Fed

31. Henning and Destler (1988) suggest that the success of the Plaza stemmed in part from the fact that negotiations were organized through the G-5 (France, Germany, Japan, the United States, and the United Kingdom). This avoided the large numbers problem that would have complicated negotiations organized through the International Monetary Fund or the Organization for Economic Cooperation and Development. This argument is consistent with the observed contrast between the 1933 World Economic Conference and the 1936 Tripartite Agreement, although some of the other episodes analyzed above fit less easily with their viewpoint.

32. Frankel (1994) observes that a devaluation of this magnitude became a focal point for discussions as a result of "a never-released 'non-paper' drafted by [Assistant Secretary of Treasury for International Affairs David] Mulford for a secret preparatory meeting of G-5 deputies in London on September 15...." Funabashi (1988) goes farther, asserting that the United States made a formal proposal to this effect that was accepted by the other governments.

had favored some form of action, including presumably sterilized intervention, to prevent and reverse excessive dollar appreciation but the Treasury, under Regan, strongly wedded to free market ideology, did not agree. Henning (1994) reminds us not to dismiss the existence of differences of opinion or at least emphasis within governments; his account is a reminder of how the Fed subsequently became more concerned than Treasury about dollar weakness (which it feared could become inflationary) and how the Bank of Japan was less alarmed than the Ministry of Finance by the increasing strength of the yen (which the Ministry of Finance feared could damage Japanese manufacturing). But the fact is that there was considerable agreement within as well as among governments about the goals of exchange rate policy, which enabled national authorities to negotiate more productively. This was very different from 1933.

Finally, the Plaza realignment worked because it was consistent with economic fundamentals. In 1936 fundamentals had pointed to a weak franc and a strong pound and dollar. The Tripartite Agreement accelerated movement in that direction and prevented governments from frustrating it. In 1985 a weaker dollar and stronger yen were consistent with the competitive positions and needs of the US and Japanese economies. The Plaza Accord accelerated movement toward exchange market levels consistent with those fundamentals and similarly prevented governments from frustrating it.

The bottom line of this historical review is that the circumstances under which exchange rate stabilization and intervention agreements can be successfully negotiated and produce desirable results are rare. Arguably, 1985 was one of these instances.

References

Angel, R.C. 1991. *Explaining Economic Policy Failure: Japan in the 1969–1971 International Monetary Crisis.* New York: Columbia University Press.

Clarke, Stephen. 1977. *Exchange Rate Stabilization in the Mid-1930s: Negotiating the Tripartite Agreement.* Princeton Studies in International Finance 41. International Finance Section, Department of Economics, Princeton University.

Clavin, Patricia. 2013. *Securing the World Economy: The Reinvention of the League of Nations, 1920–1946.* New York: Oxford University Press.

Cohen-Setton, Jérémie, Joshua Hausman, and Johannes Weiland. 2015. Supply-Side Policies in the Depression: Evidence from France. Departments of Economics at the University of California, Berkeley; the University of Michigan; and the University of California, San Diego. Photocopy.

Drummond, Ian. 1979. *London, Washington and the Management of the Franc, 1936-39.* Princeton Studies in International Finance 45. Princeton, NJ: International Finance Section, Department of Economics, Princeton University.

Drummond, Ian. 2008. *The Floating Pound and the Sterling Area 1931–1939.* Cambridge: Cambridge University Press.

Edwards, Sebastian. 2015. *Academics as Advisers: Gold, the "Brains Trust," and FDR.* NBER Working Paper 21380. Cambridge, MA: National Bureau of Economic Research.

Eichengreen, Barry. 1993. Three Perspectives on Bretton Woods. In *A Retrospective on the Bretton Woods System: Lessons for International Monetary Reform,* ed. Michael Bordo and Barry Eichengreen. Chicago: University of Chicago Press.

Eichengreen, Barry. 2015. *Hall of Mirrors: The Great Depression, The Great Recession, and the Uses—and Misuses—of History*. New York: Oxford University Press.

Eichengreen, Barry, and Caroline James. 1991. *Can Informal Cooperation Stabilize Exchange Rates? Evidence from the 1936 Tripartite Agreement*. Working Paper 91-162. Department of Economics, University of California, Berkeley.

Feldstein, Martin. 2013. An Interview with Paul Volcker. *Journal of Economic Perspectives* 27, no. 4: 105–20.

Feis, Herbert. 1966. *1933: Characters in Crisis*. Boston: Little Brown.

Frankel, Jeffrey. 1994. Exchange Rate Policy. In *American Economic Policy in the 1980s*, ed. Martin Feldstein. Chicago: University of Chicago Press.

Funabashi, Yoichi. 1988. *Managing the Dollar: From the Plaza to the Louvre*. Washington: Institute for International Economics.

Henning, Randall. 1994. *Currencies and Politics in the United States, Germany, and Japan*. Washington: Institute for International Economics.

Henning, Randall, and Mac Destler. 1988. From Neglect to Activism: American Politics and the 1985 Plaza Accord. *Journal of Public Policy* 8, no. 3/4: 317–33.

Hoover, Herbert. 1941. *The Memoirs of Herbert Hoover, vol. III: The Great Depression, 1929–1941*. New York: Macmillan.

IMF (International Monetary Fund). 2011. Did the Plaza Accord Cause Japan's Lost Decades? *World Economic Outlook* (April): 53–55. Washington.

Irwin, Douglas. 2012. Gold Sterilization and the Recession of 1937–38. *Financial History Review* 19, no. 3: 249–67.

Irwin, Douglas. 2013. The Nixon Shock after Forty Years: The Import Surcharge Revisited. *World Trade Review* 12, no. 1: 29–56.

Johnson, Harry. 1973. The International Monetary Crisis of 1971. *Journal of Business* 46, no. 1: 11–23.

Kindleberger, Charles. 1973. *The World in Depression 1929–39*. Berkeley: University of California Press.

Lewis, W. Arthur. 1949. *Economic Survey 1919–1939*. London: Allen & Unwin.

Meltzer, Allan. 2003. *A History of the Federal Reserve, vol. 1: 1913–1951*. Chicago: University of Chicago Press.

Miller, Adolph. 1935. Responsibility for Federal Reserve Policies 1927-29. *American Economic Review* 25, no. 3: 442–57.

Moggridge, Donald. 1972. *British Monetary Policy 1924–1931: The Norman Conquest of $4.86*. Cambridge: Cambridge University Press.

Rauchway, Eric. 2015. *The Money Makers: How Roosevelt and Keynes Ended the Depression, Defeated Fascism, and Secured a Prosperous Peace*. New York: Basic Books.

Rothbard, Murray N. 1963 (2002). *America's Great Depression*, 5th ed. Auburn, AL: Ludwig von Mises Institute.

Sachs, Jeffrey. 1986. The Uneasy Case for Greater Exchange Rate Coordination. *American Economic Association Papers and Proceedings* 76, no. 2: 336–41.

Sauvy, Alfred. 1967. *Histoire économique de la France entre les deux guerres*. Paris: Economica.

Volcker, Paul. 1978–79. The Political Economy of the Dollar. *Quarterly Review* (Winter): 1–12. Federal Reserve Bank of New York.

Wigmore, Barrie. 1987. Was the Bank Holiday of 1933 Caused by a Run on the Dollar? *Journal of Economic History* 47, no. 3: 739–75.

III

IMPLICATIONS OF THE PLAZA

11

Foreign Exchange Intervention since the Plaza Accord
The Need for Global Currency Rules

JOSEPH E. GAGNON

The Plaza Accord of September 1985 marked the apogee of global coordinated efforts to manage exchange rates in the floating exchange rate era.[1] It involved much more than intervention in foreign exchange markets, but such intervention was a major element in the public's eye and is the focus of this chapter.

Many economists and officials were, and remain, skeptical that intervention can have significant sustained effects on exchange rates and current account balances. The evidence from the 1980s does not refute that skepticism. However, the experience of the past 15 years shows that intervention can have important sustained effects if it is large enough. A number of countries—most notably China—have used massive and sustained intervention to hold their currencies down (sometimes in conjunction with other policies) and maintain large current account surpluses for years at a time.

At the time of the Plaza Accord, the issue was what officials could or should do when they believed that private markets had mispriced foreign exchange rates. Although that potential problem remains, a new problem has arisen: What should officials in some countries do when officials in other countries cause substantial exchange rate misalignments and trade imbalances? A further complication is that the original parties to the Plaza Accord no longer dominate the global economy as they did in the 1980s; emerging

Joseph E. Gagnon is senior fellow at the Peterson Institute for International Economics. He thanks C. Fred Bergsten, Menzie Chinn, Bill Cline, Hali Edison, Josh Felman, Russell Green, Signe Krogstrup, Marc Noland, Brad Setser, and Ted Truman for helpful comments.

1. The floating rate era is generally accepted as beginning in 1973. However, some groups of countries maintained systems of more or less fixed exchange rates with one another after 1973. The most notable example is the exchange rate mechanism in the European Community (the European Union after 1992).

economies and developing countries are increasingly important. The new global steering group is the G-20, but it is in danger of becoming irrelevant because it is unwieldy and lethargic. Now more than ever, forceful global rules on currency management are needed.

Did the Plaza Work?

One can never be sure what would have happened without the Plaza. The dollar's rise in the first half of the 1980s created a then-record US trade deficit. By 1985 officials in the United States and many other countries agreed that the dollar was overvalued.

The dollar had declined somewhat from its peaks in February (the yen) and March (the deutsche mark) 1985, but it was still at a historically high level (figure 11.1).[2] The depreciation briefly accelerated after the Plaza and then persisted for many months.

The rise of US external liabilities associated with the trade deficit probably would have contributed to downward pressure on the dollar at some point. But the evidence suggests that the Plaza helped speed the process of adjustment in an orderly manner.

The success of the Plaza had little to do with actual intervention in foreign exchange markets: G-7 official flows out of dollars (negative values) were negligible in 1985 and quickly returned to inflows in 1986 (figure 11.2).[3, 4] To the extent that the Plaza succeeded in pushing the dollar down, it had more to do with the message that was sent to financial markets about policy intentions and the implied threat of further dollar sales.

Intervention was far more pronounced (in the opposite direction) after the Louvre Accord of February 1987, in which G-7 ministers and governors stated that dollar depreciation had gone far enough. Japan conducted about half of the dollar buying that year, in a desperate attempt to cap the yen's rise. The yen did stabilize in 1988 and even depreciated a bit in 1989 (see figure 11.1). It is difficult to infer from this one episode whether intervention made a difference. Many economists were (and still are) skeptical.

---

2. The dollar's strength against the yen at this time was less apparent than it was against the deutsche mark. Japan's rapid productivity growth and low inflation in the 1980s implied that the yen should have been appreciating steadily against the dollar since 1980.

3. Quarterly data on reserve stocks suggest that net dollar outflows were limited to the last two quarters of 1985 and the first quarter of 1986 (IMF *International Financial Statistics* database).

4. In this chapter I use the concept of financial flows as defined in the IMF's *Balance of Payments Statistics*. Financial flows include purchases or sales of and accrued earnings on assets in other countries. They do not include changes in the market values of assets. Flows out of dollars are defined as the sum of US flows into foreign assets and foreign flows out of US assets. The official sector refers to general governments and central banks. Some studies use data on official foreign exchange intervention, which refers to a subset of official purchases or sales of foreign assets with the specific intent of influencing the foreign exchange market.

Figure 11.1 Exchange rate of the US dollar against deutsche mark and yen, January 1982–December 1989

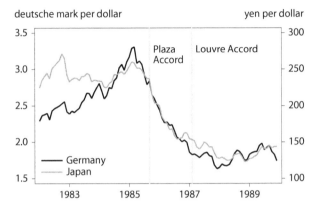

Source: IMF, *International Financial Statistics* database.

Figure 11.2 Official net dollar flows by G-7 countries, 1980–2014

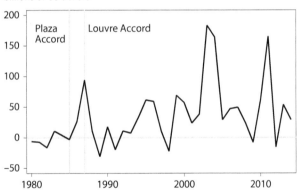

Note: G-7 net dollar flows are estimated as the sum of non-US G-7 foreign exchange reserve flows minus US reserve flows.

Source: IMF, *Balance of Payments Statistics* database.

In 1983 a report of a G-7 working group under the leadership of Philippe Jurgensen highlighted the limits of sterilized intervention.[5] According to the report, "intervention did not generally have a lasting effect"; using it to pursue exchange rate objectives that are inconsistent with economic fundamentals, including monetary and fiscal policies, "tended to be counterproductive" (Jurgensen 1983, 17).

The Jurgensen Report was at odds with the view that intervention could have an effect through lasting changes in investor portfolios. In the portfolio balance model, private investors must be offered a higher return (lower price) in order to buy more of a given asset—or conversely must be offered a lower return (higher price) in order to sell some of a given asset (Tobin 1969, Branson and Henderson 1985). When governments sell one currency in exchange for another, they alter the supplies of both currencies available to the public. According to the portfolio balance theory, such changes in relative supplies of two currencies should affect their relative price (that is, the exchange rate).

An opposing view gaining adherents at the time was that financial markets are (nearly) efficient. According to the efficient markets theory, investors do not care about the currency composition of their portfolios. In an efficient market, all that matters for exchange rates are the current and expected future interest rates on each currency as well as any other policies and factors, such as tariffs and inflation rates, that affect the long-run equilibrium exchange rate. An influential article (Meese and Rogoff 1983) published the same year as the Jurgensen Report demonstrated that predicting exchange rates was nearly impossible and that portfolio balance models in particular were not useful in explaining exchange rates. The Jurgensen Report and the Meese-Rogoff article provided considerable support to the efficient markets view.

The Plaza and Louvre sparked numerous studies of the effects of intervention. Edison (1993) surveyed the first round of studies and concluded that any effect of sterilized intervention was at most temporary. The scholarly debate then focused on the conditions under which intervention might have a significant temporary effect—by, for example, accelerating the reaction to a long-lasting change in monetary or fiscal policy through what became known as the signaling channel (Dominguez and Frankel 1993, Obstfeld 1995, Sarno and

---

5. Intervention is sterilized when it is not associated with a change in domestic interest rates, in particular the short-term interest rates closely associated with monetary policy. In this chapter, "intervention" refers to sterilized intervention. Unsterilized intervention is best described as a combination of intervention and monetary policy. In general, sterilization requires that the monetary authorities issue domestic bonds or sell domestic assets equal in value to the foreign exchange purchased. Unsterilized intervention implies a net increase in high-powered money and thus a reduction in the policy interest rate and a loosening of monetary conditions. It is widely agreed that monetary policy does have a lasting effect on the exchange rate. In practice, however, the vast majority of interventions are conducted without any change in monetary policy and are thus sterilized. In the context of a growing economy, intervention may be considered sterilized if the purchases of foreign exchange replace purchases of domestic assets that would have been necessary to keep the money supply on a steady growth path with stable interest rates.

Taylor 2001, Ito 2002, Dominguez 2003). Even the studies most supportive of intervention effectiveness were not able to show strong evidence of effects lasting beyond a few days or weeks.

By the turn of the millennium, skepticism about any independent long-term effect of foreign exchange intervention was widespread among academic economists. Truman (2003, 263) summarized the prevailing view in his comments on Dominguez (2003): "Intervention is not a separate instrument of policy that can be used regardless of the stance of other economic and financial policies; it is not effective in achieving discrete adjustments in exchange rates, moving them from one level to another and holding them there."

Intervention since the Plaza and Louvre

Coordinated intervention operations by the G-7 never returned to their intensity of 1987. The three highest points in figure 11.2 (2003, 2004, and 2011) primarily reflect unilateral dollar purchases by Japanese officials. Apparently, Japanese officials retained greater confidence in the effectiveness of intervention than the economics profession.

Figure 11.3 takes a broader perspective, displaying net official flows of nearly all countries into foreign currency assets.[6] These flows include purchases of and earnings on foreign exchange reserves and external sovereign wealth fund (SWF) assets minus official borrowing in foreign currency; reserves constitute by far the largest portion of these flows. Net official flows is the broadest measure of official intervention in foreign exchange (note that the scale in figure 11.3 is eight times larger than the scale in figure 11.2). It is the measure that the portfolio balance theory suggests is relevant for economic analysis, because it includes all government actions that affect the relative supplies of currencies. The burst of intervention with the Louvre Accord is not particularly noticeable compared with official flows after 2000.

These massive flows appear to be strongly correlated with the rise of imbalances in global trade since 2000.[7] Figure 11.4 displays aggregate data for countries with current account surpluses (the included countries change from year to year depending on whether they moved in or out of surplus).[8] Imbalances peaked in 2007 but remained at historically high levels during and after the global financial crisis of 2008, as countries resisted further current account adjustment.[9] This apparent relationship suggests that intervention may be

---

6. The primary missing countries are oil exporters with large unreported SWFs: Bahrain, Brunei, Oman, Qatar, and the United Arab Emirates. Taiwan is also missing.

7. The current account balance is the sum of the balances on trade, income, and unilateral transfers. It reflects the difference between what a country earns from abroad and what it pays to foreigners. In most countries, it is dominated by trade.

8. The imbalance is understated because of the lack of data for Bahrain, Brunei, Oman, Qatar, Taiwan, and the United Arab Emirates.

9. Incomplete data for 2014 and the first half of 2015 suggest that the aggregate current account

Figure 11.3 Global net official flows, 1980–2013

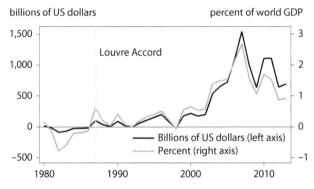

Note: Global net official flows are purchases of foreign currency reserves and other official foreign assets plus earnings on those assets minus official borrowing in foreign currency. Data exclude countries with unreported flows from sovereign wealth funds.

Source: Gagnon et al. (2015).

Figure 11.4 Aggregate net official flows and current account balance of all countries running surpluses, 1980–2013

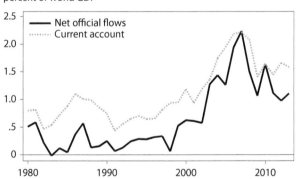

Note: See figure 11.3. Data are summed over all countries with a current account surplus in each year.

Source: Gagnon et al. (2015).

having an important sustained effect on exchange rates, which in turn affect current account balances. Perhaps the portfolio balance model is relevant after all—it just takes much larger movements in portfolios than observed in the 1980s and 1990s.

What countries are behind the rise and fall of net official flows since 2000? China is the single biggest contributor.[10] Also important are other Asian emerging economies, such as South Korea, Malaysia, the Philippines, and Singapore.[11] Oil exporters such as Kuwait, Norway, and Saudi Arabia loom large. Japan and Switzerland have made important contributions but with high volatility.

Effectiveness of Intervention Redux

Measuring the effect of intervention on the exchange rate is difficult because economists do not understand exchange rates well. An alternative approach is to look at the effect of intervention on the current account balance.

The Difficult Question of "What If Intervention Had Not Occurred?"

Figure 11.4 suggests that intervention can have a sustained and important effect, at least when conducted on a sustained and massive scale. But causality may run in both directions:

- A large intervention may hold down the exchange rate and create or sustain a current account surplus.
- An increase in the current account surplus may put upward pressure on the exchange rate, which a country may choose to resist by foreign exchange intervention.

The first possibility has causality running from intervention to the current account. The second has causality running from the current account to intervention. In the latter case, the question then becomes: What would happen if officials decided not to buy reserves? It is possible that the private sector would buy an equal volume of foreign assets (as implied by the efficient markets theory), but it is also possible that the exchange rate would appreciate and move the current account toward balance (as implied by the portfolio balance theory). To the extent that intervention reduces the appreciation that would otherwise occur, it is sustaining a current account surplus.

---

surplus has declined somewhat farther and the associated net official flows much farther since 2013. The Chinese current account surplus in particular has been increasingly supported by net private outflows.

10. Goldstein and Lardy (2009) provide a detailed account of how China's rapid economic development interacted with its exchange rate regime during the run-up of these large imbalances.

11. Subramanian and Kessler (2012) show that many Asian currencies increasingly move together with China's renminbi, perhaps reflecting a desire to remain competitive with China.

The difficulty of knowing what would have happened if a country had not intervened has been the bane of research in this area since the beginning. A key part of the problem is that exchange rates are highly volatile and nearly impossible to predict. Standard economic models suggest that changes in fundamentals often cause exchange rates to overshoot their long-run levels. Moreover, some of these fundamentals, such as expected long-run differences in price levels across countries or regulatory and institutional barriers to trade and financial flows, are difficult to measure. Exchange rates also respond to nonfundamental forces, such as financial market fads, manias, and noise trading, which are also difficult to measure

A recent paper (Adler, Lisack, and Mano 2015) finds an effect of intervention on the exchange rate that is roughly consistent with the findings I present here. According to its authors, an intervention of 1 percent of GDP that is sustained for several years will cause the exchange rate to depreciate by about 3 percent. To translate that result into an effect on the trade balance, I note that the median share of exports in GDP in the countries on which table 11.1 is based is about 40 percent. To be conservative, I focus on the share of exports that is not composed of imported parts and materials, about 70 percent, the median value for a group of advanced and emerging markets.[12] Together these data imply that domestic value added in exports has a median value of just over 25 percent of GDP. Applying a standard macro trade price elasticity of 1 to a depreciation of 3 percent at this median value implies that a sustained intervention of 1 percent of GDP increases the trade balance by 0.75 percent of GDP.

The Current Account as an Alternative Gauge

In ongoing research some colleagues and I have focused on the effects of net official flows (including intervention) on current account balances. We base our analysis on a framework that models current accounts across countries and over time in response to exogenous factors that affect desired saving and investment.

Economists have had more success in explaining current account balances than in explaining exchange rates. Current account surpluses in some countries must be associated with current account deficits in other countries because trade adds up around the world. In the absence of specific differences across countries in underlying saving and investment conditions, current account balances should be zero. Current accounts are flows, measured in the same dollars as net official flows, which makes the two concepts easier to relate to each other than to exchange rates, which are prices not flows. All of these considerations help to ease the "what if?" problem that bedevils work on the effectiveness of intervention.

---

12. Data on value added in trade are from the Organization for Economic Cooperation and Development (OECD)–World Trade Organization (WTO) Statistics on Trade in Value Added database.

A key step in addressing the "what if?" problem is to identify episodes in which a country chose to borrow or lend abroad for reasons not related to pressures on the exchange rate. In the jargon of statistics, we use "instrumental variables" for net official flows. We tried many different instruments and specifications. Table 11.1 presents results for a set of instruments that we like, but we obtained broadly similar results in a previous paper using two entirely different sets of instruments (Bayoumi, Gagnon, and Saborowski 2015). One principle we believe is useful is that official responses to exchange rate pressures are generally conducted using foreign exchange reserves as well as monetary and fiscal policy. Borrowing for development projects and flows out of SWFs proceed out of longer-term motivations; these flows are thus good instruments for net official flows.

We find that restrictions on cross-border financial flows have a powerful influence on the way the current account responds to economic factors. In the extreme case of no private capital mobility, only the government can lend or borrow abroad and the current account must equal net official flows. In this case other factors have no effect on the current account. The exchange rate moves to keep the demand for (supply of) foreign currency from net official flows equal to the supply of (demand for) foreign currency from the current account balance.[13] As channels for private capital flow open up, other factors may affect the current account and the tight link between net official flows and the current account is loosened. However, if private investors care about the currency composition of their portfolios, net official flows will affect the exchange rate, and thus the current account, even in the absence of capital flow restrictions. Our measure of capital mobility is the Aizenman-Chinn-Ito (2015) inverse index of legal barriers to capital flows, which ranges from 0 (substantial restrictions on all categories of capital flows) to 1 (no legal barriers to capital flows).[14]

Statistical Results

Table 11.1 presents averages of coefficients from instrumental variables regressions of equations 2.1 and 2.2 in Gagnon et al. (2015).[15] The current account is regressed on the variables listed on the left as well as the products of each

---

13. To some extent the government itself may create the link between official flows and the current account. It may, for example, borrow and use the proceeds to purchase machinery and equipment for a development project. In such a case the exchange rate would not need to move at all.

14. The median value in the estimation sample is 0.45. About 5 percent of observations take the value of 0, and 25 percent take the value of 1. A value of 0 does not imply the complete absence of private capital flows, and a value of 1 may still be consistent with implicit costs and barriers to capital flow.

15. The dependent variable in equation 2.1 is the current account. The dependent variable in equation 2.2 is net private flows. Net investment income is subtracted from both dependent variables. For equation 2.2 the reported coefficient on net official flows is 1 plus the estimated coefficient, based on the accounting identity that the current account equals net private flows plus net official flows.

Table 11.1 What moves the current account balance?

Dependent variable: (Current account – net investment income)/trend GDP

Variable	Capital mobility = 0	Capital mobility = 1
Inverse index of legal restrictions on capital mobility [0 – 1]	–0.01	0.05**
Share of private financial in total cross-border transactions [0 – 1]	0.01	–0.11**
Per capita GDP relative to United States	0.03	–0.02*
Projected population aging	2.79	1.51
Lagged five-year growth rate	0.04	–0.61**
Net energy exports/trend GDP	0.27**	–0.01
Fiscal balance/trend GDP	0.17**	0.54**
Net official flows/trend GDP	0.72**	0.31**
Lagged net official assets/trend GDP	–0.01	0.03**
R^2		0.49
Observations		2,053

* Statistically significant at the 5 percent level; ** statistically significant at the 1 percent level.

Note: Instrumental variables for net official flows are the nonreserves portion of net official flows and a dummy variable for external crisis in the previous three years (Laeven and Valencia 2012). Sample includes 141 countries over 1985–2014. Many countries are missing data for some years.

Source: Data from Gagnon et al. (2015).

of those variables and the index of capital mobility. The first column displays the coefficients on the listed variables; the second column displays the sums of the coefficients in the first column and the coefficients on the listed variables times capital mobility. The numbers in the first column thus reflect the effects of the listed variables when the capital mobility measure is 0. The numbers in the second column reflect the effects of the listed variables when the mobility measure is 1. For countries and years with mobility measures between 0 and 1, the implied effects lie between those of column 1 and column 2. All regressions include a full set of year effects.

The first two explanatory variables in table 11.1 are measures of capital mobility and financial market depth and integration with the rest of the world. The expected signs of the coefficients of these variables are theoretically ambiguous. Demographic and other structural factors determine whether a country is a net borrower or lender in global markets. Openness, depth, and integration of capital markets merely facilitate a country's ability to borrow or lend.

The first coefficient in the first column implies that in countries with the tightest restrictions on capital flows, increasing capital mobility has a tiny and statistically insignificant negative effect on the current account. At some point, however, the effect of removing capital flow restrictions turns positive; by the time all restrictions are removed, it has a significant effect. The coefficient of 0.05 under high capital mobility implies that, other things equal, a country with completely open capital markets will have a current account surplus of 5 percent of GDP.

The second variable is based on the depth of a country's financial market integration with the rest of the world. It is defined as the share of private financial transactions in total cross-border transactions (including exports and imports). It is another measure of the ease of borrowing and lending across a country's borders. Because it is constructed as a share, it is bounded by 0 and 1.[16] Increasing financial integration is associated with a statistically significant decrease in the current account for high-mobility countries.

The third variable is per capita GDP relative to the United States. This variable has a very small negative effect on the current account under high mobility.

The fourth variable is the projected change in the ratio of the population over the age of 64, which has an economically important but statistically insignificant positive effect on the current account. This effect presumably reflects saving for retirement.

The fifth variable is the lagged five-year economic growth rate, which is meant to proxy for trend growth potential. Fast-growing countries are expected to borrow more because they have more investment opportunities and thus a smaller current account balance. Our regressions confirm this expectation, especially when capital markets are more open for external borrowing: Under high mobility a 1 percentage point increase in trend growth reduces the current account by 0.6 percent of GDP.

The sixth variable is net energy exports, which have a moderate positive effect under low mobility and no effect under high mobility. Under low capital mobility, a $1 increase in net energy exports increases the current account $0.27.

The seventh variable is the fiscal balance. A higher fiscal balance (smaller government budget deficit) is associated with a higher current account balance. As expected this effect is larger when capital markets are more open. Under high mobility a $1 increase in the fiscal balance increases the current account by $0.54.[17]

The eighth variable is net official flows (including foreign exchange intervention). For each $1 of net official flows, the current account increases $0.72 under low mobility and $0.31 under high mobility.

The ninth variable reflects a persistent effect of past official flows, such that for each $1 of the net stock of official foreign assets (including foreign exchange reserves) the previous year, the current account is little affected under low mobility and increases $0.03 under high mobility. Because the lagged stock

---

16. The median value in the estimation sample is 0.10; 95 percent of observations take values less than 0.27.

17. This result rejects the proposition of Ricardo neutrality, which argues that private saving behavior fully offsets any saving or borrowing by governments.

of net assets is often many times greater than the net flows in a given year, this stock effect is important when mobility is high.

The coefficient on lagged net assets arises purely from the portfolio balance, which relates to the stocks of assets people own. The government's amassment of a large stock of foreign exchange (paid for with domestic currency) puts upward pressure on the value of foreign currency and downward pressure on the value of domestic currency. As long as the government retains the foreign-currency assets, private portfolios have less exposure to foreign currencies than they otherwise would. This ongoing scarcity of foreign currencies keeps their value high. Without private capital mobility, the portfolio balance effect cannot operate, which explains why the coefficient on the net asset stock increases with capital mobility.

The coefficient on the net official flow combines a portfolio balance component (this year's stock equals last year's stock plus this year's flow) with a direct effect that arises from imperfect capital mobility. As expected, when the mobility of private capital is very low, the coefficient on net official flows is close to 1. As private capital mobility increases, this coefficient decreases, as shown in table 11.1.

An issue that is not directly addressed in the regression results displayed in table 11.1 is that of dynamic adjustment or lags. The effect of intervention on the exchange rate is expected to be very rapid. In contrast, the effect of the exchange rate on trade and the current account is generally believed to take place over a period of about two years. Some of the effect of intervention ought to show up the same year as the intervention, but some ought to occur the following year, and a small amount might even linger into a third year. The residuals of the regression in table 11.1 suggest that such dynamics may be important, but it has not been possible to model them, because they appear to differ across countries and across independent variables.[18] The coefficients are best interpreted as capturing the long-run effect of intervention and other factors, not the immediate effect.

Overall, the results in table 11.1 suggest that intervention in foreign exchange markets—broadly defined as net official flows, both current and lagged—has very large effects on the current account balance but that it is hardly the only factor at work.[19]

---

18. First-order autocorrelation of the residuals in table 11.1 is about 0.7.

19. Recent research also shows that portfolio balance effects are at work in government transactions with domestic assets, in particular the new monetary tool commonly known as quantitative easing (QE). Numerous studies find that large-scale purchases of long-term bonds significantly increase the prices of (reduce yields on) bonds purchased and bonds with similar characteristics (Gagnon and Hinterschweiger 2013).

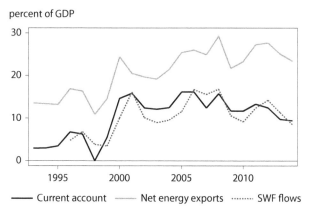

Figure 11.5 Norway's current account, net energy exports, and sovereign wealth fund (SWF) flows, 1993–2014

percent of GDP

—— Current account   — — Net energy exports   ······· SWF flows

Sources: IMF, *International Financial Statistics*; Norwegian Ministry of Finance; World Bank, *World Development Indicators*.

Case Studies

As an alternative to the dry statistics in table 11.1, it may be useful to examine historical examples of movements in net official flows and their effect on current account balances. These case studies allow the issue of causality to be studied in greater depth, providing a useful reality check on the instruments used in the statistical analysis. They help reveal how convincing the answer to the question "what if foreign exchange intervention had not occurred?" is.

The examples are not intended to be typical: I cherry-picked examples of large movements in net official flows that were associated with large movements in current account balances. The purpose is not to deny that other factors can be important and can sometimes mask the correlation between net official flows and current accounts but rather to show that in important cases when the two variables move together, the underlying motivation for the net official flows was not to stabilize the exchange rate in response to the current account. This evidence provides extra assurance that foreign exchange intervention really is having an important effect on the current account.

Sovereign Wealth Funds: Norway

Figure 11.5 displays data for Norway after it switched to a floating exchange rate in 1992. The country is a major oil exporter. In 1996, to save for future generations, the government began to set aside a portion of the revenues from oil exports in an SWF. The dark line in figure 11.5 is the current account balance; the dotted line is SWF flows into foreign assets, which are equivalent to foreign exchange intervention; and the light grey line is net energy exports. All are expressed as percent of Norwegian GDP.

The close relationship between SWF flows and the current account is striking (figure 11.5). Revenues minus expenses in the oil sector plus returns on the assets of the SWF drive flows into Norway's sovereign wealth fund. Global oil prices and long-term production plans that are essentially exogenous to the Norwegian economy drive oil revenues. Returns on the SWF assets are also exogenous to Norway. The government has taken the conservative philosophy of drawing down only about 4 percent of the value of SWF assets a year for current budgetary needs.[20]

The key point for the analysis here is that the exchange rate plays essentially no role in the setting of SWF flows. Indeed, since Norway moved to a floating exchange rate in 1992, flows into and out of foreign exchange reserves have been small. As Norway has no external official debt, SWF flows dominate net official flows.

Some observers would argue that Norway's current account surplus mainly reflects the fact that it is a net oil exporter and not that it has large net official flows. The results in table 11.1 show that energy exports have essentially no long-term effect on the current account balance of a country with high capital mobility, as Norway does. Moreover, many current and former net oil exporters—including other medium-size advanced economies, such as Australia and Canada—have run current account deficits;[21] the world's largest oil exporter, Saudi Arabia, had a current account deficit for most of the 1980s and 1990s. Although oil exports have little long-term effect on the current account, there is a significant temporary effect, which means that increases in oil revenues boost the current account and SWF flows at the same time. This temporary effect of changes in net oil revenues explains the apparent lack of any lag in the connection between SWF flows and the current account in figure 11.5.

Norway's SWF flows correspond closely to its overall fiscal balance. Based on data from Norway alone, one would not be able to determine whether the current account surplus arises from SWF flows or the fiscal surplus. However, data for other countries show that fiscal surpluses often do not lead to current account surpluses in the absence of net official flows. Australia is a case in point. Its fiscal balance moved into sustained surplus after 1997, yet its current account balance became even more negative. Other factors are surely responsible for Australia's current account deficit, but it seems unlikely that Norway's current account surplus would remain as large as it is if a substantial portion of the fiscal surplus were invested at home. The results of table 11.1 suggest that both the fiscal surplus and foreign exchange intervention (in the form of SWF flows) play roles in sustaining Norway's large current account surplus.[22]

---

20. There is some allowance for countercyclical fiscal policy, but these changes are small relative to the changes induced by oil prices.

21. In 2014 Australia had a net energy balance of 11 percent of GDP and a current account balance of –3 percent of GDP. The analogous figures for Canada were 8 percent and –2 percent.

22. These results are strong evidence against Ricardo neutrality in Norway. If Norwegian households had reduced their saving by an amount equal to the increase in public saving after 1996,

Figure 11.6   Morocco's current account, official external borrowing, and net official flows, 1975–89

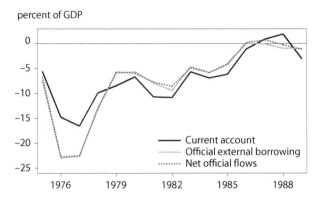

percent of GDP

Sources: IMF, *International Financial Statistics* database and yearbooks.

External Borrowing for Development: Morocco

Morocco is a medium-size rapidly growing middle-income economy. Its history is not particularly unusual. In the late 1970s the Moroccan government launched a large-scale public sector investment boom to help boost economic development. The borrowing binge continued into the early 1980s. Although the investments were not entirely wasted, they did not yield returns as high as expected, and the government had difficulty repaying its loans.

Under the tutelage of the International Monetary Fund (IMF) and the World Bank, the Moroccan government was weaned off foreign borrowing, had its debts restructured through Brady bonds, and adopted a private sector export-oriented development strategy (Friedman and Sharkey 2010). Secretary Baker started the consultative process that eventually produced Brady bonds through his 1985 Baker Plan.

Net official flows during this episode were composed almost entirely of official external borrowing (figure 11.6). Morocco bought and sold very few foreign exchange reserves at this time, but, from the viewpoint of the portfolio balance model, official borrowing in a foreign currency has effects comparable to those of negative foreign exchange intervention. According to the IMF, Morocco allowed a considerable degree of exchange rate flexibility throughout the 1980s before moving to a more tightly managed exchange rate in 1990.[23]

Norway's current account (which reflects the difference between saving and investment in Norway) would not have risen.

23. The IMF's coarse scale of exchange rate regimes (1= tight peg, 4 = freely floating) rates Morocco as a 3 for most of the 1970s and 1980s, switching to a 1 starting in 1990. Purchases of foreign exchange reserves jumped significantly with the start of the peg (see www.carmenreinhart.com/data/browse-by-topic/topics/11/ [accessed on August 20, 2015]).

As the country increased its official external borrowing, the current account moved into deep deficit.[24] As it gradually eliminated external borrowing, both net official flows and the current account returned to zero. The effect of net official flows on the current account in Morocco is very clear.

Political Pressures on Intervention Policy: South Korea

South Korea was hit hard by the Asian financial crisis of 1997–98. A sharp economic downturn and the sudden cessation of foreign capital inflows quickly turned the Korean current account deficit into a surplus by 1999. The government decided to rebuild and then greatly increase its stock of foreign exchange reserves as a war chest against future turbulence. The current account surplus was 2 percent of GDP in 2000, and net official flows, mainly reserve accumulation, totaled more than 4 percent of GDP (figure 11.7). The Korean currency (the won) bottomed out against the US dollar in 2001 and rose modestly in 2002. The Korean government gradually reduced the pace of reserve accumulation and the current account surplus remained around 1 percent of GDP in 2001 and 2002.

In 2003 Korea experienced strong demand for its exports as well as an increase in net private capital inflows. These factors put unwelcome upward pressure on the won at a time when a credit card crisis weakened domestic spending. The Korean government resisted these upward pressures by stepping up intervention markedly. Both exports and intervention continued to boom in 2004, and the government allowed only a relatively modest amount of exchange rate appreciation. The record-setting purchase of reserves in 2004 (6 percent of GDP) attracted a great deal of negative publicity amid reports that the government was losing money on the reserves as the dollar fell against the won.[25] Opposition politicians criticized the losses on reserves and questioned whether the level of reserves was excessive (Noland 2007, Kim 2011).

At least partly in response to this political pressure, the Korean government reduced intervention purchases sharply in 2005, allowing the won to appreciate more quickly.[26] Intervention declined further in 2006 and 2007, as the won continued to appreciate. Figure 11.7 clearly shows that this politically driven decision to change intervention policy had a pronounced effect on the current account balance. Declining intervention led quickly to a declining current account.

---

24. As Morocco had the lowest possible measure of capital mobility (0) from 1975 through 1985, direct government actions probably played an important role in current account outcomes. To the extent that the government and public sector corporations used the proceeds of the foreign loans directly to import machinery and supplies, the exchange rate may not have needed to move by much and the lags would have been short.

25. In 2005 the government began to report information on its derivatives position in foreign exchange, which revealed a substantial loss from won appreciation.

26. In 2005 Korea established an SWF (the Korea Investment Corporation) to earn better returns on a portion of the accumulated foreign assets.

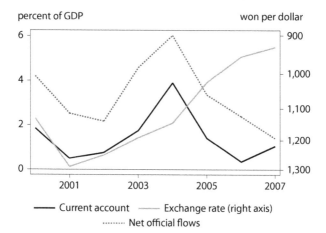

Figure 11.7 Korea's current account, exchange rate, and net official flows, 2000–07

percent of GDP   won per dollar

Legend:
—— Current account   —— Exchange rate (right axis)
········· Net official flows

Sources: IMF, *Balance of Payments Statistics* and *International Financial Statistics* databases.

The Korean experience suggests strongly that even when intervention is an endogenous response to exchange rate pressures, the answer to the "what if?" question is clear:[27] If a country chooses not to intervene, its current account will be lower than if it does intervene.

Contributions to Recent Current Account Imbalances

Table 11.2 lists the countries with the eight largest current account surpluses (excluding net investment income) in 2013 among countries that also report net official flows.[28] Despite a decline in the price of its oil exports, Russia's surplus grew as its economy slowed. Surpluses also appear to be increasing in China, Korea, and Singapore. In contrast, slow growth in the euro area and a strong currency are putting downward pressure on Switzerland's surplus. Limited data suggest that net official flows dropped sharply in 2014 and 2015 in most of these countries, reflecting both a reduction in oil revenues to be invested through SWFs and net outflows of private capital in China and

---

27. After the global financial crisis of 2008–09, in which it drew down a modest portion of its reserves, Korea decided to resume large-scale purchases of foreign exchange reserves. Its current account surplus has increased dramatically.

28. Net investment income is excluded, because the regressions in table 11.1 are based on current accounts minus net investment income. Missing data do not permit a full accounting of imbalances in 2014. Declines in oil prices led to smaller surpluses in Kuwait, Norway, and Saudi Arabia in 2014, with further declines likely in 2015. Current account estimates and projections for 2014 and 2015 are from the IMF's *World Economic Outlook* database.

Table 11.2 Contributions to global current account imbalances, 2013
(billions of US dollars)

Country	2013 current account (excluding investment income)	Model-fitted current account	Contribution of net official flows	Contribution of net official stock	Capital mobility measure
China	243	267	306	−5	0.16
Russia	101	54	−12	8	0.65
Saudi Arabia	121	97	31	13	0.70
Kuwait	58	67	27	7	0.70
South Korea	72	38	20	8	0.71
Norway	52	71	20	21	1.00
Singapore	54	38	3	21	1.00
Switzerland	35	28	5	15	1.00
Total	736	660	400	88	

Source: Table 11.1 and author's calculations.

Russia that put downward pressure on their exchange rates. It appears that, to the extent that they persisted, global imbalances in 2015 were being driven mainly by market forces rather than government intervention.

Of the countries included in table 11.2, China had the least open financial markets and the largest current account surplus ($243 billion). The fitted value of the statistical model shown in table 11.1 calls for a Chinese surplus of $267 billion, slightly more than the actual surplus but reasonably close considering that the model explains only about half the variation in current account balances. According to the model, the Chinese surplus derives entirely from Chinese net official flows, which, in turn, are composed almost entirely of foreign exchange intervention. Factors operating in the opposite direction include China's rapid trend growth and its negative net energy exports (not shown in table 11.2).

For the four major oil exporters in the sample, the model explains only about half of Russia's surplus; it does considerably better for Saudi Arabia, Kuwait, and Norway. Russia was a net seller of foreign exchange reserves in 2013. The main factors in the model that support Russia's surplus are an aging population and large net energy exports. A factor that is not in the model of table 11.1 is pessimism among investors about Russia's economic prospects in the context of Western sanctions over Ukraine. This pessimism (both inside and outside Russia) drove private financial flows out of Russia, weakening the ruble and supporting a large current account surplus. Official flows and stocks explain $44 billion of Saudi Arabia's $121 billion surplus, $34 billion of Kuwait's $58 billion surplus, and $41 billion of Norway's $52 billion surplus. Other factors contributing to surpluses in these countries include positive net energy exports and fiscal balances (not shown).

For Korea, Singapore, and Switzerland, net official flows and stocks explain 40–50 percent of the current account surpluses. Aging populations and fiscal balances explain another 25 percent in Singapore, 35 percent in Switzerland, and 50 percent in Korea of the surpluses. In Korea and Singapore, negative net energy exports and relatively rapid growth rates work in the opposite direction to reduce surpluses.

Taken together official flows and stocks explain $488 billion of the $736 billion in surpluses of these eight countries in 2013.

Policy Implications

The primary objective of this chapter is to demonstrate that foreign exchange intervention, and official financial flows more broadly, have important and lasting effects on the world economy. Indeed, net official flows are the single biggest factor behind global current account imbalances between 2000 and 2013, especially when account is taken of the lagged effect of these flows.

Official flows are not the only source of current account imbalances: Imbalances driven by market forces and economic policies other than net official flows have sometimes reached unhealthy levels. The Plaza Accord occurred at one of those times. In 2015 market forces again appeared to be driving imbalances. The evidence presented in this chapter demonstrates that foreign exchange intervention can be a useful tool to counter market-driven imbalances.

Not all current account surpluses and deficits are undesirable. Current account imbalances may reflect economic fundamentals, both cyclical and secular. Countries experiencing temporarily strong domestic demand tend to have deficits, and countries in recession tend to have surpluses. Fast-growing developing economies with relatively youthful populations should have persistent modest deficits as they borrow to finance productive capital. Conversely, slow-growing advanced economies with rapidly aging populations should have persistent modest surpluses as they save for retirement.[29] But experience shows that large imbalances often lead to financial crises, so that imbalances should normally be limited to less than 3 percent of GDP, especially for the largest economies.[30] The main exception to this rule concerns countries in which exports of nonrenewable natural resources constitute a large share of GDP. There is a strong case for saving a significant fraction of net revenues from resource extraction. When the domestic economy is small in relation to resource exports, much of these savings must flow abroad. The appropriate degree of net foreign saving will vary across resource-exporting countries, but

---

29. As an aging advanced economy, the United States should be running a current account surplus, albeit a smaller one than Japan or Europe, which are growing more slowly and aging more rapidly. The persistence of the US deficit provides further evidence of the lasting harm caused by excessive currency intervention in many countries.

30. In their widely cited work on fundamental equilibrium exchange rates, Cline and Williamson (2011) define sustainable current account balances as lying between –3 percent and +3 percent of GDP. They cite several studies that support a range of this magnitude.

in all cases it should be considerably less than 100 percent of resource revenues net of production costs. A number of oil-exporting countries had net official flows close to net resource revenues in recent years, suggestive of excessive net foreign saving. Surpluses of commodity exporters diminished sharply in 2014 and 2015.

Long after their peak in 2007, official flows and current account imbalances remained substantial by historical standards. Net official flows appear to be down sharply in 2015, but the reasons behind the decline may not be long-lived. Officials everywhere can now see that several Asian economies, a few oil-exporting countries, and Switzerland managed to sustain large current account surpluses through massive foreign exchange intervention or SWF outflows. They will be tempted to use this policy instrument to deliver growth through exports in the next economic slowdown. Even if China, Japan, and other large countries restrain themselves, as they have pledged in the G-20, many smaller economies may not.[31] Indeed, as recently as 2014, Korea had net official flows of nearly 4 percent of GDP and a current account surplus of more than 6 percent of GDP, figures that seem inconsistent with its G-20 commitments. The risk of a real currency war at some future date, with beggar-thy-neighbor policies on a large scale, is serious.

Some observers have mistakenly argued that loose monetary policy in the major advanced economies constitutes a currency war aimed at emerging markets. However, monetary policy and foreign exchange intervention are very different, in both design and effect. Monetary policy is conducted in domestic markets with domestic financial instruments. It is designed to increase spending at home. A side effect is to weaken the exchange rate, which dampens imports, but the increased domestic spending counteracts the exchange rate effect on imports and there are positive financial market spillovers. A series of reports by the IMF shows that the net effects of monetary easing in the advanced economies on emerging markets are rather small and generally positive (e.g., IMF 2015). In contrast, the purpose of foreign exchange intervention is to shift spending away from foreign competitors toward domestic producers; it has no other effects and is thus a pure beggar-thy-neighbor policy.

Because it involves the purchase of assets in foreign countries, there is a strong presumption that intervention policy should be subject to international rules. A minimum standard for rules on foreign exchange intervention would be to prevent destabilizing behavior. For example, countries with more than adequate stocks of reserves should not be allowed to buy additional reserves

---

31. At the St. Petersburg summit of September 2013, G-20 leaders declared: "We reiterate our commitments to move more rapidly toward more market-determined exchange rate systems and exchange rate flexibility to reflect underlying fundamentals, and avoid persistent exchange rate misalignments. We will refrain from competitive devaluation and will not target our exchange rates for competitive purposes." Similar statements have been made since Seoul in 2010; G-20 finance ministers reiterated this pledge in Ankara in September 2015. G-20 materials are available at https://g20.org/.

when they have a sustained current account surplus.[32] A country in such a position that has a fixed exchange rate should be required to use monetary policy to stabilize its exchange rate or revalue or float. The rule should be symmetric, in that countries with less than adequate reserves should not be allowed to sell reserves if they have a sustained current account deficit.[33]

A stronger standard would encourage proactive stabilizing behavior. Countries would agree on reference ranges for currencies designed to keep current account balances close to zero (Williamson 2007). Given the uncertainty and likely disagreement on equilibrium currency values, the reference ranges would need to be fairly wide (bands of at least 10 and probably 20 percent). When exchange rates move outside these ranges, countries would be encouraged to intervene in a stabilizing direction to encourage a return to rates within the bands. Countries would retain independent monetary and fiscal policies aimed at full employment and low inflation. Reference ranges are fully consistent with floating exchange rates, as there would be no specific target for the exchange rate or even any commitment to keep it within the range.[34] All that would be implied would be a modicum of intervention when the exchange rate fell outside a reasonable range. Occasional intervention to push exchange rates toward their equilibrium values is pretty much what the Plaza and Louvre were all about.

Conclusion

At the time of the Plaza Accord there was widespread skepticism that foreign exchange intervention was a potent tool for managing exchange rates and current account imbalances. We now know that intervention is effective—it just takes far larger magnitudes of intervention than anyone (except the Japanese) was willing to contemplate in the 1980s. Massive purchases of foreign assets by governments have been a key driver of the unprecedented current account imbalances since 2000.

---

32. Exporters of nonrenewable resources would be allowed to purchase foreign assets while running current account surpluses within agreed limits. Switzerland poses an interesting question, as it faces deflationary pressure while its short-term policy interest rate is at the zero lower bound. Svensson (2003) proposes using the exchange rate (supported by intervention) as part of a strategy for monetary easing at the zero bound. He ignores the spillover effects of his strategy on other countries. For a discussion of unconventional policy options in Switzerland, see Gagnon (2014).

33. A minimum standard along these lines would seem to follow from the IMF Articles of Agreement, which state that "members shall... avoid manipulating exchange rates or the international monetary system in order to prevent effective balance of payments adjustment or to gain an unfair competitive advantage over other members" (Article IV, Section 1). However, the IMF lacks appropriate sanctions to enforce this stricture. Even getting the IMF Executive Board to publicly identify members in violation of Article IV has proved impossible in recent years (Blustein 2013).

34. Bergsten and Williamson (1983) originated the idea of target zones for the major exchange rates. It is a stronger version of reference ranges, in that it implies some commitment to maintaining exchange rates within the zones.

Net official flows (including intervention) appear to be down sharply this year, as low commodity prices reduce outflows from SWFs and a wave of pessimism has sparked private outflows from Brazil, China, and other emerging markets. This situation is not likely to persist indefinitely, but it may present a useful opportunity, as countries are more likely to agree to forceful rules at a time when the rules would not impinge on their behavior. Countries that would benefit from forceful rules, primarily the United States, should press hard for their adoption.

The case for new and forceful rules to limit official flows is persuasive. They are needed not only to help counter market excesses but also to prevent a devastating round of beggar-thy-neighbor devaluations in the next global recession. This is no time for complacency.

References

Adler, Gustavo, Noemie Lisack, and Rui Mano. 2015. *Unveiling the Effects of Foreign Exchange Intervention: A Panel Approach.* IMF Working Paper WP/15/130. Washington: International Monetary Fund.

Aizenman, Joshua, Menzie Chinn, and Hiro Ito. 2015. The Trilemma Indexes. Available at http://web.pdx.edu/~ito/trilemma_indexes.htm (accessed on August 17, 2015).

Bayoumi, Tamim, Joseph Gagnon, and Christian Saborowski. 2015. Official Financial Flows, Capital Mobility, and Global Imbalances. *Journal of International Money and Finance* 52 (April): 146-74.

Bergsten, C. Fred, and John Williamson. 1983. Exchange Rates and Trade Policy. In *Trade Policy in the 1980s,* ed. William Cline. Washington: Institute for International Economics.

Blustein, Paul. 2013. *Off Balance: The Travails of Institutions that Govern the Global Financial System.* Waterloo, Ontario: Centre for International Governance Innovation.

Branson, William, and Dale Henderson. 1985. The Specification and Influence of Asset Markets. In *Handbook of International Economics*, vol. 2, ed. Ronald Jones and Peter Kenen. Amsterdam: Elsevier.

Cline, William, and John Williamson. 2011. *Estimates of Fundamental Equilibrium Exchange Rates, May 2011.* PIIE Policy Brief 11-5. Washington: Peterson Institute for International Economics.

Dominguez, Kathryn. 2003. Foreign Exchange Intervention: Did It Work in the 1990s? In *Dollar Overvaluation and the World Economy,* ed. C. Fred Bergsten and John Williamson. Washington: Institute for International Economics.

Dominguez, Kathryn, and Jeffrey Frankel. 1993. *Does Foreign Exchange Market Intervention Work?* Washington: Institute for International Economics.

Edison, Hali. 1993. The Effectiveness of Central Bank Intervention: A Survey of the Literature after 1982. *Special Papers in International Economics* 18. Princeton, NJ: Department of Economics, Princeton University.

Friedman, Steven, and Heather Sharkey. 2010. A Tale of Two Economic Developments: Tunisia and Morocco. *College Undergraduate Research Electronic Journal.* University of Pennsylvania Scholarly Commons.

Gagnon, Joseph. 2014. *Alternatives to Currency Manipulation: What Switzerland, Singapore, and Hong Kong Can Do.* PIIE Policy Brief 14-17. Washington: Peterson Institute for International Economics.

Gagnon, Joseph, and Marc Hinterschweiger. 2013. Responses of Central Banks in Advanced Economies to the Global Financial Crisis. In *Responding to Financial Crisis: Lessons from Asia Then, the United States and Europe Now*, eds. Changyong Rhee and Adam Posen. Washington: Peterson Institute for International Economics.

Gagnon, Joseph, Tamim Bayoumi, Juan-Miguel Londoño, Christian Saborowski, and Horacio Sapriza. 2015. Direct and Spillover Effects of Unconventional Monetary and Exchange Rate Policies. Paper presented at the 16th Jacques Polak Annual Research Conference, International Monetary Fund, Washington, November 5-6.

Goldstein, Morris, and Nicholas Lardy. 2009. The Future of China's Exchange Rate Policy. *Policy Analyses in International Economics* 87. Washington: Peterson Institute for International Economics.

IMF (International Monetary Fund). 2015. *2015 Spillover Report* (July 23). Washington.

Ito, Takatoshi. 2002. *Is Foreign Exchange Intervention Effective? The Japanese Experiences in the 1990s.* NBER Working Paper 8914. Cambridge, MA: National Bureau of Economic Research.

Jurgensen, Philippe. 1983. *Report of the Working Group on Exchange Market Intervention.* Washington: US Department of Treasury.

Kim, Woochan. 2011. *Korea Investment Corporation: Its Origin and Evolution.* Munich Personal RePEc Archive. Available at https://mpra.ub.uni-muenchen.de/44028/.

Laeven, Luc, and Fabián Valencia. 2012. *Systemic Banking Crises Database: An Update.* IMF Working Paper WP/12/163. Washington: International Monetary Fund.

Meese, Richard, and Kenneth Rogoff. 1983. Empirical Exchange Rate Models of the Seventies: Do They Fit Out of Sample? *Journal of International Economics* 14, no. 1-2: 3-24.

Noland, Marcus. 2007. South Korea's Experience with International Capital Flows. In *Capital Controls and Capital Flows in Emerging Economies*, ed. Sebastian Edwards. Chicago: University of Chicago Press.

Obstfeld, Maurice. 1995. International Currency Experience: New Lessons and Lessons Relearned. *Brookings Papers on Economic Activity* 1: 119-200.

Sarno, Lucio, and Mark Taylor. 2001. Official Intervention in the Foreign Exchange Market: Is It Effective and, If So, How Does It Work? *Journal of Economic Literature* 39 (September): 839-68.

Subramanian, Arvind, and Martin Kessler. 2012. *The Renminbi Bloc Is Here: Asia Down, Rest of the World to Go?* PIIE Working Paper WP 12-19. Washington: Peterson Institute for International Economics.

Svensson, Lars. 2003. *Escaping from a Liquidity Trap and Deflation: The Foolproof Way and Others.* NBER Working Paper 10195. Cambridge, MA: National Bureau of Economic Research.

Tobin, James. 1969. A General Equilibrium Approach to Monetary Theory. *Journal of Money, Credit, and Banking* 1, no. 1: 15-29.

Truman, Edwin. 2003. The Limits of Exchange Market Intervention. In *Dollar Overvaluation and the World Economy*, ed. C. Fred Bergsten and John Williamson. Washington: Institute for International Economics.

Williamson, John. 2007. *Reference Rates and the International Monetary System.* Policy Analyses in International Economics 82. Washington: Peterson Institute for International Economics.

12

A Rules-Based Cooperatively Managed International Monetary System for the Future

JOHN B. TAYLOR

For nearly two decades following the Plaza Accord of 1985 economic performance and stability improved in major parts of the world—a period known as the Great Moderation or simply NICE (for noninflationary consistently expansionary)—as monetary policy tended to be more focused and rules based. In contrast, during much of the past decade, monetary policy deviated from a rules-based approach and economic performance and stability deteriorated, remaining poor today. As Paul Volcker put it, "The absence of an official, rules-based, cooperatively managed monetary system has not been a great success."[1]

This chapter draws on lessons from the Plaza Accord and the three decades of economic policy and performance that followed to propose a new approach to international monetary policy. The experience of the past 30 years and basic economic reasoning suggest that a rules-based reform in each country will deliver performance akin to a rules-based international monetary system and "can better reconcile reasonably free and open markets with independent national policies [and] stability," the sensible goal called for by Volcker.[2]

I start with a review of key lessons from the Plaza Accord that are most relevant for the future of the international monetary system. Next I review the economic principles that indicate that such a rules-based policy will lead to

John B. Taylor is the Mary and Robert Raymond Professor of Economics at Stanford University, the George P. Shultz Senior Fellow in Economics at the Hoover Institution, and the former undersecretary of Treasury for international affairs (2001–05). He is grateful to David Mauler, David Papell, and Makoto Utsumi for comments and suggestions.

1. Paul A. Volcker, Remarks at the Bretton Woods Committee Annual Meeting, Washington, June 17, 2014, www.brettonwoods.org.

2. Ibid.

good global economic performance. I then provide evidence consistent with those principles, showing that adhering to more rules-based policy has been associated with good performance while deviating from rules-based policy has been associated with poor economic performance. Building on this experience and the principles, I then describe the reform proposal and its implementation.

Key Lessons from the Plaza Accord

In my view two key lessons from the Plaza Accord are most relevant for thinking about a new approach to the international monetary system. The first relates to the effectiveness of exchange market intervention. The second relates to the impact of the agreement on the strategy of domestic monetary policy in different countries.[3]

Impact of Exchange Market Interventions

The first key lesson from the Plaza Accord, as analyzed in empirical studies of the period, is that sterilized exchange market interventions have been largely ineffective in moving the exchange rate on a sustained basis.[4] To be sure, the dollar was very strong at the time of the September 22 meeting of the G-5 and the announcement at the Plaza Hotel in New York, and it depreciated for the next two years: By 1987 the dollar had largely reversed the appreciation experienced during 1981–85.[5] So a casual observer of these trends would see a strong effect of both the Plaza and the Louvre Accords. Moreover, the dollar depreciated immediately on the Monday after the Sunday Plaza meeting. Against the yen, for example, it depreciated from 240 yen/dollar to 232 yen/dollar over the weekend.

However, as Feldstein (1994) and others emphasize, the decline in the dollar had started several months before the Plaza Accord. It had reached 260 yen/dollar in February 1985 and was down to 240 yen/dollar on the Friday before the meeting at the Plaza Hotel. In their recent comprehensive history of foreign exchange market interventions in the United States, Bordo, Humpage, and Schwartz (2015, 301) "find no support for the view that intervention influences exchange rates in a manner that might force the dollar lower, as under the Plaza Accord, or maintain target zones as under the Louvre Accord.... most

---

3. A detailed review of the meetings and events surrounding the Plaza Accord and the Louvre Accord is beyond the scope of this chapter. Frankel (1994) provides an excellent review, including of important events like the September 1986 meeting between Secretary Baker and Finance Minister Miyazawa of Japan.

4. By "sterilized" I mean that either the monetary base or the policy interest rate is held steady as the central bank offsets its purchases or sales of foreign currency–denominated assets with sales or purchases of domestic assets.

5. That this reversal had gone far enough was the reason for the Louvre Accord of February 22, 1987.

of the movements in exchange rates over the Plaza and the Louvre period seem attributable to policy changes, not intervention."

In an earlier study, Obstfeld (1990) found that currency interventions could reveal policymakers' intentions to change macroeconomic policy and thus affect expectations of such a change in policy, which in turn could affect actual exchange rates. However, Bordo, Humpage, and Schwartz (2015) report that the interventions during this period had very little systematic effect on actual exchange rate changes, through changes in expectations or other channels. Their study of 129 separate interventions against the yen and the mark during the Plaza-Louvre period using different criteria finds that the impact of the interventions was insignificantly different from random.

Alan Greenspan summed up the empirical evidence well at a Federal Open Market Committee (FOMC) meeting in October 2000: "There is no evidence, nor does anyone here [at the FOMC] believe that there is any evidence to confirm that sterilized intervention does anything" (FOMC transcript, October 3, 2000, quoted in Bordo, Humpage, and Schwartz 2015, 332).

It is possible, of course, to move exchange markets temporarily even with sterilized intervention, but the impacts are uncertain. As I report in Taylor (2007a, 276), based on my experience observing every intervention by the Japanese in real time during 2002–03, "If the Japanese intervene in the markets by buying a huge amount of dollars with yen, they can usually increase the price of the dollar relative to the yen. But the impacts of such interventions are temporary and their size is hard to predict because the volume of trading in the market is many times larger than even the largest interventions." Nevertheless, I believe that these temporary effects can lead policymakers to intervene in the markets, because it is harder to detect the offsetting effects, as fundamentals soon overtake the intervention.[6]

Impact on National Monetary Policies

A second key lesson from the Plaza Accord concerns the impacts of such international agreements on monetary policy. There were differential effects on participants in the Plaza Accord, with monetary policy affected in some countries and not in others. Compare, for example, monetary policy in Japan with that of the United States and other participants. Research reported by the International Monetary Fund (IMF 2011) shows that monetary policy was excessively restrictive in Japan in 1985 and 1986 and too expansionary in 1987–90. Such a swing toward overly expansionary policy could have been a factor in the boom and subsequent collapse in Japan in the 1990s.

---

6. Not all Japanese intervention during 2003 was sterilized, in the sense that the monetary base increased during the period as part of quantitative easing. In fact, I and other officials viewed the sustained interventions during the year as a means of increasing money growth in Japan and thereby confronting deflationary pressures.

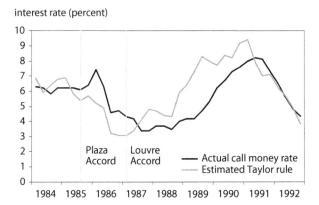

Figure 12.1   Estimated Taylor rule rate and actual call money rate in Japan, 1984–92

interest rate (percent)

Plaza Accord   Louvre Accord

— Actual call money rate
⋯ Estimated Taylor rule

1984 1985 1986 1987 1988 1989 1990 1991 1992

Source: IMF (2011), based on research by Leigh (2010).

The IMF research suggests that the Plaza Accord, at least as implemented in Japan, played a role in this swing. Figure 12.1 shows that the interest rate was too high relative to the rules-based policy in late 1985 and throughout 1986 (see also Jinushi, Kuroki, and Miyao 2000). It also shows the swing, with the policy rate set well below the rule from 1987 through 1990.

The move toward excessively restrictive monetary policy starts at the time of the Plaza meeting. Indeed, as figure 12.1 shows, the Bank of Japan increased its policy rate significantly immediately after the Plaza meeting—the opposite course of action indicated by inflation and output. Then, after a year and a half, starting around the time of the Louvre Accord, Japanese monetary policy swung in the other direction, toward excessive expansion. Figure 12.1 is remarkably clear about this move.[7] According to IMF (2011) calculations, the policy interest rate swung from up to 2¼ percentage points too high between the Plaza and the Louvre Accord to up to 3½ percentage points too low during the time between the Louvre Accord and 1990 "relative to an implicit Taylor rule based on the output and inflation outlook" (IMF 2011, 53).

Evidence of an effect of the Plaza and Louvre Accords on Japanese monetary policy can also be found in official statements. The Plaza and Louvre communiqués included specific commitments about Japanese monetary policy actions regarding the exchange rate or the interest rate. In the Plaza Accord statement, the government of Japan committed to "flexible management of monetary policy with due attention to the yen rate." In the February 22 Louvre Accord statement, "The Bank of Japan announced that it will reduce its discount rate by one half percent on February 23." Thus the deviations from

---

7. The policy rule estimates of Green, Papell, and Prodan in chapter 8 yield similar results to figure 12.1 for the period after the Plaza.

the rules-based policy, as defined here, were clearly due to the way Japan implemented the Plaza Accord and later the Louvre Accord.

The Plaza and Louvre communiqués included no similar statements about monetary policy by the Federal Reserve, the Deutsche Bank, the Bank of England, or the Bank of France. For the United States the communiqué included many supply-side or structural reforms, including the commitment to "implement revenue-neutral tax reform which will encourage savings, create new work incentives, and increase the efficiency of the economy, thereby fostering noninflationary growth," a commitment that was indeed fulfilled in the 1986 tax reforms.

Paul Volcker's comments on the Plaza Accord are particularly informative. They are an important part of the record and the lessons learned. According to Volcker (1994), the Plaza Accord had no implications for US monetary policy, either explicit or implicit. He was willing to go along with the agreement, he said, because he felt that Federal Reserve policy would not be tightened soon anyway. "In fact, it was the absence of any need or desire to tighten that provided a 'green light' for the Plaza Agreement" (Volcker 1994, 150).

To summarize, two types of international cooperation underlay the Plaza Accord. For some participants—certainly the United States but apparently also France, Germany, and the United Kingdom—international cooperation did not affect the monetary authorities' strategy. The meetings confirmed that these central banks would continue to pursue the strategies in place. The Plaza Accord statement simply said the Fed would provide "a financial environment conducive to sustainable growth and continued progress toward price stability." The Louvre statement simply said that the Fed's "monetary policy will be consistent with economic expansion at a sustainable noninflationary pace." Neither the Plaza nor the Louvre Accord statements included any mention of exchange rate actions for the Fed or any mention of deviations from the policy that the Fed had been putting in place under Volcker. Nevertheless, the dollar depreciated across the board—as much against the mark as against the yen—suggesting that the decline was part of a general reversal of the dollar appreciation experienced during 1981-85 and related to the monetary policy strategy that Volcker and his colleagues at the Fed had put in place.

This does not mean that the discussions at these or subsequent meetings were without merit. As I argue below, it is beneficial for a central bank simply to describe, clarify, and commit to a monetary strategy, including at these meetings and publicly through the communiqués issued after the meetings. Doing so enables other central banks to formulate and stick to their strategies; the information exchanged reduces uncertainty and helps create stability in global markets. Moreover, discussions among top economic and finance officials can relate to a host of other important issues, including tax policy, budget policy, and international trade policy, as they did in the case of the Plaza Accord.

In many respects, as later empirical research in Clarida, Gali, and Gertler (2002) and others showed, the monetary strategies of the American and European participants, which started around the time of the Plaza Accord, were maintained, and these strategies helped create two NICE decades following the Plaza Accord, even if they were not so NICE for Japan. Indeed, there was another form of NICE, a nearly international cooperative equilibrium, thanks to these policies that would also last for two decades, as I discuss below.

Global Benefits of Rules-Based Monetary Policy

Economic research going back to the time of the Plaza Accord shows that simple rules-based monetary policy results in good global economic performance (see Carlozzi and Taylor 1985 and Taylor 1985, for example). Global stability increases when each central bank adopts a rules-based monetary policy that predictably reacts to economic conditions (including possibly exchange market conditions) and that is optimal for its own country's price and output stability. Moreover, there is little additional gain from central banks jointly optimizing their policies; in practice such joint actions can lead to unintended suboptimal behavior (that is, deviations from the policy that is domestically optimal), as the example of Japan following the Plaza Accord illustrates. The research shows that the Nash equilibrium—in which each country chooses its monetary strategy taking other countries' strategies as given—is nearly optimal or nearly an internationally cooperative equilibrium.

In the models used in this research, capital is mobile, which is largely appropriate for the modern global economy, and rigidities, including sticky prices and wages, exist. There are cross-country linkages: The price of foreign imports affects domestic prices, and the real exchange rate affects output. Shocks from abroad can hit anywhere. Monetary policymakers face a macro-economic tradeoff between price stability and output stability, and they have the task of finding a policy strategy in which they adjust their monetary policy instrument to reach an optimal point on that tradeoff. The strategy must respond to shocks while not creating its own shocks, either domestically or internationally.

The tradeoff is like a frontier. Monetary policy cannot take the economy to infeasible positions off the frontier. But suboptimal monetary policy—as a result of deviating from good policy, reacting to the wrong variables, and so forth—can take the economy to inferior points off the tradeoff. Along the frontier, lower price variability can be achieved only with greater output variability, corresponding to different values of the reaction coefficients. The existence of such a tradeoff is quite general; the modeling framework has been used in many different monetary policy studies going back to the 1970s and continuing today.

The important result for international policy is that such models imply that the central bank's choice of domestic output and price stability along its frontier has little impact on the output and price stability tradeoff in other countries. The tradeoffs for other countries are virtually the same regardless of which of the optimal policies each country chooses. This is the sense in which there is little to be gained by countries coordinating their choice of policy rules with other countries if all are following policy rules that are optimal domestically.

The converse situation, where monetary policy in one or more countries does not follow an optimal rule, is less clear-cut theoretically, because it requires defining the nature of the deviation. Nevertheless, the tradeoff concept can be used to illustrate how such deviations from an optimal policy rule can lead to a breakdown in the international system.

Suppose a country deviates from its policy rule and moves in the direction of an inefficient policy. Its actions will have two types of impacts on other countries. First, the tradeoff in other countries shifts in an unfavorable direction, perhaps as a result of more volatile capital flows, exchange rates, commodity prices, and export demand. Second, less efficient monetary policy in one country brings about less efficient monetary policy in other countries. For example, if the policy change in one country brings about an excessively easy policy with very low interest rates, then policymakers in other countries—concerned about exchange rate appreciation—may deviate from their policy rule by setting interest rates that are too low.

The historical experience following the Plaza Accord has validated many of these theoretical predictions. As central banks in the United States and Europe moved toward rules-based monetary policies in the 1980s and 1990s, economic performance improved, especially compared with the instability of the 1970s. Clarida, Gali, and Gertler (2002) provided early evidence for this shift in policy. When central banks in many emerging market countries started moving toward more rule-like policies with their inflation-targeting approach, economic performance also improved, as De Gregorio (2014) shows.

During the past decade, policy changed. I refer here not to the lender-of-last-resort actions taken by the Fed and other central banks during the panic of the autumn of 2008, which were largely appropriate and effective in my view, but rather to the departures from rules-based policy before and after the panic. Empirical research by Taylor (2007b), Ahrend (2010), and Kahn (2010) shows that a deviation from rules-based policy in the United States and other countries started about a decade ago—well before the financial crisis. Hofmann and Bogdanova (2012) show that a "global great deviation" is continuing, especially when unconventional central bank interventions and large-scale balance sheet operations are included. Nikolsko-Rzhevskyy, Papell, and Prodan (2014) uncover these changes in policy using modern time-series techniques. Associated with the change has been deterioration in economic performance, including the Great Recession, the slow recovery, large negative international spillovers, and an increase in the volatility of capital flows and exchange rates. Policymakers in emerging-market countries, including Agustín Carstens (2015), the governor of the Bank of Mexico, have noted the adverse spillovers, and many have had to resort to unusual policy actions. Policymakers in developed economies, including Japan and Europe, have reacted to the adverse exchange rate effects of monetary policies. International economists have raised concerns about currency wars.[8]

While there is general agreement about the first shift in policy, in the early 1980s, around the time of the Plaza Accord, disagreement remains about the second and its timing. An alternative view is that monetary policies were appropriate during the past decade, even if they were not rule-like, and that the recent deterioration in economic performance was not the result of monetary policy deviating from a rules-based approach. Mervyn King, the former governor of the Bank of England, argues that the policy tradeoff in many countries shifted in an unfavorable direction because financial stability during the NICE period eventually bred instability, as investors became complacent: "Relative to a Taylor frontier that reflects only aggregate demand and cost shocks, the addition of financial instability shocks generates what I call the Minsky-Taylor frontier."[9]

There is also disagreement about international spillovers and related problems with the international monetary system. Bernanke argues that during 2009–13 it was appropriate for countries around the world to deviate from the policies that worked during the NICE period.[10]

Empirical Evidence on Global Effects

Five types of evidence can inform this shift in policy and its effects:

- econometric models of spillover effects of policy deviations
- regressions showing policy contagion and the multiplier effects of such contagion
- the spread of unconventional monetary policy as weapons in currency wars
- the impact of policy deviations on other policies that detract from economic performance
- direct evidence that global economic instability has increased.

---

8. See C. Fred Bergsten, "Currency Wars, the Economy of the United States and Reform of the International Monetary System," Stavros Niarchos Foundation Lecture, Peterson Institute for International Economics, Washington, May 16, 2013.

9. Mervyn King, "Twenty Years of Inflation Targeting," Stamp Memorial Lecture, London School of Economics, October 9, 2012.

10. Ben Bernanke, "Monetary Policy and the Global Economy," speech at the Department of Economics and Suntory and Toyota International Centres for Economics and Related Disciplines (STICERD), London School of Economics, London, March 25, 2013.

Figure 12.2   Estimated impact on output of a temporary negative shock to US interest rate rule of 0.2 percentage points: Results from the IMF's GPM6 model for 2013–23

percentage change from baseline

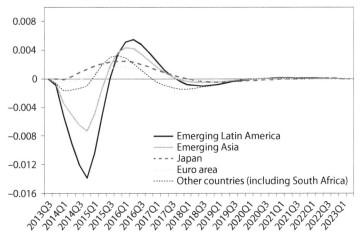

GPM6 = Global Projection Model with 6 Regions; IMF = International Monetary Fund

Note: Figure shows the impact of a deviation from a monetary policy rule in the United States on real output for Japan; the euro area; emerging Latin America (Brazil, Chile, Colombia, Mexico, and Peru); and emerging Asia (China, Hong Kong, India, Indonesia, Korea, Malaysia, the Philippines, Singapore, Taiwan, and Thailand).

Source: Simulations of the IMF's GPM6 model provided by Roberto Garcia-Saltos.

Evidence from Econometric Models on Spillovers of Monetary Policy Deviations

The IMF's main multicountry monetary model, the Global Projection Model with 6 Regions (GPM6; described in Carabenciov et al. 2013), includes the United States, other developed countries, and emerging-market countries in Latin American and Asia. Simulations of models in Volker Wieland's model database (Wieland et al. 2012) show that the IMF model is not special. Other estimated multicountry models, including the Federal Reserve's SIGMA model vintage 2008 and the New Area Wide Model (NAWM) of the European Central Bank (ECB) vintage 2008, show impacts in the same general range.

Figure 12.2 shows the impact of a deviation from the policy rule in the GPM6 model, which initially causes the US interest rate to fall by about 0.2 percentage points. The dynamics of the policy rule then lead to a gradual rise in the interest rate back to its starting point in about five quarters. According to the GPM6 model, there is a negative effect on output in the emerging-market economies of Latin American and Asia. In these simulations the interest rate change in the United States is quite small (only 20 basis points) so the impact on output in both the United States and the other countries is also small. It is best therefore to consider the foreign effects as a percentage of the US effects. Thus, for each percentage point monetary policy–induced increase in output in the United States, output falls by 0.25 percentage points in the Latin American countries and by 0.13 percentage points in the Asian countries. As described by the authors of the IMF's GPM6 model, this effect occurs because "the exchange rate channel is stronger than the direct output gap effect" (Carabenciov et al. (2013). The impact on output in other developed economies is not negative, but it is small. Japan's output, for example, increases by only about 1/20th of the US increase in the GPM6 model.

These simulations contradict the view that deviations from the rules-based policy are beneficial abroad; they do not support an enrich-thy-neighbor view. Bernanke argues that "the benefits of monetary accommodation in the advanced economies are not created in any significant way by changes in exchange rates; they come instead from the support for domestic aggregate demand in each country or region. Moreover, because stronger growth in each economy confers beneficial spillovers to trading partners, these policies are not 'beggar-thy-neighbor' but rather are positive-sum, 'enrich-thy-neighbor' actions."[11]

Evidence of Monetary Policy Contagion and Multiplier Effects

Given these simulations it is not surprising that policy deviations at one central bank put pressures on other central banks to deviate. A reduction in policy interest rates abroad causes the exchange rate to appreciate, and even with offsetting effects thanks to economic expansion abroad, the overall spillover effect may well be negative. For the emerging-market countries in Latin America and Asia, the exchange rate effect dominates. Central banks tend to resist large appreciations of their currency; one way to do so is to reduce their own policy rate relative to what it would be otherwise. Doing so reduces the difference between the foreign interest rate and the domestic interest rate and thus mitigates the appreciation of their exchange rate.

There is considerable empirical evidence of this impact of foreign interest rates on central bank decisions (see Taylor 2013). The best evidence comes from central bankers themselves, many of whom readily admit to these reactions in conversations.

The Norges Bank provides a great deal of detail about its decisions and the rationale for them. In 2010, for example, it explicitly reported that it lowered its policy interest rate because interest rates were lower abroad. The actual policy rate, at about 2 percent, was much lower than the rate implied by its domestic monetary policy rule, which called for a policy rate of about 4 percent. This deviation was due almost entirely to the very low interest rate abroad, according

---

11. Ben Bernanke, "Monetary Policy and the Global Economy," speech at the Department of Economics and Suntory and Toyota International Centres for Economics and Related Disciplines (STICERD), London School of Economics, London, March 25, 2013.

Figure 12.3   Illustration of the international monetary policy deviation multiplier

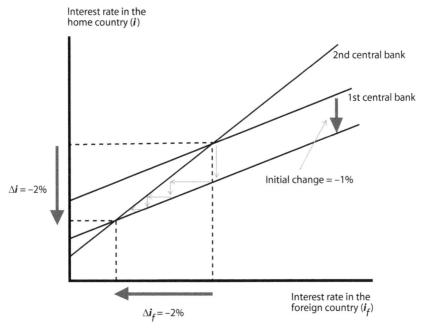

Source: Author's illustration.

to the Norges Bank. It reported that a policy rule with external interest rates included came much closer to describing the actual decisions than the policy rules without external interest rates.

Regressions or estimates of policy rules provide considerable evidence of the international spread of central bank policies. The work of Gray (2013), Carstens (2015), and Edwards (2015) is definitive. The usual approach is to estimate policy rate reaction functions in which the US federal funds rate or other measures of foreign interest rates are entered on the right-hand side as deviations from their respective policy rules. The usual finding is that the reaction coefficient on the foreign rate is positive, large, and significant. There is also evidence reported in Taylor (2009) that the Federal Reserve's interest rate policy is affected by interest rate decisions abroad.

In addition, this type of deviation from interest rate policy rules can create large international multiplier effects. The multiplier can be illustrated in the case of two countries. Assume that the size of the deviation depends on interest rate settings at the central bank in the other country. In figure 12.3 the first central bank has a response coefficient of 0.5 on the second central bank's policy interest rate, and the second central bank has a response coefficient of 1 on the first central bank's interest rate. Suppose the first central bank cuts its interest rate by 1 percentage point below its normal policy rule setting.

Figure 12.4 Yen-dollar exchange rate, 2006–15

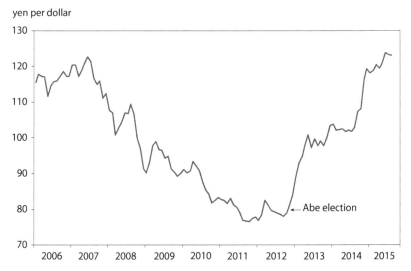

yen per dollar

Source: Federal Reserve Economic Data (FRED) at Federal Reserve Bank of St. Louis.

The second central bank will also reduce its policy rate by 1 percentage point, causing the first central bank to cut its interest rate by another 0.5 percentage point, leading to another cut at the second central bank, and so on. The end result is a 2 percentage point rate cut, or a multiplier of 2. What may have appeared as a currency competition becomes an interest rate competition.

International Transmission of Quantitative Easing and the Threat of Currency Wars

Just as interest rate policy deviations can be transmitted globally, so can quantitative easing. Consider the possible impact of quantitative easing in the United States on exchange rates, focusing on the Japanese yen. Following the financial crisis and the start of the US recovery in 2008–12, the yen significantly appreciated against the dollar, while the Fed repeatedly extended its large-scale asset purchases along with its zero interest rate policy, with little or no response from the Bank of Japan (figure 12.4).

The adverse economic effects of the currency appreciation in Japan became a key issue in the 2012 election. When the Abe government came into power, it urged the Bank of Japan to implement its own massive quantitative easing. With a new governor, the Bank of Japan did just that. As a result of this change in policy, the yen fully reversed its course and has now depreciated to levels before the panic of 2008. In this way the quantitative easing policy of one central bank appeared to beget quantitative easing by another central bank.

The moves of the ECB toward quantitative easing in the past year seem to have had a similar motivation and were likely influenced by the impacts

Figure 12.5   Euro-dollar exchange rate, 2012–15

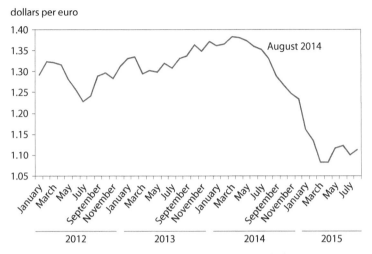

Source: Federal Reserve Economic Data (FRED) at Federal Reserve Bank of St. Louis.

of quantitative easing in Japan. An appreciating euro was, in the view of the ECB, a cause of the weak European economy. The response was to initiate another large round of quantitative easing. At the Jackson Hole conference in August 2014, Mario Draghi spoke about his concerns about the strong euro and hinted at quantitative easing, which then followed. This shift in policy was followed by a weaker euro and a stronger dollar (figure 12.5).

These exchange rate effects in Europe were accompanied—with remarkably close timing—by widespread depreciations of currencies in emerging markets. Figure 12.6 plots the dollar index against a large group of economies (Argentina, Brazil, Chile, China, Colombia, Hong Kong, India, Indonesia, Israel, Korea, Malaysia, Mexico, the Philippines, Russia, Saudi Arabia, Singapore, Taiwan, Thailand, and Venezuela). The taper tantrum of May–June 2013, in which the Fed first indicated it was going to wind down quantitative easing, is often cited as the beginning of the recent turbulence in capital flows and exchange rates, but August 2014 was a turning point for currency markets.

With these currency developments in the background, the actions of China to start to let the yuan move with other currencies and away from the dollar in August 2015 are understandable. There is also econometric evidence that quantitative easing has an impact on monetary policy decisions abroad. Chen et al. (2012, 230) find that "the announcement of QE [quantitative easing] measures in one economy contributed to easier global liquidity conditions."

Figure 12.6   Dollar index, 2012–15

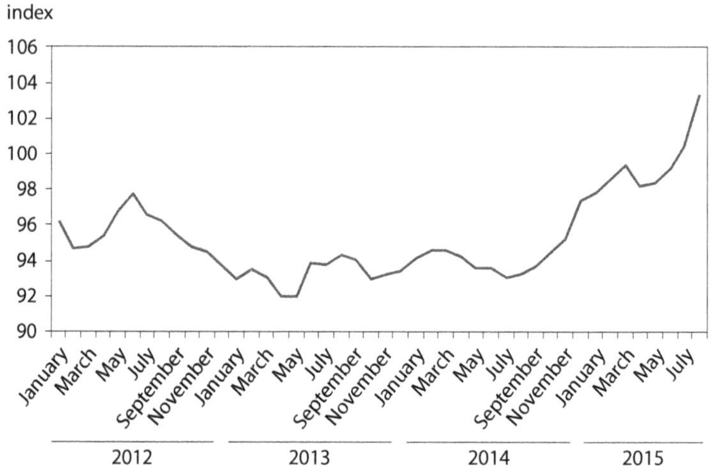

index

Note: Dollar index is the exchange rate of the dollar against the following trading partners: Argentina, Brazil, Chile, China, Colombia, Hong Kong, India, Indonesia, Israel, Korea, Malaysia, Mexico, the Philippines, Russia, Saudi Arabia, Singapore, Taiwan, Thailand, and Venezuela.

Source: Federal Reserve Economic Data (FRED) at Federal Reserve Bank of St. Louis.

Impact of Policy Deviations on Other Policies

Concerned about the ramification of deviating from their normal monetary policy, many central banks have looked for other ways to deal with the impacts of policy deviations abroad. They include imposing capital controls, using macroprudential tools, and intervening in currency markets.

Controls on capital flows—what IMF staff call *capital flow management*—are usually aimed at containing the demand for local currency and its appreciation, but they are also used to mitigate risky borrowing and volatile capital flows. Capital controls create market distortions and may lead to instability, as borrowers and lenders try to circumvent them and policymakers seek even more controls to prevent the circumventions. Capital controls are one reason why the output and price stability frontier shifts adversely, as discussed above. Capital controls also conflict with the goal of a more integrated global economy and higher long-term economic growth. Despite these drawbacks, the unusual spillovers of recent years have led even the IMF to suggest that capital controls might be used as a defense.

Currency intervention is another way countries try to prevent unwanted changes in a currency, as either an alternative or a supplement to deviations of interest rates from normal policy. Many emerging-market countries have used currency intervention widely in recent years. Although it can temporarily prevent appreciation, it can have adverse side effects. If not accompanied by capital controls, interventions require a change in monetary policy (nonsterilization) to be effective. Currency intervention also leads to an accumulation of international reserves, which must be invested somewhere. If low policy interest rates are set in the United States (as in 2003–05), the resulting gross outflow of loans is accompanied by a gross inflow of funds from central banks into dollar-denominated assets, such as US Treasury or mortgage-backed securities, which affects the prices and yields of these securities.

Macroprudential policies are another impact of policies from abroad. They are most obvious in small open economies that are closely tied to the dollar. Both Singapore and Hong Kong have had near zero short-term interest rates in recent years because the Fed has had zero rates. Their pegged exchange rate regimes and open capital markets have left no alternative. In order to contain inflationary pressures, they have had no choice but to resort to discretionary interventions in housing or durable goods markets, such as lowering required loan-to-value ratios in housing or requiring larger down payments for automobile purchases.

These policies are also becoming more popular in inflation-targeting countries with flexible exchange rates as advanced countries have deviated from rules-based policy. Discouraged from leaving interest rates at appropriate levels because of exchange rate concerns caused by the unusual policies abroad, such countries turn to such market-specific measures.

Macroprudential actions are inherently discretionary. They expand the mission of central banks and bring them closer to politically sensitive areas. They also run the risk of becoming permanent even after unconventional policies abroad are removed. A regulatory regime aimed at containing risk taking is entirely appropriate, but such a regime entails getting the levels right, not manipulating them as a substitute for overall monetary policy.

Capital Flows and Exchange Rate Volatility

The flows of capital in and out of emerging markets as well as the recent swings in exchange rates seem related in time to changes in monetary policy. Regarding the volatility of capital flows, Rey (2014, 310) writes that "our VAR [vector auto-regression] analysis suggests that one important determinant of the global financial cycle is monetary policy in the center country, which affects leverage of global banks, credit flows and credit growth in the international financial system." Figure 12.7 shows a marked increase in the volatility of capital flows to emerging markets since the recent deviation from rules-based policy began.

More work needs to be done on the correlation between the documented deviations from rules-based monetary policy and the volatility of capital flows; additional tests of causation are also important. This empirical task is made more difficult by the lack of comparable data going back to the 1980s and 1990s and the staggered timing of countries adhering to and deviating from rules-based policy.

Exchange rate movements have also become more volatile. Figure 12.8 shows the 12-month percentage change in the value of the US dollar against

Figure 12.7 Weekly capital (debt and equity) flows in emerging markets, January 2001–September 2015

billions of dollars

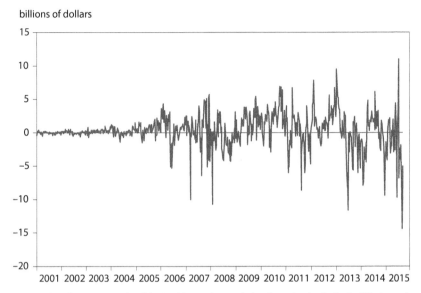

Source: Data from Emerging Portfolio Fund Research, provided to the author by the Bank of Mexico and used in Carstens (2015).

an index of "major" currencies, as defined by the Federal Reserve for the period from the end of the Plaza-Louvre Accords (January 1988) through August 2015. A marker at June 2002 indicates the approximate date of the shift away from rules-based policy.

The data show an increase in volatility in the second period. The standard deviation during the post–Plaza-Louvre period is 5.7 percent (8.3 percent in recent years). The max-min spreads also increase, from +/–12 percent in the first period to +20/–15 percent in the second. The most recent 12-month percent changes are about as large as during the global financial crisis

A New Approach

The foundation of a rules-based international monetary system is simply a rules-based monetary policy in each country. An established body of research shows that the move toward rules-based monetary policy in the 1980s led to improved national and international performance in the 1980s and 1990s. The economic evidence also indicates that the recent spread and amplification of deviations from rules-based monetary policy in the global economy are drivers of current instabilities in the international monetary system, although more research is needed. Research shows that each country following a rules-based monetary policy that is consistent with achieving national economic stability—and expecting other countries to do same—would move the world toward an

Figure 12.8   Change in the value of the dollar against an index of major currencies, January 1988–August 2015

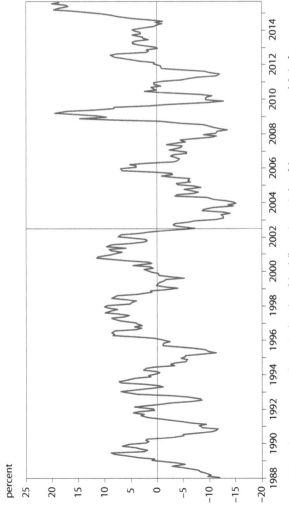

percent

Note: Figure shows percentage changes in the value of the dollar against an index of the euro, yen, pound, Swiss franc, Canadian dollar, Australian dollar, and Swedish krona over a 12-month period.

Source: Federal Reserve Economic Data (FRED) at Federal Reserve Bank of St. Louis.

international cooperative equilibrium. The more countries that follow such an approach in practice, the closer actual global conditions will be to the assumptions that underlies this research.

Lessons from the Plaza Accord indicate that the process of each country reporting on its monetary policy strategy and agreeing to commit to that strategy can be an important means of building this foundation. They also indicate that it is essential that the process not impinge on other countries' domestically optimal monetary strategies or focus on sterilized currency intervention as an instrument. In keeping with the expansion of the global economy since the Plaza Accord, emerging-market countries should be part of the process. The issue is one for the G-20 and beyond, perhaps the Bank for International Settlements (BIS), not just the G-5 or the G-7. A clear commitment by the Federal Reserve—still the world's most significant central bank, with responsibility for the world's most significant currency—to move in this rules-based direction would help start the process. The staff of the IMF or the BIS could be asked to help monitor and keep track of the strategies.

The barriers to implementing an international understanding and agreement along these lines may be surprisingly low. Of course, some form of renormalization of monetary policy, or at least intent to renormalize, is needed. After that come goals and strategies for the instruments of policy to achieve the goals. The major central banks now have explicit inflation goals, and many policymakers use policy rules that describe strategies for the policy instruments. Explicit statements about policy rules or strategies to achieve these goals are thus feasible. Such policy rules would describe the nature of adjustments of the policy instruments in response to economic conditions. That there is wide agreement that some form of international reform is needed would help move implementation along.

Such a process poses no threat to either the national or international independence of central banks. It would be the job of each central bank to formulate and describe its strategy. Participants in the process or parties to the agreement would not have a say in the strategies of central banks in other countries or currency unions. The strategies could be changed or deviated from if the world changed or there was an emergency. A procedure for describing the change in strategy and the reasons for it would presumably be part of the agreement.

Many have called for reforms of the international monetary system, reflecting concerns about instabilities, international policy spillovers, volatile capital flows, risks of crises, or simply less than stellar economic performance. The BIS has been researching the issues; Jaime Caruana, the general manager of the BIS, has made the practical case (Caruana 2012). The approach suggested here may not be the be-all and end-all of such a reform, but it is supported by experience from the Plaza Accord and extensive research over the years. It also has the key prerequisites of a good, feasible reform: Each country can choose its own independent strategy, avoid interfering with the principles of free and open markets, and contribute to the common good of global stability and growth.

References

Ahrend, Rudiger. 2010. Monetary Ease: A Factor behind Financial Crises? Some Evidence from OECD Countries. *Economics: The Open Access, Open Assessment E-Journal* 4.

Bordo, Michael D., Owen F. Humpage, and Anna J. Schwartz. 2015. *Strained Relations: US Foreign Exchange Operations and Monetary Policy in the Twentieth Century*. Chicago: University of Chicago Press.

Carabenciov, Ioan, Charles Freedman, Roberto Garcia-Saltos, Douglas Laxton, Ondra Kamenik, and Petar Manchev. 2013. *GPM6: The Global Projection Model with 6 Regions*. IMF Working Paper WP/13/87. Washington: International Monetary Fund.

Carlozzi, Nicholas, and John B. Taylor. 1985. International Capital Mobility and the Coordination of Monetary Rules. In *Exchange Rate Management under Uncertainty*, ed. J. Bhandhari. Cambridge, MA: MIT Press. Available at http://web.stanford.edu/~johntayl/Onlinepaper-scombinedbyyear/1985/International_Capital_Mobility_and_the_Coordination_of_Monetary_Rules.pdf.

Carstens, Agustín. 2015. *Challenges for Emerging Economies in the Face of Unconventional Monetary Policies in Advanced Economies*. Stavros Niarchos Foundation Lecture, Peterson Institute for International Economics, Washington, April 20.

Caruana, Jaime. 2012. Policymaking in an Interconnected World. Paper presented at the Federal Reserve Bank of Kansas City Policy Symposium on the Changing Policy Landscape, Jackson Hole, WY, August 31.

Chen, Qianying, Andrew Filardo, Dong He, and Feng Zhu. 2012. *International Spillovers of Central Bank Balance Sheet Policies*. BIS Paper. Basel, Switzerland: Bank for International Settlements.

Clarida, Richard, Jordi Gali, and Mark Gertler. 2002. A Simple Framework for International Monetary Policy Analysis. *Journal of Monetary Economics* 49, no. 5: 879–904.

De Gregorio, José. 2014. *How Latin America Weathered the Global Financial Crisis*. Washington: Peterson Institute for International Economics.

Edwards, Sebastian. 2015. *Monetary Policy Independence under Flexible Exchange Rates: An Illusion?* NBER Working Paper 20893. Cambridge, MA: National Bureau of Economic Research.

Feldstein, Martin. 1994. American Policy in the 1980s: A Personal View. In *American Policy in the 1980s*, ed. Martin Feldstein. Chicago: University of Chicago Press for the National Bureau of Economic Research.

Frankel, Jeffrey. 1994. Exchange Rate Policy: 1. In *American Economic Policy in the 1980s*, ed. Martin Feldstein. Chicago: University of Chicago Press for the National Bureau of Economic Research.

Gray, Colin. 2013. Responding to a Monetary Superpower: Investigating the Behavioral Spillovers of US Monetary Policy. *Atlantic Economic Journal* 21, no. 2: 173–84.

Hofmann, Boris, and Bilyana Bogdanova. 2012. Taylor Rules and Monetary Policy: A Global Great Deviation? *BIS Quarterly Review*, September.

IMF (International Monetary Fund). 2011. *World Economic Outlook: Tensions from the Two-Speed Recovery* (April). Washington.

Jinushi, Toshiki, Yoshihiro Kuroki, and Ryuzo Miyao. 2000. Monetary Policy in Japan since the Late 1980s: Delayed Policy Actions and Some Explanations. In *Japan's Financial Crisis and Its Parallels to US Experience*, ed. Ryoichi Mikitani and Adam S. Posen. Washington: Institute for International Economics.

Kahn, George A. 2010. Taylor Rule Deviations and Financial Imbalances. *Federal Reserve Bank of Kansas City Economic Review*, Second Quarter: 63–99.

Leigh, Daniel. 2010. Monetary Policy and the Lost Decade: Lessons from Japan. *Journal of Money, Credit and Banking* 42, no. 5: 833–57.

Nikolsko-Rzhevskyy, Alex, David H. Papell, and Ruxandra Prodan. 2014. Deviations from Rules-Based Policy and Their Effects. In *Frameworks for Central Banking in the Next Century*, ed. Michael Bordo and John B. Taylor. Special Issue of the *Journal of Economic Dynamics and Control* 49 (December): 4–18.

Obstfeld, Maurice. 1990. The Effectiveness of Foreign-Exchange Intervention: Recent Experience, 1985–88. In *International Policy Coordination and Exchange Rate Fluctuations*, ed. W. H. Branson. Chicago: University of Chicago Press.

Rey, Hélène. 2014. Dilemma not Trilemma: The Global Financial Cycle and Monetary Policy Independence. In *Global Dimensions of Unconventional Monetary Policy*. Conference volume of symposium sponsored by the Federal Reserve Bank of Kansas City, Jackson Hole, WY, August 22–24, 2013.

Taylor, John B. 1985. International Coordination in the Design of Macroeconomic Policy Rules. *European Economic Review* 28: 53–81.

Taylor, John B. 2007a. *Global Financial Warriors: The Untold Story of International Finance in the Post-9/11 World*. New York: W. W. Norton.

Taylor, John B. 2007b. Housing and Monetary Policy. In Housing, Housing Finance, and Monetary Policy, *Economic Policy Symposium Proceedings*, Federal Reserve Bank of Kansas City, September: 463–76.

Taylor, John B. 2009. Globalization and Monetary Policy: Missions Impossible. In *The International Dimensions of Monetary Policy*, ed. Mark Gertler and Jordi Gali. Chicago: University of Chicago Press for the National Bureau of Economic Research.

Taylor, John B. 2013. International Monetary Coordination and the Great Deviation. *Journal of Policy Modeling* 35, no. 3: 463–72.

Volcker, Paul A. 1994. Monetary Policy: 2. In *American Economic Policy in the 1980s*, ed. Martin Feldstein. Chicago: University of Chicago Press for the National Bureau of Economic Research.

Wieland, Volker, Tobias Cwik, Gernot J. Müller, Sebastian Schmidt, and Maik Wolters. 2012. A New Comparative Approach to Macroeconomic Modeling and Policy Analysis. *Journal of Economic Behavior and Organization* 83 (August): 523–41.

13

The International Monetary System in Perpetual Search of Stability

AGNÈS BÉNASSY-QUÉRÉ

Since the Plaza Accord, in 1985, the world economy has changed dramatically along two main lines (table 13.1). First, new countries have emerged as major economic powers, and the economy has developed in a tripolar way, with North America, Europe, and East Asia becoming its main pillars, with similar weights. Second, international capital movements have been liberalized, first in advanced economies but also to a lesser extent in emerging markets and developing countries. Subsequently, cross-border financial flows have exploded.

These two major changes in the global economy could have involved a marked evolution of the international monetary system—namely, the diversification of key currencies and expansion of freely floating exchange rate regimes. In fact, in 2013, 147 countries, representing 89 currencies and 27 percent of global GDP, were running fixed or managed exchange rate regimes.[1] The share of floating regimes increased from 6 percent of International Monetary Fund (IMF) member states in the 1980s to 23 percent in the 1990s, and it stayed stable in the 2000s, according to Ghos, Qureshi, and Tsangarides (2011).[2] Simultaneously, the US dollar has remained the main key currency of the international monetary system for international currency functions. The euro

Agnès Bénassy-Quéré is professor at the Paris School of Economics, University Paris 1 Panthéon-Sorbonne and chair of the French Council of Economic Analysis. She gratefully acknowledges efficient research assistance by Paul Berenberg-Gossler and comments by Arnaud Mehl on a preliminary draft.

1. Own calculations based on 2014 IMF *Annual Report on Exchange Arrangements and Exchange Restrictions* and World Bank GDP data in current dollars. Fixed and managed regimes include all regimes except floating and free-floating regimes. Euro area countries are excluded from the count.

2. De facto floating regimes expanded even less, with only 18 percent of all countries adopting such regimes in the 2000s (Ghosh, Qureshi, and Tsangarides 2011).

Table 13.1 Major changes in the world economy since 1985

Item	1985	Latest year available[a]
Percent of world GDP[b]		
North America	38.7	26.3
Europe	25.5	24.4
East Asia	16.2	24.6
De jure capital openness (index of capital mobility)		
Advanced economies	0.63	2.10
Emerging markets and developing countries	–0.60	0.09
De facto capital openness (foreign assets + foreign liabilities)/ GDP (expressed as percent)		
Advanced economies	46.6	227.7
Emerging markets and developing countries	42.7	80.7

a. Latest year available is 2014 for GDP, 2013 for de jure capital openness, and 2011 for de facto capital openness.
b. Calculations are based on current US dollars. Europe includes the United Kingdom. East Asia includes Japan.

Sources: GDP data are from World Bank, World Development Indicators. De jure capital openness data are from Chinn and Ito (2008, updated to 2013). De facto capital openness data are from Lane and Milesi-Ferretti (2007, updated to 2011).

has emerged as a second key currency, but with much lower "market shares" than the US dollar (table 13.2).

As for the renminbi, it has been handicapped by the slow liberalization of China's financial market. Since the mid-1990s, China has taken significant steps toward progressively internationalizing the renminbi as a means of payment and store of value. There is still a long way toward full internationalization, however. In particular, key steps need to be taken to open up the country to two-way capital flows and to establish the "rule of law" (see, for example, Dobson and Masson 2009; Eichengreen 2011; Prasad and Ye 2012; Bergsten 2014; Cohen 2014; Yu 2014; Yiping, Wang, and Fan 2015). In the long run, however, it is difficult to envisage a fully multipolar global economy without a considerable reshaping of the international monetary system (Angeloni et al. 2011; Bénassy-Quéré and Pisani-Ferry 2011). Eichengreen (2013b) considers that 10 years from now, the renminbi will likely be a "consequential" currency, something like second or third.[3]

The observed resilience on the part of the dollar was benign as long as the US economy was clearly dominant in terms of GDP, trade, and financial markets: Monetary pegs and reserve accumulation from third countries did not weigh much on global trade and capital flows. However, the share of the United States in the global economy fell from 34.3 percent in 1985 to 22.2

---

3. For a recent analysis of renminbi internationalization, see Eichengreen and Kawai (2015).

Table 13.2   International importance of the US dollar, yen, and euro, end-2014 (percent)

Function	US dollar	Yen	Euro	Other
Medium of exchange				
Foreign exchange turnover, April 2014[a]	87.0	23.0	33.4	56.6
Unit of account				
Invoicing/settlement of euro area exports of goods to non–euro area, 2014	n.a.	n.a	67.3	n.a.
Invoicing/settlement of euro area imports of goods from non–euro area, 2014	n.a.	n.a.	48.8	n.a.
Third-country currency peg, April 2014[b]	48.3	0.0	29.2	22.5
Store of value				
Allocated official reserves, 2014Q4	62.9	4.0	22.2	10.9
Outstanding international debt securities, narrow measure, 2014Q4[c]	58.2	2.9	23.4	15.5
Outstanding international debt securities, broad measure, 2014Q4[d]	44.6	2.2	34.9	18.3
Outstanding cross-border bank loans, narrow measure, 2014Q4[e]	47.8	8.2	12.5	31.6
Outstanding cross-border bank loans, broad measure, 2014Q4[f]	52.7	2.8	16.8	27.6

n.a. = not applicable

a. Since a given trade involves two currencies, the percentages sum to 200 percent in this row.
b. Out of 89 pegged or semipegged currencies.
c. Excluding domestic issuance of international debt.
d. Including domestic issuance of international debt.
e. Loans by banks outside the euro area to borrowers outside the euro area.
f. All cross-border loans.

Sources: BIS (2013); IMF (2014); ECB (2015).

percent in 2013, at current exchange rates. In 2013 countries running a fixed or managed exchange rate regime (de jure or de facto) with respect to the US dollar accounted for 18 percent of world GDP, with China (which the IMF classified as having a de facto crawling peg arrangement with the dollar) alone accounting for 12 percent of world GDP.[4]

The mismatch between a unipolar international monetary system and a multipolar real economy has at times been singled out as a key ingredient

---

4. Own calculations, see supra.

of the macroeconomic environment that led to the 2007–09 financial crisis (see, for example, Ivashina, Scharfstein, and Stein 2012). Leading policymakers have also argued that a unipolar international monetary system creates a deflationary bias, with all countries other than the key currency issuer wishing to accumulate foreign exchange reserves through current account surpluses in order to self-insure against a reversal of gross capital inflows (see UN 2009).

Another aspect of the problem is the Triffin Dilemma (Triffin 1960), revisited by Zhou (2009) and Farhi, Gourinchas, and Rey (2011) in the context of the post–Bretton Woods system. According to Farhi, Gourinchas, and Rey, the growth of emerging economies and their appetite for liquid, riskless assets increases demand for international liquidity, putting downward pressure on US interest rates and the current account. At some stage international investors will either lose confidence in US solvency or fear massive monetization of US bonds, which could trigger a crash of the dollar. To avoid such an outcome, it would be advisable to develop alternative sources of international liquidity, through either the internationalization of other currencies or the development of Special Drawing Rights (SDR) through regular allocations (Mateos y Lago, Duttagupta, and Goyal 2009).[5]

A multipolar monetary system could alleviate the Triffin Dilemma by diversifying the sources of international liquidity. Multipolarity could also act as a disciplinary device. Because they would be offered a choice between several currencies with equivalent liquidity features but issued by countries with varying depths of imbalances, international investors would no longer invest in a country displaying long-lasting deficits (Kwan 2001; Eichengreen 2010). Some experts argue, however, that a multipolar monetary system could raise exchange rate volatility, because greater substitutability across key currencies would translate into more frequent and larger portfolio reallocations (UN 2009).

This chapter reviews the potential of the euro to become a full-fledged international currency. It then analyzes the implications of a multipolar international monetary system for monetary stability.

The Euro as an International Currency

Historical experience suggests that the advantages enjoyed by the incumbent currency should not be overblown (see Eichengreen, Chițu, and Mehl 2014a, 2014b). There is room for more than one international currency.

Although creating an international currency was never the primary objective of European monetary unification, the Europeans could still expect their single currency to reach international status. Based on both the theoretical literature on currency internationalization and historical experience (see the

---

5. The decision in November 2015 to include the renminbi in the SDR basket does not change the fundamental scarcity of SDR liquidity, which represented only 2.5 percent of global reserves in 2015 according to IMF data. The implications for renminbi internationalization will depend on Chinese policies and reforms (see infra).

Table 13.3   Comparative size of the euro area, as of end-2014

Item	Euro area[a]	EU-28[b]	United States	Japan	China
Population (millions)	337	507	319	127	1,369
GDP (billions of euros at current exchange rates)	10,111	13,921	16,036	3,760	6,974
Exports of goods and services (billions of euros at current exchange rates, excluding exports within the European Union and the euro area)[c]	2,380	2,233	1,717	625	1,780

a. Austria, Belgium, Cyprus, Estonia, Finland, France, Germany, Greece, Ireland, Italy, Latvia, Lithuania, Luxembourg, Malta, the Netherlands, Portugal, Slovakia, Slovenia, and Spain.
b. Euro area + Bulgaria, Croatia, Czech Republic, Denmark, Hungary, Poland, Romania, Sweden, and the United Kingdom.
c. Data are for 2013. The share of intra-EU and intra-eurozone exports is estimated based on CEPII-CHELEM bilateral trade data for goods in 2012.
Sources: World Bank; European Commission; CEPII-CHELEM databases.

survey by Bénassy-Quéré 2015), it is possible to identify five main conditions for a currency to grow internationally:

- Be issued by a large country or monetary area.
- Be used to denominate assets that are traded in deep and liquid markets.
- Provide nominal stability both internally (low inflation) and externally (a stable or at least not depreciating exchange rate).
- Enjoy financial stability and a strong regulatory environment.
- Be backed by some attributes of noneconomic power (military force, a single voice in international forums).

The euro area meets the size criterion (table 13.3). As of 2014 it had a larger population and greater trading power than the United States, although its GDP was smaller. Looking ahead, however, the share of the euro area in global GDP is likely to decline. According to Bénassy-Quéré, Fouré, and Fontagné (2013), the share of the EU-28 in global GDP is projected to fall from 23 percent in 2010 to 17 percent in 2025, at current relative prices. The share of the United States is projected to decline from 25 to 17 percent. Over the same period the share of China is projected to rise, from 10 to 22 percent. According to the size criterion, it is China's renminbi, not the euro, that should be expected to rival the dollar in the future.

The second criterion—deep and liquid financial markets—appears only moderately favorable to the euro, for two reasons. First, the financing model of the euro area relies much more heavily on banks than does that of the United States, limiting the size of the financial market. Second, the monetary union has no fiscal backing: In contrast to the United States, the euro area's "federal" debt continues to be very limited.[6] On top of these two weaknesses, the euro area's financial markets remain fragmented, because of different regulations and tax treatments across member states.

The crisis in the euro area undoubtedly dampened the attractiveness of the euro as an international currency, at least in the short term. Paradoxically, it may also have raised the prospects for euro internationalization, thanks to the reshuffling of banking supervision (in large part transferred at the ECB level), the development of the corporate bond market (viewed as an alternative to declining bank loans), and the project of a European "capital market union" (see Véron 2014, European Commission 2015a). Additionally, the ECB largely played its role as lender of last resort during the global financial crisis and closely monitored short-term liquidity.

The third criterion for euro internationalization (nominal stability) is supportive of the euro. Its central bank is independent and has a clear mandate to maintain price stability, the Maastricht Treaty prohibits the monetization of government deficits, and fiscal rules limit national government deficits, reducing the risk of "fiscal dominance" over monetary policy. As for the exchange rate, it has proved unstable, like that of every floating currency, but no weakening trend is evident over the 1999–2014 period.

The fourth criterion (financial stability and a strong legal environment) is moving in favor of the euro, notably in view of the progress made toward establishing a banking union since the onset of the euro area debt crisis. In contrast, there have been mounting concerns over China and alleged risks raised by over-investment, stretched real estate valuations, and the shadow banking system. There is also suspicion of never-ending discretionary intervention by China's authorities in the financial market. In July 2015, and again in January 2016, sharp falls in China's stock market led the government to ban large investors from selling some listed companies and international banks from trading on the foreign exchange market, to intervene heavily through the China Securities Finance Corporation, and to temporarily suspend trading altogether. Such bold intervention was sometimes interpreted as reluctance by China's authorities to accept the volatility arising from a free market.[7] Eichengreen (2013b) and Eichengreen and Kawai (2014) mention the lack of a strong, independent legal system as a major impediment to the development of the renminbi as an international currency.[8]

---

6. Claeys et al. (2014) estimate the total volume of EU-wide public debt denominated in euros at the end of 2013 at €490 billion (€230 billion in European Financial Stability Facility [EFSF]/ European Stability Mechanism [ESM] bonds, €200 billion in European Investment Bank debt, and €60 billion in European Union debt). Although the three data sources may not be readily comparable, the figure is a fraction of the $12,600 billion of US federal government debt in 2014.

7. See *Financial Times*, July 13, 2015, and January 7, 2016.

8. At the other extreme, the extensive acceptance of extraterritoriality expressed by the US legal system in 2014, in both the Argentina and BNP-Paribas cases, may precipitate the rise of alternative currencies and jurisdictions for future debt issuance and financial transactions. On the BNP-Paribas violation of US law, see, e.g., T. Putnam, "An $8.9 billion fine shows that foreign

Table 13.4   Strengths and weaknesses of the euro and the renminbi as international currency

Requirement	Euro	Renminbi
Size of country or monetary areas	Strength	Strength
Deep and liquid financial markets	Strength	Weakness
Nominal stability	Strength	Strength
Financial stability and strong regulatory environment	Strength	Weakness
Attributes of noneconomic power	Weakness	Strength

The last criterion for the emergence of the euro (geopolitical influence) is clearly missing (Posen 2008). Europeans have retained national sovereignty over foreign affairs and military forces, and the European External Action Service introduced by the Lisbon Treaty has not proved to be game-changing. Furthermore, no single eurozone voice is to be heard, be it at the IMF (where euro members are spread over several constituencies) or at G-20 meetings. The European Commission recently proposed unifying euro area representation at the IMF through a single chair (see European Commission 2015b, 2015c). More fundamentally, external representation in economic and finance forums could be empowered by transforming the president of the Eurogroup into a full-fledged finance minister responsible to a eurozone parliament. Such transformation would require a treaty change, however, and it would not in itself produce unity on foreign affairs and military issues.

Table 13.4 summarizes the strengths and weaknesses of the euro and the renminbi in terms of the various determinants of currency internationalization. A static view suggests that the euro has more strengths than the renminbi, and the euro is already playing a significant role as an international currency. Depending on the capacity of China to make reforms, however, the dynamic view is more favorable to the renminbi, thanks to the size effect and the backing of the currency by a single sovereign state.

History shows that several international currencies can coexist over a long period of time (Eichengreen Chiţu, and Mehl 2014a, 2014b). The declining weight of the euro area in the world economy, combined with the hysteresis of the international monetary system, is not supportive of the internationalization of the euro, however. In this respect the failure of the yen to emerge as an international currency in the 1990s should act as a useful reminder. To take a more positive spin, one could argue that the drop in transactions costs (as a result of the development of international financial markets and the expansion of the foreign exchange market) has reduced the incumbent's advantage (Eichengreen 2010).

banks evade U.S. laws at their peril," *Washington Post*, June 30, 2014. On Argentina, see Halverson Cross (2014).

History also suggests a "tipping point" effect: While the emergence of the euro (or the renminbi) as an international currency may be delayed, when it happens the change could be rapid. Chinn and Frankel (2008) estimate the currency distribution of foreign exchange reserves as a function of size, nominal stability, and financial depth (as proxied by foreign exchange turnover). They find support for a nonlinear form with strong inertia. It is, however, very difficult to make predictions about currency internationalization (see, for example, Chinn and Frankel 2008 and Li and Liu 2008).

Implications of a Multipolar International Monetary System for Monetary Stability

Research on the pros and cons of different international monetary systems suffers from limited experience: Since World War II, the international monetary system has basically moved from a gold exchange standard organized around the US dollar to a dirty floating regime still centered on the US dollar. Hence there is no opportunity to estimate the impact of different monetary organizations on economic stability and growth. One is left with theoretical reasoning and narrative interpretations of historical experience.

This section analyzes the implications for monetary stability of moving the international monetary system from unipolar to multipolar. Defining monetary stability is not easy. The extensive body of literature on the impact of exchange rate volatility on trade or investment is not fully conclusive. In fact, exchange rate instability is detrimental to the real economy insofar as it (a) results from abrupt changes in exchange rates that do not allow enough time for domestic producers to adjust, (b) takes the form of long-lasting misalignments rather than short-term volatility, (c) induces retaliation from partner countries that could degenerate into trade and/or currency wars, or (d) is a side effect of asymmetric exchange rate adjustments (see below). However, monetary stability also extends to the smooth provision of international liquidity, as exemplified during the global financial crisis.

I first review the traditional "stabilizing hegemony" argument, before moving to the implications of a multipolar international monetary system in a portfolio-choice model. I then examine the nth currency problem and the risk of currency wars.

Stabilizing Hegemony

Scholars of international relations often point out that a unipolar system exhibits "hegemonic stability" properties (see Kindleberger 1981 or the critical assessment by Eichengreen 1987). This idea is rooted in the interwar experience, a period when "the international economic system was rendered unstable by British inability and US unwillingness to assume responsibility for stabilizing it" (Kindleberger 1973, 292). According to the hegemonic stability argument, the hegemon will internalize the externalities involved in the provision of a given global public good (here, monetary stability), refraining from conducting monetary policy that could destabilize the rest of the world. This discipline results from its global responsibilities and corresponding privileges.

A "leaderless" currency system could theoretically produce the global "public good" of stability, provided there is effective coordination among the players. Such coordination was missing during the interwar period and is unlikely to be effective with more than two players, especially as one player (the euro area) has yet to resolve the issue of its external representation (Cohen 2009).

However, as Walter (1991) argues, the hegemon may exploit its monetary power rather than internalize global stability in its decision-making process. The United States did act as a crisis coordination leader during the 1997 Asian crisis, and the Federal Reserve did supply other central banks with US dollars through swap agreements during the 2008 global crisis. However, the loose monetary policy of the Greenspan era may not have fully internalized the worldwide impact of cheap credit. By the same token, the Federal Reserve's decision to embark on quantitative easing in the aftermath of the crisis, while not deliberately noncooperative, failed to internalize the impact of the US stance on emerging countries (hot-money inflows).[9]

Furthermore, the incentive to preserve international stability and the capacity to do so may fade away when the hegemon's relative economic size declines.[10] In this case, Kwan (2001) and Eichengreen (2010) argue, a multiple currency system could reduce the scope for large imbalances in the issuer country (or countries) (i.e., the scope of the Triffin Dilemma). The arguments traditionally put forward in favor of the hegemonic system are therefore weaker than may appear at first sight.

Portfolio Effects

Another argument in favor of a unipolar system, of an entirely different nature, stems from the substitutability of currencies. As long as the international currency is unrivalled in terms of liquidity and risk profile, shocks to expected returns have limited impact on portfolio choices; exchange rates are relatively stable. But if one (or two) other international currencies were to share the dominant currency's liquidity and risk characteristics, all these currencies would become more substitutable. Portfolio allocations would become more sensitive to shocks to expected returns, and exchange rates would become more volatile (see, for example, UN 2009).

However, increased substitutability across currencies also means that less exchange rate adjustment is needed to accommodate a given shock to financial preferences or the current account. Based on an extension of a dynamic portfo-

---

9. Eichengreen (2013a) shows that after the end of the Bretton Woods system, the Federal Reserve appeared less influenced by international factors, except in a number of exceptional circumstances.

10. Bergsten (2014) argues that the United States is no longer able to exert leadership on the international monetary systems and that China is not yet willing to do so.

Table 13.5 Portfolio allocation in a simple three-country setting

Item	United States	Euro area	China
Wealth at initial unitary exchange rates			
Initial level	100	100	100
After transfer from United States to euro area and China	80	110	110
After transfer from United States and euro area to China	90	90	120
Portfolio allocation (shares of dollar/euro/renminbi)			
Dollar as sole international currency	100/0/0	20/80/0	20/0/80
Dollar and euro as international currencies	80/20/0	20/80/0	10/10/80
Dollar, euro, and renminbi as international currencies	80/10/10	10/80/10	10/10/80

Source: Author.

lio model introduced by Blanchard, Giavazzi, and Sa (2005), Bénassy-Quéré and Forouheshfar (2015) show that a transitory shock to the current account has less impact on exchange rates when more currencies are "international" (in the sense that they are present in international portfolios), because the impact of the wealth transfer (or portfolio shock) is spread over more numerous currencies.

We also show that a more diversified international monetary system induces more symmetric exchange rate adjustments: The exchange rate between two countries is no longer affected by a symmetric shock originating in a third country. To understand this result, consider three currency areas (the United States, the euro area, and China) initially with equal wealth (table 13.5) and study two shocks: a wealth transfer from both the United States and the euro area to China and a wealth transfer from the United States to both China and the euro area. Given the home bias in portfolio choices, these shocks will affect global demand for the three currencies.

Wealth Transfer from Both the United States and the Euro Area to China

With a symmetric monetary system, all three currencies are international in the sense that they are present in the portfolios of the three countries (last row of table 13.5). In this case, because of home bias, the wealth transfer reduces the global demand for both the dollar and the euro and increases the global demand for the renminbi (figure 13.1a, bars on the left).[11] The shock, which is symmetric for the United States and the euro area, has symmetric impact

---

11. For the detailed calculations, see the appendix to this chapter.

Figure 13.1   Impact of wealth transfer on demand for dollars, euros, and renminbi

a. Wealth transfer from the United States and the euro area to China

percent change

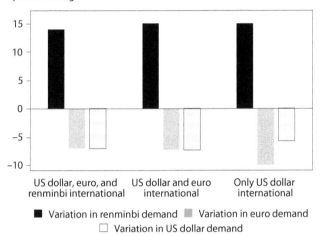

b. Wealth transfer from the United States to the euro area and China

percent change

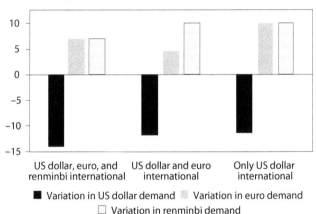

Note: In each panel, the shock is symmetric for countries in grey but asymmetric between grey and black.

Source: Author's calculations.

on the demands for their two currencies. Their bilateral exchange rate is not affected. The same symmetry is obtained when the renminbi is not international (figure 13.1a, middle bars). The only difference is a larger increase in the global demand for renminbi, because euro area and US investors do not reduce their demand for it (because they do not initially hold any).

With a unipolar system, a wealth transfer from the United States and the euro area to China results in a larger decline in the demand for the euro than for the dollar (figure 13.1a, bars on the right), because increased Chinese demand for euros does not compensate for reduced euro area demand for euros, whereas increased Chinese demand for dollars partially compensates for reduced US demand for dollars. In this case a symmetric fall in wealth in the United States and the euro area triggers a depreciation of the euro against the dollar.

Wealth Transfer from the United States to Both China and the Euro Area

With three international currencies, global demand for the dollar falls, while demand for the euro and renminbi rises in equal proportions (figure 13.1b, bars on the left). Symmetry between euro and renminbi is also obtained with a unipolar system (figure 13.1b, bars on the right) but not when only the dollar and the euro are international currencies (figure 13.1b, middle bars). In this case, a transfer of wealth from the United States to the euro area and China results in a rise in the demand for euros that is smaller than the rise in the demand for renminbi. The reason is that the United States reduces its demand for euros but not renminbi (because the renminbi is not international). The euro depreciates against the renminbi, despite the fact that the shock is symmetric for both countries.

In each experiment, a symmetric shock on two countries has asymmetric impact on the global demand for their currencies if they have different international status. The argument extends to a shock to portfolio choices: If the share of the dollar in international portfolios falls, there will be more demand for both the euro and the renminbi (if both currencies are international) but only for the euro if the renminbi is not international. In the latter case, the euro will appreciate against the renminbi. The argument also extends to a full-fledged stock-flow adjustment model with endogenous currency weights. In fact, a given depreciation of the dollar will be more stabilizing for the international portfolio balance if both the euro and the renminbi are international, because both assets will become more expensive, limiting the rise in demand for them.

Hence the instability of portfolio choices arising from more substitutability across key currencies in a multipolar system appears less convincing than it may appear at first sight. In fact, the portfolio choice model suggests that a multipolar international monetary system produces more stability than a unipolar one in a multipolar economic world.

The *n*th Currency Problem and the Risk of Currency Wars

With *n* currencies in the world, there are only *n* − 1 independent exchange rates. Either one country (the hegemonic one) must give up on exchange rate policy or the *n* countries must cooperate. It can be argued that a multipolar international monetary system will make the *n*th currency problem more acute, since there is no longer a natural monetary hegemon. In an environment of

independent central banks with a clear domestic mandate, monetary cooperation is unlikely to take place, except when financial spillovers are large enough
to spill back to the originating country (see Obstfeld 2015). Hence the risk of
"currency wars" will rise.

As Eichengreen (2013b) argues, the concept of currency wars is tricky, in
the sense that some large exchange rate movements are desirable when two
countries are hit by an asymmetric shock or when for whatever reason one
of them refrains from applying adequate monetary policy in reaction to a
symmetric shock. Quantitative easing in the United States during the global
financial crisis may be viewed as a way to "force" other central banks to ease
monetary policy in the presence of a large global shock. Taylor (2013) challenges this "positive-sum" mechanism, contending that the only way to avoid
currency wars is to return to rules-based monetary policies.

Whether or not something like a currency war exists is essentially an
empirical question. One way to measure it is to check whether the exchange
rate tends to appreciate in an economic upturn and depreciate in a downturn.
If each central bank follows a Taylor rule, then its real short-term interest rate
r_t depends on its inflation rate π_t and the level of the output gap og_t:

$$r_t = r + 0.5(\pi_t - \pi) + 0.5\ og_t \tag{13.1}$$

where r denotes the "natural" real interest rate and π (without subscript) is the
inflation objective. Denoting by q_t the logarithm of the real effective exchange
rate, q_t^e its expected value, and by star exponents the variables in the rest of the
world, the uncovered real interest parity can be written as follows:

$$r_t = r_t^* - (q_t^e - q_t) \tag{13.2}$$

Writing equation 13.1 for the rest of the world and putting the equations
together yields:

$$q_t - q_t^e = 0.5(\pi_t - \pi_t^*) + 0.5(og_t - og_t^*) + \chi \tag{13.3}$$

with $\chi = (r - r^*) - 0.5(\pi - \pi^*)$. When the output gap increases relative to the
rest of the world, the domestic central bank raises its interest rate relative to
the rest of the world. The domestic currency appreciates up to a level where it
is expected to depreciate at a pace that compensates for the return differential.

In advanced economies, the real effective exchange rate (REER) tends to
return to a constant value in the long run (see Rogoff 1996). This result is
consistent with the mean-reverting pattern of market expectations documented by, for example, Frankel and Froot (1987) and MacDonald (2000) at
medium-term horizons. The expected REER variation can be written as follows:

$$q_t^e - q_t = \theta(q - q_t), \text{ with } 0 < \theta < 1 \tag{13.4}$$

where q (without subscript) represents the long-term value of the REER. The
relationship between the REER and the output gap deviation to the rest of the
world is positive:

$$\theta \, q_t = \theta \, q + 0.5(\pi_t - \pi_t{}^*) + 0.5(og_t - og_t{}^*) + \chi \qquad (13.5)$$

Equation 13.5 expresses the reaction of the REER that is consistent with all central banks following the Taylor rule. Of course this is a partial equilibrium equation where inflation and the output gap are considered exogenous. In practice, a real exchange rate appreciation will lower both inflation and the output gap, which may dampen the positive relationships of equation 13.5. Additionally, it could be argued that a weaker REER will boost aggregate demand, increasing the output gap. The latter effect is less mechanical than the former, however, and may act with some delay. Hence to assess whether REER variations are stabilizing (i.e., whether the REER does appreciate when GDP grows faster than potential GDP), it is interesting to look at how they compare with the output gap.

Figure 13.2 plots the relationship between the output gap of four advanced economies (in deviation from the OECD average) and their REER (in deviation from the 1995–2014 average) over 1995–2014. Strikingly, only in the United States does the REER appreciate whenever the output gap is greater than the OECD average and depreciate in the reverse case. In the other three countries, there is hardly a discernible relationship between the two variables.

Figure 13.3 shows the correlation between the output gap deviation from OECD aggregate and the logarithm of the REER for 10 advanced economies over 1995–2014. With a correlation close to 0.80, the United States stands out as an outlier. The correlation is positive in four other countries, negative in four countries, and close to zero in one.

The behavior of the REER with respect to the economic cycle has received limited attention so far.[12] Further research is needed to understand how currency status interacts with the correlations shown in figure 13.2. For instance, the fact that the US dollar is a major funding currency with a large impact on global credit cycles (see Rey 2013, 2015) may amplify the impact of the Fed's monetary policy on the exchange rate through implied capital flows. The status of a "safe haven" (i.e., a currency that appreciates when global risks increase) may also play a distinct role from carry-trade reversal effects (see Hossfeld and MacDonald 2015). The evidence presented in this section suggests that only some countries benefit from the stabilizing impact of exchange rate variations; exchange rate adjustments appear destabilizing in other countries. The issues that need to be understood are the role of international currency status in this pattern and how a multipolar international monetary system could help more countries benefit from stabilizing exchange rate adjustment.

---

12. An exception is Cordella and Gupta (2015), who highlight the role of capital flows in emerging-market countries and the fact that procyclical capital flows may lead to both procyclical monetary policy (a loosening of monetary policy in good times) and a procyclical exchange rate, when the latter is flexible.

**Figure 13.2   Output gap and real effective exchange rate
in four advanced economies, 1995–2014**

a. United States

log of real effective exchange rate (deviation from
1995–2014 average in percent)

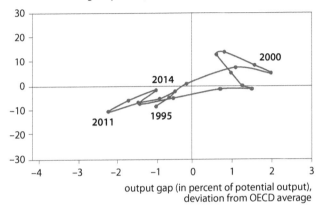

output gap (in percent of potential output),
deviation from OECD average

b. Euro area

log of real effective exchange rate (deviation from
1995–2014 average in percent)

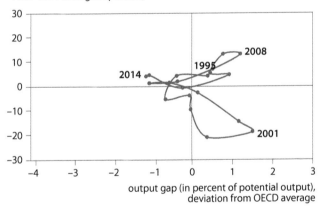

output gap (in percent of potential output),
deviation from OECD average

(figure continues)

Figure 13.2 Output gap and real effective exchange rate in four advanced economies, 1995–2014 (continued)

c. Japan

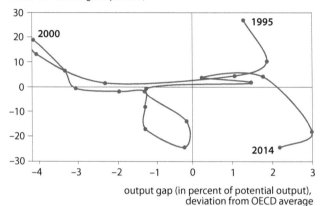

log of real effective exchange rate (deviation from 1995–2014 average in percent)

output gap (in percent of potential output), deviation from OECD average

d. United Kingdom

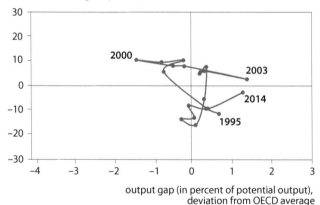

log of real effective exchange rate (deviation from 1995–2014 average in percent)

output gap (in percent of potential output), deviation from OECD average

OECD = Organization for Economic Cooperation and Development

Sources: Data from OECD *Economic Outlook* no. 97 (output gap) and Bank for International Settlements (real effective exchange rate, narrow index).

Figure 13.3   Correlation between the output gap deviation from the OECD average and the logarithm of the real effective exchange rate, 1995–2014

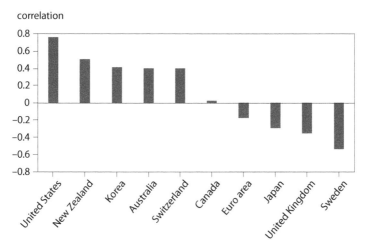

correlation

OECD = Organization for Economic Cooperation and Development

Sources: Data from OECD *Economic Outlook* no. 97 (output gap) and Bank for International Settlements (REER, narrow index).

Conclusion

A growing body of literature, mostly rooted in variants of the Triffin Dilemma, suggests that the mismatch between a unipolar international monetary system and a multipolar world is not viable in the long run. The euro has met some but not all of the required criteria suggested by the theoretical literature and experience that would enable it to rival (or complement) the dollar as an international currency. It could still achieve a status similar to that of the dollar, but the window of opportunity may not last much more than a decade before the renminbi overtakes it. Indeed, China has taken significant steps toward internationalizing its currency since the mid-2000s. Provided more liberalization takes place and a safer legal system is created, the future of the renminbi as an international currency may well be brighter than that of the euro.

The international community should not fear the move of the international monetary system toward multipolarity. In fact, a better match between the multipolar economy and a multipolar international monetary system could increase rather than decrease monetary stability. To the extent that it brings more stability, a multipolar international monetary system could reduce the need for international monetary cooperation, which has proved especially difficult since the historic Plaza Accord. By designating two or three key international currencies, such a system could also make monetary cooperation easier, because the discussion is likely to be more operational between two or three key players than among, say, the G-20. More research is needed to understand whether a multipolar international monetary system would raise or reduce the scope for "currency wars."

References

Angeloni, Ignazio, Agnès Bénassy-Quéré, Benjamin Carton, Zsolt Darvas, Christophe Destais, Jean Pisani-Ferry, André Sapir, and Vallée Shahin. 2011. *Global Currencies for Tomorrow: A European Perspective*. CEPII Research Report 2011-01/Bruegel Blueprint 13. Brussels: Bruegel.

Bénassy-Quéré, Agnès. 2015. The Euro as an International Currency. In *Handbook of the Economics of European Integration*, ed. Harald Badinger and Volker Nitsch. London: Routledge.

Bénassy-Quéré, Agnès, and Yeganeh Forouheshfar. 2015. The Impact of Yuan Internationalization on the Euro-Dollar Exchange Rate. *Journal of International Money and Finance* 57: 115–35.

Bénassy-Quéré, Agnès, Jean Fouré, and Lionel Fontagné. 2013. Modelling the World Economy at the 2050 Horizon. *Economics of Transition* 21, no. 4: 617–54.

Bénassy-Quéré, Agnès, and Jean Pisani-Ferry. 2011. What International Monetary System for a Fast-Changing World Economy? In *Reform of the International Monetary System: The Palais-Royal Initiative*, ed. Jack T. Boorman and André Icard. New Delhi: SAGE.

Bergsten, C. Fred. 2014. Currency Wars and the International Economic Order. Lecture delivered at the Stockholm School of Economics, August 22.

BIS (Bank for International Settlements). 2013. *Triennial Central Bank Survey on Foreign Exchange and Derivative Market Activity in 2013*, December. Basel, Switzerland.

Blanchard, Olivier, Francesco Giavazzi, and Filippa Sa. 2005. International Investors, the US Current Account, and the Dollar. *Brookings Papers on Economic Activity* 36, no. 2005-1: 1–66.

Chinn, Menzie, and Jeffrey A. Frankel. 2008. Why the Euro Will Rival the Dollar. *International Finance* 11: 49–73.

Chinn, Menzie, and Hiro Ito. 2008. A New Measure of Financial Openness. *Journal of Comparative Policy Analysis* 10, no. 3: 309–22.

Claeys, Grégory, Zsolt Darvas, Silvia Merler, and Guntram Wolff. 2014. *Addressing Weak Inflation: The European Central Bank's Shopping List*. Bruegel Policy Contribution 2014/05. Brussels: Bruegel.

Cohen, Benjamin J. 2009. Dollar Dominance, Euro Aspirations: Recipe for Discord? *Journal of Common Market Studies* 47, no. 4: 741–66.

Cohen, Benjamin J. 2014. *Will History Repeat Itself? Lessons for the Yuan*. ADBI Working Paper 453. Tokyo: Asian Development Bank Institute.

Cordella, T. and P. Gupta. 2015. What makes a currency procyclical? An empirical investigation. *Journal of International Money and Finance* 55: 240–59.

Dobson, Wendy, and Paul Masson. 2009. Will the Yuan Become a World Currency? *China Economic Review* 20: 124–35.

ECB (European Central Bank). 2015. *The International Role of the Euro*. Annual Report. Frankfurt.

Eichengreen, Barry. 1987. *Hegemonic Stability Theories of the International Monetary System*. NBER Working Paper 2193. Cambridge, MA: National Bureau of Economic Research.

Eichengreen, Barry. 2010. Managing a Multiple Reserve Currency World. *Insights* 8: 29–33.

Eichengreen, Barry. 2011. *Exorbitant Privilege: The Rise and Fall of the Dollar and the Future of the International Monetary System*. Oxford: Oxford University Press.

Eichengreen, Barry. 2013a. Does the Federal Reserve Care about the Rest of the World? *Journal of Economic Perspectives* 27, no. 4: 87–104.

Eichengreen, Barry. 2013b. Number One Country, Number One Currency? *World Economy* 36, no. 4: 363–74.

Eichengreen, Barry, Livia Chiţu, and Arnaud Mehl. 2014a. *Network Effects, Homogeneous Goods and International Currency Choice: New Evidence on Oil Markets from an Older Era*. ECB Working Paper 1651. Frankfurt: European Central Bank.

Eichengreen, Barry, Livia Chiţu, and Arnaud Mehl. 2014b. *Stability or Upheaval? The Currency Composition of International Reserves in the Long Run.* ECB Working Paper 1715. Frankfurt: European Central Bank.

Eichengreen, Barry, and Masahiro Kawai. 2014. *Issues for Renminbi Internationalization: An Overview.* ADBI Working Paper 454. Tokyo: Asian Development Bank Institute.

Eichengreen, Barry, and Masahiro Kawai, eds. 2015. *Renminbi Internationalization: Achievements, Prospects, and Challenges.* Asian Development Bank Institute, Tokyo and Brookings Institution, Washington.

European Commission. 2015a. Action Plan on Building a Capital Market Union. October 30, COM(2015) 468 Final. Brussels.

European Commission. 2015b. A Roadmap for Moving towards a More Consistent External Representation of the Euro Area in International Fora. October 21, COM(2015) 602 Final. Brussels.

European Commission. 2015c. Proposal for a Council Decision Laying Down Measures in View of Progressively Establishing an External Representation of the Euro Area in the International Monetary System. October 21, COM(2015) 603 Final. Brussels.

Farhi, Emmanuel, Pierre-Olivier Gourinchas, and Hélène Rey. 2011. Reforming the International Monetary System. CEPR Report, September. London: Centre for Economic and Policy Research.

Frankel, Jeffrey A., and Kenneth A. Froot. 1987. Using Survey Data to Test Standard Propositions Regarding Exchange Rate Expectations. *American Economic Review* 77, no. 1: 133–53.

Ghosh Atish R., Mahvash S. Qureshi, and Charalambos G. Tsangarides. 2011. *Words vs. Deeds: What Really Matters?* IMF Working Paper WP/11/112. Washington: International Monetary Fund.

IMF (International Monetary Fund). 2014. *Annual Report on Exchange Arrangements and Exchange Restrictions.* Washington.

Halverson Cross, K. 2014. The Extraterritorial Reach of Sovereign Debt Enforcement. Society of International Economic Law, Online Proceedings Working Paper No. 2014/28.

Hossfeld, O., and R. MacDonald. 2015. Carry funding and safe haven currencies: a threshold regression approach. *Journal of International Money and Finance,* 59: 185–202.

Ivashina, Victoria, David S. Scharfstein, and Jeremy C. Stein. 2012. *Dollar Funding and the Lending Behavior of Global Banks.* NBER Working Paper 18520. Cambridge, MA: National Bureau of Economic Research.

Kindleberger, Charles. 1973. *The World in Depression.* Berkeley: University of California Press.

Kindleberger, Charles. 1981. Dominance and Leadership in the International Economy. *International Studies Quarterly* 25, no. 2: 242–54.

Kwan, Chi Hung. 2001. *Yen Bloc: Towards Economic Integration in Asia.* Washington: Brookings Institution Press.

Lane, Philip, and Gian-Maria Milesi-Ferretti. 2007. The External Wealth of Nations Mark II. *Journal of International Economics* 73 (November): 223–50.

Li, Daokui David, and Linling Liu. 2008. RMB Internationalization: An Empirical and Policy Analysis. *Journal of Financial Research,* no. 11.

MacDonald, Ronald. 2000. Expectations Formation and Risk in Three Financial Markets: Surveying What the Surveys Say. *Journal of Economic Surveys* 14, no. 1: 69–100.

Mateos y Lago, Isabel, Rupa Duttagupta, and Rishi Goyal. 2009. *The Debate on the International Monetary System.* Staff Position Note 09/26. Washington: International Monetary Fund.

Obstfeld, Maurice. 2015. *Trilemmas and Tradeoffs: Living with Financial Globalization.* BIS Working Paper 480. Basel, Switzerland: Bank for International Settlements.

Posen, Adam. 2008. Why the Euro Will Not Rival the Dollar. *International Finance* 11, no. 1: 75–100.

Prasad, Eswar, and Lei Ye. 2012. Will the Yuan Rule? *Finance & Development* (March): 26–29.

Rey, H. 2013. Dilemma not Trilemma: The global financial cycle and monetary policy independence. Jackson Hole conference proceedings. Kansas City Federal Reserve Bank.

Rey, H. 2015. International Channels of Transmission of Monetary Policy and the Mundellian Trilemma. Mundell-Fleming Lecture, International Monetary Fund. Forthcoming in *IMF Economic Review.*

Rogoff, Kenneth. 1996. The Purchasing Power Parity Puzzle. *Journal of Economic Literature* 34: 647–68.

Taylor, John. 2013. International Monetary Coordination and the Great Deviation. *Journal of Policy Modeling* 35: 463–72.

Triffin, Robert. 1960. *Gold and the Dollar Crisis: The Future of Convertibility.* New Haven, CT: Yale University Press.

UN (United Nations). 2009. *Report of the Commission of Experts of the President of the United Nations General Assembly on Reforms of the International Monetary and Financial System.* June, New York.

Véron, Nicolas. 2014. *Defining Europe's Capital Markets Union.* Bruegel Policy Contribution 2014/12. Brussels: Bruegel.

Walter, Andrew. 1991. *World Power and World Money: The Role of Hegemony and International Monetary Order.* New York: St. Martin's Press.

Yiping, Huang, Daili Wang, and Gang Fan. 2015. Paths to a Reserve Currency: Renminbi Internationalization and Its Implications. In *Renminbi Internationalization: Achievements, Prospects, and Challenges,* ed. Barry Eichengreen and Masahiro Kawai. Asian Development Bank Institute, Tokyo, and Brookings Institution, Washington.

Yu, Yongding. 2014. Revisiting the Internationalization of the Yuan. In *Reform of the International Monetary System,* ed. Masahiro Kawai, Mario B. Lamberte, and Peter J. Morgan. Tokyo: Springer, for the Asian Development Bank Institute.

Zhou, Xiaochuan. 2009. Reform of the International Monetary System. Essay posted on the website of the People's Bank of China, April 9. Available at www.pbc.gov.cn.

Appendix 13A

Detailed Results of the Simulations

Table 13A.1 Impact of a symmetric wealth transfer from the United States and the euro area to China (amounts and percent variations at initial unitary exchange rates)

	Dollar, euro, and renminbi international			Dollar and euro international			Only dollar international		
	Before shock	After shock	Percent variation	Before shock	After shock	Percent variation	Before shock	After shock	Percent variation
Wealth									
United States	100	90	–10	100	90	–10	100	90	–10
Euro area	100	90	–10	100	90	–10	100	90	–10
China	100	120	20	100	120	20	100	120	20
Demand for US dollar									
United States	80	72	–10	80	72	–10	100	90	–10
Euro area	10	9	–10	20	18	–10	20	18	–10
China	10	12	20	10	12	20	20	24	20
Total	100	93	–7	110	102	–7	140	132	–6
Demand for euro									
United States	10	9	–10	20	18	–10	0	0	0
Euro area	80	72	–10	80	72	–10	80	72	–10
China	10	12	20	10	12	20	0	0	0
Total	100	93	–7	110	102	–7	80	72	–10

(table continues)

Table 13A.1 Impact of a symmetric wealth transfer from the United States and the euro area to China (amounts and percent variations at initial unitary exchange rates) (continued)

	Dollar, euro, and renminbi international			Dollar and euro international			Only dollar international		
	Before shock	After shock	Percent variation	Before shock	After shock	Percent variation	Before shock	After shock	Percent variation
Demand for renminbi									
United States	10	9	–10	0	0	0	0	0	0
Euro area	10	9	–10	0	0	0	0	0	0
China	80	96	20	80	96	20	80	96	20
Total	100	114	14	80	96	20	80	96	20

Source: Author's calculations.

Table 13A.2 Impact of a symmetric wealth transfer from the United States to China and the euro area (amounts and percent variations at initial unitary exchange rates)

	Dollar, euro, and renminbi international			Dollar and euro international			Only dollar international		
	Before shock	After shock	Percent variation	Before shock	After shock	Percent variation	Before shock	After shock	Percent variation
Wealth									
United States	100	80	–20	100	80	–20	100	80	–20
Euro area	100	110	10	100	110	10	100	110	10
China	100	110	10	100	110	10	100	110	10
Demand for US dollar									
United States	80	64	–20	80	64	–20	100	80	–20
Euro area	10	11	10	20	22	10	20	22	10
China	10	11	10	10	11	10	20	22	10
Total	100	86	–14	110	97	–12	140	124	–11
Demand for euro									
United States	10	8	–20	20	16	–20	0	0	0
Euro area	80	88	10	80	88	10	80	88	10
China	10	11	10	10	11	10	0	0	0
Total	100	107	7	110	115	5	80	88	10

(table continues)

Table 13A.2 Impact of a symmetric wealth transfer from the United States to China and the euro area (amounts and percent variations at initial unitary exchange rates)

(continued)

	Dollar, euro, and renminbi international			Dollar and euro international			Only dollar international		
	Before shock	After shock	Percent variation	Before shock	After shock	Percent variation	Before shock	After shock	Percent variation
Demand for renminbi									
United States	10	8	–20	0	0	0	0	0	0
Euro area	10	11	10	0	0	0	0	0	0
China	80	88	10	80	88	10	80	88	10
Total	100	107	7	80	88	10	80	88	10

Source: Author's calculations.

14

Time for a Plaza II?

C. FRED BERGSTEN

The Plaza-Louvre in Retrospect

The Plaza Accord of September 1985—and its successor Tokyo Summit and Louvre Accord over the following 18 months—represents the high-water mark of international economic policy cooperation and indeed coordination over the entire postwar period.[1] These agreements created a model that has not been replicated during the past 30 years.

Numerous other international efforts have been undertaken to correct current account imbalances and currency disequilibria. They have taken place under both fixed and flexible exchange rates, both before and after the Plaza-Louvre.

A number of emergency meetings of the G-10 sought to resolve sterling crises in the 1960s. The Franco-German imbalance was addressed in 1968–69. Much more prominently, the 1971 Smithsonian Agreement established a new set of parities after the United States suspended the convertibility of the dollar into gold and adopted an import surcharge.

C. Fred Bergsten was founding director of the Peterson Institute for International Economics from 1981 through 2012 and is now senior fellow and director emeritus there. The comments of William Cline, Charles Dallara, Jeffrey Frankel, Joseph Gagnon, Ted Truman, and John Williamson on earlier drafts of this chapter are greatly appreciated. Abir Varma provided invaluable research assistance.

1. This account of the Plaza-Louvre draws heavily on the definitive study of the period by Yoichi Funabashi (1989). Funabashi interviewed all but one of the ministers and central bank governors who negotiated the agreement (including Secretary James Baker, Assistant Secretary (later Under Secretary) David Mulford, Assistant Secretary Charles Dallara, and Fed Chairman Paul Volcker and his chief lieutenant, Ted Truman) as well as a who's who of other government officials and outside observers.

The Bonn Summit of 1978 broke new ground by implementing quantitative growth targets and energy policy initiatives to remedy international imbalances rather than addressing exchange rates per se. The dollar defense program conducted by the United States in 1978–79 relied heavily on cooperation by a few key surplus countries, especially Germany and Switzerland. The yen/dollar rate was a policy focus for the United States and Japan from the mid-1970s through the mid-1990s, before and after the Plaza-Louvre. Chinese manipulation of the relationship between the renminbi and other currencies, especially the dollar, has been a centerpiece of global concern for most of the last decade.[2]

Achievements of the Plaza-Louvre

Two characteristics distinguish the Plaza-Louvre from these other episodes. First, the Plaza Accord worked. The near-term goal of reducing the value of the dollar by 10–12 percent was achieved on time, with less intervention than countries agreed to (Gyohten 2013). The dollar ultimately fell by about 50 percent against its main targets (the yen and the deutsche mark), with 36 percent of the decline occurring between the Plaza and the Louvre Accords.

One reason for the success was the unique and, to this day, unprecedented degree of dollar overvaluation that clearly had to be corrected (see chapter 8 of this volume). Another was the complete surprise with which the initiative was launched and the shock generated by the lead of the United States, which had intervened very little in the previous five years and had made clear its hostility to the very concept.

The three main current account imbalances—the US deficit and the Japanese and German surpluses—all declined as a share of their respective GDPs by about 50 percent by 1990 (Krugman 1991, 278). The US current account deficit, which had risen to unprecedented heights—peaking at a then-record 3.4 percent of GDP in 1987, as a result of the two-year lag between currency movements and recorded trade outcomes—virtually disappeared by 1991, after prolonged doubts that the currency realignments of 1985–87 would pay off.[3] The acute protectionist pressures in Congress, which had been a major motivation for the Baker Treasury to initiate the process (see below), were largely quelled, and the relatively open world trading system was preserved. Thus the fundamental goals of the Plaza policy were almost totally achieved.[4]

---

2. Europe has experienced a series of currency crises as well, most notably the exits from the European Monetary System in 1992 and the flare-ups that have occurred in different forms since the creation of the euro. These crises affected the world economy but were primarily regional. This chapter addresses only issues that involved direct participation by wider groupings of countries.

3. Although the total elimination of the US deficit in 1991 was a one-shot result of payments of about $50 billion, which are treated as "unilateral transfers" in the balance of payments statistics and thus part of the current account, by several Gulf countries to the United States for the First Gulf War. Those payments were largely negotiated by Secretary of State James Baker.

4. Krugman (1991) analyzes the period carefully, concluding that the adjustment worked in almost precisely textbook fashion. His paper summarizes the results of a conference held by the

None of the other postwar international currency initiatives recorded remotely equivalent payoffs.[5] The new parities agreed at the Smithsonian held for only a few months, a new round of realignments was negotiated in early 1973, and generalized floating commenced within a month when they too failed. The Bonn Summit commitments were pursued in good faith, but the Iranian Revolution and second oil shock derailed them in less than a year. The US dollar defense program stopped the currency's free fall, but lasting stabilization (and indeed reversal) occurred only with the fundamental changes in monetary policy implemented by Paul Volcker after he became chairman of the Federal Reserve in 1979. Years of negotiation on the yen/dollar rate failed to appreciably reduce US and Japanese imbalances, aside from the Plaza-Louvre, or to overcome the Japan bashing of that era; only the collapse of the Japanese economy and resurgence of the US economy in the 1990s eventually accomplished the latter (Bergsten, Ito, and Noland 2001). The exchange rate of the renminbi has risen substantially and the Chinese current account surplus declined considerably in recent years. These changes occurred only after a decade of huge imbalances, however, and repeated displays of impotence by the United States and the International Monetary Fund (IMF) in resolving the problem, which produced deep congressional concern over currency manipulation, as dramatically revealed in its debate on US trade policy in 2015 (also see below).

Second, the Plaza-Louvre also produced a degree of international cooperation that remains historically unique (see chapter 10). All participating countries agreed that the markets had grossly overshot, that protectionist pressure in the US Congress posed a major risk to the world trading system and thus had to be countered, and that coordinated direct intervention in the foreign exchange markets could make a major contribution to resolving these problems. All of the other episodes cited above generated considerable enmity among the parties, both at the time the issues were addressed, usually amidst crises in the financial markets, and on a more lasting basis. The Plaza-Louvre could not avoid tensions and disputes altogether, and the degree of rancor apparently increased as the process evolved over its roughly two-year duration. But there was a true convergence of views at the initial Plaza phase that clearly separates it from its predecessors and successors.

The Plaza-Louvre had three sequential components. The Plaza Accord aimed to correct the substantial overvaluation of the dollar, especially against the yen and the deutsche mark. Its G-5 participants (France, Germany, Japan, the United Kingdom, and the United States) agreed to take significant adjust-

---

Institute for International Economics in late 1990 to assess the validity of concerns that the Plaza adjustment was not working.

5. Eichengreen (chapter 10) suggests that the much earlier Tripartite Agreement of 1936 was modestly successful in stabilizing the French franc but that none of the other interwar cases he considered had much effect.

ment initiatives, which they did not follow through on, and to intervene directly in the exchange markets to promote that outcome, which they did.[6]

The Tokyo Summit of 1986, which has received much less attention than either the Plaza or Louvre, was the most ambitious part of the entire initiative. In an attempt to both clarify the goals of the Plaza Accord and provide more policy tools to achieve them, Tokyo adopted an unprecedented (before or after) set of guidelines for international coordination of a wide-ranging set of national economic policies. While well-intentioned, those commitments soon proved to be too extensive to sustain, and most of them were never implemented.

The Louvre Accord of early 1987 reverted to the narrower exchange rate focus of the Plaza itself. It adopted a set of target zones (called "reference ranges") between the major currencies to try to limit further declines of the dollar, which were judged to have become too rapid, but also to avoid a renewed rise of the dollar, as indicated by subsequent sales of dollars by the Federal Reserve on several occasions (see chapter 9). The chief goal was to restore stability in the currency markets and the world economy more broadly. The agreed yen/dollar zone had to be rebased shortly; it held for about a year, plus or minus a few months, depending on one's definition. The mark/dollar range did not hold for long (see chapter 7). The Louvre Accord was thus less successful than the Plaza Accord, though it did head off any free fall or hard landing for the dollar.

Criticisms of the Plaza-Louvre

There are five criticisms of the Plaza-Louvre. The first is that it relied too heavily on exchange rate corrections and produced very little change in underlying policy stances ("the fundamentals"). In particular, the United States failed to explicitly address its burgeoning budget deficits. The landmark tax reform of 1986 did produce a temporary improvement of about $100 billion, however, and Secretary Baker told me at the time that "maybe 10 percent" of his success on that front could be attributed to his using the international coordination argument (see chapter 9). In addition, in late 1985 Congress passed the Graham-Rudman-Hollings procedural reforms, which placed some checks on future deficit increases. But Secretary Baker, who viewed the Plaza Accord as a "beginning" to "coordination of the fundamentals" (Baker 2006), was clearly disappointed by the meager results on that front.

The second criticism of the Plaza-Louvre is that it occurred outside the multilateral institutional framework, centered on the IMF, that obtained at the time (and now). The subgroups (the G-5 and later the G-7 [the G-5 plus Canada and Italy]) that carried out those initiatives, however, had come to be

6. The G-5 deputy from Japan, Toyoo Gyohten, visited my office on the day after the Plaza Accord was signed. From my office he called his lieutenants in Tokyo, instructing them to sell $1 billion, a very large (unprecedented?) intervention at the time. Ito reports that Japanese dollar sales on that first post-Plaza market day in Tokyo amounted to $1.3 billion (see chapter 7).

widely regarded as legitimate steering committees for the system, including the IMF itself; they had been the locus of all former currency cooperation efforts. Confidentiality concerns alone required keeping the operations as small as possible. Indeed, the powerful impact on markets of the Plaza and Louvre Accords was caused largely by their shock effects. The IMF did come into the process extensively for the Tokyo Summit. The entire process was multilateral, in the sense that almost all the major players of the time were involved.

The third criticism, raised by Martin Feldstein and others (including Taylor, in chapter 12), is that the Plaza had no real effect on exchange rates and that the dollar correction would have occurred anyway solely through market forces. In fact, the markets had gone wildly off course in overvaluing the dollar in the first place, and the dollar had begun rising again (after several months of depreciation) just before the accord. No one can know the counterfactual.

A very specific fourth criticism is that the stock market crash of late 1987 resulted partly from disagreement between the United States and Germany over implementation of the Louvre Accord. In fact, that event had very little impact on the real economy.

The fifth—and most profound and probably most lasting—criticism of the Plaza-Louvre is that it "forced" bad policy choices on Japan that set the stage for that country's financial crash in the early 1990s and subsequent "lost two decades." That interpretation has been widely cited in China, for example, to justify its rejection of proposals by the United States and others over the past decade to let its currency strengthen substantially to help address the very large imbalances of the recent period.

This argument, especially its application to the more recent Chinese and other undervaluation cases, has several major flaws (see also chapter 7). First, if anything, the Plaza led the Japanese to maintain excessively high interest rates to help strengthen the yen rather than the low interest rates that brought on the bubble (see chapter 12). Second, although the Louvre arguably led to Japanese interest rates that were too low, Japan could have stimulated its economy at the time, to counter the dampening effect of Plaza-induced appreciation, through fiscal rather than monetary policy; it was only the (since corrected) bureaucratic control of the Ministry of Finance over the Bank of Japan that produced the erroneous policy mix. No such parallels could be envisaged in the recent situation with China anyway, as the goal would have been to emulate the Plaza (that is, to strengthen the renminbi) rather than Louvre (that is, to weaken it). Third, the Japanese crash resulted primarily from a failure of financial regulation rather than changes in monetary policy. Hence this view, which is still heard, does not detract from the success of the Plaza or even the Louvre Accord.

The bottom line is that the Plaza-Louvre was a uniquely successful and relatively harmonious interlude in the generally ineffectual and contentious history of postwar international economic and monetary relations, which continues to this day. Secretary Baker (2006) did not overstate the case when, upon leaving the Treasury in 1988, he told President Reagan that "a new system of multilateral economic policy coordination" would be one of his three initiatives that "will be widely judged to have lasting significance" (the other two were tax reform and the United States–Canada Free Trade Agreement).

On the 30th anniversary of that initiative, it is thus instructive to assess its implications for contemporary and prospective policy. In the next section, I attempt to do so. In the section that follows I argue that, while it is not yet time for a Plaza II, we may need its equivalent in the relatively near future to address the new set of international imbalances and currency misalignments that are already developing, could expand much farther, and so far have failed to stimulate any similarly constructive policy response.

Lessons from the Plaza-Louvre

Six lessons can be drawn from the Plaza and Louvre Accords.

Lesson 1: The United States Must Lead

The United States failed to participate actively in international monetary cooperation, let alone lead it, during the first Reagan administration. Coming on top of a sharp rise in budget deficits and consequent continuation of sky-high interest rates (the Reagan-Volcker policy mix), that failure permitted—indeed strongly encouraged—the massive dollar appreciation and buildup of huge (for that time) imbalances that triggered intense congressional protectionist pressure and necessitated the Plaza Accord.[7] The other limited successes cited above, from the Smithsonian to the more recent yen and renminbi cases, occurred only because the United States pushed for them (with greater or lesser skill and determination). There is no example of successful global monetary cooperation that was not led by the United States.

It is unclear whether, even if it tried, US leadership could prevail today as it did in 1985–87. The United States failed to satisfactorily resolve the yen and, especially, renminbi problems in more recent decades (albeit partly because it did not really try to mobilize international coalitions on these issues as the Baker team, led by assistant secretaries Mulford and Dallara, did so effectively before Plaza, as described in their chapters in this volume). Like the global political order, the international monetary system has become increasingly multipolar, and the relative power of the United States has declined. Monetary affairs appear to be moving, over the next decade or two, toward an essentially tripartite structure resting on the euro (if the zone recovers, as I think it will) and the renminbi along with the dollar (see chapter 13).

---

7. I predicted those consequences of Reaganomics in my testimony before the House Subcommittee on International Economic Policy and Trade of the Committee on Foreign Affairs, on February 24, 1981, just after Reaganomics was launched, and in subsequent articles. The only comparable analysis was by Otto Eckstein, but he expected the high interest rates that would accompany the Reagan budget deficits to crowd out private investment and cause an economic downturn rather than the boom that was enabled by the huge inflow of foreign capital, the rising dollar, and the soaring trade deficits that I predicted (Bergsten 1981).

The United States is nevertheless likely to remain primus inter pares for the foreseeable future, especially as the eurozone continues to falter and China maintains a measured pace in internationalizing the renminbi and faces its own economic problems. We may, however, increasingly experience a no-leadership, or G-0, world. Kindleberger (1973) blamed the Great Depression largely on the advent of a leaderless nonsystem in the 1930s, when "the United Kingdom was no longer able to lead and the United States was not yet willing to do so." As a result, no one provided the necessary global public goods (open markets, adequate lending, an international currency) to ward off the proliferation of competitive currency devaluations and trade restrictions that cut world commerce in half between 1930 and 1933 and converted national recessions into the Great Depression.

The United States continues to provide those global public goods today, running large (and again growing) current account deficits, thanks in part to its open markets and the key currency role of the dollar, which permit the rest of the world to enjoy export-led growth. The United States, however, has its own pressing problems of lagging employment, wage stagnation, and worsening income distribution. The antiglobalization backlash of the past two decades raises the question of whether unilateral US leadership of the traditional type will be sustainable for much longer—an issue to which I return in the next section.

Lesson 2: The Other Key Players Must Cooperate

Unilateral actions by the United States via the "Nixon shocks" forced the far-reaching currency realignments and eventual systemic adoption of floating exchange rates in the early 1970s. Exchange rates are inherently two-sided, however; the grudging acquiescence of France, Germany, and Japan was essential even then. The willingness, indeed eagerness, of the other key players was central to the success of the Plaza-Louvre.[8] Japan was especially helpful, particularly with respect to supportive domestic (notably monetary) policies, presumably because it was the primary target of congressional trade pressure and thus had the biggest stake in reducing currency misalignments.

Even the surplus countries with undervalued currencies (especially Germany and Japan in that case), which are usually the least willing to cooperate, were ready to participate. Their economies were doing reasonably well at the time, which helped a great deal. So did the patient and persistent efforts of top Treasury officials, including David Mulford and Charles Dallara, to build a plan of action through three months of "long and exhaustive" negotiations before the Plaza Accord (see chapter 3). The increasing doubts of Germany after the Louvre were key to its erosion. The lessons are that there can be no leadership without followership but also that effective leadership can beget followership.

---

8. The Europeans had already intervened on their own to weaken the dollar in early 1985.

The continuing trend toward multipolarity renders such cooperation even more essential today. The inability of the United States over at least a decade, dating from 2003, to get China to let the renminbi appreciate more quickly and more extensively is the current exemplar of that reality. That failure included the inability to win enough support from its usual allies to produce meaningful policy response through the IMF (Blustein 2013). The fiasco of US opposition to the creation of the Asian Infrastructure Investment Bank in early 2015, when most of its traditional supporters in Asia and Europe abandoned it, makes the point even more forcefully.

The advent of China means that the traditional reliance on the G-7 (or previously the G-5 or G-10) of high-income democracies is no longer adequate. The G-20 has become the predominant steering committee for the world economy, but it is too large to function effectively as an operational body. A de facto G-3 (the United States, the eurozone, and China) or G-4 (adding Japan) is needed to restore any prospect for effective international monetary cooperation. No Plaza II could be envisaged without China; indeed there were calls for a "new Plaza Accord" about a decade ago, including by Secretary Baker (2006), when the major systemic need was an appreciation of most or all of the Asian currencies, which would have required cooperation from several Asian countries (Cline 2005).[9]

Lesson 3: Domestic Politics, Especially Trade Policy, Drive Most Major International Monetary Initiatives

In their memoirs and their chapters in this volume, James Baker and David Mulford write that the threat of congressional protectionism was the main cause of their switch from the "benign neglect" exchange rate policy of the first Reagan administration to the Plaza Accord (Baker 1996, Mulford 2014). The sharp deterioration of US price competitiveness generated by the soaring dollar, which brought unprecedented and rapidly growing trade and current account deficits, had already triggered the passage of protectionist bills in the House and threatened the global trading system. Congressman Bill Frenzel, the highly respected ranking minority member of both the full Ways and Means Committee and its subcommittee on trade, commented later that "the Smoot-Hawley Tariff itself would have passed the Congress" had it come to the floor during this period. This congressional pressure provided the administration with enormous leverage over the other countries (Baker 2006). Fortunately, they understood the risk and shared the desire of the Baker Treasury to counter it constructively and effectively through currency action rather than new restrictions on trade. The use of a multilateral forum, the G-5, added to the policy's antiprotectionist impact in Congress by demonstrating that other

---

9. The IMF sponsored a multilateral consultation on global imbalances in 2006–07 that included those G-4 countries plus Saudi Arabia (representing the oil exporters). There were no noticeable results.

key countries (including oft-targeted Japan) were helping the United States and acting to resolve the problem.

Somewhat similar developments marked the other major US foray into aggressive exchange rate action in 1971. On that occasion there were genuine external pressures from actual and threatened dollar conversions into gold by some foreign central banks. Then, too, however, the House had passed protectionist bills, notably the Mills bill of 1971, with its import quotas on textiles and shoes, and the "Byrnes basket," which could have established quotas in numerous other sectors.[10] In addition, the Burke-Hartke bill, which would have limited foreign direct investment by US firms as well as imports across the board, was being prepared and attracting widespread attention. In both 1985 and 1971, the administrations of the day were rightly motivated by a desire to maintain control of trade and currency policy rather than letting it shift by default to Congress, as well as by the desire to maintain an open trading system (and prevent the United States from being blamed for replicating the huge policy errors it made in the 1930s).

The current situation has clear echoes of these past episodes. An important part of the congressional opposition to the Trade Promotion Authority (TPA) legislation in 2015 and the subsequent Trans-Pacific Partnership (TPP) agreement was motivated, or at least justified, by the rise in the US trade and current account deficits to record levels—as a share of GDP, twice the levels that prompted the Plaza Accord in 1985—a few years earlier and especially the currency misalignments, driven by overt manipulation by China and a few others, that helped generate them. Congressional initiatives usually lag real-world events by several years; imbalances had fortunately declined considerably by the time Congress began acting on these trade policy issues in mid-2015. The Obama administration therefore felt able to reject this Plaza (and 1971) lesson and to largely stonewall Congress rather than respond positively to its concerns or even take preemptive action, even though that jeopardized its own trade policy legacy. The carryover impact has nevertheless been substantial enough to force significant changes in US currency policy, which I describe below.

This lesson is very important, because most of the analytical work on the sustainability of exchange rates focuses on its international financial dimension (i.e., whether a given level of external deficits and debt can attract adequate funding to avoid problems or, in extreme cases, "sudden stops" and currency crises). There is also a critically important domestic political dimension to currency sustainability; the domestic constraint can sometimes bind before (or even in the absence of) its international counterpart. The Plaza was motivated by just such a pattern, as is the contemporary debate in the United States. There was no shortage of external financing for the US deficits in either case—indeed, the deficits were being overfinanced, as indicated by the strong rise of the dollar, but the overvaluation of the day was aggressively attacked from within.

---

10. C. Fred Bergsten, "Crisis in U.S. Trade Policy," *Foreign Affairs,* July 1971.

Lesson 4: The Fed Must Be on Board

The Plaza program to drive down the dollar largely ended—prematurely, as it soon turned out—when the Federal Reserve decided to let market interest rates rise in early 1987, after a renewed depreciation of the dollar (triggered to some extent by another round of jawboning from the Treasury) became excessive in the view of Chairman Volcker and his colleagues (or, as Truman puts it, the Plaza Accord "overperformed"). The definition of a hard landing for a currency—which all officials, including US officials via the Plaza-Louvre, seek to avoid—is that interest rates rise while the exchange rates decline.[11] Even more immediately, and with an eye on the upcoming 1988 elections, the administration of the day did not want to see higher interest rates. The other countries were also ready to call a halt to the dollar's decline. Secretary Baker and his team made the best of their circumstances by working out the Louvre Accord, putting in place the new target zones to at least protect against a renewed rise (as well as disorderly fall) in the dollar.

The lesson is that successful international monetary cooperation requires internal as well as external coordination by a US administration (and especially Treasury). US law authorizes the secretary of the Treasury to determine the country's exchange rate policy, but the Federal Reserve views its independence in conducting monetary policy as providing it with autonomy in the currency area as well (Volcker and Gyohten 1992, 233–35). Volcker, in fact, concludes that "the net result (between Treasury and the Fed) is a kind of mutual veto that in practice gives the last word to the agency that is most reluctant to intervene," confirming that they must work out a compact if any intervention initiative is to succeed.[12, 13]

Lesson 5: Exchange Rates Are Less Difficult than Macroeconomic or Structural Policies to Coordinate Internationally

The Plaza worked. The Louvre worked to some extent. Tokyo never got off the ground. The lesson is that currency cooperation or even coordination, difficult as it is, is much more likely to succeed than similar efforts centered on the alternative (and more fundamental) macro and structural policy areas.

Numerous other examples support this conclusion. The "Nixon shocks" of 1971 and the subsequent Smithsonian Agreement succeeded to a degree on

---

11. Under normal circumstances, an increase in interest rates can be expected to strengthen a country's currency. It is the major policy instrument usually used for that purpose. A hard landing for an economy has much wider implications.

12. Ironically, Volcker would have supported pre-Plaza intervention to counter the sharp rise of the dollar toward the end of the first Reagan administration, but Treasury vetoed it (see chapter 2). He then vetoed Treasury's decision to continue pushing the dollar down in 1987 and forced the stabilization agreement of the Louvre.

13. For his part, Secretary Baker indicated the need for Fed concurrence privately to me in 1987 and in his memoirs (Baker 2006).

exchange rates, including ultimately changing the exchange rate system, but on little else. The Europeans could create a common currency, but, despite having previously agreed on a comprehensive customs union and extensive internal liberalization, they have been unable to support their monetary union with an economic union. The Bonn Summit potentially provided a counterexample, but its accord on macroeconomic goals and policies was aborted by the second oil shock.

This lesson can be carried further. Exchange rate cooperation, perhaps embodied in firm rules, can be deployed in an effort to forge internationally compatible and thus more sustainable domestic economic policies, at least in the major countries. This was the basic concept underlying both the gold standard and the "fixed" exchange rates of the original Bretton Woods system. Thoughtful European leaders believed that creating a common currency would inexorably lead to the additional reforms needed to create an optimal currency area. The Plaza Accord sought to expand its agreement on currency into cooperation on much broader "fundamentals" at Tokyo and, to a degree, in the Louvre. None of these agreements worked perfectly, to put it mildly, but they seemed to run more successfully from exchange rates to macro/structural policies than vice versa. At the same time, based on his careful examination of a number of historical episodes, Eichengreen (chapter 10) cautions that it is a huge mistake to maintain inappropriate domestic policies to support "arbitrary exchange rate targets." Great care must be exercised to design any currency regime accordingly.

Lesson 6: Ideas Matter

The Plaza Accord was initiated in part to promote an orderly realignment of the major currencies of the day and to avert the risk of a hard landing for the dollar. That concern, which was deeply shared by Fed Chairman Volcker (see chapter 2), had been propagated most vocally by Stephen Marris (1983, 1987), the former chief economist of the Organization for Economic Cooperation and Development (OECD), with strong support from me.[14] A more immediate push for such action came in the statements by me, Richard N. Cooper, and Paul Krugman at the annual Jackson Hole conference sponsored by the Federal Reserve Bank of Kansas City (1985) less than a month before the Plaza Accord itself.

John Williamson and I invented target zones, which were actively discussed by top US and other officials in the period just before the initiation of the Plaza-Louvre (Bergsten and Williamson 1983). At a briefing session hosted for him by the Institute for International Economics in early 1985, Deputy Treasury Secretary Richard Darman embraced the idea but indicated that target zones would be called something else, in order to avoid endorsing its sponsors.

---

14. Marris (1991) later explained how the hard landing was averted, importantly including via the Plaza-Louvre initiative itself.

The term "reference ranges" was developed for that purpose. (Darman's only other objection to the scheme was that it gave too big a role to central banks, a concern that turned out to be justified—from his standpoint at Treasury—as indicated above.)

Williamson and Miller (1987) subsequently concluded that the "reference ranges" of the Louvre failed to persist because they differed from the proposed target zones in five important ways:

- The ranges were not publicly announced; private capital flows were therefore not mobilized to support them.

- The bands were too narrow, limited to +/–2½–5 percent instead of 10 percent.

- They were defined as nominal bilateral exchange rates against the dollar instead of real effective exchange rates (REERs).

- They had a provisional rather than permanent nature, as indicated by their early "rebasing," which reflected the fundamental problem that they did not rest on any analysis of sustainable equilibrium levels; they were simply set "around current levels," because that is what the negotiators at the Louvre could agree on and deemed least disruptive to the markets.

- The only obligation when a rate reached the edge of the zone was to consult rather than to implement a prespecified policy action.

The lesson is that concepts and proposals that are developed outside official circles can often have important and even decisive policy impact, even, or perhaps especially, over relatively brief periods of time if the need for new ideas is as acute as when crises of the magnitude of 1985–87 arise. But the lesson is also that official adoption of outside policy proposals can misfire if applied incorrectly, as at the Louvre and in the latest debate, when the currency issue came uncomfortably close to derailing the entire TPP negotiation.[15]

Is There a Need for Plaza II?

Does it matter that the Plaza success has not been replicated in 30 years? Have there been any problems of similar type and magnitude that called for such a policy response? Is there any practical need to absorb the lessons from the Plaza-Louvre?

The international imbalances run by the United States and the largest surplus country of the day, China, reached shares of GDP in the mid-2000s

---

15. Ideas developed outside government also heavily influenced that debate. The unusual letters to the president on the issue from bipartisan majorities of both the House and Senate in 2013, which triggered the debate on linking currency policy to trade agreements, cited and largely rested on the analysis in Bergsten and Gagnon (2012). Some of the mandates that survived the legislative process derived directly from Bergsten (2014), although I, unlike some supporters of including "enforceable currency disciplines" in the TPP itself, never argued that TPP should be rejected unless it included such provisions.

that were far higher than those that motivated the Plaza Accord in 1985. The US current account deficit hit about 6 percent in 2006 and remained near 5 percent in 2007–08, compared with its earlier peak of 3.4 percent in 1987. The Chinese current account surplus peaked at 9.8 percent in 2007–08, almost three times the surpluses of Germany and Japan in 1985. Other Asian countries were also running large surpluses at the time that cumulated to a total about equal to that of China. The US economy was doing well (although edging toward the crisis that hit in 2008), however, and the dollar remained below its long-term average. Congressional support for new trade restrictions was not as great as in the earlier period although the Schumer-Graham proposal for a sizable import surcharge against China attracted considerable attention in 2005–07. The Chinese felt sufficient pressure to let the renminbi start appreciating gradually in mid-2005.

The Great Recession intervened in 2008, deflecting attention away from the international imbalances (Blustein 2013) and sharply reducing them (though taking the US deficit down to only a little below the level at which it had peaked in 1985–87). The issue arose again, in Congress and through its pressure on the administration, in 2010–11, when the muted recovery from the recession was under way. The House and Senate separately passed currency bills in 2010 and 2011, respectively, authorizing the use of countervailing duties against undervalued currencies (especially if they were "manipulated"), with the Senate bill adding "remedial currency intervention" by the United States itself (see below). Largely as a result, China let the renminbi start appreciating again. Congress ratcheted up the pressure even more intensively in 2013–15, when it began addressing the TPP trade agreement and the associated TPA legislation, acquiring substantial leverage in dealing with the administration on the issue. But the administration rejected the lesson from the Plaza-Louvre that suggested preemptive currency action to protect the trade agenda, arguing instead that its "quiet diplomacy" had largely resolved the major problem (China) and that linking the issue to trade policy could torpedo the TPP negotiations.

Notably absent from these latest congressional concerns were the factors that drove the trade policy backlash and thus the Plaza initiative in 1985: large changes in exchange rates driven by market reactions to sharp differences in national growth rates and monetary policies. In the mid-1980s, the US economy boomed as a result of the massive fiscal stimulus provided by the Reagan administration and the sky-high US interest rates that made sure that rapid inflation would not return (the Reagan-Volcker policy mix). In the mid-2010s, the United States was again growing considerably faster than Europe and Japan, and US monetary policy had begun to tighten (the end of quantitative easing) while monetary policy in Europe and Japan was still easing aggressively. The dollar soared in the 1980s and strengthened sharply from late 2014 into 2015.

Congressional anxiety over exchange rates on this occasion focused solely on "manipulation," defined as direct intervention in the currency markets by foreign monetary authorities. It was viewed as an unfair trade practice as well as a monetary distortion and thus fully appropriate for consideration by trade policy, especially in the context of new liberalization (TPP), to make sure that deliberate currency moves did not undermine it. The G-7 and IMF made a clear distinction between these two sources of potential currency misalignment, condemning "manipulation" but largely exonerating market-driven movements, despite the protests of some countries on the receiving end (most vocally Brazil) that the effects on their economies are identical (see chapter 11). Congress, and the US political process more broadly, accepted this distinction and thus did not criticize the sharp general run-up in the dollar. This reaction may have been in part because, in light of the lags between currency movements and subsequent trade effects, the US trade and current account deficits had yet to climb very much or do much additional damage to the US economy, which was recovering and moving steadily if slowly back toward full employment, as conventionally defined. It also presumably reflected the fact that, in light of the limited alternatives to the dollar and the preference of weak economies around the world for a strong dollar to enhance their own competitiveness, the United States has had no difficulty financing its imbalances (and was thus again running "deficits without tears").

The questions going forward are whether continued large and rising dollar overvaluation and external deficits are sustainable domestically for both the US economy and US politics, as Congress will presumably have to vote on both the TPP (probably in 2016 or 2017) and subsequently the Transatlantic Trade and Investment Partnership (TTIP) (probably in 2018 or beyond). In economic terms the United States is approaching full employment. The requirements of the TPA/fast-track legislation sharply limit the ability of Congress to tie its approval of the pending trade deals to currency questions. However, the expansion remains moderate, wage growth is modest, income distribution continues to worsen, and the employment ratio remains disturbingly low. The US economic situation is thus far from satisfactory. An external imbalance headed back toward 5 percent of GDP by 2020 (Cline 2015b), at the exchange rates of late 2015 and likely to evolve in 2016, raises questions that are only likely to intensify (including as the political campaigns heat up during the course of 2016).

The dollar could, of course, rise significantly if the United States maintains, or even increases, its growth advantage over Europe and Japan. It could do so if Fed tightening proceeds, especially if that tightening turns out to be quicker and larger than anticipated by markets. The dollar could rise especially if the currencies of key emerging markets, including China, weaken as Fed tightening and their own economic problems promote capital outflows.

Is the dollar significantly overvalued, as it was in 1985? In his May 2015 estimates of "fundamental equilibrium exchange rates," using the methodology developed at the Peterson Institute for International Economics, my colleague William Cline concludes that the dollar is only modestly overvalued (by about 8 percent) and that the euro and yen are only modestly undervalued (by about 3 percent each) (Cline 2015a). He posits no misalignment in the exchange rate of the renminbi.

But the traditional approach of Cline (and the Institute) seeks only to keep countries' current account positions within 3 percent, plus or minus, of their GDPs. Hence the US deficit (4.3 percent), eurozone surplus (3.8 percent), and Japanese surplus (3.4 percent) that he projects for 2020 called for only minor corrections, which would presumably not require an international initiative like the Plaza Accord. China's even smaller projected surplus (2.5 percent) would require no change at all.[16]

The rationale for this analytical approach is that only deficits larger than 3 percent of GDP are likely to produce increases in a country's foreign debt position that could become unsustainable, from an international financial standpoint, and that symmetry calls for permitting surpluses of similar magnitudes. In the real world, the projected imbalances are very large in absolute terms: almost $1 trillion for the United States, more than $500 billion for the eurozone, and about $400 billion for China. These imbalances can make a great deal of difference to the world economy.

Moreover, there are sound reasons to believe that the United States, as a mature high-income country, should again become a net capital exporter and thus run current account surpluses. There are equally powerful reasons to believe that China, as a low-income developing country, should again become a net capital importer and thus run current account deficits. The IMF, as part of its 2015 External Sector Report (IMF 2015), has not gone quite that far, but it has suggested current account "norms" of a much smaller deficit for the United States of 1.6 percent of GDP, a zero balance for China and Japan, and a surplus of 2.25 percent of GDP for the euro area.

Using these IMF norms, let alone setting current account targets at zero for the four main economies, produces a dramatically different picture of whether current exchange rates, let alone future rates that moved further away from equilibrium levels, reflect underlying economic fundamentals. Tables 14.1 to 14.4 set current account targets on both bases and use Cline's model and parameters to calculate the implied misalignments for the four major currencies. Table 14.5 summarizes their main implications.

In essence, today's misalignments are in the same ballpark as the two negotiated currency corrections of the earlier postwar period (Plaza and Smithsonian).[17] The dollar came down by about 50 percent against both the deutsche mark and the yen after the Plaza Accord. Its trade-weighted depreciation was about 30 percent, compared with an overvaluation of 18–25

---

16. In his subsequent update, in November 2015, Cline (2015b) took account of the further rise of the dollar in late 2015 and concluded that the US current account deficit would rise to 4.8 percent of its GDP by 2020. This level would approach its previous highs and substantially exceed its pre-Plaza level.

17. Using a completely different methodology, Green, Papell, and Prodan (chapter 8 of this volume) reach the same conclusion.

Table 14.1 Target current account positions for 2020 using IMF Staff norms for China, Japan, euro area, and United States

Country	IMF projection of 2015 current account (percent of GDP)	IMF 2020 GDP forecast (billions of US dollars)	IMF 2020 current account forecast (percent of GDP)	Cline (2015a) adjusted 2020 current account (percent of GDP)	Target current account[a] (percent of GDP)
Pacific					
Australia	-4.0	1,491	-3.4	-2.6	-2.6
New Zealand	-4.8	240	-4.6	-4.9	-3.0
Asia					
China	3.2	16,157	3.0	2.5	0.0
Hong Kong	2.0	438	3.1	1.6	1.6
India	-1.3	3,640	-2.5	-2.7	-2.7
Indonesia	-3.0	1,307	-2.6	-2.3	-2.3
Japan	1.9	4,933	2.3	3.4	0.0
Korea	7.1	2,012	3.6	4.8	3.0
Malaysia	2.1	538	1.4	4.9	3.0
Philippines	5.5	510	3.0	1.5	1.5
Singapore	20.7	390	14.5	15.5	3.0
Taiwan	12.4	776	9.9	10.8	3.0
Thailand	4.4	504	0.7	0.2	0.2

Middle East/Africa					
Israel	4.5	315	3.8	4.5	3.0
Saudi Arabia	−1.0	902	5.4	5.9	5.9
South Africa	−4.6	409	−4.2	−3.5	−3.0
Europe					
Czech Republic	1.6	203	−0.7	0.2	0.2
Euro area	3.3	14,160	2.5	3.8	2.3
Hungary	4.8	165	1.2	−0.4	−0.4
Norway	7.6	502	4.8	5.2	5.2
Poland	−1.8	673	−3.5	−3.1	−3.0
Russia	5.4	2,081	4.3	1.5	1.5
Sweden	6.3	677	5.6	6.9	3.0
Switzerland	5.8	769	5.3	3.7	3.0
Turkey	−4.2	1,012	−5.0	−5.1	−3.0
United Kingdom	−4.8	3,731	−3.3	−2.3	−2.3
Western Hemisphere					
Argentina	−1.7	631	−1.5	−2.6	−2.6
Brazil	−3.7	2,354	−3.2	−1.9	−1.9
Canada	−2.6	2,044	−1.8	1.0	1.0
Chile	−1.2	325	−2.4	−1.6	−1.6
Colombia	−5.8	483	−3.6	−2.2	−2.2
Mexico	−2.2	1,653	−2.3	1.0	1.0
United States	−2.3	22,489	−2.6	−4.3	−1.6
Venezuela	−4.7	274	1.4	2.3	2.3

a. IMF (2015) for current account targets for China, Japan, euro area, and the United States; Cline (2015a) for the rest.

Sources: Cline (2015a); IMF (2015).

Table 14.2 FEER estimates based on IMF Staff norms for current accounts of China, Japan, euro area, and United States

| Country | Changes in current account as percent of GDP | | Change in REER (percent) | | Dollar exchange rate | | FEER-consistent dollar rate |
	Target change	Change in simulation	Target change	Change in simulation	Actual April 2015	Percent change from actual April 2015 rate to FEER	
Pacific							
Australia*	0.0	0.2	0.0	-1.2	0.77	22.1	0.94
New Zealand*	1.9	2.1	-7.2	-8.2	0.76	12.3	0.85
Asia							
China	-2.5	-2.2	10.3	9.2	6.20	27.8	4.85
Hong Kong	0.0	0.3	0.0	-0.6	7.75	24.5	6.23
India	0.0	0.2	0.0	-1.0	62.7	15.3	54.4
Indonesia	0.0	0.2	0.0	-1.1	12,946	24.1	10,428
Japan	-3.4	-3.3	23.0	21.9	120	41.1	85
Korea	-1.8	-1.4	4.2	3.3	1,086	23.8	878
Malaysia	-1.9	-1.4	3.8	2.7	3.63	27.3	2.86
Philippines	0.0	0.2	0.0	-1.0	44.4	23.3	36.0
Singapore	-12.5	-11.9	25.1	23.9	1.35	44.9	0.93
Taiwan	-7.8	-7.4	17.6	16.7	31.0	39.6	22.2
Thailand	0.0	0.5	0.0	-1.1	32.5	21.4	26.8

Middle East/Africa

Israel	−1.5	−1.3	5.0	4.3	3.93	19.1	3.30
Saudi Arabia	0.0	0.3	0.0	−0.8	3.75	19.8	3.13
South Africa	0.5	0.7	−2.2	−2.9	11.99	15.0	10.43
Europe							
Czech Republic	0.0	0.3	0.0	−0.6	25.4	19.0	21.3
Euro area*	−1.5	−1.2	6.3	4.8	1.08	21.0	1.31
Hungary	0.0	0.3	0.0	−0.6	277	18.1	235
Norway	0.0	0.2	0.0	−0.7	7.88	17.8	6.69
Poland	0.1	0.4	−0.3	−1.1	3.72	17.8	3.16
Russia	0.0	0.2	0.0	−0.6	53.0	15.4	45.9
Sweden	−3.9	−3.5	10.2	9.3	8.63	26.8	6.81
Switzerland	−0.7	−0.5	1.7	1.1	0.96	20.2	0.80
Turkey	2.1	2.3	−8.7	−9.4	2.65	6.3	2.50
United Kingdom*	0.0	0.2	0.0	−0.8	1.50	16.8	1.75
Western Hemisphere							
Argentina	0.0	0.2	0.0	−1.1	8.86	14.0	7.77
Brazil	0.0	0.2	0.0	−1.3	3.05	15.4	2.64
Canada	0.0	0.1	0.0	−0.4	1.23	7.3	1.15
Chile	0.0	0.3	0.0	−1.0	614	16.7	526
Colombia	0.0	0.1	0.0	−0.8	2,493	10.0	2,266
Mexico	0.0	0.1	0.0	−0.4	15.2	7.4	14.2
United States	2.7	2.9	−16.4	−17.6	1.00	0.0	1.00
Venezuela	0.0	0.2	0.0	−0.6	6.29	9.5	5.75

FEER = fundamental equilibrium exchange rate; REER = real effective exchange rate

* The currencies of these countries are expressed as dollars per currency. All others expressed as currency per dollar.

Sources: Cline (2015a); table 14.1.

percent today. The euro and yen are now undervalued against the dollar by 20–40 percent and 40–50 percent, respectively, with the yen approaching its 1985 peak, according to Green, Papell, and Prodan (see chapter 8). Fortunately, their trade-weighted average exchange rates (their real effective exchange rates, or REERs) are undervalued by much less, because they would need to rise by roughly equivalent amounts against the dollar and thus by very little vis-à-vis one another (and against most other currencies).

In terms of the magnitude of today's projected imbalances and misalignments, there is thus a strong case for a Plaza II. Tables 14.1 to 14.5 show that the current situation is very similar to the one that prevailed before the Plaza. The dollar is substantially overvalued, not only in the aggregate but vis-à-vis every significant currency. The currencies of China and several other Asian economies, notably Korea and Taiwan, are substantially undervalued (especially against the dollar) and should be included in order to avoid their free-riding on the agreement.[18] These economies, especially China and Japan, are the major targets of congressional ire. The absence of any significant currency intervention by the United States for more than 15 years suggests that a Plaza-type initiative would have substantial shock and thus market impact. The main participants would need to be the same countries as at the Plaza itself (the United States; Germany, through the eurozone; and Japan).

The policy issue is whether a Plaza-type agreement to correct these misalignments is now called for. There are three major arguments against it. The most compelling is the relatively good economic performance of the United States, a major source of the dollar's strength. Despite its large and gradually (so far) growing external deficit and the problems cited above, the US economy is performing much better than the economies of Europe and Japan (itself a major cause of the rising trade imbalance). China is looking shaky, with its slowdown and stock market fall in 2015 and early 2016. At the time of the Plaza Accord, by contrast, US growth and monetary policy were easing while German and Japanese growth were picking up and monetary policy was tightening. Hence a Plaza-type agreement at this time to raise the value of the euro, yen, and renminbi to anything like the equilibrium levels suggested above would be inconsistent with "fundamentals" and thus difficult to justify, as Eichengreen argues in chapter 10.

A second argument is that until recently, the major imbalances have been moving in the right directions. The Plaza took place as the US deficit, and the European and Japanese surpluses, had been soaring to record highs for several years. In contrast, in 2015 both the US deficit and the Chinese surplus remained significantly below their recent peaks (though both were starting to

---

18. After the Plaza Accord, Korea and Taiwan retained their dollar pegs; their currencies depreciated sharply with the dollar on a trade-weighted basis. They began running sizable surpluses as a result (Korea for the first time) and soon became the targets of global currency policy (Balassa and Williamson 1987), including via the Louvre communiqué, which led to substantial "catch-up" appreciations of their own exchange rates.

Table 14.3 Target current account positions for 2020 using zero targets for China, Japan, euro area, and United States

Country	IMF projection of 2015 current account (percent of GDP)	IMF 2020 GDP forecast (billions of US dollars)	IMF 2020 current account forecast (percent of GDP)	Cline (2015a) adjusted 2020 current account (percent of GDP)	Target current account[a] (percent of GDP)
Pacific					
Australia	-4.0	1,491	-3.4	-2.6	-2.6
New Zealand	-4.8	240	-4.6	-4.9	-3.0
Asia					
China	3.2	16,157	3.0	2.5	0.0
Hong Kong	2.0	438	3.1	1.6	1.6
India	-1.3	3,640	-2.5	-2.7	-2.7
Indonesia	-3.0	1,307	-2.6	-2.3	-2.3
Japan	1.9	4,933	2.3	3.4	0.0
Korea	7.1	2,012	3.6	4.8	3.0
Malaysia	2.1	538	1.4	4.9	3.0
Philippines	5.5	510	3.0	1.5	1.5
Singapore	20.7	390	14.5	15.5	3.0
Taiwan	12.4	776	9.9	10.8	3.0
Thailand	4.4	504	0.7	0.2	0.2

(table continues)

Table 14.3 Target current account positions for 2020 using zero targets for China, Japan, euro area, and United States *(continued)*

Country	IMF projection of 2015 current account (percent of GDP)	IMF 2020 GDP forecast (billions of US dollars)	IMF 2020 current account forecast (percent of GDP)	Cline (2015a) adjusted 2020 current account (percent of GDP)	Target current account[a] (percent of GDP)
Middle East/Africa					
Israel	4.5	315	3.8	4.5	3.0
Saudi Arabia	–1.0	902	5.4	5.9	5.9
South Africa	–4.6	409	–4.2	–3.5	–3.0
Europe					
Czech Republic	1.6	203	–0.7	0.2	0.2
Euro area	3.3	14,160	2.5	3.8	0.0
Hungary	4.8	165	1.2	–0.4	–0.4
Norway	7.6	502	4.8	5.2	5.2
Poland	–1.8	673	–3.5	–3.1	–3.0
Russia	5.4	2,081	4.3	1.5	1.5
Sweden	6.3	677	5.6	6.9	3.0
Switzerland	5.8	769	5.3	3.7	3.0
Turkey	–4.2	1,012	–5.0	–5.1	–3.0
United Kingdom	–4.8	3,731	–3.3	–2.3	–2.3

Western Hemisphere

Argentina	-1.7	631	-1.5	-2.6	-2.6
Brazil	-3.7	2,354	-3.2	-1.9	-1.9
Canada	-2.6	2,044	-1.8	1.0	1.0
Chile	-1.2	325	-2.4	-1.6	-1.6
Colombia	-5.8	483	-3.6	-2.2	-2.2
Mexico	-2.2	1,653	-2.3	1.0	1.0
United States	-2.3	22,489	-2.6	-4.3	0.0
Venezuela	-4.7	274	1.4	2.3	2.3

a. Author's current account targets for China, Japan, euro area, and the United States; Cline (2015a) for the rest.

Sources: Cline (2015a); IMF (2015).

Table 14.4 FEER estimates based on zero targets for current accounts of China, Japan, euro area, and United States

Country	Changes in current account as percent of GDP		Change in REER (percent)		Dollar exchange rate		FEER-consistent dollar rate
	Target change	Change in simulation	Target change	Change in simulation	Actual April 2015	Percent change from actual April 2015 rate to FEER	
Pacific							
Australia*	0.0	0.1	0.0	-0.4	0.77	32.0	1.02
New Zealand*	1.9	1.9	-7.2	-7.5	0.76	21.8	0.92
Asia							
China	-2.5	-2.4	10.3	9.9	6.20	37.1	4.52
Hong Kong	0.0	0.1	0.0	-0.2	7.75	34.2	5.78
India	0.0	0.1	0.0	-0.4	62.7	24.3	50.5
Indonesia	0.0	0.1	0.0	-0.4	12,946	33.9	9,671
Japan	-3.4	-3.3	23.0	22.6	120	50.2	80
Korea	-1.8	-1.6	4.2	3.8	1,086	32.7	818
Malaysia	-1.9	-1.7	3.8	3.4	3.63	36.9	2.65
Philippines	0.0	0.1	0.0	-0.4	44.4	32.8	33.5
Singapore	-12.5	-12.3	25.1	24.6	1.35	54.7	0.87
Taiwan	-7.8	-7.7	17.6	17.3	31.0	48.8	20.9
Thailand	0.0	0.2	0.0	-0.4	32.5	30.8	24.9

Middle East/Africa							
Israel	−1.5	−1.5	5.0	4.7	3.93	29.3	3.04
Saudi Arabia	0.0	0.1	0.0	−0.3	3.75	29.2	2.90
South Africa	0.5	0.6	−2.2	−2.4	11.99	25.3	9.57
Europe							
Czech Republic	0.0	0.1	0.0	−0.2	25.4	35.9	18.7
Euro area*	−3.8	−3.6	15.5	15.0	1.08	40.9	1.52
Hungary	0.0	0.1	0.0	−0.2	277	33.6	207
Norway	0.0	0.1	0.0	−0.3	7.88	32.1	5.97
Poland	0.1	0.2	−0.3	−0.6	3.72	34.0	2.78
Russia	0.0	0.1	0.0	−0.2	53.0	26.8	41.7
Sweden	−3.9	−3.7	10.2	9.8	8.63	41.4	6.10
Switzerland	−0.7	−0.7	1.7	1.5	0.96	35.4	0.71
Turkey	2.1	2.1	−8.7	−9.0	2.65	17.9	2.25
United Kingdom*	0.0	0.1	0.0	−0.3	1.50	30.6	1.95
Western Hemisphere							
Argentina	0.0	0.1	0.0	−0.4	8.86	23.9	7.15
Brazil	0.0	0.1	0.0	−0.5	3.05	25.4	2.43
Canada	0.0	0.0	0.0	−0.2	1.23	11.6	1.11
Chile	0.0	0.1	0.0	−0.4	614	25.9	488
Colombia	0.0	0.1	0.0	−0.3	2493	16.8	2,134
Mexico	0.0	0.0	0.0	−0.2	15.2	11.5	13.6
United States	4.3	4.4	−26.1	−26.5	1.00	0.0	1.00
Venezuela	0.0	0.1	0.0	−0.2	6.29	15.0	5.47

FEER = fundamental equilibrium exchange rate; REER = real effective exchange rate

* The currencies of these countries are expressed as dollars per currency. All others expressed as currency per dollar.

Sources: Cline (2015a); table 14.3.

Table 14.5   Currency misalignments in 2015

Economy	Trade-weighted average		Bilateral rates against dollar (equilibrium level)	
	To achieve:		To achieve:	
	IMF norms	Zero balances	IMF norms	Zero balances
United States	−17.6	−26.5	—	—
Euro area	+4.8	+15.0	+21.0 (1.31)	+40.9 (1.52)
China	+9.2	+9.9	+27.8 (4.85)	+37.1 (4.52)
Japan	+21.9	+22.6	+41.1 (85)	+50.2 (80)

Note: + means undervaluation and thus needed appreciation; – means overvaluation and thus needed depreciation. The numbers in parentheses are the implied equilibrium levels of the bilateral dollar rates for the euro, renminbi, and yen.

trend up again as the year progressed, toward the much larger imbalances projected for 2020, and the Chinese surplus had already doubled as a share of its GDP from 2013 through the first half of 2015). The surpluses of the large oil exporters had dropped sharply with the fall in world energy prices. The surpluses of the eurozone, especially Germany, continued to climb, but the overall pattern of imbalances was not getting much worse.

The third argument against early action is the slackening, at least for the moment, of protectionist pressure in Congress. The TPA votes were very close in both houses, and fairly intrusive currency amendments lost by even smaller margins in the Senate Finance Committee and on the Senate floor (see next section). But the administration largely won that battle, and little appetite to reopen the issue has yet developed or is likely to develop, at least directly on the trade bills themselves, when the TPP and TTIP legislation come up for approval, because of the up-or-down and time-limited nature of those votes under TPA/fast-track procedures.

It is thus likely that Plaza II ideas will come onto the policy agenda only under three conditions: the US economy turns down, in part as a result of rising trade deficits; the dollar takes another sharp upward climb, producing widespread complaints from US firms and workers about the impact on their competitiveness; and/or Congress begins to worry again about growing trade deficits caused by dollar overvaluation, whatever its causes.

How much further dollar appreciation would be needed to trigger these reactions? Cline's model indicates that every 10 percent rise in the dollar adds about $350 billion to the trade deficit and reduces the level of US economic activity by about 1.65 percent (with a corresponding loss of about 1.5 million jobs, although easier monetary policy could in principle produce a full offset, unless interest rates are already at the zero lower bound). On these parameters, the current account deficit was headed toward $1 trillion, with the dollar at the levels of late 2015. A further rise of 10 percent in the dollar would take the imbalance close to $1.5 trillion a year by 2020, with correspondingly higher output and job losses.[19] This increase would presumably attract considerable attention and spur calls for action in some quarters.

When, if ever, might such further dollar appreciation occur? The timing probably depends on four key variables: the extent of Fed tightening, the speed of Fed tightening, differences between economic growth in the United States on the one hand and Europe and Japan on the other, and the success of China's reforms in sustaining rapid growth without which they will both lose further market confidence and be tempted to revert to export expansion via renewed manipulation. One can imagine combinations of these variables that would push the dollar significantly up or down. It can move a great deal in a short period (between August 2014 and August 2015 it rose about 15 percent on a real trade-weighted average basis). Policy should be ready to respond if it does. Each of the two major dollar appreciations of the postwar period—from 1978 to 1985 and from 1995 to 2002—took seven years. The current appreciation has proceeded for only four years, so a good deal more could still be in store.

The developments most likely to produce a sharp new rise in the dollar and thus make the case for a Plaza II—namely, a sharp tightening of Fed policy and continued stagnation in Europe and Japan, as the United States becomes an island of growth in a weak world economy, and continued lags in reform in China—would simultaneously reinforce the case against such an initiative, however, as indicated above. Cooperation from the other key countries to weaken the dollar, and thus strengthen their own currencies and further cloud the outlook for their economies, would be highly unlikely in such circumstances. Any US currency initiative in such a setting, perhaps driven by renewed congressional pressure, would almost certainly have to be unilateral—which could undermine its provision of the needed global public goods described above. The final question is thus the current status of US currency policy in the wake of the debate in Congress in 2015, the most active public discussion of the topic since the Plaza-Louvre period itself.

Does the United States Have a New Currency Policy?

Currency was a central topic in the trade policy debate in both the Senate and House in May–June 2015. That debate was foreshadowed by letters conveyed by unusual bipartisan majorities of both houses to the president and his top officials in 2013 calling for "enforceable disciplines" on currency manipulation in the TPP and all future US free trade agreements.

The currency debate itself encompassed five major features. The first was the direct linkage of the currency issue to trade policy, which was largely unprecedented (Bergsten 2014). Congress found the lever to address currency, which it had been seeking for some time, when the administration was forced to approach it for negotiating authority to pursue the TPP and TTIP. There

---

19. The market consensus in late 2015 was for a trade-weighted average dollar appreciation of about 2.6 percent in 2016, including rises of 7–10 percent against the euro and yen.

was also compelling logic in the linkage, despite the administration's continuous denial and delayed recognition of it: For the past decade, currency manipulation has distorted trade flows far more than any tariff or conventional tool of trade policy (Bergsten and Gagnon 2012; chapter 11 of this volume). Paul Volcker famously opined that trade flows respond more to 10 minutes of movement in exchange rates than to 10 years of trade negotiations.

The second feature was the focus on currency manipulation as an "unfair trade practice" as well as a monetary distortion. This outcome stemmed directly from the linkage to trade policy. No attention was paid to the sharp market-driven rise in the dollar, in response to differential growth rates and monetary policies, that was occurring just as the congressional debate was getting under way in early 2015. This ignoring of aggregate misalignments was presumably in part because the inevitable sharp increase in the US current account deficit had not yet taken place, because of the usual time lag of two to three years between currency change and trade outcomes and the fact that the deficit had declined sharply from its recent peak. Complaints from adversely affected US firms and even labor unions were limited. The muted reaction to macro-induced dollar appreciation also probably occurred because the Republican majorities in both houses believe in flexible exchange rates and respect the outcomes generated in them by market forces even when they may be objectively excessive.

The administration implicitly endorsed this clear distinction between "manipulation" (defined as direct intervention in the foreign exchange markets to limit a currency's appreciation) and market-driven movements in exchange rates. It did so because it feared that any new constraints on "manipulation" might be used to attack its own macroeconomic policies, especially quantitative easing by the Federal Reserve, which some countries view as affecting their exchange rates just as much as (or more than) direct intervention by China. Some members of Congress shared this fear. Both the IMF and the G-7 have drawn a clear distinction between the two types of policy action. However, as the impact on recipient countries can appear very similar, some might very well accuse the United States (and other countries deploying quantitative easing) of currency manipulation. Hence the administration reinforced the congressional focus on manipulation as it emphasized this distinction.

A third interesting feature was the country focus of the debate. China had, of course, been the major target of congressional (and administration) concerns on the currency front over the preceding decade, and Senator Schumer and some others continued to emphasize its previously heavy intervention. However, the renminbi had risen substantially over the preceding five years, especially on a trade-weighted basis, and it had recently appreciated with the dollar, to which it remained essentially pegged, against most other currencies. The Chinese current account surplus had dropped from almost 10 percent of GDP at its peak in 2007–08 to less than 3 percent. Chinese intervention in 2015 shifted from primarily buying dollars, to keep the renminbi from strengthening further, to largely selling dollars, to keep the renminbi from departing its fixed exchange rate on the downside in the face of large private capital outflows. While rhetorically maintaining its traditional position that China should let market forces determine its exchange rate, the administration in practice reinforced this "reverse intervention" by letting China know that it would be displeased with a "disorderly" or sharp fall in the renminbi, especially after China engineered a small devaluation in August 2015, undoubtedly using the congressional pressures (some of which resurfaced for a short time after that Chinese action) as usual to reinforce its case. The administration could thus claim with some validity that its policy of patient diplomacy had succeeded, and the decline in manipulation probably weakened congressional concern over the issue (although some members had simply used it as an excuse to justify antitrade positions that were based on other considerations).

These changes in circumstances, including the sharp decline in the US deficit as well as the Chinese surplus from the levels of 7 to 10 years ago, also probably meant that no countries (and almost certainly no TPP countries with the possible exception of Singapore) could reasonably be indicted for manipulation any time soon. The anti-Chinese invective that had been common in earlier years declined substantially, and Congress quite sensibly came to view the legislation as a potential vehicle to provide deterrence against future bad behavior on the currency front, especially vis-à-vis countries that were about to enjoy increased access to the US market via new trade agreements, rather than a trigger for immediate retaliation.

The chief political driver of the currency issue was the automobile industry, especially Ford Motor Company, whose emphasis was on Japan and, to a lesser extent, Korea. Japan had not been guilty of overt manipulation for more than a decade, as even the auto companies acknowledged. The incoming Abe government in late 2012 had vigorously talked down the yen by about 30 percent, however, with subsequent "validation" by the aggressive quantitative easing monetary policy adopted by the Bank of Japan (but also with stern rebukes by the Treasury and a strong G-7 statement in February 2013 that committed Japan, along with the other members, to avoid targeting exchange rates and indeed all currency intervention without prior consultation with the group).[20] In its most recent semiannual currency reports, the Treasury Department had singled out Korea as the major intervener over the past year or so (though Treasury did not label it a "manipulator," any more than it had China for the previous decade, and noted that it, like China, had also recently intervened on the other side of the market to keep its exchange rate from weakening further).

---

20. Frankel (chapter 6) calls this G-7 statement an "anti-Plaza agreement" because it "rules out intervention." The statement clearly permits intervention, including joint intervention, that is agreed to by the group, however; it therefore also authorizes a repetition of the (agreed) Plaza strategy. More generally, Frankel fails to distinguish between intervention that is agreed to and intervention that is adopted unilaterally and may therefore be guilty of contributing to "currency wars."

A fourth feature is the fact that the issue remained bipartisan to an important extent. Democrats provided most of the votes for strong action on currency in the Senate (there were no recorded votes in the House), but Republicans took the lead on key aspects of the issue. Senator Rob Portman, the former US Trade Representative under President George W. Bush, led the effort in both the Finance Committee and on the floor to require that "enforceable disciplines" against manipulation be negotiated in the TPP (the vote lost by very small margins in both). Senator Lindsey Graham continued to cosponsor, with Senator Schumer, the amendment that would authorize the application of countervailing duties against imports subsidized by currency manipulation (the measure passed the Senate by a wide majority as part of separate legislation but was dropped in the conference committee as a result of opposition by the House leadership).

A fifth feature was the administration's adamant opposition to any new legislation that would be legally binding on either it or its trading partners in the TPP. The strategy was risky, because it appeared at several points that such stonewalling could block passage of the entire TPA bill, possibly killing the TPP negotiations. But the administration claimed that its consultations with TPP partners indicated that US insistence on binding currency rules would itself kill the negotiations. (It is impossible to validate that claim, because the administration never sought agreement on binding rules; to the contrary, the trading partners knew that the administration opposed such rules, so they could have simply been giving it ammunition to use in the congressional debate.) It also feared, as noted above, that other countries might attack the macroeconomic policies of the United States, especially quantitative easing by the Fed, as constituting currency manipulation. In the end the administration conceded enough ground on nonbinding alternatives (see below) to persuade just enough advocates of new currency action to support the TPA legislation that permitted the trade policy agenda to move ahead. However, the absence of stronger action on currency is emphasized by many opponents of the TPP itself and could jeopardize congressional approval of that agreement.

Where does the congressional debate leave US currency policy? There were four major components of that debate (and a fifth that was considered informally). First, Congress inserted two "principal negotiating objectives" into the TPA legislation itself: an insistence that TPP members "avoid manipulating exchange rates to prevent effective balance of payments adjustment or to gain an unfair competitive advantage" and "establish accountability with respect to unfair currency practices... by other parties to a trade agreement." Both provisos authorize the administration to adopt various techniques to achieve its purposes, including "enforceable rules." Neither objective needs to be achieved through the TPP itself, however, and the law also authorizes such softer options as "cooperative mechanisms, reporting, monitoring, transparency or other means."

The administration's primary response was to negotiate a Joint Declaration of the Macroeconomic Policy Authorities of Trans-Pacific Partnership Countries that reaffirms their commitments, from the IMF Articles of Agreement and numerous G-7 and G-20 communiqués, to avoid "manipulating exchange rates or the international monetary system in order to prevent effective balance of payments adjustment or to gain an unfair competitive advantage," "persistent exchange rate misalignments," "competitive devaluation," and targeting of "its country's rate for competitive purposes." Countries also commit to greater transparency and reporting, including public disclosure of their foreign exchange reserves and intervention data. They also agree to create a Group of TPP macroeconomic officials that consults with one another at least annually on macroeconomic, including currency, issues and to issue reports on its results. All of this will take place outside the TPP itself and with no legal obligations.[21]

The other TPP countries acknowledged the US need for some such initiative to respond to the new Congressional mandate and broader currency pressures. They were pleased that the concept of "enforceable disciplines" in the TPP itself was dropped. But they were not enthusiastic about the watered-down version either, which an aggressive US administration could use to put considerable pressure on them. Japan publicly expressed doubt about it.[22] It remains to be seen what, if any, practical impact the new group will have. Treasury will, of course, continue its bilateral efforts and its use of existing forums, including the G-7 and G-20, to pursue US currency goals.

Second, the proposed Portman-Stabenow amendment greatly strengthened the "negotiating objectives" by requiring their implementation through "enforceable disciplines" in the TPP itself. This approach, maintaining the insistence of the congressional letters of 2013, elicited the strongest opposition from the administration and indeed a pledge by Treasury Secretary Jacob Lew to recommend that the president veto any TPA bill that included it (though never a veto threat from the president himself) on the grounds that it would torpedo the entire TPP negotiation. The amendment lost by a narrow margin both in the Senate Finance Committee (18–14) and on the floor (51–48).

The two other alternatives considered by Congress were, through a parliamentary maneuver to protect the TPA bill, included in a parallel customs and enforcement bill that was initially adopted in different forms by the two houses. The stiffer of the two was the Schumer-Graham amendment authorizing countervailing duties against exports subsidized by currency manipulation. It passed the Senate by a large majority (after passing both the House and Senate in separate bills in 2010 and 2011, respectively) but was strongly opposed by the Republican leadership in the House (as well as by the administration). It was dropped when the conference committee met to reconcile the two versions of the full bill and in the final legislation, which passed in early 2016.

---

21. For more details, see Bergsten and Schott (2016).

22. The G-7 antimanipulation statement of February 2013, whose main target was Japan, can be viewed as a US-Japan precursor to the joint TPP declaration in the same way that the Baker-Miyazawa bilateral agreement of late 1986 on the yen/dollar exchange rate was a precursor to the broader target zones agreed by the G-7 at the Louvre.

The less aggressive alternative, and the one most likely to have a lasting impact on US currency policy, is the Bennet-Hatch-Carper amendment, worked out by the administration and the key committees, particularly the Senate Finance Committee (where most of the detailed discussion took place). It has three parts: specification of the criteria that will lead a country to be confronted for currency manipulation; a new procedure to guide such confrontation, culminating in "enhanced engagement" by the United States; and a series of remedies to be considered once such engagement is undertaken.

The amendment requires Treasury to include in its semiannual reports an "enhanced analysis" of any major trading partner of the United States that has "a significant bilateral trade surplus with the United States... a material current account surplus and... engaged in persistent one-sided intervention in the foreign exchange market." It goes on to require that "the President, through the Secretary of the Treasury, *shall* [emphasis added] commence enhanced bilateral engagement with each country for which an enhanced analysis... is included in the report...." It is difficult to see how Treasury could have evaded these criteria with respect to China and a number of other countries over the past decade. However, the "enhanced bilateral engagement" has no required outcome; the closest is the requirement to "develop a plan with specific actions to address [the] undervaluation and surpluses." The bill also includes a clause authorizing the Treasury secretary to waive the requirements for economic or national security reasons.[23]

In addition, if the secretary determines that a country has failed to adopt appropriate policies to correct its undervaluation and surpluses after a year, the president *shall* [emphasis added] take "one or more" of four specified actions. One is to instruct the US executive director at the IMF to call for that institution to undertake "additional rigorous surveillance and, as appropriate, formal consultations on findings of currency manipulation" (though the United States of course cannot force the IMF to do so). Another is to "take [such failure] into account" in determining whether to pursue a bilateral or regional trade agreement with that country. This proviso, which acknowledges the linkage between currency and trade, might prove to be a powerful deterrent to manipulation by Korea, or even China, if it decides to seek membership in a second phase of the TPP. The secretary has discretion to determine whether a country has "failed to adopt appropriate policies," although the same objective criteria that require "enhanced analysis" in the first place would still presumably obtain.[24]

---

23. The most likely immediate targets would be Korea and Taiwan, the same economies that were labelled "manipulators" in Treasury's first report after the previous law was passed, in 1988.

24. A fifth, much more informal and limited, policy consideration during the congressional debate was my proposal (first presented June 25, 2003, in testimony before the House Committee on Small Business ["The Correction of the Dollar and Foreign Intervention in the Currency Markets"]) for "countervailing currency intervention." Under this mechanism, the United States would buy the currencies of manipulators in amounts equal to their purchases of dollars, in order to neutralize

It may be a while before we know what impact, if any, the recent congressional debate will have on US currency policy. It could result in new procedures, both domestically (especially at Treasury) and internationally (including via the committee of TPP monetary authorities), but little or no new substance. Alternatively, it could lead to a tougher stance against recent (Korea?) and potential future (China or Japan again?) manipulators that would effectively deter such practices. The outcome will depend heavily on the degree of continuing congressional pressure on the administration, which in turn will depend at least partially on the extent of actual currency manipulation by countries that are major trade competitors of the United States.

More subtly, the congressional debate itself—especially the close votes regarding insistence on "enforceable disciplines" in the TPP and authorization of countervailing duties against all manipulators—may deter future manipulation, at least for a while. The extent and amount of manipulation has declined substantially in recent years (as Gagnon notes in chapter 11). The decline reflects market forces, where the flipside of strong dollar appreciation is the weakening of the currencies of most emerging-market economies and thus the disappearance of much (if not all) of the need for them to buy dollars to avoid appreciation. Many countries, such as China and Korea, have indeed been operating on the other side of the market—selling dollars on at least some occasions to limit the depreciation of their exchange rates. But the sharp decline in manipulation is also probably at least partially the result of the stepped-up concern over the issue voiced in Congress and more broadly in the United States and around the world. It may be sustained if that concern is maintained, as is likely to be the case. The test will come only when market pressures again start promoting stronger exchange rates for the renminbi and the currencies of other traditional manipulators, as they surely will, but the global currency regime may thus have achieved at least a bit of progressive de facto reform.

Conclusion

Recent developments regarding currency policy relate to prospects for a future Plaza II or similar initiative by the United States, which lessons from the Plaza Accord suggest would have to lead any such effort. Such initiatives do not require legislative authorization. But congressional pressure—especially related to trade policy—has been a central feature of past US efforts of this type, including the Plaza itself. On the most recent occasion, Congress stopped just short of forcing the administration to take new steps. Its widespread senti-

---

and thus deter their manipulation. Such an authorization was passed by the Senate as "remedial currency intervention" in 2011 but never formally addressed by the House. Key members of the Senate Finance and House Ways and Means Committees raised the idea with top administration officials during the latest debate. They strongly opposed it, and the idea was not pursued further. It would be useful to add this remedy to the list authorized for deployment against countries subjected to "enhanced engagement."

ment for a more aggressive stance was clear, however, and has already led to potentially significant policy changes. This congressional attitude is likely to have continuing and even growing impact as the US trade and current account deficits increase as a result of the sizable recent (and potential future) run-up in the exchange rate of the dollar and as trade policy issues remain before Congress for action.

The congressional focus on manipulation by individual surplus countries, rather than on generalized currency problems in response to macroeconomic conditions and monetary policies, could on the other hand reduce the likelihood of multilateral action. It is possible that intervention by surplus countries could again become sufficiently widespread to warrant such an approach, as some analysts advocated a few years ago (Cline 2005, Bergsten and Gagnon 2012). But the thrust of US currency policy since the Plaza-Louvre period has been country specific and ad hoc, and that pattern is likely to prevail unless and until the conditions hypothesized in the previous section prevail again.

It is thus not yet time for a Plaza II. However, the underlying imbalances are about as great as the ones that triggered the Plaza Accord itself. The problem of currency misalignments remains acute. It would be desirable to erect new deterrents to manipulation (though it is likely to remain only part of the broader adjustment problem), including enforceable disciplines in trade agreements, if they could be negotiated, and the institution of a policy of countervailing currency intervention by the United States itself.

In the meanwhile it is extremely useful to recall the successes and lessons of the Plaza Accord. Secretary Baker and the Baker Institute for Public Policy are to be greatly commended for sponsoring this project to do so—and thus to remind current and future policymakers that a model exists for responding to such problems. It would probably take another Secretary Baker and an equally talented team to engineer such a replication, however. Future administrations should take note in assembling their lineups.

References

Baker, James A., III. 2006. *Work Hard, Study... And Keep Out of Politics! Adventures and Lessons from an Unexpected Public Life.* New York: Penguin Group.

Balassa, Bela, and John Williamson. 1987. *Adjusting to Success: Balance of Payments Policy in the East Asian NICs.* Washington: Institute for International Economics.

Bergsten, C. Fred. 1981. US International Economic Policy in the 1980s. Hearing before the Subcommittee on International Economic Policy and Trade of the Committee on Foreign Affairs. House of Representatives, 97th Congress, 1st session, February 24.

Bergsten, C. Fred. 2014. *Addressing Currency Manipulation through Trade Agreements.* Policy Brief 14-2. Washington: Peterson Institute for International Economics.

Bergsten, C. Fred, and Joseph E. Gagnon. 2012. *Currency Manipulation: The US Economy and the Global Economic Order.* PIIE Policy Brief 12-25. Washington: Peterson Institute for International Economics.

Bergsten, C. Fred, Takatoshi Ito, and Marcus Noland. 2001. *No More Bashing: Building a New Japan–United States Economic Relationship.* Washington: Institute for International Economics.

Bergsten, C. Fred, and Jeffrey J. Schott. 2016. TPP and Exchange Rates. In *Assessing the Trans-Pacific Partnership—Volume 2: Innovations in Trading Rules*. PIIE Briefing 16-4. Washington: Peterson Institute for International Economics.

Bergsten, C. Fred, and John Williamson. 1983. Exchange Rates and Trade Policy. In *Trade Policy in the 1980s*, ed. William R. Cline. Washington: Institute for International Economics.

Blustein, Paul. 2013. *Off Balance: The Travails of Institutions that Govern the Global Financial System.* Waterloo, ON: Centre for International Governance Innovation.

Cline, William R. 2005. *The Case for a New Plaza Agreement.* Policy Brief 05-4. Washington: Institute for International Economics.

Cline, William R. 2015a. *Estimates of Fundamental Equilibrium Exchange Rates, May 2015*. Policy Brief 15-8. Washington: Peterson Institute for International Economics.

Cline, William R. 2015b. *Estimates of Fundamental Equilibrium Exchange Rates, November 2015*. Policy Brief 15-20. Washington: Peterson Institute for International Economics.

Federal Reserve Bank of Kansas City. 1985. *The U.S. Dollar: Recent Developments, Outlook and Policy Options.* Kansas City.

Funabashi, Yoichi. 1989. *Managing The Dollar: From the Plaza to the Louvre*, 2nd ed. Washington: Institute for International Economics.

Gyohten, Toyoo. 2013. *En no Koubou: Tsu ka Mafia no Dokuhaku* [*The Rise and Fall of the Yen: Monologue of a "Currency Mafia"*]. Tokyo: Asahi Shimbun Publishing Co.

IMF (International Monetary Fund). 2015. *2015 External Sector Report*, July 27. Washington.

Kindleberger, Charles P. 1973. *The World in Depression.* Berkeley: University of California Press.

Krugman, Paul R. 1991. Has the Adjustment Process Worked? In *International Adjustment and Financing: The Lessons of 1985–1991*, ed. C. Fred Bergsten. Washington: Institute for International Economics.

Marris, Stephen. 1983. The Coming Dollar Crisis. *Fortune.* December.

Marris, Stephen. 1987. *Deficits and the Dollar: The World Economy at Risk,* 2nd ed. Washington: Institute for International Economics.

Marris, Stephen. 1991. Why No Hard Landing? In *International Adjustment and Financing: The Lessons of 1985-91,* ed. C. Fred Bergsten. Washington: Institute for International Economics.

Mulford, David. 2014. *Packing for India: A Life of Action in Global Finance and Diplomacy.* Lincoln, NE: Potomac Books.

Volcker, Paul, and Toyoo Gyohten. 1992. *Changing Fortunes: The World's Money and the Threat to American Leadership.* New York: Times Books.

Williamson, John, and Malcolm Miller. 1987. *Targets and Indications: A Blueprint for the International Coordination of Economic Policy.* Washington: Institute for International Economics.

About the Contributors

James A. Baker, III, served in senior government positions under three US presidents. He was the nation's 61st secretary of state from January 1989 through August 1992 under President George H. W. Bush. During his tenure at the State Department, he traveled to 90 countries as the United States confronted the unprecedented challenges and opportunities of the post–Cold War era.

Baker was the 67th secretary of the Treasury from 1985 to 1988 under President Ronald Reagan. As Treasury secretary, he was also chairman of the President's Economic Policy Council. In 1985, he coordinated the Plaza Accord. From 1981 to 1985, he served as White House chief of staff to President Reagan.

Baker's record of public service began in 1975 as undersecretary of commerce to President Gerald Ford. It concluded with his service as White House chief of staff and senior counselor to President Bush from August 1992 to January 1993. Long active in American presidential politics, Baker led presidential campaigns for Presidents Ford, Reagan, and Bush over the course of five consecutive presidential elections from 1976 to 1992.

A native Houstonian, Baker graduated from Princeton University in 1952. After two years of active duty as a lieutenant in the United States Marine Corps, he entered the University of Texas School of Law. He received his JD with honors in 1957 and practiced law with the Houston firm of Andrews and Kurth from 1957 to 1975.

Agnès Bénassy-Quéré is professor at the Paris School of Economics–University of Paris 1 Panthéon Sorbonne and chair of the French Council of Economic Analysis. She worked for the French Ministry of Economy and Finance, before moving to academic positions successively at universities of

Cergy-Pontoise, Lille 2, Paris-Ouest, and École Polytechnique. She also served as deputy director and director of CEPII and is affiliated with CESIfo. She is a member of the Commission Économique de la Nation (an advisory body to the finance minister), the French macroprudential authority, and the Banque de France's board. She was a member of the Shadow ECB Council and columnist at France Culture. Her research interests focus on the international monetary system and European macroeconomic policy.

C. Fred Bergsten was founding director of the Peterson Institute for International Economics from 1981 through 2012 and is now senior fellow and director emeritus there. He has been a member of the President's Advisory Committee on Trade Policy and Negotiations since 2010. He was formerly assistant secretary for international affairs of the US Treasury (1977–81), functioned as undersecretary for monetary affairs (1980–81), and was assistant for international economic affairs to the National Security Council (1969–71). He was chairman of the Competitiveness Policy Council created by Congress (1991–95) and chairman of the APEC Eminent Persons Group (1993–95). This is the 44th book he has written, coauthored, or edited, including most recently *India's Rise: A Strategy for Trade-Led Growth* (2015), *Addressing Currency Manipulation through Trade Agreements* (2014), *Bridging the Pacific: Toward Free Trade and Investment Between China and the United States* (2014), and *The Coming Resolution of the European Crisis* (2012).

Bergsten has received the Meritorious Honor Award of the Department of State (1965), Exceptional Service Award of the Treasury Department (1981), Legion d'Honneur from the Government of France (1985), an honorary fellowship in the Chinese Academy of Social Sciences (1997), the Distinguished Alumni Leadership Award from the Fletcher School (2010), the Order of the Polar Star from the Government of Sweden (2013), the Officer's Cross of the Order of Merit of the Federal Republic of Germany (2014), the Swedish American of the Year for 2014, and the 1st Class of the Order of Diplomatic Service Merit "Gwanghwa Medal" from the Republic of Korea (2016).

Charles H. Dallara is vice chairman of Partners Group Holding's board of directors and chairman of the Americas. He has 39 years of experience in global finance and economics. He is also a member of the board of directors of Scotiabank, the investment advisory board at Holowesko Partners, the board of directors of the Bertelsmann Foundation North America, the senior advisory board of Oliver Wyman Financial Services, and the international advisory board of Lingnan College, SunYat-Sen University, as well as director at large of the National Bureau of Economic Research, vice chair of the board of advisors of the Fletcher School of Law and Diplomacy, and vice president of the International Finance Forum.

Prior to joining Partners Group, he was managing director and CEO of the Institute of International Finance (IIF) (July 1993–January 2013). In this capacity, he built the IIF into one of the most influential global associations of financial institutions. He played a leading role in the handling of many sovereign debt issues, including in the Greek debt restructuring. He was also substantially involved in global regulatory reform working closely with regulators, central bank governors, and leaders of financial institutions to strengthen the global regulatory framework for financial services.

Previously, he was managing director at J.P. Morgan & Co. (1991–93). He also served in the US Treasury Department from 1976 to 1991. During this time, he held a variety of senior positions in the Ronald Reagan and George H.W. Bush administrations, including assistant secretary of the Treasury for international affairs, assistant secretary of the Treasury for policy development and United States executive director of the International Monetary Fund. In these capacities, he played a role in key US economic policy initiatives such as the Plaza Accord and the Brady Plan. He holds a Master of Arts, a Master of Arts in Law and Diplomacy, and a PhD from the Fletcher School of Law and Diplomacy at Tufts University and a bachelor's degree in economics and an honorary doctorate from the University of South Carolina.

Barry Eichengreen is professor of economics and professor of political science at the University of California, Berkeley. He is a research associate at the National Bureau of Economic Research, research fellow at the Centre for Economic Policy Research, a fellow of the American Academy of Arts and Sciences, and a columnist for Project Syndicate. He was named one of *Foreign Policy* magazine's 100 Leading Global Thinkers in 2011. His recent books are *Hall of Mirrors: The Great Depression, The Great Recession, and the Uses—and Misuses—of History* (2015); *From Miracle to Maturity: The Growth of the Korean Economy* with Dwight Perkins and Kwanho Shin (2012); *The World Economy after the Global Financial Crisis*, coedited with Bokyeong Park (2012); and *Exorbitant Privilege: The Rise and Fall of the Dollar and the Future of the International Monetary System* (2011).

Jeffrey Frankel is James W. Harpel Professor of Capital Formation and Growth at Harvard University's Kennedy School. He directs the program in International Finance and Macroeconomics at the National Bureau of Economic Research and is also on its Business Cycle Dating Committee, which officially declares US recessions. Frankel served in the President's Council of Economic Advisers (CEA) in 1983–84 and 1996–99. As CEA member, he was responsible for macroeconomics, international economics, and the environment. Before joining Harvard in 1999, he was professor of economics at the University of California, Berkeley. He was born in San Francisco, graduated from Swarthmore College, and received his PhD in economics from MIT.

Joseph E. Gagnon is senior fellow at the Peterson Institute for International Economics and former associate director of the Division of International Finance at the Federal Reserve Board. He also served at the US Treasury Department and taught at the Haas School of Business, University of California, Berkeley. He is author of *Flexible Exchange Rates for a Stable World*

Economy (2011) and *The Global Outlook for Government Debt over the Next 25 years: Implications for the Economy and Public Policy* (2011). He has published numerous articles in economics journals, including the *Journal of International Economics, Journal of Monetary Economics, Review of International Economics,* and *Journal of International Money and Finance,* and has contributed to several edited volumes. He received a BA from Harvard University in 1981 and a PhD in economics from Stanford University in 1987.

Russell A. Green is the Will Clayton Fellow in International Economics at Rice University's Baker Institute and an adjunct assistant professor in the economics department there. His current research focuses on exchange rate policies, financial market development in emerging-market economies, and India's development challenges. Prior to joining the Baker Institute, Green spent four years in India as the US Treasury Department's first financial attaché to that country. He was previously the deputy director of the US Treasury's Office of International Monetary Policy, where he led efforts to strengthen International Monetary Fund exchange rate policies and international reserve management. Green holds a BA from Pomona College and PhD from the University of California, Berkeley.

Takatoshi Ito is professor at the School of International and Public Affairs, Columbia University. He has taught extensively both in the United States and Japan since finishing his PhD in economics at Harvard University in 1979. He taught at the University of Minnesota (1979–88), Hitotsubashi University (1988–2002), and the University of Tokyo (2004–14) before assuming his current position in 2015. He held visiting professor positions at Harvard University, Stanford University, Columbia Business School, and the University of Malaya. Among his distinguished academic and research appointments are president of the Japanese Economic Association in 2004, fellow of the Econometric Society since 1992, and research associate at the National Bureau of Economic Research since 1985. Ito served as senior adviser in the Research Department of the International Monetary Fund, as deputy vice minister for international affairs at the Ministry of Finance of Japan, and as a member of the Prime Minister's Council on Economic and Fiscal Policy. He is the author of many books, including *The Japanese Economy,* and more than 60 refereed journal papers. He frequently contributes op-ed columns to the *Financial Times.* The government of Japan awarded him the National Medal with Purple Ribbon in June 2011 for his excellent academic achievement.

David C. Mulford is vice chairman international of Credit Suisse, rejoining in March 2009 after spending five years as US ambassador to India. Before being nominated as the US ambassador to India, he served as chairman international and member of the executive board of Credit Suisse from 1992 to 2003. He was undersecretary and assistant secretary of the US Treasury for international affairs from 1984 to 1992. He served as the senior international economic policy official at the Treasury under Secretaries Regan, Baker, and Brady. Before his government service, Mulford was managing director and head of international finance at White, Weld & Co., Inc., from 1966 to 1974. He was then seconded to the Saudi Arabian Monetary Agency (SAMA), where he served as senior investment advisor from 1974 to 1983. He also served as a special assistant to the secretary and deputy secretary of the Treasury as a White House Fellow from 1965 to 1966.

Mulford received his PhD from Oxford University, MA in political science from Boston University, and BA in economics, cum laude, from Lawrence University in Appleton, WI. He pursued graduate studies at the University of Cape Town, South Africa, in 1960 and has published two books on Zambia. He received an honorary Doctor of Laws degree from Lawrence University; the Legion d'Honneur from the President of France; the Distinguished Alumni Award from Boston University; the Alexander Hamilton Award, the highest honor to be bestowed by the secretary of the Treasury for extraordinary service and benefit to the Treasury Department and the nation; the Order of May from the President of Argentina; and the Officer's Cross of the Medal of Merit from the President of Poland.

In 2007 the US Department of State awarded him the Sue M. Cobb Award for Exemplary Diplomatic Service in recognition of his extraordinary efforts as a noncareer ambassador in using private sector leadership and management skills to make a significant impact on US-India bilateral relations. In 2011 he received the Oxford Cup for lifetime professional achievement, the highest award given by the Beta Theta Pi national fraternity.

In 2012 he served as co-chair of the Joint Committee on Strengthening the Framework for Sovereign Debt Crisis Prevention and Resolution, whose report was delivered to the G-20 at the annual meeting of the International Monetary Fund and World Bank in Japan in October 2012 and published by the Institute of International Finance in Washington. Mulford is a member of the Council of Foreign Relations and the Economic Club of New York and has authored two books on Central Africa. He is also the author of *Packing for India—A Life of Action in Global Finance and Diplomacy* (2014).

David Papell is the Joel W. Sailors Endowed Professor and chair of the Department of Economics at the University of Houston, where he has taught since 1984. His fields of expertise are macroeconomics, international economics, and applied time-series econometrics. He previously taught at the University of Florida and has held visiting positions at the University of Pennsylvania, the University of Virginia, and the International Monetary Fund. He received a BA from the University of Pennsylvania and a PhD from Columbia University. He has published more than 60 articles in refereed journals including the *American Economic Review, Review of Economics and Statistics, Journal of International Economics*, and *Journal of Monetary Economics*, and has served as an associate editor for the *Journal of International Economics, Journal of Money, Credit, and Banking*, and *Empirical Economics*.

Ruxandra Prodan is clinical assistant professor of economics at the University of Houston. She holds a PhD degree in economics from the University of Houston. She has taught courses in international finance, econometrics, and forecasting. Prodan's research focuses on international finance, time-series econometrics, and macroeconomics. Her research has been published in journals such as *Journal of Money, Credit and Banking, Journal of Business and Economics Statistics, The B.E. Journal of Macroeconomics,* and *Journal of Economic Dynamics and Control.*

John B. Taylor is the Mary and Robert Raymond Professor of Economics at Stanford University and the George P. Shultz Senior Fellow in Economics at Stanford's Hoover Institution. An award-winning researcher and teacher specializing in macroeconomics, international economics, and monetary policy, he has served as a senior economist (1976–77) and member (1989–91) of the President's Council of Economic Advisers and as undersecretary of the Treasury for international affairs (2001–05). His book *Getting Off Track* was one of the first on the financial crisis. He won the 2012 Hayek Book Prize for *First Principles: Five Keys to Restoring America's Prosperity.*

Edwin M. Truman, nonresident senior fellow at the Peterson Institute for International Economics since 2013 and senior fellow from 2001 to 2013, served as assistant secretary of the US Treasury for international affairs from December 1998 to January 2001 and as counselor to the secretary from March to May 2009. He directed the Division of International Finance of the Board of Governors of the Federal Reserve System from 1977 to 1998. He has taught at Yale, Amherst, and Williams and is the author of *Economic Policy Coordination Reconsidered* (forthcoming).

Makoto Utsumi is the chairman of the Global Advisory Board of Tokai Tokyo Financial Holdings, Inc. He served at Japan's Ministry of Finance from 1957 to 1991 and held various positions including director-general of the International Finance Bureau and vice minister of finance for international affairs. Utsumi was named Policy Maker of the Year by *International Economy* magazine in 1989. He was also awarded Commandeur de la Legion d'Honneur by France in 2007. He graduated from the University of Tokyo with a bachelor of law degree in 1957 and was a professor at Keio University (1992–2000).

Index

Plaza Accord II and, 274-75, 286-88
and timing of Plaza Accord, 113, 218, 265
in portfolio balance model, 245-48, 246t, 247f,
   257t-260t
sterling/dollar stabilization
       1925 attempt, 174-78
       1933 attempt, 178-81
US Trade Representative (USTR), 98
US Treasury
   initiation of Plaza Accord by, 12-13, 148,
    262
   international area of, 34, 43, 168
Utsumi, Makoto
   Dallara on, 43
   official recollections, 45-49, 74
   role of, 20

Versailles Summit (1982), 56, 140
Viner, Jacob, 182
Volcker, Paul
   Baker on, 19
   on current account balance, 158
   on dollar overvaluation, 148, 154
   on effect of Plaza Accord, 154, 270
   on exchange rate policy, 186
   on global currency, 21
   on gold window, 185

inflation-fighting efforts, 129
on interest rates, 82, 150
on lessons learned, 221
monetary policy, 55, 146, 155, 157, 165, 263,
   266, 273
official recollection, 25-31
on Plaza Accord communiqué, 75
at Plaza Accord press conference, 25, 26f
on policy shift, 10, 271
on rules-based system, 217
on trade flows, 288
on US intervention, 143

Warburg, James, 179n
wealth transfer, in portfolio balance model,
   245-48, 247f, 257t-260t
White, Harry Dexter, 182
Williamsburg Summit (1983), 42n, 56, 143
Working Group on Exchange Market
    Intervention, 140
World Bank, 20, 207
World Trade Organization (WTO), 98
World War I, 174-76
World War II, 20

Yellen, Janet, 31